Lecture Notes
in Business Information Processing   **212**

Series Editors

More information about this series at http://www.springer.com/series/7911

Casper Lassenius · Torgeir Dingsøyr
Maria Paasivaara (Eds.)

Agile Processes,
in Software Engineering,
and Extreme Programming

16th International Conference, XP 2015
Helsinki, Finland, May 25–29, 2015
Proceedings

 Springer

Editors
Casper Lassenius
Aalto University
Espoo
Finland

Maria Paasivaara
Aalto University
Espoo
Finland

Torgeir Dingsøyr
SINTEF
Trondheim
Norway

ISSN 1865-1348   ISSN 1865-1356 (electronic)
Lecture Notes in Business Information Processing
ISBN 978-3-319-18611-5   ISBN 978-3-319-18612-2 (eBook)
DOI 10.1007/978-3-319-18612-2

Library of Congress Control Number: 2015938434

Springer Cham Heidelberg New York Dordrecht London

Printed on acid-free paper

Springer International Publishing AG Switzerland is part of Springer Science+Business Media
(www.springer.com)

Preface

This volume contains the papers presented at XP 2015: the 16th International Conference on Agile Software Development held during May 25–29, 2015 in Helsinki, Finland.

While agile development already has become mainstream in industry, it is a field that is constantly evolving and that continues to spur an enormous interest both in industry and academia. The XP conference series has, and continues to play, an important role in bridging the academic and practitioner communities, providing a forum for both formal and informal sharing and development of ideas, experiences, and opinions.

The theme of XP 2015 — Delivering value: Moving from Cyclic to Continuous Value Delivery reflects the modern trend toward organizations that are simultaneously very efficient and flexible in software development and delivery.

The XP 2015 program includes research papers, experience reports, industry and practice sessions, scientific workshops, panels, lightning talks, technical demos, posters, and a doctoral symposium. In total over all submission types, we received almost 300 proposals, showing that the XP community indeed is vibrant and active.

This proceedings volume contains the full research papers, short research papers, and experience reports. In addition, we included the abstracts of select posters, extended abstracts of the PhD symposium presentations, as well as the position statements of the panel participants.

All of the submitted research papers went through a rigorous peer-review process. Each paper was reviewed by three members of the Program Committee. We received 44 research papers, out of which 15 (34%) were accepted as full papers and 7 as short papers.

We received 45 experience report proposals, out of which 11 (24%) were accepted following the review process. Each accepted experience report proposal received the guidance of an experienced shepherd in writing the final paper.

We would like to extend our thank you to all the people who have contributed to XP 2015 and helped make it a success: the authors, the sponsors, the reviewers, the volunteers, and the chairs. We hope you enjoy the conference!

March 2015

Casper Lassenius
Torgeir Dingsøyr
Maria Paasivaara

Organization

XP 2015 was organized by the Department of Computer Science, Aalto University, Finland.

Organizing Committee

General Chair

Maria Paasivaara   Aalto University, Finland

Academic Chairs

Torgeir Dingsøyr   SINTEF, Norway
Casper Lassenius   Aalto University, Finland

Scientific Workshops

Daniela S. Cruzes   SINTEF, Norway
Casper Lassenius   Aalto University, Finland

Industry and Practice Track

Jutta Eckstein   IT Communications, Germany
Diana Larsen   FutureWorks Consulting, USA

Experience Reports

Rebecca Wirfs-Brock   Wirfs-Brock Associates, USA
Ken Power   Cisco Systems, Ireland

Executives and Managers Track

Jaana Nyfjord   Swedsoft SICS, Sweden
Henri Kivioja   Ericsson, Finland
Paul D. Tolchinsky   Performance Dev. Partners, USA

Bridging Research and Practice

Morten Elvang   DELTA, Denmark
Nils Brede Moe   SINTEF, Norway
Jaana Nyfjord   Swedsoft SICS, Sweden

Technical Demos

Kari Systä   Tampere University of Technology, Finland

Short Talks and Lightning Talks

Johanna Hunt   Aptivate, UK
Jussi Markula   Prominda Revolution, Finland

Panels

Steve Fraser   Independent Consultant, USA

Open Space

Charlie Poole   Independent Consultant, USA

Doctoral Symposium

Peggy Gregory   University of Central Lancashire, UK
Helen Sharp   The Open University, UK

Posters

Andrey Maglyas   Lappeenranta University of Technology, Finland
Ville T. Heikkilä   Aalto University, Finland

Student Volunteer Coordination

Ville T. Heikkilä   Aalto University, Finland
Pilar Rodriguez   University of Oulu, Finland

Local Organization

Local Organizing Chair

Juha Itkonen   Aalto University, Finland

Event Manager

Mary-Ann Wikström   Aalto University, Finland

Web Masters

Ville T. Heikkilä   Aalto University, Finland
Eero Laukkanen   Aalto University, Finland

Program Committee (Research Papers)

Adolph, Steve	Development Knowledge, Canada
Ali Babar, Muhammad	The University of Adelaide, Australia
Aoyama, Mikio	Nanzan University, Japan
Counsell, Steve	Brunel University, UK
Desouza, Kevin	Arizona State University, USA
Dorairaj, Siva	Software Education, New Zealand
Dybå, Tore	SINTEF, Norway
Ebert, Christof	Vector Consulting
Erdogmus, Hakan	Carnegie Mellon University Silicon Valley, USA
Garbajosa, Juan	Universidad Politecnica de Madrid / Technical University of Madrid (UPM), Spain
Goldman, Alfredo	University of São Paulo - USP, Brazil
Greer, Des	Queens University Belfast, UK
Hoda, Rashina	The University of Auckland, New Zealand
Holmström Olsson, Helena	Malmö University, Sweden
Iivari, Juhani	University of Oulu, Finland
Kruchten, Philippe	University of British Columbia, Canada
Madeyski, Lech	Wroclaw University of Technology, Poland
Marchesi, Michele	DIEE - University of Cagliari, Italy
Martin, Angela	The University of Waikato, New Zealand
Mishra, Alok	Atilim University, Turkey
Moe, Nils Brede	SINTEF, Norway
Nerur, Sridhar	University of Texas at Arlington, USA
Noble, James	Victoria University of Wellington, New Zealand
Nyfjord, Jaana	Swedsoft, Sweden
Prechelt, Lutz	Freie Universitaet Berlin, Germany
Pries-Heje, Jan	Roskilde University, Denmark
Prikladnicki, Rafael	PUCRS, Brazil
Rodriguez, Pilar	University of Oulu, Finland
Rolland, Knut	The Norwegian School of IT, Norway
Rossi, Matti	Aalto University School of Economics, Finland
Rumpe, Bernhard	RWTH Aachen University, Germany
Schneider, Kurt	Leibniz Universität Hannover, Germany
Sharp, Helen	The Open University, UK
Sjøberg, Dag	Department of Informatics, University of Oslo, Norway
Tonelli, Roberto	University of Cagliari, Italy
Van Solingen, Rini	Delft University of Technology, Netherlands
Van Vliet, Hans	VU University Amsterdam, Netherlands
Vidgen, Richard	University of Hull, UK
Wang, Xiaofeng	Free University of Bozen-Bolzano, Italy
Yague, Agustin	Universidad Politecnica de Madrid, Spain

Reviewers and Shepherds (Experience Reports)

Heikkilä, V.
Lassenius, C.
Paasivaara, M.
Power, K.

Wirfs-Brock, R.
Davies, R.
Eckstein, J.
Freudenberg, S.

Itkonen, J.
Lehtinen, T.
Soares Cruzes, D.

Reviewers (Industry and Practice)

Eckstein, J.
Larsen, D.
Andrea, J.
Asproni, G.
Bache, E.
Baldauf, C.
Bless, M.
Dorairaj, S.
Dubinsky, Y.
Favaro, J.
Freeman, S.

Freudenberg, S.
Garbajosa, J.
Hassa, C.
Holyer, S.
Hunt, J.
Juncu, O.
Kua, P.
Laing, S.
Light, A.
Little, T.
Moe, N.

North, D.
Norton, M.
Peraire, C.
Provaglio, A.
Putman, D.
Rose, S.
Sharp, H.
Trincardi, M.
Turhan, B.
Wild, W.

Sponsoring Institutions

Platinum Sponsors

Aalto University, Finland
Ericsson, Finland
Reaktor, Finland

Gold Sponsors

Nitor, Finland
Nokia, Finland
Omenia, Finland

Silver Sponsor

Agilefant, Finland

Contents

Full Research Papers

A Duplicated Code Refactoring Advisor 3
Francesca Arcelli Fontana, Marco Zanoni, and Francesco Zanoni

Expectations and Challenges from Scaling Agile in Mechatronics-Driven
Companies – A Comparative Case Study. 15
Christian Berger and Ulrik Eklund

An Industrial Case Study on Test Cases as Requirements 27
Elizabeth Bjarnason, Michael Unterkalmsteiner, Emelie Engström,
and Markus Borg

What Do Practitioners Vary in Using Scrum? 40
Philipp Diebold, Jan-Peter Ostberg, Stefan Wagner, and Ulrich Zendler

Key Challenges in Early-Stage Software Startups. 52
Carmine Giardino, Sohaib Shahid Bajwa, Xiaofeng Wang,
and Pekka Abrahamsson

Agile Challenges in Practice: A Thematic Analysis 64
Peggy Gregory, Leonor Barroca, Katie Taylor, Dina Salah,
and Helen Sharp

UX Work in Startups: Current Practices and Future Needs 81
Laura Hokkanen and Kaisa Väänänen-Vainio-Mattila

Why the Development Outcome Does Not Meet the Product
Owners' Expectations? 93
Timo O.A. Lehtinen, Risto Virtanen, Ville T. Heikkilä, and Juha Itkonen

Functional Size Measures and Effort Estimation in Agile Development:
A Replicated Study. 105
Valentina Lenarduzzi, Ilaria Lunesu, Martina Matta, and Davide Taibi

Software Development as an Experiment System: A Qualitative Survey
on the State of the Practice 117
Eveliina Lindgren and Jürgen Münch

Would You Mind Fixing This Issue? An Empirical Analysis of Politeness
and Attractiveness in Software Developed Using Agile Boards 129
Marco Ortu, Giuseppe Destefanis, Mohamad Kassab, Steve Counsell,
Michele Marchesi, and Roberto Tonelli

Coordinating Expertise Outside Agile Teams   141
  Mawarny Md. Rejab, James Noble, and Stuart Marshall

Transitioning Towards Continuous Delivery in the B2B Domain:
A Case Study   154
  Olli Rissanen and Jürgen Münch

DevOps: A Definition and Perceived Adoption Impediments   166
  Jens Smeds, Kristian Nybom, and Ivan Porres

Scaling Kanban for Software Development in a Multisite Organization:
Challenges and Potential Solutions   178
  *Nirnaya Tripathi, Pilar Rodríguez, Muhammad Ovais Ahmad,
  and Markku Oivo*

Short Papers

The Two Faces of Uncertainty: Threat vs Opportunity Management
in Agile Software Development   193
  Denniz Dönmez and Gudela Grote

Management Ambidexterity: A Clue for Maturing in Agile
Software Development   199
  *Rafaela Mantovani Fontana, Victor Meyer Jr., Sheila Reinehr,
  and Andreia Malucelli*

Towards Predictable B2B Customer Satisfaction and Experience
Management with Continuous Improvement Assets and Rich Feedback   205
  Petri Kettunen, Mikko Ämmälä, and Jari Partanen

Dimensions of DevOps   212
  Lucy Ellen Lwakatare, Pasi Kuvaja, and Markku Oivo

Towards Introducing Agile Architecting in Large Companies:
The CAFFEA Framework   218
  Antonio Martini, Lars Pareto, and Jan Bosch

Optimal Refactoring   224
  Susanne Siverland, Roger C.S. Wernersson, and Charlotte Sennersten

Agile and the Global Software Leaders: A Perfect Match?   230
  Stavros Stavru and Sylvia Ilieva

Experience Reports

High Level Test Driven Development – Shift Left   239
  *Kristian Bjerke-Gulstuen, Emil Wiik Larsen, Tor Stålhane,
  and Torgeir Dingsøyr*

Shorter Feedback Loops By Means of Continuous Deployment   248
  Arjan Claassen and Laurens Boekhorst

On a Different Level of Team   254
  Johanna Hunt

Applying Agile and Lean Elements to Accelerate Innovation Culture
in a Large Organization – Key Learnings After One Year Journey   262
  Jari Partanen and Mari Matinlassi

It Has Been a Long Journey, and It Is Not Over Yet   270
  Avraham Poupko

Organizational Culture Aspects of an Agile Transformation   279
  Shlomi Rosenberg

The Guide Board, an Artefact to Support the Continuous Improvement
of an Agile Team's Culture   287
  Matti Schneider

Testing Modtalk   294
  Josh Fridstrom, Adam Jacques, Kurt Kilpela, and John Sarkela

Building Learning Organization Through Peer Hands-on Support
Community and Gamification   302
  Tomáš Tureček, Martin Chmelař, Roman Šmiřák, and Jan Krchňák

From Sprints to Lean Flow: Management Strategies
for Agile Improvement   310
  Marcelo Walter, Ramon Tramontini, Rafaela Mantovani Fontana,
  Sheila Reinehr, and Andreia Malucelli

Mob Programming – What Works, What Doesn't   319
  Alexander Wilson

Panels

Continuous Delivery – From Concept to Product: Trade-offs in Effectiveness
and Efficiency?   329
  Steven Fraser, Ismo Aro, Henri Kivioja, Erik Lundh, Ken Power,
  Linda Rising, Werner Wild, and Rebecca Wirfs-Brock

Learning from Disaster and Experience: Evolving
Software Professionalism   334
  Steven Fraser, Janne Järvinen, Erik Lundh, Ken Power, Linda Rising,
  Werner Wild, and Rebecca Wirfs-Brock

Practical Applications of the Agile Fluency Model   339
  Diana Larsen, Steve Holyer, Jutta Eckstein, Antti Kirjavainen,
  and Olli Sorje

Doctoral Symposium Abstracts

Improving Processes by Integrating Agile Practices   345
  Philipp Diebold

Assurance Case Integration with An Agile Development Method   347
  Osama Doss and Tim Kelly

Data-Driven Decision-Making in Product R&D   350
  Aleksander Fabijan, Helena Holmström Olsson, and Jan Bosch

Combining Kanban and FOSS: Can It Work?   352
  Annemarie Harzl and Wolfgang Slany

Paradigm Shift from Large Releases to Continuous Deployment
of Software: Designing a Reference Model for Continuous Deployment   354
  Teemu Karvonen, Markku Oivo, and Pasi Kuvaja

How to Adopt Continuous Delivery? A Research Proposal   356
  Eero Laukkanen and Casper Lassenius

Posters

Teaching Scrum – What We Did, What We Will Do and What Impedes Us   361
  Emil Alègroth, Håkan Burden, Morgan Ericsson, Imed Hammouda,
  Eric Knauss, and Jan-Philipp Steghöfer

Agility in Dynamic Environments: A Case Study for Agile Development . . .   363
  Simon Brooke and Dina Allswang

Introducing SafeScrum   365
  Geir Kjetil Hanssen, Ingar Kulbrandstad, and Børge Haugset

Revisit – A Systematic Approach to Continuously Improve Agile Practices
in Large-scale and Fast-expanding R&D Center   367
  Peng Liu and Yuedong Zhao

Applying Randori-Style Kata and Agile Practices
to an Undergraduate-Level Programming Class   369
  Chitsutha Soomlek

Continuous Strategy Process in the Context of Agile and Lean
Software Development   371
    Tanja Suomalainen and Jenni Myllykoski

Automatizing Android Unit and User Interface Testing   373
    Juha-Matti Vanhatupa and Mikko Heikkinen

Author Index   375

Full Research Papers

A Duplicated Code Refactoring Advisor

Francesca Arcelli Fontana, Marco Zanoni[✉], and Francesco Zanoni

University of Milano-Bicocca, Viale Sarca, 336, 20126, Milano, Italy
{arcelli,marco.zanoni}@disco.unimib.it,
f.zanoni1@campus.unimib.it

Abstract. Refactoring is one of the key practices in Extreme Programming and other agile methods. Duplicated code is one of the most pervasive and pungent smells to remove from source code through refactoring. Duplicated code has been largely studied in the literature, and different types of duplications, or "clones", have been identified. Some studies analyzed in details the problems caused by clones in the code, others outlined also the difficulties in removing clones, and the cases in which it could be better not removing them. The refactoring cost for removing clones can be very high, also due to the different choices on the possible refactoring steps. In this paper, we describe our approach and tool developed with the aim to suggest the best refactorings to remove clones in Java code. Our approach is based on the classification of the clones in terms of their location in a class hierarchy, and allows to choose among a restricted set of refactorings, which are then evaluated using multiple criteria. We provide a validation of the effectiveness of the approach.

Keywords: Clone refactoring · Refactoring advisor · Empirical study

1 Introduction

Different tools and techniques can be used for agile development. In our work, we focus our attention on the development of a tool to select and suggest the best refactorings of duplicated code. Duplicated code involves all non-trivial software systems; the percentage of involved duplicated lines is usually estimated between 5 % and 20 %, sometimes reaching even 50 % [1,2]. Fowler [3] suggests that code duplication is a bad smell and one of the major indicators of poor maintainability.

With the concept of "clone" we mean a code fragment duplicated in several locations within a software system with several similarity degrees. We consider "Cloning" as a synonym of "duplicating code", both identifying the activity of introducing clones of a code fragment within a software system. Anyway, a shared definition of "similarity" does not exist, resulting in the lack of a rigorous definition of clone [1,2]. Different types of cloned have been identified in the literature, providing a clone classification involving the amount and the way a code fragment is duplicated. The most commonly accepted classification is the one of Roy et al. [4], which identifies four types of clones (we describe Type-1 and Type-3 of clones, the ones we detect through our approach, in Section 3.2).

© Springer International Publishing Switzerland 2015
C. Lassenius et al. (Eds.): XP 2015, LNBIP 212, pp. 3–14, 2015.
DOI: 10.1007/978-3-319-18612-2_1

The main problems related to code duplication are, e.g., the uncontrolled spread of yet-to-know bugs, resulting in heavy correction time cost when discovered, and heavy update time cost, when modification of an important part of a code fragment implies modification of all duplicated fragments.

Even if duplication may not always be avoided, it is considered a serious problem, mainly from a maintenance perspective. Many works investigated in depth the factors causing its insertion, or provided taxonomies according to several criteria and detection techniques, but just few works examined its management procedures [1]. Many sources suggest to fully delegate correction activities to developers' experience and judgement [1,2], and assert the importance of the "human in the loop" concept [3,5]. These assertions follow the awareness that every modification to a software system must consider and respect the design choices of that system. Furthermore, design choices are not easily captured within automated procedures. During duplicated code management, two main decisional steps involve design aspects:

1. the choice of which instances are worth to be refactored and which are not,
2. the choice of which technique should be applied to remove a duplication instance, once the instance has been evaluated as refactoring-worthy.

In this paper, we introduce our approach and a tool developed to suggest "the best" refactoring of Java code clones. The tool is called Duplicated Code Refactoring Advisor (DCRA) and is composed of four modules. We use for clone detection a well known tool, NiCad [6], and we define a post-processor for its output, called Clone Detailer, which adds information characterizing every clone, e.g., the location of the clone in the class hierarchy, its size and type. Then, through the Refactoring Advisor module, we suggest the refactorings able to remove the clones, and provide a ranking of their quality. Refactorings are chosen by considering the location of the clone and the variables contained in the clone; they are sorted by considering different features, i.e., the variation of Lines of Code (LOC), and an evaluation of the quality resulting from its application, in terms of the exploitation of OOP constructs. Finally, a module called Refactoring Advice Aggregator provides a summary of the most interesting information about clones, i.e., the clones having greater size, and the ones which should be simpler or more convenient to remove.

Through our approach, we aim to filter clone pairs worthy of refactoring from unworthy ones, and to suggest the best refactoring techniques for worthy ones. We experimented the Clone Detailer module on 50 systems of the Qualitas Corpus [7]. All the modules of our DCRA tool have been validated on 4 systems of the Qualitas Corpus.

The paper is organized through the following Sections: Section 2 reports some related works, pointing out the differences with our approach; Section 3 contains a general description of DCRA's features; Section 4 describes the architecture of DCRA; Section 5 reports the validation of the tool on four systems; Section 6 makes an overall conclusion on DCRA, outlining some future developments.

2   Related Work on Code Clone Refactoring

In the literature, we can find many papers on clones and on clone detection tools [8]. Here, we focus our attention only on some works which consider and propose approaches or techniques for clone refactoring.

Fowler [3] provides a generic approach for duplicate code refactoring based on the description of different refactoring steps. His approach is intentionally generic and agrees with the common practice of delegating all solution choices and details to developers. The same approach is summarized and slightly extended by Zibran and Roy [1], by reporting many duplicated code classifications and taxonomies, each considering different sets of duplication features. Their duplication classification is based on refactoring opportunities. A more detailed approach was defined by Golomingi [5]: a precise and motivated set of locations ("scenarios") within class hierarchies is used to classify duplications, which are linked to a precise and motivated set of refactoring techniques. Only general refactoring selection criteria are then provided, committing further considerations to developers. The strong point is the association of refactoring techniques to specific scenarios, whereas Fowler favours a much more generic approach. The "human in the loop" concept still holds, since no assessment is made on the actual techniques applicability, but it provide more guidance than Fowler's approach. The tool implemented by Golomingi, called Supremo, provides further help to developers through a graphical representations of all entities involved and their relationships. At last, Giesecke [9,10] further generalizes several scenarios and selects functions/methods as the best duplication granularity, reducing the number of scenarios and refactoring techniques.

Our approach, implemented in DCRA, mainly draws inspiration from the described works, by extending the duplication and classification categories of Golomingi and by adapting the approach to Java. Furthermore, automated evaluation, classification and suggestion of refactoring techniques are added.

3   DCRA Approach

The main features characterizing our approach are the following:

- the extension of Golomingi's [5] scenario set with further recurring locations,
- the analysis of the location of each clone pair, resulting in a specific set of applicable refactoring techniques (see Tables 1 and 2),
- the ranking of the applicable refactoring techniques, based on a score weighting different criteria,
- the aggregation of the information about clones and refactorings, on the more critical clones, and on the best refactorings, according to numerical criteria.

The automatic evaluation of the applicability of refactoring techniques is the central point of this work, since it helps reducing the human involvement. The evaluation is achieved by defining a specific set of criteria and by translating them

Table 1. DCRA refactoring techniques

Refactoring technique	Description
Extract method (EM) [3]	extract a subset of the statements of a method as a new method
Replace method with method object (RMMO) [3]	a.k.a. "Extract utility class" [1], considered in its simplest version (**private** or **protected** class with **public** attributes and only one method: the constructor)
Merge method (MM)	delete one of the two identical copies of a method
Pull up method (PUM) [3]	move a method to the superclass
Pull up method object (PUMO)	combination of "Pull up method" and "Replace method with method object"
Form template method (FTM) [3]	introduce a Template Method design pattern to manage behaviour variation in subclasses
Leave unchanged (LU)	do not refactor at all

Table 2. DCRA locations and refactoring suggestions (remaining locations have only the LU suggestion)

Location	EM	FTM	LU	MM	PUM	PUMO	RMMO
SAME METHOD	×	·	×	·	·	·	×
SAME CLASS	×	·	×	×	·	·	×
SIBLING CLASS	·	×	×	·	×	×	·
SAME EXTERNAL SUPERCLASS	·	×	×	·	×	×	·

into suitable numeric values. Currently, DCRA evaluates refactoring techniques according to the following two criteria: *1)* lines of code variation and *2)* OOP principles compliance: encapsulation, inheritance and polymorphism.

3.1 Locations and Refactoring Techniques

In Table 1, we report the list of the refactorings we consider in DCRA with a short description. Refactorings without a reference were defined by us during the development of DCRA; the last one, "Leave unchanged", is actually the suggestion to avoid refactoring. Since locations are the starting point of the whole procedure and refactoring techniques are the ending point, Table 2 outlines these elements and the way they are related (refactorings listed in the headers of the table are defined in Table 1). Some of Golomingi's and Fowler's refactoring suggestions were not included: *1)* "Substitute algorithm", because Type-4 clones (code fragments implementing the same algorithm in different ways) were not considered, and *2)* "Push down method", because DCRA does not currently manage the *SUPERCLASS* location.

We added to Golomingi's location set [5] the *SAME EXTERNAL SUPER-CLASS* location: it describes all clones located within sibling classes extending a

Table 3. Distribution of clone types and granularity in locations in 50 systems

Location	Type-1		Type-3		Block		Method		Total
	#	%	#	%	#	%	#	%	
ancestor class	13	4.4	281	95.6	120	40.8	174	59.2	294
common hierarchy class	970	23.5	3,152	76.5	968	23.5	3,154	76.5	4,122
first cousin class	416	12.2	2,980	87.8	473	13.9	2,923	86.1	3,396
same class	5,645	9.9	51,308	90.1	17,096	30.0	39,857	70.0	56,953
same external superclass	4,384	6.2	66,391	93.8	31,534	44.6	39,241	55.4	70,775
same method	569	10.4	4,901	89.6	5,449	99.6	21	0.4	5,470
sibling class	2,721	16.4	13,868	83.6	2,830	17.1	13,759	82.9	16,589
superclass	91	8.4	981	91.6	431	40.2	641	59.8	1,072
unrelated class	2,758	7.3	35,035	92.7	23,103	61.1	14,690	38.9	37,793
Total	17,567	8.9	178,897	91.1	82,004	41.7	114,460	58.3	196,464

common external class, i.e., a class belonging to external libraries. This addition is significant; in fact, our dedicated analysis reported in Section 3.2 revealed that over 1/3 of all detected duplications is related to this location. Golomingi's approach classifies those instances as *UNRELATED CLASS*, therefore not manageable through an automatic procedure. *SAME EXTERNAL SUPERCLASS* and *SIBLING CLASS* have similar characteristics, and share the same refactoring suggestions. Anonymous classes are recurring examples of *SAME EXTERNAL SUPERCLASS* instances, since they usually extend class `Object`.

3.2 Qualitas Corpus Analysis

To determine the most recurring characteristics featured by duplication instances, a statistical assessment was achieved by analyzing 50 software projects, included in the Qualitas Corpus [7] (v. 20120401). Software projects were analyzed by the Clone Detector and the Clone Detailer modules of DCRA (see Section 4). This assessment analyzed three aspects of duplicated code: clone pair types, clone pair locations and clone pair granularity. Clones are grouped in pairs, and the Clone Detector was configured to look for clones of blocks of code, which include also clones of methods.

Table 3 counts the clone pairs found in the analyzed systems, classifying them by location, type and granularity. Most ($\sim$75 %) clone pairs belong to the locations listed in Table 2. Type-3 clone pairs (code fragments with added, removed or modified statements) are the most recurrent because, intuitively, when a code fragment is duplicated, it is also slightly modified, as it rarely matches the functionalities needed in both positions.

As for the granularity of clones, we classified the detected clone pairs as block-only or method clones (block clones contain both cases). On average, function/method clones are more respect to block clones, supporting the choice of function/method granularity made by Giesecke [9,10]. Methods are also more cohesive units than blocks, featuring higher reusability. As a result, the detection procedure of DCRA was configured to detect:

- Type-1 (identical code fragments, only white space differences allowed) and Type-3 clones (code fragments with added, removed or modified statements);
- block-level clones, for their diffusion, and because they include method-level clones.

The design and implementation efforts were focused on the locations reported in Table 2. Also Fowler's suggestions are mainly related to these four locations. For all other locations, only "Leave unchanged" is suggested.

3.3   Refactoring Technique Implementation

Refactoring techniques reported in Table 1 are terms naming the generic strategy to apply to correct clone pairs. Some refactorings need a further customization, to be applied to a particular case. For example, the "Extract method" refactoring has a "Flag" strategy, applied to Type-3 clones: to create a method usable from all original positions, a flag parameter is added to the extracted method signature and is checked by conditional branches within the extracted method body. This kind of refactoring approach is not described in the literature; Roy and Cordy's survey [2] implicitly reports only Type-1 clones may be refactored with the "Extract method" technique, since, if a flag parameter is introduced, the class interface actually changes, and the risk of encapsulation reduction increases.

Every refactoring was decomposed in one or more implementation steps, to compute the change of the code size (LOC variation) when a refactoring is applied. Every implementation step is associated to a function, which computes the LOC resulting after the application of the step. By computing the LOC for each implementation step belonging to a refactoring, it is possible to estimate the size of a clone pair after the refactoring.

4   Duplicated Code Refactoring Advisor

DCRA outputs a suitable list of techniques to be applied on the most problematic duplications. The tool consists of four components:

- *Clone Detector*: external tool detecting clone pairs;
- *Clone Detailer*: analyzes the Clone Detector output to add all necessary clone pair details;
- *Refactoring Advisor*: chooses the possible refactoring techniques related to each clone pair;
- *Refactoring Advice Aggregator*: aggregates the available information about clones and refactorings, grouping by class or package, and sorting by refactoring significance or clone pair impact.

Before the execution of DCRA, the end of line characters of the analyzed source code are standardized, to allow a precise line count, and a more correct evaluation of the solutions. A "toy example" of a clone pair, shown in Listing 1, will be used throughout the section to show how the analysis works.

Listing 1. DCRA toy example: clone pair

```
public class SuperClass {}
public class SubCls1
    extends SuperClass {
  public void method() {
    int a = 0;
    int b = 1;
    a++;
    b++;
    System.out.print(a + b);
  }
}
public class SubCls2
    extends SuperClass {
  public void method() {
    int a = 0;
    int b = 1;
    a++;
    b++;
    System.out.print(a + b);
  }
}
```

Listing 2. DCRA toy example: refactoring preview of the clone pair

```
public class SuperClass {

  public void method() {
    int a = 0;
    int b = 1;
    a++;
    b++;
    System.out.print(a + b);
  }

}

public class SubCls1
    extends SuperClass{}

public class SubCls2
    extends SuperClass{}
```

4.1 Clone Detector

NiCad [6] was chosen as the clone detector because it allows choosing between function- and block-level clones. We setup the tool with these parameters:

- block-level granularity is chosen, since more manageable clones are detected;
- a minimum clone length of 5 lines, a commonly used value in the literature [2];
- a maximum dissimilarity percentage between code fragments of 30 % (NiCad's default); no common agreement appears to exist yet [1] on this parameter;
- no renaming allowed, since a large set of unmanageable clone pairs would result; only Type-1 and the consequent Type-3 subset are detected;
- clones grouped in pairs, since they are easier to manage than n-ary groups; this is common in the literature [5,9] and in many clone detection tools.

4.2 Clone Detailer

This component adds to clone pairs all details needed to select refactoring techniques. Some of the relevant details it adds are:

- variables used in each clone, labelled using their declaration position and usage;
- length of each clone, cloned lines and different lines (NiCad only reports the total length of the longest clone);

- clone pair location (introduced in Section 3.1);
- clone pair granularity: method or block;
- clone pair type: Type-1 or Type-3.

Regarding the first point, the declaration position was classified in the following categories: *1)* inside the clone, *2)* outside the clone but within its container method, *3)* class attribute, *4)* inherited attribute; the usage, instead, was classified using these other categories: *1)* used after clone but within its container method, *2)* read within clone, *3)* modified within clone. These criteria were taken from Higo et al. [11], and applied to our location-based classification, obtaining a more precise characterization of each clone pair.

4.3   Refactoring Advisor

The Refactoring Advisor uses the Clone Detailer output to choose the possible refactoring techniques for each clone pair.

We introduce now the "coupled entity" concept: when clones access variables or attributes from their local scope (e.g., their container class or method), and the application of a refactoring would move the code in a different scope, the reference to those variables or attributes may increase the coupling level of the refactored clone. A coupled entity is any of these variable or attribute references. They are evaluated differently for each refactoring kind, because each refactoring applies different transformations to the code. Coupled entities make the application of a refactoring more costly, or not possible without changing the visibility or placement of variables in the system.

The Refactoring Advisor works independently on each clone pair. First, it selects all refactoring techniques applicable to the clone pair on the base of its location, granularity, type and coupled entities. Second, it ranks the selected techniques, relying on a score based on two criteria: *i)* relative LOC variation, *ii)* compliance to OOP (inheritance, polymorphism and encapsulation). The score is calculated as the average of two weights, one for each criterion, evaluating the compliance to each principle. In our example, "Pull up method" would modify the code as shown in Listing 2. We compute the two weights by evaluating the code after the refactoring w.r.t. the original. In the following, we explain how the two weights, i.e., LOC variation and OOP compliance are computed.

Equation 1 defines the refactoring evaluation score. The LOC variation is obtained (Equation 2) as the ratio of LOC before and after the application of the refactoring, normalized to the $[-1, +1]$ range. OOP compliance (Equation 3) is calculated as the average of the values assigned to its three principles: encapsulation, inheritance, polymorphism; each value is in the $[-1, +1]$ range, and has been manually determined for each refactoring during the assessment phase of the DCRA development. Values $(-1, 0, +1)$ correspond respectively to: the maximum possible deterioration, no variation, the maximum improvement.

Table 4. Refactoring Advisor computation example

PUM Evaluation: 0.66	OOP Compliance: 0.33		encapsulation:	0
			inheritance:	1
			polymorphism:	0
	LOC Variation:	1	LOC before:	10
			LOC after:	5
LU Evaluation: −0.33	OOP Compliance: −0.66		encapsulation:	0
			inheritance:	−1
			polymorphism:	−1
	LOC Variation:	0	LOC before:	10
			LOC after:	10

$$Evaluation = \frac{LOCVar + OOP}{2} \tag{1}$$

$$LOCVar = \frac{LOCBefore}{LOCAfter} - 1 \tag{2}$$

$$OOP = \frac{Encap + Inh + Polym}{3} \tag{3}$$

In our clone pair example, the values assigned and derived for each variable of the two refactorings are resumed in Table 4 (every value depends on the ones on its right). Our approach allows to give different relative weights to the different criteria used to produce an evaluation, allowing to tune the refactoring selection towards, e.g., more OOP quality or more LOC saving.

4.4   Refactoring Advice Aggregator

This component summarizes all advices and clone pair details, providing to the developers the selected sets of refactoring techniques or clone pairs, sorted by their weight: techniques are sorted by effectiveness, clone pairs by length. Effectiveness is measured by combining the evaluation of each technique with the length of the clone pair. Grouping by package was considered because it can help developers to quickly identify the most problematic subsystems. A class or package is considered refactorable if it contains effective refactorings, and is considered affected if it participates to clone pairs.

For each clone pair, only the first refactoring (the one with the higher evaluation) is considered, and its weight is normalized according to its clone pair length (the maximum length of the clones in the pair), to make the comparison of different refactoring applications coherent. For instance, if the first technique for a 5 lines-long duplication is evaluated as 1, and the first technique for a 20 lines-long duplication is evaluated as 0.5, the second refactoring will better improve system quality, since the respective weight values would be 5 and 10.

Table 5. Systems used for validation

Project	LOC	Pairs	Cloned LOC	Cloned LOC %
fitjava-1.1	3,643	27	218	5.98
jgrapht-0.8.1	9,086	53	736	8.10
nekohtml-1.9.14	6,149	81	1,130	18.38
oscache-2.4.1	5,786	70	982	16.97

Table 6. Assessment results for clones in the same class

Location	Type	EM	RMMO	MM	LU		Total	
SAME METHOD	1	2/2	1/1	0/0	0/0	3/3		44/46
	3	8/10	0/0	0/0	33/33	41/43		
SAME CLASS	1	6/6	0/0	0/0	0/0	6/6		97/106
	3	81/90	0/0	0/0	10/10	91/100		
Total	1	8/8	1/1	0/0	0/0	9/9		
	3	89/100	0/0	0/0	43/43	132/143		
		97/108	1/1	0/0	43/43			141/152

The Refactoring Advice Aggregator provides as output the: top N most effective refactorings; top N most harmful clone pairs; top N most refactorable packages and classes; top N most affected packages and classes. The value of N is currently set to 20.

5 Validation

DCRA was tested on four projects of different size belonging to the Qualitas Corpus [7], reported in Table 5[1]. The Refactoring Advisor provided advices for more than 80 % of clone pairs[2]. All refactoring suggestions were then assessed by hand, to verify their usefulness. The results of the assessment are reported in Table 6 and Table 7 for different locations, since different locations mean different possible refactoring sets. In the tables, the number of advices is classified by location, type, and refactoring suggestion. The shown numbers represent the ratio of accepted advices (accepted/total), e.g., in Table 6, 81 suggestions out of 90 were accepted for clones in the *SAME CLASS* location, Type-3, and "Extract method" suggestion.

The criteria producing the advices proved to be mostly effective, since mainly refactoring-worthy duplications were proposed. The suggested refactorings were accepted in most cases, in particular for "Extract method", "Leave unchanged", "Replace method with method object". Actually, we rejected only 8 % of the whole advices. This led to suitably refactor 66 % of all duplications found in

---

[1] LOC were computed by the tool CLOC 1.56.

[2] The other ones are not managed in the current version of DCRA.

Table 7. Assessment results for clones in sibling classes

Location	Type	PUM	PUMO	FTM	LU	Total	
SIBLING CLASS	1	2/2	0/0	0/0	0/0	2/2	3/6
	3	0/2	0/0	1/2	0/0	1/4	
SAME EXTERNAL SUPERCLASS	1	8/9	0/0	0/0	0/0	8/9	16/37
	3	0/0	0/3	8/25	0/0	8/28	
Total	1	10/11	0/0	0/0	0/0	10/11	
	3	0/2	0/3	9/27	0/0	9/32	
		10/13	0/3	9/27	0/0		19/43

the analyzed software systems. Refactoring suggestions in some categories were less effective than others. For example, 9/32 refactoring advices regarding Type-3 clone pairs between sibling classes (see Table 7), were actually not worth of application. In particular, "Form template method" was often rejected because it was suggested for too few cloned lines; "Pull up method" was usually preferred in these cases. To prevent this issue, a higher lower bound to clone LOC is needed. Another category of clone pairs having (minor) issues were the Type-3 ones within the same class (see Table 6). In this case, the issue is that refactorings with low rank were often application-unworthy, because of the small size of clones; as in the previous consideration, a higher lower bound to cloned LOC is needed for this scenario. Another result of the validation is that the "Replace method with method object" and "Pull up method object" refactoring techniques were suggested only a few times, as they are very line-expensive.

As a conclusion, our validation outlines that DCRA is effective for suggesting refactorings in most cases. All the issues found during the validation can be corrected by adjusting the thresholds of specific criteria.

6   Conclusions and Future Works

This work suggests it is possible to help developers towards the refactoring of duplicated code, with the aim of improving the design quality, resulting in increased manageability and consequently reducing valuable time spent in code inspection phases. Our technique can be used to suggest the best refactoring to apply to code clones, considering different properties of the code.

The proposed approach may be summarized as an automated technique selecting the best refactorings, based on a classification of code clones, with the aim to concretely reduce the human involvement during duplicated code refactoring procedures. We apply a scenario-based approach classifying clone pairs by their location: a set of possible refactoring techniques is suggested for each location, leaving only the other details to developers. Our approach extends an existing set [5] of classification categories; the extension allows to automatically suggest refactoring techniques for a large amount of duplications, which were considered hardly manageable by the original approach.

In future work, we plan to extend DCRA to manage all remaining locations, and to refine the parameter settings, in particular the minimum clone length and the minimum dissimilarity percentage. A planned enhancement of the Clone Detailer is the tracking of read or modified coupled entities, to obtain more detailed clues for the refactoring decision. Finally, we are investigating an extension of the approach, allowing to consider clone groups in addition to clone pairs. Another interesting topic of investigation regards the analysis of the impact of refactoring of code clones on different software quality metrics. We started a research in this direction [12] with the aim of prioritizing the clones to remove.

References

1. Zibran, M.F., Roy, C.K.: The road to software clone management: A survey. Technical Report 2012–03, The Univ. of Saskatchewan, Dept. CS, February 2012
2. Roy, C.K., Cordy, J.R.: A survey on software clone detection research. Technical Report 2007–541, Sch. Computing, Queen's Univ., Kingston, Canada, September 2007
3. Fowler, M.: Refactoring: Improving the Design of Existing Code. Addison-Wesley Longman Publishing Co. Inc., Boston (1999)
4. Roy, C.K., Cordy, J.R., Koschke, R.: Comparison and evaluation of code clone detection techniques and tools: A qualitative approach. Science of Computer Programming **74**(7), 470–495 (2009). Special Issue on ICPC 2008
5. Golomingi Koni-N'Sapu, G.: Supremo – a scenario based approach for refactoring duplicated code in object oriented systems. Master's thesis, Inst. of Computer Science, Faculty of Sciences, Univ. of Bern, June 2001
6. Roy, C., Cordy, J.: NICAD: accurate detection of near-miss intentional clones using flexible pretty-printing and code normalization. In: Proc. the 16th IEEE Int'l Conf. Program Comprehension (ICPC 2008), pp. 172–181. IEEE CS, Amsterdam (2008)
7. Tempero, E., Anslow, C., Dietrich, J., Han, T., Li, J., Lumpe, M., Melton, H., Noble, J.: The qualitas corpus: a curated collection of java code for empirical studies. In: Proc. the 17th Asia Pacific Software Eng. Conf., pp. 336–345. IEEE CS, Sydney, December 2010
8. Rattan, D., Bhatia, R., Singh, M.: Software clone detection: A systematic review. Information and Software Technology **55**(7), 1165–1199 (2013)
9. Giesecke, S.: Clone-based Reengineering für Java auf der Eclipse-Plattform. Diplomarbeit, Carl von Ossietzky Universität Oldenburg, Dept. für Informatik, Abteilung Software Eng., Germany (2003)
10. Giesecke, S.: Generic modelling of code clones. In: Koschke, R., Merlo, E., Walenstein, A. (eds.) Duplication, Redundancy, and Similarity in Software. Dagstuhl Seminar Proc., vol. 06301. Int'les Begegnungs- und Forschungszentrum für Informatik (IBFI), Germany (2007)
11. Higo, Y., Kusumoto, S., Inoue, K.: A metric-based approach to identifying refactoring opportunities for merging code clones in a java software system. J. Software Maintenance and Evolution: Research and Practice **20**(6), 435–461 (2008)
12. Arcelli Fontana, F., Zanoni, M., Ranchetti, A., Ranchetti, D.: Software clone detection and refactoring. ISRN Software Eng. **2013**, 8 (2013)

Expectations and Challenges from Scaling Agile in Mechatronics-Driven Companies – A Comparative Case Study

Christian Berger[1]([✉]) and Ulrik Eklund[2]([✉])

[1] Department of Computer Science and Engineering, University of Gothenburg,
Gothenburg, Sweden
christian.berger@gu.se
[2] Department of Computer Science, Malmö University, Malmö, Sweden
ulrik.eklund@mah.se

Abstract. Agile software development is increasingly adopted by companies evolving and maintaining software products to support better planning and tracking the realization of user stories and features. While convincing success stories help to further spread the adoption of Agile, mechatronics-driven companies need guidance to implement Agile for non-software teams. In this comparative case study of three companies from the Nordic region, we systematically investigate expectations and challenges from scaling Agile in organizations dealing with mechatronics development by conducting on-site workshops and surveys. Our findings show that all companies have already successfully implemented Agile in their software teams. The expected main benefit of successfully scaling agile development is a faster time-to-market product development; however, the two main challenges are: (a) An inflexible test environment that inhibits fast feedback to changed or added features, and (b) the existing organizational structure including the company's mind-set that needs to be opened-up for agile principles.

Keywords: Scaling agile · Agile · Software development process · Mechatronics · Comparative case study

1 Introduction

Developing high-quality software products that better match a customer's expectations is successfully supported by Agile [1]. Key advantages over other development approaches are short and fixed periods consisting of development, integration, and testing, small team sizes, and active communication within the software team while also including the customer. A flexible development approach allows a team to get frequent feedback to newly added features from the end-user but also enables reprioritization of user stories and feature requests whenever the stakeholders' needs change over time.

© Springer International Publishing Switzerland 2015
C. Lassenius et al. (Eds.): XP 2015, LNBIP 212, pp. 15–26, 2015.
DOI: 10.1007/978-3-319-18612-2_2

The typical habitat for adopting Agile are pure software-driven companies with prominent examples being Google and Amazon. Implementing Agile in environments where the final product combines software, hardware, and mechanics is more challenging considering the different nature of the involved artifacts.

1.1 Problem Domain and Motivation

In the mechatronics domain there are two opposing trends affecting R&D: Manufacturing and hardware development is a mature domain, which has been optimized for more than fifty years, but still having long lead-times, typically years. Focus during R&D is on predictability, i.e. meeting the start-of-production (SOP) with the required mechanical quality, which in practice is achieved by stage-gate/waterfall processes. In contrast, software development today is characterized by increasing speed and being more nimble while keeping quality. This typically enables lead-times of weeks or months, and many agile methods are a response to this. There are no established solutions to solve the intersection between the aforementioned trends, but the necessity to resolve them in the mechatronics domain motivates further studies.

1.2 Research Goal

The goal for this comparative study is to systematically investigate expectations and challenges from scaling Agile outside software teams on the example of three companies from the Nordic region developing and manufacturing embedded and mechatronic products. Specifically, we are interested in the following subgoals:

1. Unveiling expectations and challenges originating between teams, departments, and divisions,
2. Unveiling challenges from mechatronics-related development-, project-, and product-processes, and
3. Understanding expectations from key stakeholders like teams, managers, and organizations at large.

1.3 Contributions and Scope

We designed and conducted a comparative case study at three companies and report about our findings according to Runeson and Höst (cf. [2]). The main contributions of this work are:

1. Defining a methodology to systematically unveil and compare expectations and challenges for scaling Agile in mechatronics-driven organizations,
2. Presenting results from individual on-site workshops at the three different mechatronics companies, and
3. Summarizing results from a joint follow-up survey at all companies based on the results from the individual workshops.

1.4   Structure of the Article

The rest of the article is structured as follows: Section 2 presents related work in this field. Section 3 describes the design of the comparative case study and the embodied methods followed by the results from the comparative case study in Section 4. Section 5 presents conclusions from our study.

2   Related Work

Originally, agile methods evolved to meet the needs of small and co-located development teams [3]. They typically emphasize close customer collaboration, iterative development, and small cross-functional development teams. Also, team autonomy and end-to-end responsibility are reported as important characteristics permeating the methods [4]. Most companies introduce agile methods to increase the frequency in which they release new features and new products, and as a way to improve their software engineering efficiency. According to Dingsøyr et al. [5], agility embraces lean processes with an emphasis on realizing effective outcomes, and common for agile methods is that they entail the ability to rapidly and flexibly create and respond to change in the business and technical domains [5].

Due to many successful accounts [6,7], agile methods have become attractive also to companies involved in large-scale development of embedded systems, and several attempts to extend agile methods to include development of embedded systems are seen [8–10].

While convincing success stories from industry help to further spread the adoption of Agile, there are few studies of agile development focusing on the mechatronics domain. There are examples of some companies successfully introducing agile practices at the team level, typically characterized by individual teams defining their own ways-of-working to facilitate speed, short iterations, and delivery quality when developing their components. The experiences thereof are generally positive according to two literature reviews by [11] and [12]. There are also some publications stating that a third of German and American automotive development teams using agile practices reported in a commercial survey [13]. However, with characteristics such as hardware-software interdependencies, heavy compliance to standards and regulations, and limited flexibility due to real-time functionality [14], the development of embedded and mechatronic systems seems to challenge common practices of agile development.

3   Comparative Case Study Design

We addressed the aforementioned research goal by designing a comparative case study, where we collected data from three different mechatronics-driven companies.

3.1 Research Questions

We derived the following research questions for the comparative case study:

RQ-1: Which practices from Agile are in use in a mechatronics-driven organization?

RQ-2: How is the current implementation of Agile perceived in a mechatronics-driven organization?

RQ-3: What are the expectations from scaling Agile within a mechatronics-driven organization?

RQ-4: What are the main foreseeable challenges when scaling Agile in mechatronics-driven organizations to achieve the expected benefits?

3.2 Case and Subjects Selection

We conducted our research in the context of the Software Center[1]. The Software Center is a cooperation environment where different companies from the Nordic region collaborate with selected universities on research topics and technology transfer from academia to industry. The participating companies in the Software Center cover domains like Automotive, Telecommunication, Mobile Phones, and Defense.

For our comparative case study, we selected three large companies who are mainly mechatronics-driven in their business to which we are referring to as company A, B, and C. The companies employ between approximately 18,000 and 93,000 people and their respective yearly manufacturing of mechatronic products ranges from 0.4 to over 16 million units according to their respective annual reports from 2013. These companies can be considered to be representative due to their individual market shares. Furthermore, all companies have already adopted Agile at team-level in their R&D departments and apply it since several years during the software development of projects with varying sizes. For the workshops and surveys, participants covered experienced developers and managers from software development, hardware development, integration, and testing.

3.3 Data Collection Procedure

The data collection was conducted threefold: (a) We planned and conducted individual on-site workshops at the respective companies in the first phase; (b) the collected data from these individual workshops was analyzed to design a joint survey that was subsequently distributed to key stakeholders within the respective companies in a second phase to enlarge the population for data collection; (c) the feedback from the survey was used to plan and conduct a joint workshop with key representatives from all three companies in the third phase involving an external expert on Agile practices to follow-up on selected key challenges for scaling Agile and to identify topics where to proceed internally at the companies.

---

[1] http://www.software-center.se

Individual On-Site Workshops. The individual workshops were conducted separately for each company. The respective workshop's duration was approximately 3 hours and was moderated by one researcher while the other researcher took notes during the discussion phases. The workshop addressed in a qualitative manner the following two main questions:

1. What would be the biggest benefits if your company successfully scales Agile?
2. What are the challenges for your organization to achieve these benefits?

The participants from different teams (software development, hardware development, and testing) had approximately 20min to write their answers on two-colored sticky notes. The notes were subsequently collected, presented to the audience by the workshop moderator, and clustered during a joint discussion about the respective matter. The resulting topic maps were summarized to identify the key topics for the two aforementioned questions.

Survey. Afterwards, we designed a survey based on the results from three individual on-site workshops according to the guidelines by from Singer et al. published in Shull et al. [15]. The survey was realized as an online questionnaire to reach out to more participants who could not join the on-site workshops[2]. The questionnaire consisted of the following five sections:

1. General data about the role of the participant in the company
2. Use of Agile practices in the company
3. Evaluating the use of Agile in the company
4. Expectations from scaling Agile outside the software development teams
5. Expectations about challenges to be solved when scaling Agile

The first section contained three open-ended questions; the second section contained eight questions to be ranked as *Yes, No,* and *Not applicable* and an optional open-ended text field; the third section consisted of eight pairs that needed to be weighted on a scale from 1 to 7, where 1 means that the entire focus is on the left aspect of the pair and 7 that the entire focus is on the right aspect of the pair; additionally, an optional comment field was available. The fourth section consisted out of 16 expectations for benefits to be ranked on the 6-Likert-scale *very important, important moderately important, of little importance, unimportant,* and *not relevant*; this section was complemented with two optional questions asking for further benefits and drawbacks when scaling Agile. The last section consisted of 21 potential challenges collected during the workshops to be ranked on the same 6-Likert-scale as before; this section was also complemented with an optional question asking for further challenges.

The questionnaire was piloted with the single-points-of-contact (SPoC) from the involved companies to improve its logical structure and the overall understanding. The target group for this study contains the attendees of the on-site workshops extended in snowball manner (cf. Goodman [16]) by the SPoCs to reach out to more employees who are affected when scaling Agile.

---

[2] The survey can be found as supplementary material here: http://goo.gl/yJNez1

Joint Workshop. After conducting on-site workshops and the survey, we organized a joint workshop where we invited delegates from all companies. These delegates covered different departments not only focusing on software development. The goal for the workshop was to present the findings from the separate workshops and the survey, to jointly discuss and complement with missing challenges, and to identify first steps towards initiating initiatives for scaling Agile outside software development teams. For the workshop, we invited an external Agile expert as moderator so that we could follow the discussions among the participants from an observer perspective according to the guidelines from Seaman as published in Shull et al. [15].

3.4 Analysis Procedure

Individual On-Site Workshops. Notes were taken during the separate on-site workshops alongside with capturing the resulting topic maps. The notes were structured and summarized as separate reports that were sent to the SPoCs afterwards. The collected clustered topics as well as key statements served as basis for designing the survey.

Survey. The survey was realized as online questionnaire that allowed post-processing of the data in the statistical environment R. The data was split according to the different sections in the survey and open-ended responses were separated. Likert-visualization was chosen for the range-, pair-focusing, and Likert-scale answers; for the pair-focusing answers, Fisher's exact test (cf. [17]) was chosen to test for differences pairwisely between all companies as this test is robust and applicable even to smaller data sets.

Joint Workshop with External Agile Expert. During the joint workshop, notes were also taken to complement and structure the existing data. The main results from the joined workshop were summarized and sent to attendees afterwards.

3.5 Validity Procedure

To ensure validity in our comparative case study, we applied both, method and data triangulation: For the former, (a) we initially conducted individual on-site workshops to explore the topic at the three different sites, followed by (b) separate surveys at the respective companies with a broad set of recipients, and complemented by (c) a joint workshop from the observer perspective, where we presented results from the first two steps. For the joint workshop, (a) we collected input from different, independent companies, and (b) let the final workshop be moderated by an external person to avoid influencing the workshop outcome.

4   Results

In the following, we are presenting the joint results from the three aforementioned data sources. As the notes from the individual on-site workshops were used to design and structure the survey, they are not reported here explicitly. The survey was completed by 11 respondents from company A, 19 respondents from company B, and 16 respondents from company C resulting in 46 responses in total.

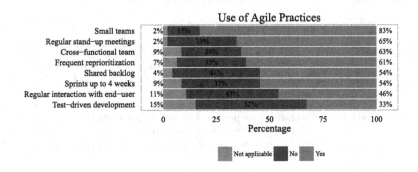

Fig. 1. Familiarity and usage of agile principles over all companies

Results to RQ-1: Fig. 1 depicts the familiarity and usage of agile principles over all companies. While having *small teams* is apparently present to a large extent, test-driven development is only applied at one third of the respondents.

Fig. 2. Where do companies put their emphasis on? Respondents could express their emphasis on a scale from 1 to 7 to describe their level of favoring one topic over the other

Results to RQ-2: The survey's next section asked to estimate where their own company puts its emphasis regarding pairs from opposite aspects regarding agile and non-agile values. Fig. 2 visualizes the responses.

We conducted a test to pairwisely compare the companies as shown in Tab. 1, and we could not observe any pairwise difference in the responses from the three different companies.

Table 1. Fisher's exact test with a p-value of 0.05: There is no difference in perceiving a company's emphasis between the responses from pairwisely comparing the companies

Where does your organization put emphasis on?	Companies		
	A/B	A/C	B/C
Individuals and interactions over processes and tools	$p = 0.691$	$p = 0.077$	$p = 0.072$
Working implementation over comprehensive documentation	$p = 1.000$	$p = 0.400$	$p = 0.272$
Customer collaboration over contract negotiation	$p = 0.433$	$p = 0.192$	$p = 0.694$
Responding to change over following a plan	$p = 1.000$	$p = 0.666$	$p = 0.476$
Product implementation over product delivery	$p = 0.380$	$p = 1.000$	$p = 0.440$
Product implementation over product integration	$p = 0.354$	$p = 0.642$	$p = 0.054$
Flexibility over predefined plan	$p = 0.679$	$p = 1.000$	$p = 0.452$
Teams over overall enterprise	$p = 0.411$	$p = 1.000$	$p = 0.710$

Results to RQ-3: The expected benefits when scaling Agile are presented in the following. As shown in Fig. 3, all companies expect with almost 90% a higher quality of the work products.

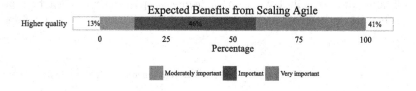

Fig. 3. Higher quality is expected from all companies

Fig. 4 depicts further expected benefits when scaling Agile where the top responses expect faster time-to-market and shorter lead-times during the development.

Results to RQ-4: The expected challenges when scaling Agile are depicted in Fig. 5. The most difficulties are expected in the existing test facilities, which is in line with the low adaptation rate for test-driven development, followed by adapting the organizational structure.

The joint workshop with the external expert on Agile resulted after a discussion phase among the involved companies in the following four cluster areas for

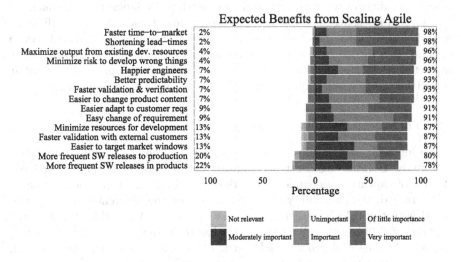

Fig. 4. Expected benefits from scaling agile over all companies

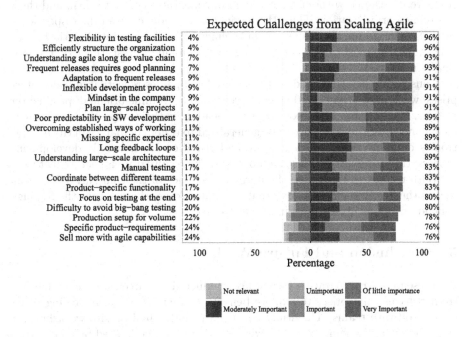

Fig. 5. Expected challenges when scaling Agile over all companies

expected challenges when scaling Agile: Leadership, Collaboration, Focusing on System, and Focusing on Customer. From these four topic areas where different possible change initiatives were jointly identified, there was consensus between all companies for (a) *improving collaboration between all disciplines involved in product development* and (b) *changing the overall mindset in the organization* as initial steps towards scaling Agile outside software development teams.

4.1 Threats to Validity

In the following, we are discussing threats to the validity of our comparative case study. Considering construct validity, our method triangulation reduced the risk of capturing incomplete data that would render in misleading results; in this regard, the plausibility of the findings from the different stages was validated with the SPoCs and the final joint workshop. A possible threat to the construct validity is that the survey was based on the underlying assumption that scaled agile development would actually have benefits for the organization, and that assumption may not be shared by respondents to the survey. Furthermore, the authors had only limited influence on the selection of the participants for the workshops.

Regarding internal validity, responses to the expected benefits from scaling Agile were gathered without associating implementation costs to them and thus, enforcing a prioritization. Thus, there might be a tendency from the respondents to wish or hope for all benefits from scaling Agile. As for initial initiatives to scale Agile, the most important challenges are of main interest, this risk, though, can be neglected.

Considering external validity, the selected companies reflect large scale enterprises with more than $15,000$ employees and a volume-oriented production process. Furthermore, these companies are leading in their respective market segments and thus, the findings can be generalized to other companies in the mechatronics domains that have a lengthy and traditionally non-agile development process; this observation is also supported by the results from Fisher's exact test.

With respect to reliability, the iterative feedback of the company's SPoCs as well as the involvement of an external expert for Agile, the risk that the findings depend on the involved researchers was tackled.

5 Conclusion and Future Work

We presented a comparative case study conducted at three large-scale, mechatronics-driven enterprises to explore benefits and challenges from scaling Agile to non-software teams. The study consisted of individual on-site workshops, a large survey, and a joint workshop with all companies moderated by an external expert on Agile. While all companies have implemented elements from Agile, main findings are that (a) the expected main benefit is a faster time-to-market product development, (b) an inflexible test environment, though, inhibits fast feedback to changed or added features and thus, prevents scaling Agile outside the software development team, and (c) the existing organizational structure including the company's mind-set needs to be adapted to beneficially scale Agile.

Relation to Existing Evidence. Our results of the need for an agile mindset and the importance of the testing environment in mechatronics systems is confirmed by other studies. [18] concludes that observed resistance towards working agile was partially based on a lack of an agile mindset, caused by extensive experience with non-agile methods, something also common among the companies in our study. [19] also identified the challenge of realizing continuos integration testing with a wide variety of platforms. One example they mention is the difficulty to reproduce reported faults with the right testing environment including released hardware.

The other main challenge on adjusting the organizational structure confirms what many scaled methods aim for, and is also the topic of both recent research (e.g. [18,20]) and of industrial frameworks such as Disciplined Agile Delivery [21].

Impact/Implications. This comparative case study is the first of its kind reporting about explorative results regarding expected benefits and challenges from scaling Agile at large scale, mechatronics-driven companies. Its findings have an apparent impact to companies with a similar development and manufacturing structure.

Limitations. All involved companies are at an comparable stage regarding scaling Agile. Thus, this comparative case study focuses primarily on the expected benefits and the foreseeable challenges when initiating initiatives for scaling Agile outside the software development teams.

Future Work. Future work needs to be done in continuously accompanying the enterprises during their initiatives for scaling Agile to collect and analyze more data towards guidelines and best practices for adopting and scaling Agile in mechatronics companies. Furthermore, comparisons with other domains would be possible to plan and guide such initiatives.

Acknowledgments. We are grateful to the companies who significantly supported this study in the context of Software Center.

References

1. Beck, K., Beedle, M., van Bennekum, A., Cockburn, A., Cunningham, W., Fowler, M., Grenning, J., Highsmith, J., Hunt, A., Jeffries, R., Kern, J., Marick, B., Martin, R.C., Mellor, S., Schwaber, K., Sutherland, J., Thomas, D.: Manifesto for the Agile Software Development (2001)
2. Runeson, P., Höst, M.: Guidelines for conducting and reporting case study research in software engineering. Empirical Software Engineering **14**(2), 131–164 (2008)

3. Kettunen, P., Laanti, M.: Combining agile software projects and large-scale organizational agility. Software Process: Improvement and Practice **13**(2), 183–193 (2008)
4. Dybå, T., Dingsøyr, T.: Empirical studies of agile software development: A systematic review. Information and Software Technology **50**(9–10), 833–859 (2008)
5. Dingsøyr, T., Nerur, S., Balijepally, V., Moe, N.B.: A decade of agile methodologies: Towards explaining agile software development. Journal of Systems and Software **85**(6), 1213–1221 (2012)
6. Abrahamsson, P., Warsta, J., Siponen, M., Ronkainen, J.: New directions on agile methods: a comparative analysis. In: Proceedings of the International Conference on Software Engineering, pp. 244–254 (2003)
7. Holmström Olsson, H., Alahyari, H., Bosch, J.: Climbing the "stairway to heaven". In: Proceeding of the Euromicro Conference on Software Engineering and Advanced Applications, Cesme, Izmir, Turkey (2012)
8. Kerievsky, J.: Industrial XP: Making XP work in large organizations. Executive Report, vol. 6, no. 2, Cutter Consortium (2005)
9. McMahon, P.: Extending agile methods: a distributed project and organizational improvement perspective. In: Systems and Software Technology Conference (2005)
10. Lagerberg, L., Skude, T., Emanuelsson, P., Sandahl, K., Stahl, D.: The impact of agile principles and practices on large-scale software development projects: a multiple-case study of two projects at ericsson. In: ACM/IEEE International Symposium on Empirical Software Engineering and Measurement, Baltimore, MD, USA, pp. 348–356 (2013)
11. Albuquerque, C.O., Antonino, P.O., Nakagawa, E.Y.: An investigation into agile methods in embedded systems development. In: Murgante, B., Gervasi, O., Misra, S., Nedjah, N., Rocha, A.M.A.C., Taniar, D., Apduhan, B.O. (eds.) ICCSA 2012, Part III. LNCS, vol. 7335, pp. 576–591. Springer, Heidelberg (2012)
12. Shen, M., Yang, W., Rong, G., Shao, D.: Applying agile methods to embedded software development: a systematic review. In: Proceedings of the International Workshop on Software Engineering for Embedded Systems, pp. 30–36. IEEE (2012)
13. Müller, M., Sazama, F., Debou, C., Dudzic, P., Abowd, P.: Survey - State of Practice "Agile in Automotive". Technical report, KUGLER MAAG CIE GmbH (2014)
14. Kaisti, M., Mujunen, T., Mäkilä, T., Rantala, V., Lehtonen, T.: Agile principles in the embedded system development. In: Cantone, G., Marchesi, M. (eds.) XP 2014. LNBIP, vol. 179, pp. 16–31. Springer, Heidelberg (2014)
15. Shull, F., Singer, J., Sjøberg, D.I.K. (eds.): Guide to Advanced Empirical Software Engineering. Springer London, London (2008)
16. Goodman, L.A.: Snowball Sampling. The Annals of Mathematical Statistics **32**(1), 148–170 (1961)
17. Fisher, R.A.: On the Interpretation of χ^2 from Contingency Tables, and the Calculation of P. Journal of the Royal Statistical Society **85**(1), 87 (1922)
18. van Manen, H., van Vliet, H.: Organization-wide agile expansion requires an organization-wide agile mindset. In: Jedlitschka, A., Kuvaja, P., Kuhrmann, M., Männistö, T., Münch, J., Raatikainen, M. (eds.) PROFES 2014. LNCS, vol. 8892, pp. 48–62. Springer, Heidelberg (2014)
19. Petersen, K., Wohlin, C.: A comparison of issues and advantages in agile and incremental development between state of the art and an industrial case. Journal of Systems and Software **82**(9), 1479–1490 (2009)
20. van Waardenburg, G., van Vliet, H.: When agile meets the enterprise. Information and Software Technology **55**(12), 2154–2171 (2013)
21. Ambler, S.W., Lines, M.: Disciplined Agile Delivery. 1 edn. IBM Press (2012)

An Industrial Case Study on Test Cases as Requirements

Elizabeth Bjarnason[1(✉)], Michael Unterkalmsteiner[2],
Emelie Engström[1], and Markus Borg[1]

[1] Lund University, SE-221 00, Lund, Sweden
{elizabeth.bjarnason,emelie.engstrom,markus.borg}@cs.lth.se
[2] Blekinge Institute of Technology, SE-371 79, Karlskrona, Sweden
mun@bth.se

Abstract. It is a conundrum that agile projects can succeed 'without require-ments' when weak requirements engineering is a known cause for project fail-ures. While Agile development projects often manage well without extensive requirements documentation, test cases are commonly used as requirements. We have investigated this agile practice at three companies in order to under-stand how test cases can fill the role of requirements. We performed a case study based on twelve interviews performed in a previous study. The findings include a range of benefits and challenges in using test cases for eliciting, vali-dating, verifying, tracing and managing requirements. In addition, we identified three scenarios for applying the practice, namely as a mature practice, as a de facto practice and as part of an agile transition. The findings provide insights into how the role of requirements may be met in agile development including challenges to consider.

Keywords: Agile development · Behaviour-driven development · Acceptance test · Requirements and test alignment · Case study

1 Introduction

Agile development methods strive to be responsive to changing business requirements by integrating requirements, design, implementation and testing processes [1][2]. Face-to-face communication is prioritised over written requirements documentation and cus-tomers are expected to convey their needs directly to the developers [3][4]. However, weak customer communication in combination with minimal documentation is reported to cause problems in scaling and evolving software for agile projects [4].

Requirements specifications fill many roles. They are used to communicate among stakeholders within a software development project, to drive design and testing, and to serve as a reference for project managers and in the evolution of the system [6]. Due to the central role of requirements in coordinating software development, there exists a plethora of research on how to document requirements with varying degrees of formality depending on its intended use. This spans from formal requirements specifications [7] and requirements models [8], over templates [9] to user stories [10] and requirements expressed using natural language. At the formal end of the spec-trum, requirements specifications can be automatically checked for consistency [11]

© Springer International Publishing Switzerland 2015
C. Lassenius et al. (Eds.): XP 2015, LNBIP 212, pp. 27–39, 2015.
DOI: 10.1007/978-3-319-18612-2_3

and used to derive other artefacts, e.g. software designs [12] or test cases [13]. For the less formal approaches, requirements documentation is driven by heuristics and best practices for achieving high quality [14] requirements.

The coordination of evolving requirements poses a challenge in aligning these with later development activities including testing [5]. In a previous study we identified the use of test cases as requirements (TCR) as one of several industrial practices used to address this challenge [5]. In this paper, we investigate this practice further by a more detailed analysis of the interview data from the three case companies (of six) that explicitly mentioned this practice. The case study presented in this paper investigates how the practice may support the role of requirements engineering (RE) by investigating **RQ1** How does the TCR practice fulfil the role of requirements? and **RQ2** Why and how is the TCR practice applied?

The rest of this paper is organized as follows. Section 2 describes related work. Section 3 presents the case companies and Section 4 the applied research method. The results are reported in Section 5, while the research questions are answered in Sections 6 and 7. The paper is concluded in Section 8.

2   Agile RE: Test Cases as Requirements Documentation

In agile software development requirements and tests can be seen as two sides of the same coin. Martin and Melnik [15] hypothesize that as the formality of specifications increases, requirements and tests become indistinguishable. This principle is taken to the extreme by unit tests [16] where requirements are formalized in executable code. Practitioners report using unit tests as a technical specification that evolves with the implementation [17]. However, unit tests may be too technical for customers and thereby lack the important attribute of being understandable to all relevant stakeholders.

Acceptance tests are used to show customers that the system fulfils the requirements [18]. However, developing acceptance tests from requirements specifications is a subjective process that does not guarantee that all requirements are covered [18]. This is further complicated by requirements documentation rarely being updated [19], leading to potentially outdated acceptance tests. In agile development, automated acceptance tests (AATs) drive the implementation and address these issues by documenting requirements and expected outcomes in an executable format [4][20]. This agile practice is known, among others, as customer tests, scenario tests, executable/automated acceptance tests, behaviour driven development and story test driven development [21].

Some organisations view and use the AATs as requirements thereby fully integrating these two artefacts [15]. AATs are used to determine if the system is acceptable from a customer perspective and used as the basis for customer discussions, thus reducing the risk of building the wrong system. However, the communication might be more technical and require more technical insight of the customer. Melnik et al. [22] found that customers in partnership with software engineers could communicate and validate business requirements through AATs, although there is an initial learning curve.

The conceptual difficulty of specifying tests before implementation [23][24][25] led to the conception of behaviour-driven development (BDD) [26]. BDD incorporates aspects of requirements analysis, requirements documentation and communication, and automated acceptance testing. The behaviour of a system is defined in a domain-specific language (DSL); a common language that reduces ambiguities and misunderstandings. This is further enhanced by including terms from the business domain in the DSL.

Haugset and Hansen studied acceptance test driven development (ATDD) as an RE practice and report on its benefits and risks [20]. Our work extends on this by also investigating companies that use the TCR practice without applying ATDD principles.

3 Case Companies

The three case companies all develop software using an agile development model. However, a number of other factors vary between the companies. These factors are summarised in Table 1 and the interviewees are characterised in Table 2.

Table 1. Overview of the case companies

Company	A	B	C
Type of company	Softw. develop., embedded products	Consulting	Softw. develop., embedded products
#employees in softw development	125-150	135	1,000
#employees in typical project	10	Mostly 4-10, but varies greatly	Previously: 800-1,000 person years
Distributed	No	No	Yes
Domain / System type	Computer networking equipment	Advisory/technical services, appl. management	Telecom
Source of reqts	Market driven	Bespoke	Bespoke, market driven
Main quality focus	Availability, performance, security	Depends on customer focus	Performance, stability
Certification	Not software related	No	ISO9001
Process Model	Agile	Agile in variants	Agile with gate decisions Previous: Waterfall
Project duration	6-18 months	No typical project	Previously: 2 years
#requirements in typical project	100 (20-30 pages HTML)	No typical project	Previously: 14,000
#test cases in typical project	~1,000 test cases	No typical project	Previously: 200,000 for platform, 7,000 for system
Product Lines	Yes	No	Yes
Open Source	Yes	Yes incl. contributions	Yes (w agile dev model)

3.1   Company A

Company A develops network equipment consisting of hardware and software. The software development unit covered by the interview study has around 150 employees. The company is relatively young but has been growing fast during the past few years. A typical software project has a lead time of 6-18 months, around 10 co-located members and approximately 100 requirements and 1,000 system test cases. A market-driven requirements engineering process is applied. The quality focus for the software is on availability, performance and security. Furthermore, the company applies a product-line approach and uses open-source software in their development.

A product manager, a project manager, and a tester were interviewed at Company A, all of which described how the company manages requirements as test cases.

3.2   Company B

Company B is a consultancy firm that provides technical services to projects that vary in size and duration. Most projects consist of one development team of 4-10 people located at the customer site. The requirements are defined by a customer (bespoke).

The three consultants that were interviewed at Company B can mainly be characterised as software developers. However, they all typically take on a multitude of roles within a project and are involved throughout the entire lifecycle. All three of these interviewees described the use of the TCR practice.

3.3   Company C

Company C develops software for embedded products in the telecommunications domain. The software development unit investigated in this study, consists of 1,000 people. At the time of the interviews, the company was transitioning from a waterfall process to an agile process. Projects typically run over 2 years and include 400-500 people. The project size and lead time is expected to decrease with the agile process. The projects handle a combination of bespoke and market-driven requirements. Including the product-line requirements, they handle a very complex and large set of requirements.

Six of the interviewees (of 15) discussed the practice, namely one requirements engineer, two project managers, two process managers and one tester.

Table 2. Interviewees per company. Experience in role noted as S(enior) = more than 3 years, or J(unior) = up to 3 years. Interviewees mentioning the TCR practice are marked with **bold**. Note: For Company B, software developers also perform RE and testing tasks.

Role	A	B	C
Requirements engineer			**C1:S**, C6:S, C7:S
Systems architect			C4:S
Software developer		**B1:J, B2:S, B3:S**	C13:S
Test engineer	A2:S		C9:S, **C10:S**, C11:J, C12:S, C14:S
Project manager	A1:J		**C3:J, C8:S**
Product manager	A3:S		
Process manager			**C2:J, C5:S**, C15:J

4   Method

We used a flexible exploratory case study design and process [27] consisting of four stages: 1) *Definition*, 2) *Evidence selection*, 3) *Data analysis* and 4) *Reporting.*

Definition of Research Questions and Planning. Since we were interested in how agile development can be successful 'without requirements' we selected to focus on the practice of using test cases as requirements. We formulated the research questions, (RQ1) How does the TCR practice fulfil the role of requirements? and (RQ2) Why and how is the TCR practice applied?

Evidence Selection. We selected to use word-by-word transcriptions from our previous study of RE-Testing coordination. The research questions of this paper are within the broader scope of the previous study [5], which also included agile processes. In addition, the semi-structured interviews provided rich material since the interviewees could freely describe how practices were applied including benefits and challenges. Data selection was facilitated by the rigorous coding performed in the previous study. We selected the interview parts coded for the TCR practice. In addition, the transcripts were searched for key terms such as 'acceptance test', 'specification'.

Data Analysis. The analysis of the selected interview data was performed in two steps. First the transcripts were descriptively coded. These codes were then categorised into benefits and challenges, and reported per case company in Section 5. The analysis was performed by the first author. The results were validated independently by the third author. The third author analysed and interpreted a fine-grained grouping of the interview data produced in the previous study, and compared this against the results obtained by the first researcher. No conflicting differences were found.

5   Results

Two of the investigated companies apply the TCR practice while the third company plan to apply it. The maturity of the practice thus varied. The interviewees for Company B provided the most in depth description of the practice, which is reflected in the amount of results per company. Limitations of the findings are discussed in Section 5.4.

5.1   Company A: A De Facto Practice

Test cases have become the de facto requirements in company A due to weak RE (A2[1]), i.e. the RE maturity in the company is low while there is a strong competence within testing. Formal (traditional) requirements are mainly used at the start of a project. However, these requirements are not updated during the project and lack traceability to the test cases. Instead, the test cases become the requirements in the sense that they verify and ensure that the product fulfils the required behaviour.

---

[1]   Mentioned by this interviewee, see interviewee codes in Table 2.

Benefits. Efficient way of managing requirements in a small and co-located organisation that does not require managing and maintaining a formal requirements specification once test design has been initiated (A1). In addition, the structure of the test specifications is closer to the code simplifying navigation of these 'requirements' once the implementation has started (A1).

Challenges. As the company grows, the lack of traces to formal requirements is a problem in communication of requirements changes to the technical roles (A1, A2) and in ensuring correct test cases (A2). In addition, the test cases lack information about requirements priority, stakeholders etc., needed by the development engineers when a test case fails (A2) or is updated (A3). The untraced artefacts do not support either ensuring test coverage of the formal requirements (A1, A3), or identifying the test cases corresponding to the requirements re-used for a new project (A2).

5.2   Company B: An Established Practice

Company B actively applies the TCR practice through behaviour-driven development supported by tools. The customer and the product owner define product and customer requirements. Then, for each iteration, the development engineers produce acceptance criteria (user scenarios) and acceptance test cases from these requirements. These 'requirements test cases' are iterated with the business roles to ensure validity (B1), and entered into an acceptance test tool that produces an executable specification. The interviewees described that the acceptance criteria can be used as a system specification. However, interviewee B3 stated that the acceptance criteria can be read 'to get an impression. But, if you wonder what it means, you can look at the implementation', i.e. this documentation is not fully stand-alone.

Benefits. The interviewees stated that the main benefits are improved customer collaboration around requirements, strengthened alignment of business requirements with verification, and support for efficient regression testing. The customer collaboration raises the technical discussion to a more conceptual level while also improving requirements validity, since, as an engineer said, 'we understand more of the requirements. They concretize what we will do.' (B1) This alignment of business and technical aspects was experienced to also be supported when managing requirements changes by the use of acceptance test cases as formal requirements (B2, B3). At the end of a project the acceptance test cases show 'what we've done' (B2). Furthermore, the executable specification provided by this practice, in combination with unit tests, acts as a safety net that enables projects to 'rebound from anything' (B1) by facilitating tracking of test coverage, efficiently managing bugs and performance issues.

Challenges. The interviewees mentioned several challenges for the practice concerning active customer involvement, managing complex requirements, balancing acceptance vs. unit tests and maintaining the 'requirements test cases'. Over time the company has achieved active customer involvement in defining and managing requirements with this practice, but it has been challenging to ensure that 'we spoke the same language' (B3). The interviewees see that customer competence affects the communication and the outcome. For example, interviewee B3 said that non-technical customers seldom focus on quality requirements. Similarly, getting the customer to work directly with requirements (i.e. the acceptance test cases) in the tool has not been achieved. This is further complicated by issues with setting up common access across networks.

Complex interactions and dependencies between requirements, e.g. for user interfaces (B1) and quality requirements (B2), are a challenge both to capture with acceptance test cases and in involving the customer in detailing them. Furthermore, automatically testing performance and other quality aspects on actual hardware and in a live testing environment is challenging to manage with this approach.

All interviewees mentioned the challenge in balancing acceptance vs. unit test cases. It can be hard to motivate engineers to write acceptance-level test cases. Furthermore, maintenance of the acceptance test cases needs to be considered when applying this practice (B1, B2, B3). Interviewee B3 pointed out that test cases are more rigid than requirements and thus more sensitive to change. There is also a risk of deteriorating test case quality when testers make frequent fixes to get the tests to pass (B2).

5.3   Company C: Planned Practice as Part of Agile Transition

The agile transition at the company included introduction of this practice. Requirements will be defined by a team consisting of a product owner, developers and testers. User stories will be detailed into requirements that specify 'how the code should work' (C8). These will be documented as acceptance test cases by the testers and traced to the user stories. Another team will be responsible for maintaining the software including the user stories, test cases and traces between them. In the company's traditional process, test cases have been used as quality requirements, as a de facto practice. Interviewee C1 describes an attempt to specify these as formal requirements that failed due to not reaching an agreement on responsibility for the cross-functional requirements within the development organisation.

Benefits. The practice is believed to decrease misunderstandings of requirements between business and technical roles, improve on the communication of changes and in keeping the requirements documentation updated (C5, C10).

Challenges. Integrating the differing characteristics and competences of the RE and testing activities are seen as a major challenge (C5, C10) in the collaboration between roles and in the tools. RE aspects that need to be provided in the testing tools include noting the source of a requirement, connections and dependencies to other requirements and validity for different products (C5).

5.4   Limitations

We discuss limitations of our results using guidelines provided by Runeson et al. [27].

Construct Validity. A main threat to validity lies in that the analysed data stems from interviews exploring the broader area of coordinating RE and testing. This limits the depth and extent of the findings to what the interviewees spontaneously shared around the practice in focus in this paper. In particular, the fact that the practice was not yet fully implemented at Company C at the time of the interviews limits the insights gained from those interviews. However, we believe that the broad approach of the original study in combination with the semi-structured interviews provide valuable insights, even though further studies are needed to fully explore the topic.

External Validity. The findings may be generalized to companies with similar characteristics as the case companies (see Section 3), by theoretical generalization [27].

Reliability. The varying set of roles from each case poses a risk of missing important perspectives, e.g. for Company B the product owner's view would complement the available interview data from the development team. There is a risk of researcher bias in the analysis and interpretation of the data. This was partly mitigated by triangulation; two researchers independently performing these steps. Furthermore, a rigorous process was applied in the (original) data collection including researcher triangulation of interviewing, transcription and coding, which increases the reliability of the selected data.

6   Test Cases in the Role of Requirements (RQ1)

We discuss how the TCR practice supports the main roles of RE and the requirements specification according to roles defined by Lauesen [28], i.e. the elicitation and validation of stakeholders' requirements; software verification; tracing; and managing requirements. The discussion is summarised in Table 3.

Table 3. Summary of benefits and challenges per role of RE

Benefits	Challenges
Elicitation and Validation	
Cross-functional communication	Good Customer-Developer relationship
Align goals & perspectives between roles	Active customer involvement
Address barrier of specifying solutions	Sufficient technical and RE competence
	Complex requirements
Verification	
Supports regression testing	Quality requirements
Increased requirements quality	
Test coverage	
Tracing	
Requirements - test case tracing in BDD	Tool integration
Requirements Management	
Maintaining RET alignment	Locating impacted requirements
Requirement are kept updated	Missing requirement context
Communication of changes	Test case maintenance
Efficient documentation updates	

6.1   Elicitation and Validation

The TCR practice supports elicitation and validation of requirements by its direct and frequent communication between business and technical roles for all companies. The customer involvement in combination with increased awareness of customer perspectives among the technical roles supports defining valid requirements. This confirms observations by Melnik and Maurer [29], Park and Maurer [30], Haugset and Hanssen [20] and Latorre [31]. Furthermore, at Company B, the use of the acceptance criteria format led to customers expressing requirements at a higher abstraction level instead of focusing on technical details. Thus, this practice can address the elicitation barrier of requesting specific solutions rather than expressing needs [28].

Nevertheless, the TCR practice requires good customer relations, as stated by interviewees in Company B. Active customer involvement is a known challenge for agile RE due to time and space restrictions for the customer, but also due to that this role requires a combination of business and technical skills [4][31]. Business domain tools can be used to facilitate the customers in specifying acceptance tests [30]. For example, Haugset and Hanssen [20] report that customers used spread-sheets to communicate information and never interacted directly with actual test cases.

Eliciting and validating requirements, in particular complex ones, relies on competence of the roles involved. At Company B limited technical knowledge affected the customer's ability to discuss quality requirements. This can lead to neglecting to elicit them altogether [4]. Similarly, capturing complex requirements with acceptance test cases is a challenge, in particular for user interactions and quality requirements.

6.2   Verification

The TCR practice supports verification of requirements by automating regression tests as for Company B. The AATs act as a safety net that catches problems and enables frequent release of product-quality code. This was also observed by Kongsli [32], Haugset and Hanssen [20], and Latorre [31]. The practice ensures that all specified requirements (as test cases) are verified and test coverage can be measured by executing the tests.

The verification effort relies on verifiable, clear and unambiguous requirements [6]. Test cases are per definition verifiable and the format used by Company B supports defining clear requirements. Nevertheless, Company B mentioned quality requirements as a particular challenge for embedded devices as this requires actual hardware. This confirms previous findings by Ramesh [4] and Haugset and Hanssen [20] that quality requirements are difficult to capture with AATs.

6.3   Tracing

Tracing of requirements and test cases is supported by the TCR practice, however the benefits depend on the context. Merely using test cases as de facto requirements (as in Company A) does not affect tracing. For the BDD approach applied at Company B, the tools implicitly trace acceptance criteria and test cases, although there are no traces between the original customer requirements and the acceptance criteria. Hence, as the requirements evolve [33] this knowledge is reflected purely in the test cases.

At Company C, where user stories were to be detailed directly into acceptance test cases, tracing remains a manual, albeit straight forward task of connecting acceptance test cases to the corresponding user stories. Furthermore, the responsibility for these traces is clearly defined in the development process, a practice identified by Uusitalo [34] as supporting traceability. However, it is a challenge for the company to identify tools which provide sufficient support for requirements and for testing aspects, and for the integration of the two.

6.4   Requirements Management

The TCR practice provides benefits in managing requirements in an efficient way throughout the life-cycle. As mentioned for Companies A and B, the practice facilitates a joint understanding of requirements that provides a base for discussing and making decisions regarding changes. However, the practice also requires effort in involving development engineers in the requirements discussion. The optimal balance between involving these technical roles to ensure coordination of requirements versus focusing on pure development activities remains as future work.

The challenge of keeping requirements updated after changes [5] is addressed by a close integration with test cases, as for Company B, since the test cases are by necessity updated throughout the project. Furthermore, since the requirements are documented in an executable format, conflicting new or changed requirements are likely to cause existing test cases to fail. However, locating requirements in a set of test cases was mentioned as a challenge for Company B due to badly structured test cases. The difficulty of organizing and sorting automated tests has also been reported by Park [21].

Contextual requirements information, e.g. purpose and priority [28], is seldom retained in the test cases but can support, for example, impact analysis and managing failed test cases. Without access to contextual information from the test cases, additional effort is required to locate it to enable decision making.

7   The Reasons for and Contexts of the Practice (RQ2)

Each case company applies the practice differently and for different reasons. At Company A it has become a *de facto practice* due to strong development and test competence, and weak RE processes. However, merely viewing test cases as requirements does not fully compensate for a lack of RE. Company A faces challenges in managing requirements changes and ensuring test coverage of requirements. The requirements documentation does not satisfy the information needs of all stakeholders and staff turnover may result in loss of (undocumented) product knowledge. As size and complexity increase so does the challenge of coordinating customer needs with testing effort [5].

Company B applies the practice *consciously using a full BDD approach including tool support*. This facilitates customer communication through which the engineering roles gain requirements insight. The AATs provide a feedback system confirming the engineers' understanding of the business domain [30]. However, it is a challenge to get customers to specify requirements in the AAT tools. Letting domain experts or customers provide information via e.g. spread-sheets may facilitate this [30].

The third practice variant is found at Company C, where it is consciously *planned as part of a transition to agile processes* applying story test driven development [21]. The practice includes close and continuous collaboration around requirements between business and development roles. However, no specific language for expressing the acceptance criteria or specific tools for managing these are planned. In contrast to the de facto context, Company C envisions this practice as enabling analysis and maintenance of requirements. To achieve this, requirements dependencies and priorities need to be supported by the test management tools.

8   Conclusions and Future Work

Coordinating and aligning frequently changing business needs is a challenge in software development projects. In agile projects this is mainly addressed through frequent and direct communication between the customer and the development team, and the detailed requirements are often documented as test cases.

Our case study provides insights into how this practice meets the various roles that the requirements play. The results show that the direct and frequent communication of this practice supports eliciting, validating and managing new and changing customer requirements. Furthermore, specifying requirements as acceptance test cases allow the requirements to become a living document that supports verifying and tracing requirements through the life cycle. We have also identified three contexts for this practice; as a de facto practice, part of an agile transition and as a mature practice.

The results can aid practitioners in improving their agile practices and provide a basis for further research. Future work includes investigating how to further improve the RE aspects when documenting requirements as test cases.

Acknowledgement. We want to thank the interviewees. This work was funded by EASE (ease.cs.lth.se).

References

1. Sommerville, I.: Integrated requirements engineering: a tutorial. IEEE Softw. **22**, 16–23 (2005)
2. Layman, L., Williams, L., Cunningham, L.: Motivations and measurements in an agile case study. J. Syst. Archit. **52**, 654–667 (2006)
3. Beck, K.: Manifesto for Agile Software Development. http://agilemanifesto.org/
4. Ramesh, B., Cao, L., Baskerville, R.: Agile requirements engineering practices and challenges: an empirical study. Inf. Syst. J. **20**, 449–480 (2010)

5. Bjarnason, E., Runeson, P., Borg, M., et al.: Challenges and practices in aligning requirements with verification and validation: a case study of six companies. Empir. Softw. Eng. **19**, 1809–1855 (2014)
6. Davis, A.M.: Just Enough Requirements Management: Where Software Development Meets Marketing. Dorset House, New York (2005)
7. van Lamsweerde, A.: Formal specification: a roadmap. In: Conf. on The Future of Software Engineering, pp. 147–159. ACM, Limerick (2000)
8. Pohl, K.: Requirements Engineering - Fundamentals, Principles, and Techniques. Springer, Heidelberg (2010)
9. Mavin, A., Wilkinson, P.: Big ears (the return of "easy approach to requirements engineering"). In: 18th Int. Reqts. Engineering Conf., pp. 277–282. IEEE, Sydney (2010)
10. Cohn, M.: User Stories Applied: For Agile Software Development. Addison-Wesley Professional, Boston (2004)
11. Heitmeyer, C.L., Jeffords, R.D., Labaw, B.G.: Automated Consistency Checking of Requirements Specifications. ACM Trans. Softw. Eng. Methodol. **5**, 231–261 (1996)
12. Dromey, R.G.: From requirements to design: formalizing the key steps. In: 1st Int'l Conf. on Software Engineering and Formal Methods, pp. 2–11. IEEE, Brisbane (2003)
13. Miller, T., Strooper, P.: A case study in model-based testing of specifications and implementations. Softw. Test. Verification Reliab. **22**, 33–63 (2012)
14. Davis, A., Overmyer, S., Jordan, K., et al.: Identifying and measuring quality in a software requirements specification. In: 1st Int. Softw. Metrics Symp., Baltimore, USA, pp. 141–152 (1993)
15. Martin, R.C., Melnik, G.: Tests and Requirements, Requirements and Tests: A Möbius Strip. IEEE Softw. **25**, 54–59 (2008)
16. Whittaker, J.A.: What is software testing? And why is it so hard? IEEE Softw. **17**, 70–79 (2000)
17. Runeson, P.: A survey of unit testing practices. IEEE Softw. **23**, 22–29 (2006)
18. Hsia, P., Kung, D., Sell, C.: Software requirements and acceptance testing. Ann. Softw. Eng. **3**, 291–317 (1997)
19. Lethbridge, T.C., Singer, J., Forward, A.: How software engineers use documentation: the state of the practice. IEEE Softw. **20**, 35–39 (2003)
20. Haugset, B., Hanssen, G.K.: Automated acceptance testing: a literature review and an industrial case study. In: Agile Conf., pp. 27–38. IEEE, Toronto (2008)
21. Park, S., Maurer, F.: A literature review on story test driven development. In: 11th Int. Conf. on Agile Processes in Softw. Engin. and Extreme Progr., pp. 208–213 (2010)
22. Melnik, G., Maurer, F., Chiasson, M.: Executable acceptance tests for communicating business requirements: customer perspective. In: IEEE Agile Conf., USA, pp. 35–46 (2006)
23. Causevic, A., Sundmark, D., Punnekkat, S.: Factors limiting industrial adoption of test driven development: a systematic review. In: 4th Int'l Conf. on Software Testing, Verification and Validation, pp. 337–346. IEEE, Berlin (2011)
24. George, B., Williams, L.: A structured experiment of test-driven development. Inf. Softw. Technol. **46**, 337–342 (2004)
25. Janzen, D.S., Saiedian, H.: A leveled examination of test-driven development acceptance. In: 29th Int'l Conf. on Software Engineering, pp. 719–722. IEEE, Minneapolis (2007)
26. North, D.: Behavior Modification: The evolution of behavior-driven development (2006)
27. Runeson, P., Höst, M., Rainer, A., Regnell, B.: Case Study Research in Software Engineering: Guidelines and Examples. Wiley, Hoboken (2012)

28. Lauesen, S.: Software Requirements: Styles & Techniques. Addison-Wesley Professional, Harlow (2002)
29. Melnik, G., Maurer, F.: Multiple perspectives on executable acceptance test-driven development. In: Concas, G., Damiani, E., Scotto, M., Succi, G. (eds.) XP 2007. LNCS, vol. 4536, pp. 245–249. Springer, Heidelberg (2007)
30. Park, S., Maurer, F.: Communicating domain knowledge in executable acceptance test driven development. In: Abrahamsson, P., Marchesi, M., Maurer, F. (eds.) Agile Processes in Software Engineering and Extreme Programming. LNBIP, vol. 31, pp. 23–32. Springer, Heidelberg (2009)
31. Latorre, R.: A successful application of a Test-Driven Development strategy in the industrial environment. Empir. Softw. Eng. **19**, 753–773 (2014)
32. Kongsli, V.: Towards agile security in web applications. In: 21st ACM SIGPLAN Symp. on Object-oriented Progr. Systems, Languages, & Appl., Portland, USA, pp. 805–808 (2006)
33. Mugridge, R.: Managing Agile Project Requirements with Storytest-Driven Development. IEEE Softw. **25**, 68–75 (2008)
34. Uusitalo, E.J., Komssi, M., Kauppinen, M., Davis, A.M.: Linking requirements and testing in practice. In: 16th Int. Conf. Reqts. Engineering, pp. 265–270. IEEE, Catalunya (2008)

What Do Practitioners Vary in Using Scrum?

Philipp Diebold[1], Jan-Peter Ostberg[2], Stefan Wagner[2]($^{(\boxtimes)}$),
and Ulrich Zendler[2]

[1] Fraunhofer Institute for Experimental Software Engineering IESE,
Kaiserslautern, Germany
philipp.diebold@iese.fraunhofer.de
[2] University of Stuttgart, Stuttgart, Germany
{jan-peter.ostberg,stefan.wagner,ulrich.zendler}@iste.uni-stuttgart.de

Abstract. *Background*: Agile software development has become a popular way of developing software. Scrum is the most frequently used agile framework, but it is often reported to be adapted in practice. *Objective*: Thus, we aim to understand how Scrum is adapted in different contexts and what are the reasons for these changes. *Method*: Using a structured interview guideline, we interviewed ten German companies about their concrete usage of Scrum and analysed the results qualitatively. *Results*: All companies vary Scrum in some way. The least variations are in the Sprint length, events, team size and requirements engineering. Many users varied the roles, effort estimations and quality assurance. *Conclusions*: Many variations constitute a substantial deviation from Scrum as initially proposed. For some of these variations, there are good reasons. Sometimes, however, the variations are a result of a previous non-agile, hierarchical organisation.

Keywords: Agile processes · Scrum variations · Industrial case study

1 Introduction

Nowadays, agile software development has become a common way of developing software, especially in the information systems domain. A survey on agile development [7] shows that, although there are many agile process frameworks, only few are regularly used: *Scrum, Extreme Programming* (XP) and *Kanban*. Scrum is the most frequently used agile process framework with more than 70% of the answering companies using it [7]. Yet, only 55% use "pure" Scrum as it has been initially described. Practitioners apply a combination of Scrum and other approaches or processes, e.g. XP or Kanban, as well as adaptations. Ken Schwaber, one of the Scrum inventors, states that around "75% of companies that claim using Scrum, do not really use Scrum" [2].

Therefore, our research objective is to understand these variations in the application of Scrum in practice. We investigate **which** variations were introduced and **why** they are used. To do so, we interviewed employees of ten German software companies from different domains and with different sizes and analysed the answers qualitatively.

© Springer International Publishing Switzerland 2015
C. Lassenius et al. (Eds.): XP 2015, LNBIP 212, pp. 40–51, 2015.
DOI: 10.1007/978-3-319-18612-2_4

2 Scrum Background

To be able to identify *variations*, we need to establish what the *standard* is. We use the "Scrum Guide" [13] as our basis for comparison. Thus, we will summarise the aspects that are most important for this paper:

The roles involved in Scrum are: **Scrum Master**, **Product Owner** and **Development Team**. The Scrum Master is responsible for the team sticking to the rules of Scrum and for organising the events. It is his or her task to introduce changes to optimise the productivity of the Development Team. The Product Owner is the interface between the Development Team and the stakeholders of the project. It is his or her task to collect all requirements and add them to the **Product Backlog**, the list of known requirements and related tasks. The Product Owner has to prioritise the requirements in the Product Backlog. She or he is the only one authorised to change the Product Backlog, and "the Product Owner is one person, not a committee" [13]. The Development Team has a size of three to nine developers who are self-organising and cross-functional.

The product is developed in iterations called **Sprints** taking two to four weeks with a fixed length (that could vary over the teams). A Sprint can only be abandoned by the Product Owner if the aim of the Sprint does not match the aim of the project anymore. At the end of each Sprint, a releasable working (software) product is available.

Each Sprint contains the following events:

- The **Sprint Planning** defines the aim of the Sprint: The Product Owner presents the backlog items with the highest priority, and the Team estimates how many of them can be accomplished in the next Sprint. This results in the **Sprint Backlog** containing all requirements the team committed to accomplish.
- During the Sprint, the Development Team holds a **Daily Scrum** of 15 minutes maximum supervised by the Scrum Master. In this event three questions are answered: *What have I accomplished yesterday to fulfil the Sprint aim? What will I do today to approach the Sprint aim? Did I encounter a problem which could interfere with the progress?*
- In the **Sprint Review**, at the end of each Sprint, the Sprint results are presented to the stakeholders and accepted based on a common definition of "Done". The stakeholders give feedback about the new increment and further progress is discussed.
- In the **Sprint Retrospective**, the Development Team reflects about the Sprint to detect problems and develop solutions.

3 Case Study Design

3.1 Research Questions

Our research objective is to better understand the variations of Scrum in practice and the reasons for these variations. Thus, our study goal is:

> *Analyse the **Scrum framework** to explore its **industrial usage** with respect to its **variations** from the perspective of **practitioners**.*

We broke down this research goal, which still covers a wide area, into research questions (RQ) for a detailed analysis. Based on the description of Scrum (Section 2) as the standard for comparison, we ended up with the following research questions focusing on the variations and reasons of their application to Scrum:

- **RQ1:** What and why do they vary in the **Development Team**?
   - **RQ1.1:** What and why do they vary in the **role** of **Product Owner**?
   - **RQ1.2:** What and why do they vary in the **role** of **Scrum Master**?
- **RQ2:** What and why do they vary in the **Sprints**?
- **RQ3:** What and why do they vary in the **events**?
- **RQ4:** What and why do they vary in **requirements engineering**?
- **RQ5:** What and why do they vary in **quality assurance**?

3.2   Case and Subjects Selection

We selected the cases and subjects based on the availability and willingness of the interview partners. The cases, the specific projects where Scrum is applied, depend on the study subjects, the interview participants, because they can only provide experience from their past or current projects. We also aimed to maximise variation by asking companies from different domains.

3.3   Data Collection Procedure

We conducted semi-structured interviews with the subjects about their most recent projects in which they applied Scrum. The guiding questions we used in the interviews are available in [4] and are aligned with common available Scrum checklists [9]. Nonetheless, we did not use such checklists, because the reasoning behind the variations of Scrum is not in their scope.

We conducted all interviews by one of the authors as interviewer together with one company employee as interviewee. Within the interviews (1) we first explained the idea behind this work to the participants. (2) We informed them that we handle their answers anonymously. (3) We gave them the interview questions and started discussing and answering. The result of the data collection were the final notes from each interview.

3.4   Analysis Procedure

We analysed the notes of the interviews purely qualitatively. First, we distilled categories with short answers into a table. For example, we collected the Sprint length, the duration of the events or the team size for each case. Second, we extracted and combined the answers for each of the research questions from the notes. We discussed and refined these answers among all researchers. For further discussion, we also checked possible connections between the asked questions and a mapping study for the usage of agile practices [3].

3.5   Validity Procedure

Our main action was to build and use the structured interview guideline to support the validity of the results. We selected the study subjects so as to avoid any interference between them. At the beginning, we stated the purpose of the interview, and we assured them that the results would be treated anonymously which gave the interviewees the freedom to give honest and open answers. As we did not record the interviews, we offered the interviewees the possibility to check the notes after the interview.

All researchers read and discussed the interview notes as well as the extracted answers. For part of the table presenting the results, an independent re-extraction of the answers from the interview notes was conducted by two researchers to find and resolve discrepancies in the interpretation.

4   Results

4.1   Case and Subject Description

We conducted 10 interviews. The German companies of our interviewees cover a wide range from one very small start-up (4 employees) up to companies with around 130,000 employees. Six of the companies had a size between 100 and 350 employees. The remaining three companies are large corporations with several thousand employees. Most of the companies (except the smallest one) work and sell their products or services internationally. Besides the size and internationality of the organisations, we were interested in the different domains they were working in to further increase the variation. Yet, nine companies are working in different information systems domains and the other one in embedded systems. Our interviewees were all developers or development managers but are not necessarily representative for other Scrum teams in the same company.

4.2   Overview

We were able to give short answers for 14 aspects of the interview notes. These are shown in Table 1. We provide the team size (excluding Scrum Master and Product Owner), if tasks are outsourced, i.e. given to people outside of the team, and if the team is at only one location. We show if there is a Scrum Master and a Product Owner. For all the event types, we give the durations and, for the Daily Scrums, also if discussions are allowed beyond the answers to the three questions. For the Sprint planning, we report the Sprint lengths, if there is a buffer in the plan, if there is a release plan and whether stories not completed in a Sprint are put back into the Product Backlog, split or continued. If we could not clearly determine the answer from the notes, we mark the cell with an "?".

Table 1. Results of the Interviews

No.	Team Size	Tasks Out-sourced	Team Local	Scrum Master	Product Owner	Daily Scrum Duration	Daily Scrum Discussions
1	3–7	yes	yes	yes, is also project lead	no	15 min, partly every second day	no
2	5	yes	yes	yes, is also developer	yes, but also PO for the whole system	30 min, only when needed	brief
3	2–7	no	(yes)[1]	yes	yes	15 min, but story related	no
4	4–10	no	?	yes, had additional tasks	no, divided between several people	15 min	no
5	20–25 split into 2 teams	no	yes	no, divided between 3 people	yes	30 min	yes
6	10	yes	yes	yes, is also developer	no	15 min	yes
7	2–4	no	yes	yes	yes, but is also developer	?	?
8	5 + tester	yes	(yes)[2]	yes, is also team-leader	no	15 min	yes
9	10	yes	yes	no	yes	15 min	no
10	4	no	(yes)[3]	no	no, role split between architect and customer	15 min	yes

[1] Two adjacent rooms   [2] same floor   [3] If everybody is present

No.	Duration of Event Planning	Review	Retrospective	Sprint Length	Buffer	Release Plan	Incomplete Stories[4]
1	30 min	both together 1h		4 weeks	10%	yes	back/split
2	1 day	both together 1 day		4 weeks	none	yes	back/cont.
3	1 day	1h	1.5h	2 weeks	none	yes	back
4	4–7h	30 min	1h	2 weeks	none	no	split
5	3h	3h	?	3 weeks	20%	yes	cont.
6	?	?	?	4 weeks, 3 × 2 weeks	none	yes	?
7	1 day	1 day	?	1–4 weeks	25%	no	split
8	1.5h	1.5h	1.5h	2 weeks	no	no	split
9	4h	1h–1.5h	1h	2 weeks	no	yes	split
10	all three together 3–4h			1–2 weeks	yes	yes	split

[4] back = Back to the Backlog; cont. = Continue in the next Sprint; split = story is split up and unfinished work has to be planned again

4.3 Team, Product Owner, and Scrum Master

The team is a central part of Scrum and an important constraint is the size of the team. We found that several of the companies stretch the team size below and above the recommended 3–9 people. Two of the companies have teams with only two members. Three companies work with teams of up to ten members; one of these even with more than 10 members. The reason is that originally, there was a classical team of 25 people.

Some teams have dedicated experts for specific topics while others are generalists. The teams with experts explain their choice by the extraordinary technical depth and higher efficiency. The oddest case was a "classical" Scrum team and an additional team for writing specifications. The company considers this necessary, because they implement the core of a very large project with many other teams relying on them. The specifications team is responsible for acquiring information about all interfaces and from all the other teams. On the other hand, the teams with generalists argue that it reduces the problem of unavailable people and allows the team balance responsibilities better.

Most of the companies run cross-functional teams with all expertise necessary for the successful completion of the project. Two of the companies outsourced some aspects, e.g. UI design or manual testing.

Ionel [8] found similar conclusions. He points out, as a possible cause for this, that smaller teams might work more effectively due to better communication, but the additional effort to coordinate a bunch of small teams increases significantly. So companies tend to increase the team size instead.

Half of the companies follow the standard idea of a **Product Owner** in their projects. Often, the Product Owner is a business analyst responsible for one or more teams (to reduce effort for communication between them). One company also had a hierarchy of Product Owners. Two companies even had a Product Owner directly from the customer. In contrast, in one company, the Product Owner was both, the business expert and the project manager. In one company, there were two Product Owners: one being the internal software architect and one being the external customer. Others reported that they either do not have a dedicated Product Owner at all and receive requirements directly from stakeholders or have a separate product management (department). Finally, in one company, a developer took this role because of the company size of four people.

It is interesting that not all interviewed companies had a Product Owner, as e.g. Moe and Dingsøyr [12] stress that the Product Owner is crucial for the communication of the product vision.

Almost all interviewees stated that they use the role of the **Scrum Master** in some way. However, the implementation differs: Companies fill this role with an existing project manager or team lead, split it between project manager and software architect or have one of the developers as Scrum Master. Thus, the main difficulty seems to be that being Scrum Master for only one team is not a full-time job. Two companies report that having one of the developers as Scrum Master works well with a strong-minded and experienced developer, because such a person has a better insight into the technicalities of the project.

This also increases his acceptance with the rest of the developers. In another company, where the Scrum Master is mainly a developer, the role degenerated to an event organiser. Only one company does not name a Scrum Master explicitly. In all companies without a dedicated Scrum Master, the costs seem to play a major role. They avoid reducing the overall capacity by assigning a developer as full-time Scrum Master. Another possible cause for a "shared" Scrum Master is presented by Moe and Dingsøyr [12]. The role is shifted in the direction of a project manager, because the team members are working on many different projects simultaneously, and so the Scrum Master is also in charge of managing the progress of different projects.

4.4 Sprint

All interviewees reported that their companies run fixed-**length** Sprints. The length of these Sprints is mostly four weeks but some also used two or three weeks. The smallest company uses a fixed Sprint length in a project but varies over projects. They sometimes even run one-week Sprints. One company reported that they separate "normal" Sprints of four weeks from subsequent two-week Sprints for clean-up work. All interviewees reported that exceptions are rare, e.g. for public holidays. One company handles new product generations more flexibly but has fixed-length Sprints for established products. One interviewee reported that the Sprint is not shielded from outside changes to let the product management remove stories from or push stories into ongoing Sprints.

Most companies do not calculate a **buffer** in the work assigned to a Sprint. But two interviewees report that they only calculate with 80% workload for the developers to account for sick leave or uncertainties. One company uses a fixed 10% buffer. Another reserves 25% for bug fixing, grooming and any unforeseen work. Another company has a varying buffer for technological risks.

4.5 Events

Although the **Daily Scrum** is a central means of communication in Scrum, we found that most of the companies do not follow [13]. Some companies hold events of 30 minutes instead the 15 minutes. We also have results that the event is done every other day or only once a week, if there are not enough news. One company allows members and Scrum Masters of other teams, who are responsible for interfaces, to be present at the Daily Scrum. This should make agreements on these interfaces easier. Furthermore, several interviewees reported that discussions are allowed during their Daily Scrums. The reason is that then they discuss issues relevant for everyone on the team and decisions can be made. One interviewee described that they hold the event structured according to the currently relevant User Stories and discuss them one by one because of higher efficiency.

A reason why the time span between Daily Scrums is increased might be the increased team size. As Ionel [8] stated, the increased event time also holds the risk of team members becoming uninterested. Companies might try to compensate for that by not holding the events daily, thus increasing the information content to keep it interesting for everyone.

All companies hold explicit **Sprint planning** events with varying topics from the current Sprint up to several Sprints. Most companies also follow the proposed structure of (1) fixing the stories for the Sprint and then (2) refining them into tasks. Six companies reported that they use planning poker for estimating User Stories. Sometimes, the planning poker sessions are held outside the planning. If they have very unclear stories, one company inserts a pre-planning phase of up to five days. Some companies skip the second part of the event. The small company even does not define any acceptance criteria because of the vaguely defined User Stories and the missing Product Owner taking care of that. Most companies reserve a whole day for the event and report that this investment pays off by accurate planning and estimates. One company reported only 30 minutes but we assume that they do not perform a proper planning.

All interviewees reported that their companies hold some kind of **Review** event. In several companies, other stakeholders are not always present at the Review. In one company it is a means to get feedback about missing functionality from the Product Owner. Two companies have the strategy to conduct two Reviews: One Review is internal with other developers reviewing the results. The second Review contains other stakeholders and in particular the customer. The reason is that the team has the possibility to make smaller changes and corrections based on first feedback before the customer sees the increment.

Finally, the **Retrospective** is held in most companies. We found only one company that does not use Retrospectives at all. Another company holds them only rarely. All interviewees report that the Retrospectives are held together or at least on the same day as the Review. In this event, however, only the team participates. The length of the combined Review and Retrospective events range from 1 to 3.5 hours. Only the small company has a full day Review event.

4.6 Requirements

All interviewees use a **Product Backlog** as a central means of capturing requirements. As Scrum suggests, all companies keep the requirements in the Product Backlog rather vague and high-level. One interviewee stated that one of the aims is to give an overview of the project. Several of the projects use *JIRA*[1] for handling the Product Backlog. Microsoft Excel is in use alternatively.

The more concrete requirements in the **Sprint Backlog** are handled mostly as proposed in the Scrum Guide. Almost all interviewees described that the team selects and refines requirements from the prioritised list in the Product Backlog. Only one company does not allow the team to decide on that but the Product Owner, architect and project leader select and prioritise the requirements. This is a relic from the older, hierarchical development process.

---

[1] https://www.atlassian.com/software/jira

The common way to specify requirements is by **User Stories**. In most companies, the team defines some more or less sharp acceptance criteria per User Story. Only one team in our study had an actual Definition of Done in the Scrum sense. In one company, the acceptance criteria are defined during Sprint planning. One company does not consequently use User Stories as means of describing requirements. They state that they use them only for a better understanding but not for all requirements. The reason is, again, the small size of the company and the missing Product Owner. If a User Story cannot be completed in a Sprint, there are two strategies in the analysed companies: Either the whole User Story is pushed back to the Product Backlog and reprioritised, or the team tries to split the User Story into something shippable now and tasks that are done in the next Sprint. The effort for a User Story is estimated either in story points or person-hours. The companies using person-hours argue that they found story points too abstract and prefer to work with a more specific unit.

4.7 Quality Assurance

All interviewees described the usage of automated tests in their companies. They are usually part of a continuous integration and nightly builds. Only four companies explicitly mention additional code reviews and automated static analysis. Four interviewees explicitly mentioned manual tests. One company emphasised that they also do a review of each User Story they define. Scrum has no explicit constraints on the used quality assurance techniques.

The work of Fontana, Reinehr and Malucelli [6] revealed that agile quality assurance can be added at any level of maturity. It is possible that the companies with less QA techniques in their development processes are at the beginning of their personal development in the agile world and so focus first on the essential parts, e.g. the involved customer or agile planning.

These quality assurance techniques are used to check the definition of done. This is an important concept in Scrum. The acceptance of a User Story with acceptance criteria and a definition of done is practiced in the analysed companies. It varies, however, how strictly the Definition of Done is defined and who is deciding acceptance. Several interviewees stated that the acceptance criteria are not clearly specified. In some companies, the Product Owner decides if the User Story is accepted. If there is no Product Owner, the team makes this decision.

4.8 Evaluation of Validity

The interview guidelines proved to be helpful for focussing during the interviews but even more so during analysis as the interviews were not audio taped. We used the categories as a guiding structure in the analysis and write-up. Additionally, the interview guidelines reduced the risk of a misinterpretation and increased the objectivity of the notes taken, because it was always possible to fall back to the basic question in the guideline. The remaining threat of subjective filtering by the interviewers is in our opinion negligible. We did not notice any major misunderstandings. For example, some interviewees were not directly aware of what the three questions in the Daily Scrum are but a short explanation could resolve this. Furthermore, we had the impression that the assurance of anonymity led the interviewees to answer freely and openly.

The independent re-extraction of several of the answers in the main results table (Table 1) revealed few differences in our interpretation. For example, we judged differently under which circumstances we describe a case as having a Scrum Master or Product Owner. A discussion resolved these differences. For the roles, we decided to stick to the Scrum Guide and not accept a Scrum Master or Product Owner, if the role is shared by several people. Therefore, we are confident that the contents of the table are valid. For the further textual results descriptions, we cannot rule out that there are smaller misinterpretations. Yet, all researchers reviewed these parts and we discussed unclear issues.

Despite we only interviewed German development teams, we believe that our qualitative results should be well generalisable for other companies applying Scrum, especially in information systems. We expect the variations and reasons will occur in other companies, maybe among others. Still, there might be a cultural impact, which we are investigating in this study.

5   Related Work

In contrast to our purely outside view on the topic, Kniberg [10] reports from his experience how Scrum and XP is used in the real world. He discusses essential parts of the process in detail, including some of the alterations we have seen in the interviews.

Kurapati, Manyam and Petersen [11] did an extensive survey of agile practices. Among other topics, they also looked into compliance to the Scrum framework. But while Kurapati et al. stopped at the level of how many Scrum practices were used, we go one step further and investigate in detail which practices are used and how and why they are altered.

Moe and Dingsøyr [12] examined the team effectiveness effects of Scrum. They formulated the alterations of the company involved in the case study as problems. This is a different perspective compared to our work, but it still shows which kind of alterations are made and why.

Dorairaj, Noble and Malik [5] studied the behaviour of distributed agile development teams. They focused on the dynamics of cooperation in the teams and presented six strategies the teams adopt to make up for the difficulties in communication in distributed teams. Their data also provided support for our results concerning the topic of team size as a frequently violated Scrum rule and the almost complete commitment to the Sprint length of 2–4 weeks.

Barabino et al. [1] conducted a survey on the use of agile methodologies in web development. From the Scrum practices, they found that the Daily Scrum is used most often and that aspects connected to the releases, like continuous delivery, are taken care of less. This matches our results, as we see that the daily events are used by all of our interviewees with little changes and process parts, e.g. the release plan, are used seldom and only in a very vague form.

Ionel [8] discusses key features of Scrum, like the team size or the Sprints, and potential effects of deviations from these key features. For example, he states that a team of more than 10 people will have increasing difficulties in communicating and implementing changes. Yet, splitting a larger team into several smaller teams leads to a large coordination effort (Scrum-of-Scrums).

Fontana, Reinehr and Malucelli [6] thought about what defines maturity in agile development. They argue that maturity in agile is not about following a predefined path but to find what fits your agile development style. They still see some essential agile practices enforced by most of the mature agile users. While this is on a higher abstraction level then our work, the effect of maturity stated here might be the reason of some of the changes we see in Scrum.

6   Conclusions and Future Work

Based on the ten interviews performed with different companies about their applications of Scrum, we can confirm the statement of Schwaber that most often it is not used as proposed. Our results show that (1) none of the companies conforms to the Scrum Guide (only one is close) and (2) there is at least one company deviating from the standard for each aspect. Additionally, the results of the interviews gave us several reasons for these variations. In some cases, we found pragmatic justifications such as "the team found it more efficient". For example, short discussions during the Daily Scrum seem to be useful in some companies. Other deviations seem more like a legacy from more hierarchical, non-agile processes. For example, one company has a specification team and an implementation team as well as the Scrum Master role split between a project leader and a chief architect.

In addition to the comparison with related work, we conclude by relating our results to the overall results of a mapping study on agile practices [3]. The results concerning the **Sprints** and their lengths showed similar results as in the literature: all companies are using a time box. The partial variation of the Sprint length is also similar in literature. Of the events performed **Sprint Planning** is most often mentioned in literature, followed by the **Retrospective** and less often, the **Review**. In contrast, our results show the opposite: Retrospectives are used less by the interview partners. The common use of **Daily Scrums** is confirmed by our results and the mapping study and the few deviations in the event durations can be found in literature too.

Regarding requirements, again a similarity to [3] can be seen, as **User Stories** are used by all of the interview partners. They only vary the way of writing. Additionally, our results show the different variations of dealing with the concepts of Product Backlog and Sprint Backlog. The mapping study covers all agile methods, also XP including the on-site customer which is rarely used. This explains the deviation from our **Product Owner** results. Product Owners are often used but frequently in slightly adapted ways. The QA aspects show the largest deviation between the mapping study and our interview results, because literature often mentions explicit the absence of pair programming, whereas our results give more details about which QA practices are used within Scrum. This matches the partial usage of QA practices reported in [3].

Based on our results we would like to extend this case study to companies with more varying background. Additionally, it would be helpful to interview companies from different countries. Then a detailed comparison with domain data of [3] would be possible, and we might be able to give practitioners guidance on when to vary which aspects of Scrum.

References

1. Barabino, G., Grechi, D., Tigano, D., Corona, E., Concas, G.: Agile methodologies in web programming: a survey. In: Cantone, G., Marchesi, M. (eds.) XP 2014. LNBIP, vol. 179, pp. 234–241. Springer, Heidelberg (2014)
2. Callanan, M.: Ken schwaber on scrum (2010). http://blog.mattcallanan.net/2010/02/ken-schwaber-on-scrum.html
3. Diebold, P., Dahlem, M.: Agile practices in practice: a mapping study. In: Proc. 18th International Conference on Evaluation and Assessment in Software Engineering (EASE 2014). ACM (2014)
4. Diebold, P., Ostberg, J.-P., Wagner, S., Zendler, U.: Interview guidelines for "what do practitioners vary in using Scrum?". doi:10.5281/zenodo.12856
5. Dorairaj, S., Noble, J., Malik, P.: Understanding team dynamics in distributed agile software development. In: Wohlin, C. (ed.) XP 2012. LNBIP, vol. 111, pp. 47–61. Springer, Heidelberg (2012)
6. Fontana, R.M., Reinehr, S., Malucelli, A.: Maturing in agile: what is it about? In: Cantone, G., Marchesi, M. (eds.) XP 2014. LNBIP, vol. 179, pp. 94–109. Springer, Heidelberg (2014)
7. VersionOne Inc. 8th annual state of agile survey (2013). http://stateofagile.versionone.com/
8. Ionel, N.: Critical analysys of the Scrum project management methodology. Annals of the University of Oradea, Economic Science Series **17**(4), 435–441 (2008)
9. Kniberg, H.: The unofficial Scrum checklist (2011). https://www.crisp.se/wp-content/uploads/2012/05/Scrum-checklist.pdf
10. Kniberg, H.: Scrum and XP from the trenches. Lulu.com (2007)
11. Kurapati, N., Manyam, V.S.C., Petersen, K.: Agile software development practice adoption survey. In: Wohlin, C. (ed.) XP 2012. LNBIP, vol. 111, pp. 16–30. Springer, Heidelberg (2012)
12. Moe, N.B., Dingsøyr, S.: Scrum and team effectiveness: theory and practice. In: Abrahamsson, P., Baskerville, R., Conboy, K., Fitzgerald, B., Morgan, L., Wang, X. (eds.) XP 2008. LNBIP, vol. 9, pp. 11–20. Springer, Heidelberg (2008)
13. Sutherland, J., Schwaber, K.: The Scrum guide: The definitive guide to Scrum: The rules of the game (2013). http://scrumguides.org

Key Challenges in Early-Stage Software Startups

Carmine Giardino[1]([✉]), Sohaib Shahid Bajwa[1], Xiaofeng Wang[1],
and Pekka Abrahamsson[2]

[1] Free University of Bozen-Bolzano, Piazza Domenicani 3, 39100, Bolzano, Italy
cgiardino@unibz.it
http://www.unibz.it
[2] Norwegian University of Science and Technology, NTNU, 7491 Trondheim, Norway

Abstract. Software startups are newly created companies designed to grow fast. The uncertainty of new markets and development of cutting-edge technologies pose challenges different from those faced by more mature companies. In this study, we focus on exploring the key challenges that early-stage software startups have to cope with from idea conceptualization to the first time to market. To investigate the key challenges, we used a mixed-method research approach which includes both a large-scale survey of 5389 responses and an in-depth multiple-case study. The initial findings reveal that thriving in technology uncertainty and acquiring the first paying customer are among the top challenges, perceived and experienced by early-stage software startups. Our study implies deeper issues that early-stage software startups need to address effectively in validating the problem-solution fit.

Keywords: Software startups · Early-stage · Challenges · Validated learning · Customer value

1 Introduction

Software startups are newly created companies with little or no operating history, producing cutting-edge products[1]. The environment of software startups is extremely dynamic, unpredictable and even chaotic. A systematic mapping study (SMS) [1] identifies the most frequently reported contextual features of a startup: general lack of resources, high reactiveness and flexibility, intense time-pressure, uncertain conditions and tackling fast growing markets. Even though startups share several similar contexts (e.g. small and web companies), the co-existence of all these features poses a new, unique series of challenges [2], especially in their early stage (i.e. from idea conceptualization to first time to market).

Despite several studies reveal the need of early-stage startups to understand the problem/solution fit [3,4], actual executions prioritize development. Results in [5] show a necessity to improve practices for a more effective process to obtain validated learning. However, to achieve this an understanding of the key challenges faced by startuppers is needed.

---

[1] In this study we refer to products as software products or services.

© Springer International Publishing Switzerland 2015
C. Lassenius et al. (Eds.): XP 2015, LNBIP 212, pp. 52–63, 2015.
DOI: 10.1007/978-3-319-18612-2_5

This study aims at understanding the key challenges that are perceived and experienced by software startuppers at the early stage of their startup initiatives. The main research question asked in our study is:

RQ: what are the key challenges that early-stage software startups face?

To answer the research question, a mixed-method research approach was employed, including both survey and case study. We first conducted a survey to obtain a general overview of the challenges that early-stage software startups face. A multiple case study was then undertaken to achieve a deeper contextual understanding of the key challenges identified in the survey.

The rest of this paper is organized as follows: in Section 2, background and related work are presented drawing upon relevant software engineering and business literature. Section 3 presents the empirical research design. It is followed by the presentation of the survey and case study findings in Section 4. The findings are further discussed in Section 5, together with the limitations of the study. The paper is summarized in Section 6 outlining the future research.

2   Background

Sixty percent of startups do not survive in the first five years, whilst 75 percent of venture capital funded startups fail [6]. A study [5], trying to understand the failure of two early-stage startups, presents some anecdotal challenges that are posed to them due to neglecting learning processes. In the two case studies presented in the paper, the startups invested in product/market fit strategies prematurely given that users were not yet sold on the product. Involving the customer to activate the learning process has also been discussed by Yogendra [7] as an important factor to encourage an early alignment of business concerns to technology strategies. Learning mechanisms (e.g. learning about one's strengths, weaknesses, skills etc.) have been widely researched by Cope [8], who reveals a deeper conceptualization of the process of learning from venture failures.

However, a SMS [1] reveals that little rigor and relevance exist in the studies about software startups, and they are not focused on investigating issues and challenges. Bosch et al. [9] claim that challenges in early-stage startups are related to the decision of when to abandon an idea. However the focus of the study shifts on methodologies to develop multiple products, rather than clarifying the nature of the challenges.

Based on the observed knowledge gap that there is a scarcity in the literature to investigate the challenges faced by early stage software startups, we focus our study on discovering and understanding the key challenges, using the four dimensions discussed in [10] and the product development and learning stages [3] to make sense of them.

In order to classify the challenges we make use of a framework, draw upon the study of MacMillan et al. [10], applied in startup contexts. Four holistic dimensions are taken into consideration to present how the challenges impact on the different development and learning stages. The first dimension is the **team**, as the main driver of development. The **product**, as often startups are developing technologically innovative solution [2]. The **financial** and the way it evolves can set the company growth and its place in the market [11]. Ultimately knowing the **market** is essential to evaluate the needs of the final customers [3].

In order to position the challenges we make use of the customer development methodology stages. Blank [3] presents the objectives of scaling a business concept, who discusses that the first learning process is concerned in understanding the problem/solution fit. The learning process is presented as follows: defining or observing a problem; evaluating the problem; defining a solution; and evaluating the solution. Also the product stages are defined as: conceptualization phase; development phase; working prototype; full-functional product. It is worth emphasizing that these stages are not linear.

3   Research Approach

We have employed a mixed-method research approach by combining both survey and case study, which provides more richness of data and more reliable results [12]. Survey results can be greatly improved when combined with other qualitative research methods (e.g. case study) [13].

We first conducted a web-based survey (available at www.leanstartup.bz) advertised by means of blogs and attendance at workshops and competitions related to software startups. The questionnaire contained four main parts. The first part was introductory, providing a definition and examples of software startups. In the second part, the respondents were asked to provide background information about their organizations, including the principal domains, the countries they work in, and their roles within the organization. The third part contained the questions related to learning processes and product development status. The fourth part asked about their perceived challenges. The questions were in the form of multiple choices, with one open-ended option. The participants were asked to provide the most significant perceived challenge. The terminology used in the questionnaire is based on two exploratory studies [1,5]. The participants were not obliged to answer all the questions, in order to maintain response quality when they were not sure about the involved concepts. The data collection lasted for approximately one year, from September 2013 until September 2014. In total 8240 responses were received, among which 5389 responses (i.e. 65,40%) have completely answered questions on background information and the perceived challenges, which are mandatory for us. As the first step of analysis, we obtained a list of key challenges by calculating the frequency of them in the responses.

In the second phase, we conducted a qualitative study by means of two cases, to provide a deeper contextual understanding of the key challenges identified in the large-scale survey. The case study approach improves the degree of realism to the research phenomenon [14]. A multiple case design allows us to apply literal and theoretical logic through the comparison and contrast of multiple cases that are analyzed through the same lens [15]. For the purpose of this study, we selected the two cases that represent two early stage software startups, EasyMedicine and MovyNext. The interviewees include the two CEOs of the startups and a developer from EasyMedicine. First, we conducted a first round of interviews as a pilot study in these two startups. The initial results of the pilot study established the two startups as suitable cases for further investigation. Then we conducted a second round of interviews. Both rounds of interviews were semi-structured with open-ended questions. They lasted between 30 minutes to 1 hour, and interviews were recorded and transcribed verbatim for the analysis purpose. The specific data analysis technique, for within-case analysis, was coding using the identified challenges in the survey as seed categories. An online tool[2] was used to manage interview data and coding process. In the cross-case comparison, the challenges that EasyMedicine and MovyNext face were compared and contrasted.

4 Results

4.1 Key Challenges Perceived by Early-Stage Software Startups

Based on the frequency calculation of the challenges perceived by the respondents, we obtained a list of top 10 challenges (contained in 4709 responses, i.e. 87,38% of the 5389 complete responses). The startups in the 4709 sample vary in different market sectors (predominately in the consumer market, such as mobile and Internet, i.e. 64,40%). They come from 90 countries around the world (the majority is from United States 52,60%, Canada 7,94%, United Kingdom 6,71%, Israel 5,30%, India 4,50%). These startups are young, on average 10 months, and small in size, predominatly having 2 founding members.

The top 10 critical challenges are presented in Table 1.

To make better sense of the challenges, we plotted the occurrence of the top 10 challenges along the two stages [3]: product development stage and learning process stage that the software startups were at when the survey was responded. The result is shown in Figure 1. The Figure is a bubble chart ("x-y scatter plots with bubbles in categories' intersections"), where the size of the bubble is determined by the number of challenges corresponding to the x-y coordinates.

Inspecting Figure 1, we can notice a malformed distribution: the respondents perceive the importance of challenges during their problem evaluation phase, however there is not a corresponding perception during the first phases of product development (e.g. only 3 out of 10 before having a working prototype).

In order to enhance the granularity of the distributions of the challenges we also present a multi-dimensional chart (see Figure 2) in which the 10 challenges are grouped into four Macmillan et al. mentioned dimensions. A close look at Figure 2 reveals that the most common perceived challenge is related to *market* and *product* (both representing the 30% of the challenges).

While market and product related challenges are equally important in the problem evaluation stage, in the mature stage of the product development the market significantly impact their perception. This might be expected, however,

---

[2] Dedoose is a tool for analyzing qualitative data, available at www.dedoose.com.

Table 1. The list of top 10 challenges

Challenge	Description	#	Dimension
Thriving in Technology Uncertainty	developing technologically innovative products, which require cutting-edge development tools and techniques	1132	Product
Acquiring First Paying Customers	persuading a costumer to purchase the product, e.g. converting traffic into paying accounts	870	Market
Acquiring Initial Funding	acquiring the needed financial resources, e.g. from angel investors or entrepreneurs' family and friends	682	Financial
Building Entrepreneurial Teams	building and motivating a team with entrepreneurial characteristics, such as the ability to evaluate and react to unforeseen events	436	Team
Delivering Customer Value	defining an appropriate business strategy to deliver value*	393	Market
Managing Multiple Tasks	doing too much work in a relatively short time, e.g. duties from business to technical concerns	351	Team
Defining Minimum Viable Product	capturing and evaluating the riskiest assumptions that might fail the business concept	307	Product
Targeting a Niche Market	focusing on specific needs of users willing to take risks on a new product, such as early-adopters and innovators	212	Market
Staying Focused and Disciplined	not being particularly sensitive to influences from different stakeholders, such as customers, partners, investors and competitors (both actual and potential)	165	Team
Reaching the Break-even Point	balancing losses with enough profits to continue working on the project	161	Financial

*The difference between what a customer gets from a product, and what he or she has to give in order to get it (www.businessdictionary.com).

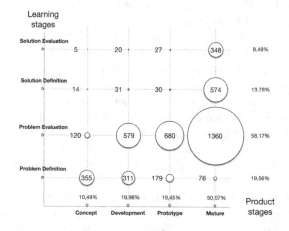

Fig. 1. Challenges map - learning and product stages

challenges related to the market, such as strategies to acquire the first customers can reasonably be considered from the very early stages of a startup company.

In the following subsection, the top 10 perceived challenges are further illustrated in two real startup settings that were investigated in our multiple-case study, to provide a richer and contextual description of the challenges.

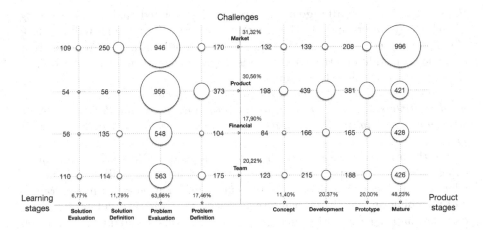

Fig. 2. Challenge map along the four dimensions

4.2 Key Challenges Experienced in Two Early-Stage Software Startups

EasyMedicine is a software startup that offers a mobile app for travellers to solve their health problems during their trips abroad. This app aims at helping travellers to find medicine, that they normally take in their home country, when abroad.

MovyNext is a software startup that has developed a web-based movie recommendation system as a "better movie filter", customized according to viewers' interests.

The profiles of the two cases are presented in Table 2

Table 2. Profile of two cases

Profile	EasyMedicine	MovyNext
Idea/Business domain	Health	Entertainment
When started	Idea: July 2013, Development: November 2013	Idea: July 2012, Development: December 2013
No. of founding team members	4	4
Current composition of team	2 (Pharmacists), 2 (Businessmen)	1 mentor (from an incubator), 4 Software developers, 1 designer (Free lancer)
Current Product Development Stage	Mature	Prototype
Current Learning Process Stage	Solution evaluation	Solution evaluation
Application Nature	Android Mob app	Website

Both EasyMedicine and MovyNext have experienced the key challenges identified in the survey. They are re-organized under the four dimensions of MacMillan et al. [10] and presented with case contexts.

Product related challenges: The first product related challenge is thriving in technology uncertainty. In the EasyMedicine case, it is manifested as a lack of supporting technologies in collecting specific drug information from different countries. In addition, the CEO of EasyMedicine commented on the lack of resources to tackle this challenge:

"Our search criteria to find medicine was not efficient. We wanted to implement multiple search criteria with optimized search within the database, but we were unable to implement it because of not enough resources available for these problems."

On the other hand, even though all of the founders of MovyNext were quite experienced in developing recommendation systems, they still had issues in adopting a new crawling algorithm for accurate information about movie trailers and providing an effective user-interface design for their early adopters. Moreover, the implementation technologies were not flexible to adapt to unforeseen changes or alternative breakthroughs.

Both EasyMedicine and MovyNext initially developed their MVPs based on their own intuitions and experiences. In the case of MovyNext, as a consequence of not properly defining MVP, the team spent a lot of time on developing the features (e.g. server side optimization) that users were not interested in. They tried by prototyping to gather early feedback and to address their technology uncertainty, however the novel solutions had negative impact on the early adopters, without engaging them effectively to obtain useful feedback.

Market related challenges: Attracting customers to buy a startup product is a challenging endeavor. In the case of EasyMedicine, the travellers were treated as paying customers initially. The CEO observed:

"There was positive feedback at the beginning. We got some downloads and we were satisfied. But it became quite apparent after a while that we were not making lots of progress. Lots of nice perks at the beginning, and lots of frustration in weeks after, but as soon as you launch, you discover."

Meanwhile the interviewed developer mentioned:

"If we are not getting users, we should analyze the reason. There can be many reasons e.g. difficulty in using the application, application with low quality etc."

In the case of MovyNext, the team did not have a specific type of paying customer in their mind when they developed their application. They did not have a specific strategy to attract them, as illustrated by the comment from the CEO:

"You think that your product is cool. Friends are using it, and that's it. Paying customers are not coming. How to get this? that's a challenge."

Targeting a niche market is particularly critical in the case of EasyMedicine. The CEO commented:

"At this moment, pharmacies are not seeing big numbers (users). They are saying, why should I invest, if you don't have lots of users. This is a two sided platform. If you don't see people on the other side, you don't want to be part of it. Pharmacists want to see more users."

In terms of delivering customer value, both EasyMedicine and MovyNext did not define and validate the needs of their potential customers. In the EasyMedicine case, also their understanding of customers was changing. In a similar manner, MovyNext did not have any customer acquisition strategy when they started developing the application either.

Financial challenges: EasyMedicine was in critical need of initial funding to continue their project, as the CEO commented:

"It's a challenge especially in a small city. There are not so many people to invest in startups if there is not a clear product/business plan. In software business, it is more challenging. You can create, change, and revolutionize several times. There were many apps similar to our app in our case."

In contrast, since MovyNext grabbed the opportunity to work in an incubator in Oxford, acquiring initial funding is less of an issue. The CEO said:

"The goal of startups should be to enter an incubator. Because this is kind of validation of your idea that it works."

Reaching the break-even point is important to keep the business running. However, neither EasyMedicine nor MovyNext has enough customers yet to be self-sustainable.

Team related challenges: Building an entrepreneurial team implies several challenges related to teamwork and team motivation. It also includes appropriate composition of the team. For example, in the case of EasyMedicine, it was about keeping people involved. The CEO recalled:

"We did not update our developer for the past two months. We lost him and he took another assignment. He is not available anymore".

In comparison, the challenge in building an entrepreneurial team faced by MovyNext is more related to a lack of diversity in the team composition. The CEO described the situation:

"We are all computer scientists. There is no one, who work on user experience. To build product/feature, this is one part of the business. You need people, that market it, sell it, reach to customer, perform user based experiment. In our case, we don't have them."

Moreover the entrepreneurial teams in the two case studies are overburdened with lots of activities in a short time. In the case of EasyMedicine, for example, the team identified that they needed to conduct interviews with the stakeholders e.g. pharmacists and practitioners. The data from these sources was needed for the improvement of their business. However, all of the four founders were doing this as a part-time job, and they did not have time to conduct interviews. Similarly, MovyNext was also overburdened by various activities. There were some features (e.g. movie recommendations according to users' preferences) that they wanted to add to their website, but they were unable to do so due to a lack of time. As the CEO said:

"We know what we want to do, but we are overhelmed by other work. There is no time. Everybody is extremely busy and no one would dedicate full time to that."

Staying focused and disciplined is not easy for these two startup teams. If any team member were less focused or lacked self-discipline, he would have affected the whole team, as the CEO of EasyMedicine commented:

"Two of the co-founding team members could not dedicate time to the project for three months because of personal commitments. The issue is that you do not only lose productivity. The remaining team becomes less motivated too."

In the case of MovyNext, three of the co-founders were geographically distant. Hence, this decreased coordination among the team members, and self-discipline became even more crucial. Everyone needed to work hard and contribute, as the CEO commented:

"Nobody respects you if you don't do anything, especially in a startup where the team is small. Everybody has to contribute."

In summary, there are many challenges that are common to both the cases e.g. acquiring first customers, building an entrepreneurial team, delivering customer value, etc. MovyNext is fortunate enough that they do not have financial issues being in an incubator, however they are not yet self-sustainable. In contrast, EasyMedicine is in severe need of initial funding to continue operating.

5 Discussion

Among the challenges identified in our survey, the most prominent one is thriving in technology uncertainty. This is consistent with the nature of software startups, who are often chasing new technological changes, disrupting the software industry. In turn, developing new technologies might require innovative tools and techniques with little community support. EasyMedicine has evidenced such lack of support.

However, focusing only on technological solutions will not guarantee survival and success. In order to develop something valuable for customers, startups need to understand their real problems [3]. However, startups are not consulting the necessary processes for this need. Both EasyMedicine and MovyNext have not obtained the necessary validated learning in this aspect. This can be a potential root cause for other key challenges revealed in the survey, including acquiring the first paying customers. As presented in Figure 2, often the concept of product/market fit significantly impacts the operational decisions of early-stage startups. During a previous study [5], we explored how rushing to market can lead a startup to a misalignment between business and development activities, without prioritizing the evaluation of the challenged problem.

In order to learn fast from failures, Ries [16] suggests: try an initial idea and then measure it to validate the effect. This implies an evolutionary approach to gather knowledge by feedback from stakeholders. He states "Validated learning is a rigorous method for demonstrating progress when one is embedded in the soil of extreme uncertainty in which startups grow. It is the process of demonstrating empirically that a team has discovered valuable truths about a startup's present and future business prospects." When uncertainty is high, startups should focus on knowledge acquisition. As presented in Section 4.1, during the problem evaluation stage, there is a relatively high number of perceived challenges. Yet, during the development of the product, the main challenges are predominantly present in the mature stage.

Making use of user interface prototypes and technical spikes or experiments are current practices for gathering knowledge and reducing risks. Many studies have been focusing on finding low footprint methodologies towards Lean and Agile principles [17,18]. However, presenting just debt-laden features, as discussed by Tom et al. [19], can frequently impact users, which will cost real money in support (for motivated evaluators/customers), sales (through turned-off evaluators), and renewals (through dissatisfied customers). Lack of structure and time pressure lead startups to lose their focus, investing resources in ineffective practices. In the case of EasyMedicine, they were trying to get more users showing prototypes without any strategy to persuade potential customers, and get paid for their product. Similarly, MovyNext did not have validated learning process, and spent huge amount of time on developing features that users were not interested in.

Effective requirements elicitation would improve knowledge acquisition by engaging stakeholders in understanding the product concept and underlying problems that need to be addressed [20]. Besides specific features, requirements elicitation would identify system boundaries and goals especially during the early-stage of a startup. In this regard, studies about how to support effective practices during or before development are still lacking and the topic requires further investigation [1]. Examples of starting validating the problem statement even before investing on development solutions are the use of pre-orders [21] or evaluation techniques through crowd-funding projects (e.g. Kickstarter and Indiegogo) [22]. Identifying the valuable but missing knowledge early in the project and by defining/tailoring the SE processes to focus on getting/creating the required knowledge can shift development paradigms in the early phases and thus reduce the investment in developing ineffective solutions. It is critical to investigate practices for knowledge acquisition. When uncertainty is reduced, a startup can gradually focus more and more on customer value. By employing learning process on the problem statement since the very early-stage, startuppers can provide more value to their customers [23].

The validity threats to our study design and findings are hereby discussed. One threat to validity is the selection of subjects. We centered our results on respondents' opinions. In order to mitigate this threat, we selected interviewees holding the position of CEO. Their broad perspectives on their startup organization were the only data taken into consideration in the study. In addition, we employed a two-dimensional research approach by integrating on-line surveys and multiple case studies. However, threats might be the bias by contextual factors, such as type of product, competitive landscape etc. To mitigate this threat, we constructed the framework using Macmillan et al. dimensions, widely used in previous software engineering studies [24,25], enabling a broader reasoning related to the factors that hinder the success of software startups.

6   Conclusions

Software startups are able to produce cutting-edge software products with a wide impact on the market, significantly contributing to the global economy. Software development, especially in the early-stages, is at the core of the company's daily activities. Despite their severely high failure-rate, the quick proliferation of software startups is not supported by a scientific body of knowledge [1]. This paper provides an initial explanation of the perceived and experienced challenges by means of an online survey and multiple-case studies based on two software startups, focusing on early-stage activities, from the *product, market, financial* and *team* perspectives.

A large-scale survey, with 5389 complete responses, shows that thriving in technology uncertainty (21,01%) and acquiring first paying customers (16,14%) are among the top challenges that most software startups are facing at their early stage. In conjunction with the multiple-case study, we described how early-stage startups are still too keen to develop mature products without understanding the business problem. When it comes to validating the problem/solution fit, they continue to develop software, with little focus on the learning process.

To continue the current study we will conduct a more in-depth analysis to reveal the linkages among the described challenges and with other factors, such as user growth rate. We call for further investigations on improving validated learning processes for more accurate and comprehensive evaluation of business problems from the first stages of product development.

References

1. Paternoster, N., Giardino, C., Unterkalmsteiner, M., Gorschek, T., Abrahamsson, P.: Software development in startup companies: A systematic mapping study. Information and Software Technology **56(10)**, 1200–1218 (2014)
2. Sutton, S.M.: The role of process in software start-up. IEEE Software **17**(4), 33–39 (2000)
3. Blank, S.: The four steps to the epiphany, 1st edn. CafePress (2005)
4. Crowne, M.: Why software product startups fail and what to do about it. In: Proceedings of International Engineering Management Conference (IEMC), pp. 338–343 (2002)
5. Giardino, C., Wang, X., Abrahamsson, P.: Why early-stage software startups fail: a behavioral framework. In: Lassenius, C., Smolander, K. (eds.) ICSOB 2014. LNBIP, vol. 182, pp. 27–41. Springer, Heidelberg (2014)
6. Nobel, C.: Why companies fail-and how their founders can bounce back. Working Knowledge, Harvard Business School, Boston (2011). http://hbswk.hbs.edu/item/6591.html (accessed August 29, 2013)
7. Yogendra, S.: Aligning business and technology strategies: a comparison of established and start-up business contexts. In: Proceedings of Internal Engineering Management Conference (IEMC), pp. 2–7 (2002)
8. Cope, J.: Entrepreneurial learning from failure: An interpretative phenomenological analysis. Journal of Business Venturing **26**(6), 604–623 (2011)

9. Bosch, J., Holmström Olsson, H., Björk, J., Ljungblad, J.: The early stage software startup development model: a framework for operationalizing lean principles in software startups. In: Fitzgerald, B., Conboy, K., Power, K., Valerdi, R., Morgan, L., Stol, K.-J. (eds.) LESS 2013. LNBIP, vol. 167, pp. 1–15. Springer, Heidelberg (2013)

10. Macmillan, I.C., Zemann, L., Subbanarasimha, P.: Criteria distinguishing successful from unsuccessful ventures in the venture screening process. Journal of Business Venturing **2**(2), 123–137 (1987)

11. Yu, Y.W., Chang, Y.S., Chen, Y.F., Chu, L.S.: Entrepreneurial success for high-tech start-ups - case study of taiwan high-tech companies. In: Proceedings of the Sixth International Conference on Innovative Mobile and Internet Services in Ubiquitous Computing (IMIS), pp. 933–937 (2012)

12. Mingers, J.: Towards critical pluralism. John Wiley and Sons (1997)

13. Gable, G.G.: Integrating case study and survey research methods: an example in information systems. European Journal of Information Systems **3**, 112–126 (1994)

14. Runeson, P., Höst, M.: Guidelines for conducting and reporting case study research in software engineering. Empirical Software Engineering **14**(2), 131–164 (2009)

15. Yin, R.: Case Study Research: Design and Methods. SAGE Publications (2003)

16. Ries, E.: The Lean Startup: How Today's Entrepreneurs Use Continuous Innovation to Create Radically Successful Businesses. Crown Business (2011)

17. Coleman, G., O'Connor, R.: An investigation into software development process formation in software start-ups. Journal of Enterprise Information Management **21**(6), 633–648 (2008)

18. Kuvinka, K.: Scrum and the Single Writer. In: Proceedings of Technical Communication Summit, pp. 18–19 (2011)

19. Tom, E., Aurum, A., Vidgen, R.: An exploration of technical debt. Journal of Systems and Software **86**(6), 1498–1516 (2013)

20. Nuseibeh, B., Easterbrook, S.: Requirements engineering: a roadmap. In: Proceedings of the Conference on the Future of Software Engineering, pp. 35–46. ACM (2000)

21. Walling, R.: Start Small, Stay Small: A Developer's Guide to Launching a Startup. The Numa Group LLC (2010)

22. Kuo, P.Y., Gerber, E.: Design principles: crowdfunding as a creativity support tool. In: CHI 2012 Extended Abstracts on Human Factors in Computing Systems, pp. 1601–1606. ACM (2012)

23. Woodruff, R.B.: Customer value: the next source for competitive advantage. Journal of the Academy of Marketing Science **25**(2), 139–153 (1997)

24. Kakati, M.: Success criteria in high-tech new ventures. Technovation **23**(5), 447–457 (2003)

25. Hui, A.: Lean change: Enabling agile transformation through lean startup, kotter and kanban: An experience report. In: Proceedings of Agile Conference, pp. 169–174 (2013)

Agile Challenges in Practice: A Thematic Analysis

Peggy Gregory[1](✉), Leonor Barroca[2], Katie Taylor[1], Dina Salah[2], and Helen Sharp[2]

[1] University of Central Lancashire, Preston PR1 2HE, UK
{ajgregory,kjtaylor}@uclan.ac.uk
[2] The Open University, Walton Hall, Milton Keynes MK7 6AA, UK
{leonor.barroca,dina.salah,helen.sharp}@open.ac.uk

Abstract. As agile is maturing and becoming more widely adopted, it is important that researchers are aware of the challenges faced by practitioners and organisations. We undertook a thematic analysis of 193 agile challenges collected at a series of agile conferences and events during 2013 and 2014. Participants were mainly practitioners and business representatives along with some academics. The challenges were thematically analysed by separate authors, synthesised, and a list of seven themes and 27 sub-themes was agreed. Themes were Organisation, Sustainability, Culture, Teams, Scale, Value and Claims and Limitations. We compare our findings against previous attempts to identify and categorise agile challenges. While most themes have persisted we found a shift of focus towards sustainability, business engagement and transformation, as well as claims and limitations. We identify areas for further research and a need for innovative methods of conveying academic research to industry and industrial problems to academia.

Keywords: Agile methods · Challenges: evidence-based software engineering

1 Introduction

Successfully adopting and using agile approaches within an organisation is challenging. As agile approaches mature and their use becomes more widespread [1], the nature of the challenges that practitioners and organisations face is changing. New challenges are emerging and the focus of existing challenges is shifting, reflecting the current state of practice. Some activities that used to be regarded as challenging, for example setting up a Scrum team, are well understood, and are no longer regarded that way. There is now a growing body of research literature, experience reports, books and guidelines providing suggestions for those seeking help. Even so, some known challenges still pose problems in practice. Additionally, new challenges are emerging as organisations push the boundaries of existing techniques and try new approaches or move into unknown territory.

The Agile Research Network (ARN), www.agileresearchnetwork.org, is a collaboration between the authors' institutions and an industry body, the DSDM Consortium. We believe that in order for our research to have relevance, we need to work on problems that have been identified by practitioners. We work with organisations in the following way: we identify a relevant challenge, conduct a case study to explore the

© Springer International Publishing Switzerland 2015
C. Lassenius et al. (Eds.): XP 2015, LNBIP 212, pp. 64–80, 2015.
DOI: 10.1007/978-3-319-18612-2_6

challenge within its organisational context, and conduct a literature review to identify suggested solutions. We discuss our findings with the organisation, engage in a dialogue with them about mitigation strategies and undertake research into changes made. We then publish our findings as academic papers for the research community [2-4] and as white papers for the practitioner community [5, 6]. In order to find out what topics are most challenging for organisations, we have developed a 'Challenge Wall' (see Figure 1), deployed at five Agile Conferences and events between October 2013 and October 2014. We have used this challenge wall to collect agile challenges from a range of attendees. In this paper we report our approach and present a thematic analysis of our findings.

2   Related Work

A series of papers have charted the progress of agile research since its early days. In 2003 Abrahamson et al found 'a jungle of emerged software development methods', and a lack of empirical evidence to support ideas [7]. In 2008, Dingsøyr et al [8], stated that the primary challenge for agile research was to combine academic rigour with industrial relevance, suggesting that researchers could use research methods such as action research as a way to increase relevance and impact. In a systematic review in the same year, Dybå and Dingsøyr concluded that there was a need for more empirical research, and suggested that researchers should aim to understand the drivers of agile adoption as well as its effects [9]. The call for more research continued in 2009 by Abrahamson et al. [10], who also identified a need for more rigour and industrial studies, as well as highlighting a lack of clarity about what was meant by agility. More recently the research landscape has changed. Both Dingsøyr et al in 2012 [11] and Chuang et al in 2014 [12] have reported an increase in published research, indicating a maturing field.

Fig. 1. The Challenge Wall at ABC 2013

A number of systematic literature reviews have investigated specific topic areas within agile: by reviewing the state of research, synthesising research themes and identifying challenges. For example, a 2011 review of agile global software engineering literature [13] concluded that research was increasing but there was a predominance of industrial experience reports which report on modifications to practice based on contextual factors. A 2014 review of communication in agile global software development identified seven research themes, and reported that about half of the chosen papers were experience reports [14]. Other systematic reviews have appraised topics in agile software development such as user-centred design [15, 16], Scrum challenges in global software engineering [17], governance [18] and embedded software [19].

Research overviews and systematic literature reviews usually focus on the state of research from an academic viewpoint, although in the agile field the importance of industrial relevance and practical impact is widely acknowledged. However, academics and practitioners value different aspects of research. Academics tend to value methodological rigour and the building of theory whereas practitioners look to research to provide answers to specific practical problems and evidence to show which approaches are most effective.

A number of authors have noted the predominance of industrial experience reports in the agile literature [13, 14, 20]. Experience reports are extremely useful as they tell a coherent and contextualised story about an organisation, and in doing so describe practice, suggest practical techniques, and provide guidelines. However, one of the limitations of this type of literature is that experience reports usually tell positive stories of problems solved rather than describing persistent difficulties, worsening situations or failures. As a result they give us snapshots of successful practice, but almost certainly do not represent the state-of-the-practice. Indeed, few papers describe major unresolved problems or failures, resulting in a general publication bias towards only reporting success. Since many lessons are learnt in response to mistakes and failures, this bias, although unsurprising, is not helpful. This problem is not specific to the agile area, and has been noted in other disciplines [21].

During a panel discussion at XP2010 practitioners said that researchers did not always address questions they wanted answering. During the rest of the conference delegates were asked to suggest and vote on topics that should be researched, in order to create a prioritised list of 'burning issues' for the agile research community [22]. During an XP2013 workshop Dingsøyr and Moe elicited and ranked research challenges for large-scale agile software development [23] from a mixture of practitioners and academics. Taking this approach to identifying research questions is a more direct way of ensuring research relevance, but how relevant the challenges are to practice depends on who is suggesting the challenges.

Several attempts have been made to categorise challenges faced in the application of agile. Gandomani et al. [24] categorise the challenges faced by organisations when migrating to agile into four main categories: organisation and management; people; process; and tools related challenges. This classification is based solely on existing literature. Using grounded theory, van Waardenburg and van Vliet [25] investigated the challenges caused by the co-existence of agile methods and plan-driven development, and discussed mitigation strategies for those challenges. This work is based on 21 interviews with agile practitioners from two large enterprises in the Netherlands. They organised the challenges under two categories: 'increased landscape complexity' and 'lack of business involvement'. The paper exposes consequences of the former category as 'problems with communication', 'dependent definition of done', and 'difficulties to create change'. The consequences of the latter category are problems with requirements gathering, slow reaction to change, problems with requirements prioritisation and limited feedback from the business. For both challenge categories, mitigation strategies were proposed that focused on communication between the agile and traditional part of the organisation, and the communication timing.

Conboy et al [26] identified nine themes for challenges experienced by 17 large multinational organisations using agile methods. The research focused on challenges encountered by people involved in the agile development process. The themes were: developer fear as a result of the transparency of skill deficiencies; the need for developers to be "master of all trades"; dependency on social skills; deficiency of developers' business knowledge; the need to understand and learn values and principles of agile, not just the practices; lack of developer motivation to use agile methods; implications of devolved decision-making; the need for agile compliant performance evaluation; and absence of specific recruitment policies and absence of trained IT graduates for agile. Cohn and Ford [27] focused on the challenges related to the transition from plan-driven processes to agile processes and the wider impact of this transition not only on the development team members, but also on management, other departments, and other agile teams. They proposed several approaches for introducing agile to organisations. These focused on recommendations related to the different roles and factors impacting the transition to agile.

3   Method

The ARN deployed a 'Challenge Wall' at five Agile Conferences and events between October 2013 and October 2014. This section discusses the challenges collected and how they were analysed.

3.1   Data Collection

When we ran a challenge wall we positioned an ARN poster in a visible place in the conference or event venue and provided a stack of pens and small cards on which each challenge was written. Delegates were encouraged to fill out the cards anonymously (see Figure 2), and these were then attached to the wall next to the poster for others to read. Delegates wrote one challenge per card, and could fill in as many cards as they wished. The challenge wall gradually grew throughout the event, and became a trigger for discussions between delegates and the ARN team about the nature and context of the challenges identified. After each event the cards were removed from the wall and the contents were typed up into a spreadsheet.

The first agile challenge wall was set up at the Agile Business Conference in 2013. We soon realised that we had uncovered a powerful way of identifying issues of concern. As a result, we subsequently ran the challenge wall at several agile events in order to build up a larger set of data for analysis.

We collected challenges using the challenge wall at five different events during 2013 and 2014. These events were: the Agile Business Conference, London, October 2013 (www.agileconference.org); DSDM Members Day, Manchester, November 2013 (www.dsdm.org); XP, Rome, May 2014 (www.xp2014.org); AgileNorth, Preston, June 2014 (www.agilenorth.org); and the Agile Business Conference, London, October 2014 (www.agileconference.org).

3.2   Participants

The attendees at the five events were mostly agile practitioners and business representatives rather than academics, except for the XP Conference in 2014 that was attended by a mixture of practitioners and academics. Practitioner and business attendees represented a range of organisational roles. An analysis of attendance data from the 2014 ABC Conference (the only event about which we had access to such data), showed that 34% of attendees were managers, 14% were from business roles, 12% were executive-level managers, 12% were developers, 8% were consultants, 8% were project

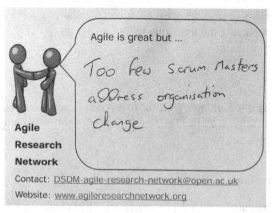

Fig. 2. A Challenge Card

managers, 5% were analysts, 3% were coaches and 4% were from other roles (including some students and academics). It is likely that ABC 2013 and the DSDM Members day had a similar mix of attendees.

3.3   Data Analysis

We used a thematic analysis approach for data analysis. This is a data synthesis method that identifies, analyses and reports patterns (themes) within data. It describes and organises the data set in rich detail and interprets different aspects related to the research topic [28]. The data is first labeled and coded, and those codes are then inspected resulting in some relabeling, dropping and merging of codes. Finally, codes are translated into themes.

Three of the authors, Salah, Gregory and Barroca each completed an independent thematic analysis of the challenges, then Taylor and Sharp, reviewed these. They verbally clarified the meaning of the descriptors used by the other authors, and created a new spreadsheet with a merged list of sub-themes. Merging started by looking at sub-theme names and their associated challenges, and went on to identify high-level themes, which were used as grouping mechanisms for the more detailed sub-themes. Discussion focussed on whether to merge or split sub-themes, finding appropriate names for sub-themes, and identifying broad themes at the right level of granularity. For example, 'culture' and 'changing mindsets/culture' had been identified as sub-themes by two of the independent analysts, but a distinction between organisational culture and national culture had not been made, so the reviewers created these as themes. They regrouped the data into nine themes and 27 sub-themes. This set of themes was revised again through discussions between all authors using Skype calls and emails, and the final set of seven themes and 27 sub-themes was agreed. For example, through group discussion at this final stage it was decided that 'organisational culture' and 'national culture' would be more appropriate as sub-themes grouped under the broader theme of 'Culture'.

4   Results

We collected 194 challenge cards, of which one was disregarded as inappropriate. As a result of the thematic analysis described in Section 3.3 the remaining 193 challenges determined the seven themes and 27 sub-themes. Table 1 below shows the themes and sub-themes along with a description and an example challenge from each sub-theme. The table is ordered, largest first, by the number of challenges in the themes and sub-themes, with the number of challenges in each group provided in brackets.

Table 1. Themes and Sub-Themes identified from our Challenge Cards

	Main Theme	Sub Themes	Description of Sub Themes	Example Challenge
1	Claims and Limitations (n=46)	Misconceptions (n=23)	The multi-faceted aspects of agile are open to many different interpretations	"Shallow Adoption" where practices or processes are followed mechanically without deep insight into underlying values
		Shortcomings (n=14)	Areas where information is sparse, limited or where methods are used inappropriately	Credibility in areas it has not traditionally used (e.g. public sector)
		Hype (n=8)	Misleading or excessive claims about agile approaches	It's become a buzzword and as such threatening its own existence. It has to be implemented thoroughly and comprehensively to get great outcomes
		Failure (n=1)	Only limited evidence is available about failures	Some believe it to be a "silver bullet" to their problems, only to realise and not like that it just exposes their existing issues
2	Organisation (n=45)	Business & IT transformation (n=11)	Requires business and IT to collaborate to establish agility throughout the entire value chain	It's still seen as an IT methodology. It needs the business teams to buy into it and join the party
		Management buy-in & understanding (n=11)	Traditional management may see agile as just another IT method that can be implemented and structured to 'fit' existing organisational norms	Misconceptions of what 'agile' means. Perceived as quicker by business owners
		Agile in a non-agile environment (n=10)	Teams successfully adopt agile but operate in an environment where wider organisational structures are more traditional	IT is agile but most of the business are not
		Commitment/ Engagement (n=10)	Success can be challenged by lack of awareness or commitment from other stakeholders	It only works if all stakeholders get involved and support the agile process
		Adoption (n=5)	Concerns around 'how to' introduce agile ways of working either into teams or into the wider organisation	What is the holistic business case to move to agile?
		Fear (n=2)	Fear of change and the unknown as agile appears less structured with people 'doing their own thing' whilst using a whole new set of jargon	Traditional practitioners may fear and resist the change given control moves to the team (self- organising teams)
3	Culture (n=31)	Organisational culture (n=13)	The organisation requires a philosophical belief in people over process	Changing from a command and control/mechanistic worldview to a future of autonomous, self-managed agents in a systemic organisation is too much if the system does not change itself – including leaders
		Changing mindsets (n=8)	Agile is more than a set of practices used by IT requiring wide ranging change to work patterns	It's a mind set not a methodology. Without a change in mind set the result will not be met
		National culture (n=5)	Differences in national culture, particularly between East and West, compound issues with organisational culture	Is it possible to do agile with all nationalities and cultures?

Table 1. (Continued)

	Culture contd.	Distributed teams (n=5)	Business realities are often contrary to the agile need for co-located teams, with teams distributed across the UK, Europe or worldwide	*It requires co-location in a digital world, where travel is too expensive*
		Trust (n=1)	Providing a safe environment to develop and innovate	*What is the cost for not investing in trust?*
4	Teams (n=24)	Team practices (n=11)	Uncertainty and perhaps lack of training in specific practices or techniques	*How to estimate/ better estimate the effort to support planning?*
		Leadership (n=5)	Traditional project management approaches of 'command and control' need to be replaced by a facilitation style of leadership	*That the manifesto lacks Leadership over Management*
		Finding good people (n=4)	Agile requires skilled, self-directed and motivated team players	*Getting the right people interested- decision makers and users*
		Individual motivation (n=4)	Agile philosophies are often at odds with organisational reward structures that value individuals	*It sometimes marginalises lonely problem solvers*
5	Sustainability (n=23)	Process improvement (n=15)	Once adopted, agile requires on-going change and commitment in order to become sustainable and embedded within teams and the organisation	*If it is codified it becomes "bureaucratic" and if not it is too diverse to be taken seriously*
		Documentation (n=4)	Tensions arise when management sees documentation as a way to demonstrate control whilst developers focus on code over documents	*That it has become an excuse not to do any documentation or planning beyond the sprint and product backlog*
		Contracts (n=3)	Standard contracts require detailed upfront specifications that are contrary to the evolving approach of agile	*Some think they need a contract*
		Knowledge sharing (n=1)	Needs a positive learning environment to motivate individual commitment in order to establish effective knowledge sharing	*We innovate but we don't really share innovations*
6	Scaling (n=15)	Large projects (n=10)	Working at programme level where team practices need to scale across multiple teams in large complex projects	*Agility in large projects effecting several applications, platforms, techniques*
		Governance (n=5)	Traditional mechanisms that ensure projects achieve regulatory or legal compliance are often process driven and bureaucratic	*Have not yet found any clear view on how the 'governance' at Business Case level works or could work in relation to outcomes, costs and benefits*
7	Value (n=7)	Business value (n=4)	To counter criticism of waterfall approaches where organisations tended to focus on process rather than product, agile projects must demonstrate value	*Ensuring that projected value is achieved*
		Measurement (n=3)	Many organisation use wide ranging metrics but these are not always appropriate or necessary to agile projects	*The lack of well formulated and defined measurement practices*

5   Discussion

Research interest in agile has been growing steadily as indicated by the publication of over 200 peer-reviewed journal articles in the period between 2001 and 2012 [12]. Amongst these many publications we have seen: a systematic literature review identifying the areas being researched [9]; a prioritisation of research needed in the form of a preliminary roadmap [8]; and a prioritised list of the areas of research that practitioners would like to see addressed [22].

Here we discuss how the challenges we have gathered are related to previous literature reviews in the area. First we compare our themes and sub-themes with areas identified in Dybå and Dingsøyr's 2008 systematic literature review [9] and investigate research on specific sub-themes by undertaking a title search of the papers listed by Chuang et al [12] in their 2014 systematic literature review (section 5.1). Second, we compare our findings with the research areas Dingsøyr et al [8] established as goals for research achievements by 2015 (section 5.2). Third, we discuss how practitioner concerns have evolved over time by comparing the challenges we have collected with those collected at XP2010 by Freudenberg and Sharp [22] (section 5.3). Finally we discuss the limitations of our approach (section 5.4). All italicised quotes in this section are verbatim transcriptions from challenge cards.

5.1   Are These Challenges Reflected in Research Literature?

The seven themes and 27 sub-themes identified in our challenge set represent a mix of familiar and less familiar topics found in the literature.

Of the familiar topics, Organisation, Sustainability, Culture and Teams are themes that have been subjects of research interest for some time. For example the topic groupings identified in Dybå and Dingsøyr's systematic review [9] are reflected in these four themes from our challenge set (Table 2).

However some sub-themes within these four main themes, such as Business and IT transformation, Fear, Contracts, Documentation and Leadership, do not seem very evident in the literature searches we have conducted for our industrial partners. This would, however, need to be confirmed by a more up-to-date systematic literature review. The need for business as well as IT transformation, was of particular concern in our challenge set, with 11 challenge cards identifying this topic. Examples of challenges identified included:

> 'Its take up outside of the delivery function. That it is has been coined by IT for IT without the business guys. Which organisational changes are triggered by IT without anybody noticing/caring/managing those changes?'; and
> 'That everyone seems to think that it starts and stops in software development. How other disciplines blend in is a big challenge'.

Scaling is also a topic that has been written about and discussed by practitioners [29, 30]. Through a title search of Chuang et al [12] we found seven papers on scaling, including large or complex projects (searching on 'scale', 'large', 'complex') and none on governance (searching on 'governance', 'PMO'). Dingsøyr and Moe reported from an XP2013 Workshop at which research challenges in large-scale agile development were discussed, that there were few research studies on the topic [23]. A recent systematic literature review on agile governance, identified a small but growing research base [18].

Table 2. Comparison of our themes and sub-themes with Dybå and Dingsøyr's topics [9]*

Dybå and Dingsøyr topics	Themes from this study	Sub-themes from this study
Introduction and adoption		
Introduction and adoption	Organisation	Adoption
Development process		*(Not mentioned in our challenge list)*
Knowledge and project management	Sustainability	Knowledge sharing
Human and social factors		
Organisational culture	Culture	Organisational culture
Collaborative work	Teams	Team practices
Team characteristics	Teams	Finding good people
Perceptions of agile		
Customer perceptions	Organisation	Commitment/engagement
Developer perceptions	Teams Organisation	Individual motivation Adoption
Student perceptions		*(Not mentioned in our challenge list)*
Comparative studies		
Project management	Organisation Sustainability	Management buy-in and understanding Process improvement
Productivity	Sustainability	Process Improvement
Product quality		*(Not mentioned in our challenge list)*
Work practices and job satisfaction	Teams	Team practices

* Dybå and Dingsøyr identify four topic groups and 13 topics, which we map to four of our themes and nine of our sub-themes.

The two themes Value, and Claims and Limitations identified in our challenge set are generally less commonly reported in the empirical research literature, although some of the associated sub-themes are more researched. In a title search of Chuang et al [12] we found no papers on the topic of business value (searching on 'value'); eight discussing measurement ('metrics', 'measurement'); and none on claims or limitations ('misconception', 'shortcoming', 'fail', 'hype', 'lack', 'claim', 'limitation').

Our participants identified 46 challenges on the theme of Claims and Limitations. Comments indicate a certain amount of frustration, but range over a number of topics, including:

> *'Religious approach';*
> *'Everyone wants to reinvent it';*
> *'Throwing away some of the old useful ideas'; and*
> *'The lack of a project management framework for coordinating multiple teams and or work.'*

While there is some literature about the concept of agility [31, 32], there is very little about misconceptions, hype and failure.

Agile hype is discussed by Janes and Succi [33] who suggest agile has followed the Gartner Hype Cycle, and is stuck in the 'Trough of Disillusionment' as a result of what they call the 'guru phenomenon'. In a grounded theory study of agile practitioners Hoda et al [34] identify agile hype and scepticism as factors that negatively affected customer involvement in agile projects. There are some discussions in the consultant literature [35], however we could find no empirical research that specifically focussed on investigating this topic.

Additionally there is very little research into agile failure. McAvoy and Butler [36] report the failure of a team to adopt an agile method, identifying ineffective decision-making and actions, which occurred as a result of the team's desire to become more cohesive, as one of the key drivers of the failure. This is a gap, and has been mentioned by other researchers [12]. It is somewhat surprising as anecdotally it is not uncommon to hear stories of failure and organisational abandonment of agile.

5.2   Challenges and the Goals Set for 2015

Dingsøyr et al in their preliminary roadmap [8] assess the state of agile research in 2008 and suggest a goal for agile research for 2015. They indicate some areas for priority in research: maturity, coverage, understanding and impact. They assess that research was having little impact on everyday practice in industry and suggest that "increased application of research methods like action research [37] can be helpful ensuring the relevance, and help provide a larger body of knowledge that can lead to a broader impact on industry."

Research has been growing significantly [12], action research is being used [2, 38] and research may be getting more relevant and is definitely increasing the body of knowledge. However, some perspectives from our challenge list are:

> *'That there is no academic research supporting the claimed success';* and,
> *'It is isolated from many fields, e.g., a good research could be about bringing information visualisation theory and methods into agile project management in a systematic way.'*

This suggests that even if research has been done, the gap between research and what industry wants to know has not yet been bridged.

5.3   Persistence of Challenges over Time

We discuss how Freudenberg and Sharp's [22] top ten research questions from practitioners feature in our challenge set; we start by looking at those that persist.

'Agile and large projects' was the top research question in the 2010 paper. Scaling is still a theme for our challenges, not only in terms of large projects:

'How do you scale up to a large project over many months or even years?';

but also in relation to complexity and the size of the organisation:

'Scaling due to complexity (rather than large projects)'; and

'Scaling across a large enterprise/companies.'

Table 3. Comparison of our themes with practitioners' top ten research questions from [22]

Freudenberg and Sharp top ten research questions	Themes/Sub-themes
1. Agile and large projects	Scaling
2. What factors can break self-organization?	Culture/Organisational culture
3. Do teams really need to always be collocated to collaborate effectively?	Culture/Distributed teams
4. Architecture and agile—how much design is enough for different classes of problem?	Scaling/Large projects
5. Hard facts on costs of distribution (in $,£,€ and so on)	Culture/Distributed teams
6. The correlation between release length and success rate	Claims and Limitations/Shortcomings Sustainability/Process Improvement
7. What metrics can we use with minimal side effects?	Value/Measurement
8. Distributed agile and trust—what happens around 8–12 weeks?	Culture/Distributed teams
9. Statistics and data about how much money/time is saved by agile	*(Time mentioned in several challenges from different themes)*
10. Sociological studies—what were the personalities in successful/failed agile teams?	Teams/ Finding good people

Collocation and distribution appeared in 2010 related to: effective work e.g. 'Do teams really need to always be collocated to collaborate effectively?'; cost e.g. 'Hard facts on costs of distribution (in $, £, €, and so on)'; and trust e.g. 'Distributed agile and trust—what happens around 8–12 weeks?'.

Distributed teams appear in our challenges as a sub-theme still raising the issue of trust:

'Why does trust decline if people are not meeting in person for more than 12 weeks?'

and, to a lesser extent, the issue of cost (travel cost in one single challenge):

'It requires co-location in a digital world, where travel is too expensive'.

However, distributed teams no longer seem to raise challenges of effective collaboration. This may suggest that distributed teams are an accepted reality that has to be dealt with rather than opposed.

Trust appears today under new contexts, not limited to distributed teams:

> *'What is the cost for not investing in trust?'*

One other research question that persists is that of metrics – 'What metrics can we use with minimal side-effects?' The Value theme gathers challenges not so much related to side effects but rather to what management wants and how to measure value:

> *'Agile is about measuring value, but management want efficiency, defect metrics etc. How to demonstrate team is efficient and improving efficiency?';*
> *'Can be difficult to define a value metric';* and
> *'The lack of well formulated and defined measurement practices.'*

These challenges suggest a wider concern of agile within a large traditional enterprise, as agile is becoming more established and having to cohabit with more or less hostile environments.

Some research questions do still appear as challenges, but with less frequency and emphasis. That is the case of 'What factors can break self-organisation?':

> *'Changing from a command and control/mechanistic worldview to a future of autonomous, self-managed agents in a systemic organisation is too much if the system does not change itself – including leaders.'*

The concern here seems also to be more about the context of the organisation rather than the internal functioning of agile teams.

Also of less importance are the issues of more detailed agile practice such as 'Architecture and agile—how much design is enough for different classes of problem?' with one single mention of architecture:

> *'Dealing with emergent architecture which can be F*agile!'*

Two other research issues appear only in one or two challenges. One is 'The correlation between release length and success rate' with the two following challenges:

> *'Cost of release, cannot release code easily';* and
> *'Agile on aged technology, environment stacks -> prevents early release to test and promotes waterfall of dev handing over to test period.'*

The other is 'Sociological studies—what were the personalities in successful/failed agile teams?' with a single challenge mentioning personality:

> *'Would like to understand the personality type of a coach in order to make better hiring decisions.'*

For the remaining research question – 'Statistics and data about how much money/time is saved by agile.' – we didn't encounter any mention of quantifying savings in time and cost. There are, however, several challenges mentioning the time it takes for agile to get established:

> *'It takes practice and time so needs some serious commitment'*;
> *'It is geriatric time to innovate'*;
> *'It takes practice and time so needs some serious commitment'*;
> *'Business managers only hearing on time delivery and not putting time in to deliver/write stories'*; and
> *'I have been on a two day course. It is common scene, I am an expert. You are not. It takes time and experience'*.

The discussion above suggests that the concerns of practitioners now are less about moving into agile, or about how to do agile, but rather about sustaining agile. Agile is here to stay, sometimes in environments that are not always supportive, but within which agile development needs to coexist.

5.4   Limitations

Collecting challenges at these agile events was opportunistic. As a result the data cannot be seen as fully representative of the community of agile practitioners. The challenge cards were filled in anonymously so we cannot link each one with a particular job role. We had conversations with a majority of respondents and although some cards may have been completed by academics, practitioners completed most. Most of the data comes from the UK, apart from that collected at the XP Conference in Rome.

We are aware of some limitations in our comparison of themes from our data with those found in previous literature. The Dybå and Dingsøyr systematic literature review [9] is now six years old and reviewed publications up to and including 2005. Although the Chuang et al [12] systematic literature review is recent, there is no thematic topic review in the paper, so we were not fully able to compare our findings with those and had to rely on a review of titles. We believe, however, that these limitations rather than invalidating some of the suggestions made in the discussion, point to a need for more updated research in some areas.

6   Conclusions

If research is to have real impact in the practitioner community, researchers need to understand and address the challenges that this community faces. However, it is not simply a matter of identifying challenges and setting up research programmes to address them. The landscape of practitioner challenges is complex and multi-faceted, and while some challenge areas have persisted for many years, some have evolved, and others are new.

Through its mission to bridge the gap between industry and academia, the ARN has collected 193 challenges at practitioner-focused events during 2013 and 2014 and analysed them. This analysis allows us to make four observations:

1. Some challenges areas have persisted for many years, and are just hard to address successfully. These challenge areas would benefit from further research. For example, identifying and measuring agile value, and understanding cultural change are highly contextual and complex.

2. Some challenge areas appear to have persisted for many years, but our analysis shows that the focus of the challenge has in fact shifted. For example, concerns around scaling and distributed teams have changed. The agile field is maturing, and practitioners are less concerned about adopting agile and more concerned about sustaining agile. Research in these areas needs to have a specific and relevant focus.

3. Some challenge areas have not been widely researched. These areas include: sustainability, governance, business engagement and transformation, failure, and the impact of claims and limitations. Future research would be beneficial in some of these areas, but it is not the answer to all of them as some would best be addressed by further or different education and training – e.g. those challenges classified as misconceptions and hype.

4. Some challenge areas have been addressed by research but practitioners still see them as a challenge. Although research is being done, it is still not having the expected impact. This means that either practitioners are not aware of this work and it needs further dissemination, or the research is not ready for practitioner implementation.

The observations above point both to the need for further research and for improvements in knowledge transfer. The ARN addresses the latter by developing more innovative methods of conveying academic research to industry and industrial problems to academia, bridging the gap between research and practice. We have developed a model of collaboration [39] where researchers engage with collaborators in an in-depth way, spending time in the organisation to understand the context, and suggesting alternative ways of working. This promotes the transfer of knowledge in a way that takes into account the context of each organisation individually, and requires an in-depth knowledge of existing research. This approach also generates opportunities to contribute to further research based on the data generated in the collaborations.

Acknowledgements. We would like to thank all those who contributed to our challenge walls and to DSDM Consortium for supporting the Agile Research Network.

References

1. West, D.: Water-Scrum-Fall is the Reality of Agile for most Organizations Today, in, Forrester Research Report (2011). http://www.cohaa.org/content/sites/default/files/water-scrum-fall_0.pdf

2. Gregory, P., Plonka, L., Sharp, H., Taylor, K.: Bridging the gap between research and practice: the agile research network. In: European Conference on Research Methods, London, UK (2014)

3. Sharp, H., Plonka, L., Taylor, K.J., Gregory, P.: Overcoming challenges in collaboration between research and practice. In: Proceedings of the International Workshop on Software Engineering Research and Industrial Practices at ICSE 2014, pp. 10–13, Hyderabad, India (2014)

4. Plonka, L., Sharp, H., Gregory, P., Taylor, K.: UX design in agile: a DSDM case study. In: Cantone, G., Marchesi, M. (eds.) XP 2014. LNBIP, vol. 179, pp. 1–15. Springer, Heidelberg (2014)

5. The Agile Research Network, LShift: Integrating UX Design into a DSDM Project: Challenges, Working Practices and Lessons Learned (2013). http://agileresearchnetwork. org/publications/

6. The Agile Research Network: Agile Projects in a Non-agile Environment: What is Your Experience? (2014). http://agileresearchnetwork.org/publications/

7. Abrahamsson, P., Warsta, J., Siponen, M.T., Ronkainen, J.: New directions on agile methods: a comparative analysis. In: International Conference on Software Engineering. IEEE, Portland (2003)

8. Dingsøyr, T., Dybå, T., Abrahamsson, P.: A preliminary roadmap for empirical research on agile software development. In: Proceedings of AGILE, pp. 83–94. IEEE, Toronto (2008)

9. Dybå, T., Dingsøyr, T.: Empirical Studies of Agile Software Development: A Systematic Review. Information and Software Technology 50, 833–859 (2008)

10. Abrahamsson, P., Conboy, K., Wang, X.: "Lots Done, More To Do": The Current State of Agile Systems Development Research. European Journal of Information Systems 18, 281–284 (2009)

11. Dingsøyr, T., Nerur, S., Balijepally, V., Moe, N.B.: A Decade of Agile Methodologies: Towards Explaining Agile Software Development. The Journal of Systems and Software 82, 1213–1221 (2012)

12. Chuang, S., Luor, T., Lu, H.: Assessment of Institutions, Scholars, and Contributions on Agile Software Development (2001-2012). Journal of Systems and Software 93, 84–101 (2014)

13. Jalili, S., Wohlin, C.: Global Software Engineering and Agile Practices: A Systematic Review. Journal of Software Maintenance and Evolution: Research and Practice (2011)

14. Alzoubi, Y.I., Gill, A.Q.: Agile global software development communication challenges: a systematic review. In: PACIS14 (2014)

15. Salah, D., Paige, R., Cairns, P.: A systematic literature review on agile development processes and user centred design integration. In: EASE14. ACM, London (2014)

16. da Silva, T.S., Martin, A., Maurer, F., Silveira, M.: User-centered design and agile methods: a systematic review. In: Proceedings of AGILE, pp. 77–86 (2011)

17. Hossain, E., Babar, M.A., Paik, H.: Using scrum in global software development: a systematic literature review. In: International Conference on Global Software Engineering. IEEE (2009)

18. de O. Luna, A.J.H., Kuruchten, P., de E. Pedrosa, M.L.G., de Almeida Neto, H.R., de Moura, H.P.: State of the Art of Agile Governance: A Systematic Review. International Journal of Computer Science & information Technology 6, 121–141 (2014)

19. Shen, M., Yang, W., Rong, G., Shao, D.: Applying agile methods to embedded software development: a systematic review. In: The 2nd International Workshop on Software Engineering for Embedded Systems (SEES), pp. 30–36. IEEE, Zurich (2012)

20. Ferreira, J.: User Experience Design and Agile Development: Integration as an On-going Achievement in Practice, in, Ph.D thesis. Open University (2011)

21. Dwan, K., Altman, D.G., Arnaiz, J.A., Bloom, J., Chan, A., Cronin, E., Decullier, E., Easterbrook, P.J., Von Elm, E., Gamble, C., Ghersi, D., Ioannidis, J.P.A., Simes, J., Williamson, P.R.: Systematic Review of the Empirical Evidence of Study Publication Bias and Outcome Reporting Bias. PloS one **3**, e3081 (2008)

22. Freudenberg, S., Sharp, H.: The Top 10 Burning Research Questions from Practitioners, IEEE Software, 8–9 September/October 2010

23. Dingsøyr, T., Moe, N.B.: Research Challenges in Large-Scale Agile Software Development. ACM SIGSOFT Software Engineering Notes **38**, 38–39 (2013)

24. Gandomani, T.J., Zulzalil, H., Ghani, A.A.A., Sultan, A.B.M., Nafchi, M.Z.: Obstacles in Moving to Agile Software Development Methods: At a Glance. Journal of Computer Science **9**, 620–625 (2013)

25. van Waardenburg, G., van Vliet, H.: When Agile meets the Enterprise. Information and Software Technology **55**, 2154–2171 (2013)

26. Conboy, K., Coyle, S., Wang, X., Pikkarainen, M.: People over Processes: Key Challenges in Agile Development. IEEE Software **28**, 48–57 (2011)

27. Cohn, M., Ford, D.: Introducing an Agile Process to an Organization. Computer **36**, 74–78 (2003)

28. Braun, V., Clarke, V.: Using Thematic Analysis in Psychology. Qualitative Research in Psychology **3**, 77–101 (2006)

29. Eckstein, J.: Agile Software Development in the Large: Diving into the Deep. Dorset House Publishing, New York (2004)

30. Sutherland, J.: Agile Can Scale: Inventing and Reinventing SCRUM in Five Companies. Cutter IT Journal **14**, 5–11 (2001)

31. Conboy, K.: Agility from First Principles: Reconstructing the Concept of Agility in Information Systems Development. Information Systems Research **20**, 329–354 (2009)

32. Lyytinen, K., Rose, G.M.: Information System Development Agility as Organisational Learning. European Journal of Information Systems **15**, 183–199 (2006)

33. Janes, A., Succi, G.: The darker side of agile software development. In: International Symposium on New Ideas, New Paradigms, and Reflections on Programming and Software, pp. 215–228. ACM (2012)

34. Hoda, R., Noble, J., Marshall, S.: The Impact of Inadequate Customer Collaboration on Self-Organising Agile Teams. Information and Software Technology **53**, 521–534 (2011)

35. Brousseau, J.: Beyond the hype of a new approach. In: Cutter IT Journal, Cutter Consortium, pp. 25–30 (2004)

36. McAvoy, J., Butler, T.: A Failure to learn in a software development team: the unsuccessful introduction of an agile method. In: Wojtkowski, W., Wojtkowski, G., Lang, M., Conboy, K., Barry, C. (eds.) Information Systems Development: Challenges in Practice, Theory and Education. Springer US (2010)

37. Avison, D., Lau, F., Myers, M.D., Nielsen, P.A.: Action Research. Communications of the ACM **1**, 94–97 (1999)

38. Svejvig, P., Nielsen, A.D.F.: The dilemma of high level planning in distributed agile software projects: an action research study in a danish bank. In: Agility Across Time and Space, pp. 171–182. Springer (2010)

39. Barroca, L., Sharp, H., Salah, D., Taylor, K.J., Gregory, P.: Bridging the Gap between Research and Agile Practice: An Evolutionary Model. International Journal of Systems Assurance Engineering and Management **6** (2015), (in press)

UX Work in Startups: Current Practices and Future Needs

Laura Hokkanen[⊠] and Kaisa Väänänen-Vainio-Mattila

Department of Pervasive Computing, Tampere University of Technology,
Korkeakoulunkatu 1, 33720, Tampere, Finland
{laura.hokkanen,kaisa.vaananen-vainio-mattila}@tut.fi

Abstract. Startups are creating innovative new products and services while seeking fast growth with little resources. The capability to produce software products with good user experience (UX) can help the startup to gain positive attention and revenue. Practices and needs for UX design in startups are not well understood. Research can provide insight on how to design UX with little resources as well as to gaps about what kind of better practices should be developed. In this paper we describe the results of an interview study with eight startups operating in Finland. Current UX practices, challenges and needs for the future were investigated. The results show that personal networks have a significant role in helping startups gain professional UX advice as well as user feedback when designing for UX. When scaling up startups expect usage data and analytics to guide them towards better UX design.

Keywords: User experience · Startup · Lean

1 Introduction

A startup is a team of people that try to find a scalable business model, and is also defined to be only a temporary organization [3, 17]. Startups are getting a lot of attention and are seen as a way to create new opportunities for work and business. Startups offer an interesting domain for research to understand what methodologies and ways of working are helping the success of these small teams with limited resources. Startups work in a fast-changing environment and what matters to UX work is that they do not have the possibility to spend a lot of time working on design when the whole product might still change significantly.

Software development practices in startups have gained some attention [16] but research on UX practices is lacking. The traditional approach to UX design based on the principles of human-centered design [10] has a lot of upfront work before starting the implementation. Some books [12, 8] have been written to offer tools for UX design in lean startups but the past academic research is limited to some case descriptions with UX practices [15, 18].

Research that would recognize the best practices for UX work in startups is missing. It could offer valuable information on how startups could optimize the resources put to UX work for creating UX that would enable growth. It is also of interest to

© Springer International Publishing Switzerland 2015
C. Lassenius et al. (Eds.): XP 2015, LNBIP 212, pp. 81–92, 2015.
DOI: 10.1007/978-3-319-18612-2_7

understand if these ways of working are transformable to be used in established companies when they need to innovate fast. This paper presents the results of our research that aimed to understand the role of UX work in startups developing ICT products. UX work includes user needs gathering, designing UX and user tests for feedback collection. Designing UX covers both choosing the right functionality and designing the user interface for the product. In this research we wanted to understand (1) what practices startups currently have for UX work, (2) what challenges startups have in UX work and (3) what kind of needs the startups expect to have regarding UX research and design in the future when they scale up.

To address these questions, we conducted an interview study with eight startups on their approaches to UX work. As a conclusion, we will propose implications for startups on how they could incorporate UX practices in their product development. The results can be used to further investigate and develop UX practices that would help startups succeed.

2   Related Work

Previous research on the specific topic of UX work in startups is very limited. In this section we briefly go through the related work on UX practices in industry, lean UX and product development in startups.

2.1   UX Practices in Industry

Practical work towards good user experience – often also referred to as usability –is rooted in human-centered design (HCD) approach, as defined for example by the ISO standard [10]. This approach emphasizes upfront user research and design activities, strong user involvement, iterative design and multifunctional design teams. While such approach has been well adopted in the research of user experience, industrial product development projects have often used more limited practices.

In their survey of user-centered design practice in industry [20], Vredenburg et al. found out that iterative design is a widely used approach and that usability evaluation is the most commonly adopted user-centered method in industry. Analyzing user tasks and conducting field studies were also often used in user-centered design. A survey by Gulliksen et al. [9] conducted in Sweden revealed that usability professionals appreciated low-fidelity prototyping, field studies and think-aloud tests with end-users the best methods to use. The survey furthermore indicated that management support is essential for the usability professionals and that user involvement often has low priority in the projects. In a more recent study in Italy, Ardito et al. [1] found out that that several companies still do not conduct any form of usability evaluation, because they require a lot of resources in terms of cost, time and people. The advantage of usability work for the usability of software was still clearly recognized in the studied companies.

In summary, while the value of user experience work is in general well understood also in industry, it is still often neglected when other pressures of product development are considered to be more important.

2.2 Lean UX

Lean development is used to describe a philosophy that concentrates on removing waste from the process while delivering value to customers. It started with manufacturing but has since been adapted to many other fields as well. One of these adaptations is the concept of Lean Startup that emphasizes fast learning with small risks while building new businesses [17]. Academic research on the topic is very scarce.

Lean UX book [8] identifies three parts for the Lean UX philosophy: the design thinking movement, Lean startup method [17] and Agile software development. Lean UX aims to produce a product extremely fast and with little resources but without compromising the customer satisfaction. According to Gothelf [8], Lean UX applies the four principles of Agile development to product design [2] and 15 principles for Lean UX. The Lean UX Manifesto [19] was published in early 2014. It was composed by collecting ideas from UX professionals including and forming them into a list much like in the Agile manifesto [2]. The Lean UX manifesto [19] has six principles: (1) **Early customer validation** over releasing products with unknown end-user value, (2) **Collaborative design** over designing on an island, (3) **Solving user problems** over designing the next "cool" feature, (4) **Measuring KPIs** over undefined success metrics, (5) **Applying appropriate tools** over following a rigid plan and (6) **Nimble design** over heavy wireframes, comps or specs.

The use of lean principles in UX work has been reported by [15], [14], [5]. [14] and [5] report positive overall experiences when adapting lean philosophy in established companies. May [15] reports a case of a startup where experienced UX designers were involved. She emphasizes as one of the lessons learned the early planning of UX, design and customer validation. May [15] also stresses continuous testing in every step of business idea and product development.

Agile-UX methodologies have been studied more thoroughly [11] than Lean UX. The academic research on Agile-UX serves as a basis for Lean UX research. Different aspects such as making the UX work more efficient while also paying attention to management and sales aspects [13] should also be understood in startup context.

2.3 Product Development in Startups

The term startup is used inconsistently [16] but some characteristics have been recognized to be common in describing startups. Giardino et al [6] have listed recurring themes in software startups such as lack of resources, innovation, rapidly evolving, small and low-experienced team, and time pressure. The product development is there by effected by these factors. The constant change makes the processes in startups evolutionary and software development practices are adopted only partly and in later stages [16]. Members of a startup team are often able to have different roles and affect significantly the outcome of product development. The background of persons involved in creating the software development process influence the most the adopted process [4].

The Lean Startup method [17] suggests startups should base their activities on validated learning with constant cycles of Build-Measure-Learn (BML). Experimenting ideas with little risk involved helps the startup reach a sustainable business model. With experimentation, a startup should be able to find the right problem/solution fit. Giardino et al [7] report that the learning seems to slow down when awareness of competitive environment increases.

3   An Interview Study of UX Work in Startups

The aim of this research was to gain insights of the current practices and future needs of startups in their UX work. We interviewed 11 participants from eight startups. The qualitative research was conducted in Finland over a period of two months (October-November 2014). In this section we first describe the startups that participated in the interviews and then the research methods used.

3.1   Participating Startups

Eight startups operating from Finland participated in study. Two of the startups had team members also in other countries. Altogether 11 persons were interviewed - in three startups two persons participated in the interviews. The interviews were semi-structured. We aimed at having startups at different stages, and with different products and markets. The participating startups were required to have a software component in the product or service they were developing. The startups were found through a local startup community by advertising the interview request them and by asking the participating startups to recommend other teams that might be willing to take part in the interviews. A summary of the startups is presented in Table 1.

Table 1. Summary of the startups

Startup	Interviewees	Company established	Size of startup	Product
SU1	H1 (CEO), H2	2014	3	Web service
SU2	H3	2014 (To be established)	3	Mobile app
SU3	H4 (CEO)	2013	3	Mobile app
SU4	H5	2013	5	SaaS
SU5	H6 (CEO), H7	2014	3	Web service
SU6	H8 (CEO), H9	2014	3	Web service
SU7	H10 (CEO)	2014	4	Software
SU8	H11 (CEO)	2013	3	Mobile app

We interviewed CEOs from six startups (SU1, SU3, SU5, SU6, SU7, SU8). From SU4 we interviewed the person responsible for online marketing, user analytics and customer acquisition. SU2 was not yet officially founded and we interviewed the inventor of the business idea. Four startups had people with experience or training in human-centered design (SU3, SU4, SU6, SU8). The size of startups varied between 3-5 people and five startups (SU1, SU4, SU5, SU6, SU8) had had someone leave the company since they started. Startups were small enough for everyone to know what others were doing and interviewees were able to answer questions about all the activities of the startup, not just about their own.

All the startups but SU8 had started with a different product idea than the one they were currently developing. Startups SU2, SU3 and SU8 had a mobile application as their product. Startup SU7 offered a technical solution that did not yet have a visible user interface. Other startups (SU1, SU4, SU5, SU6) were offering SaaS or web applications.

3.2   Method

The semi-structured interviews consisted of three parts. The first part was about understanding the business and product ideas, the team structure and the current stage of the startup. The second part of the interview was about the practices involving understanding the end user, user data collection and designing UX. This part also covered the challenges they had in these fields. The last part of the interview was about the future of UX practices and needs when scaling up. The interviews lasted 45-90 minutes. The interviews were done by one researcher and they were all recorded. One of the interviews (SU3) was conducted over Skype using a webcam. The recordings were then transcribed for analysis. Altogether, the data consisted of 71 pages of transcribed interviews. The analysis was done by iterative thematic coding of the qualitative data. The themes were formed into the main sections of the results, and populated with subtopics and individual findings from the data.

4   Results

The results are presented in three parts. The first part describes the current practices the startups have regarding understanding user needs, collecting user feedback and designing UX. The second part presents the challenges the startups have faced when collecting meaningful information about end users and designing for them. The last part addresses the needs that startups have for future and their plans for UX work.

4.1   Current Practices

Understanding User Needs. Interviewees from five startups described the product to be a direct solution to their personal needs (SU1, SU3, SU4, SU6, SU8). One startup (SU5) based their design on what they assumed the average user of the product to expect.

Startups used personal contacts and unofficial discussions to gain feedback about the product idea and the product design. Friends were mentioned as a reliable source of feedback (SU2, SU3, SU4) since the interviewees believed them to give honest feedback instead of only complimenting out of courtesy. The problem with testing the product and seeking feedback from friends was that they were not always the real users of the product so their opinions of the content were not seen as important. Other startups, investors and experts of various fields, including UX design were part of the local startup community and were used to get feedback and ideas. Discussions about how other people perceived UX of competitors' products also motivated some startups (SU1, SU2, SU5) to put effort in differentiating with better UX.

Interviews to understand the needs of users and the context of use were conducted by five startups (SU02, SU04, SU05, SU06, SU08). The interviews were done for different purposes. Startup number SU2 had interviewed friends in a very light way to understand their current use of possible competing products whereas startups SU4 and SU8 had done thorough interviews with 15 potential users. Startups SU6 and SU7 had interviewed possible business partners but had not reached end-user customers before starting the implementation.

Gaining Feedback. Startups used a wide variety of practices to gain feedback. The summary of used practices is presented in Table 2. Three startups (SU3, SU4, SU8) had **test users** for their prototype or beta version. Test users used the product the way they wanted or with some instructions but specific tasks were not given to them. Startup SU3 used friends (15 people) and potential end-users (15 people) found by visiting Meetup.com group meetings as test users. Startup SU8 had two test users who had the health condition their application was designed for. They were found from a support group. Startup SU6 had made a pilot with a partner that provided users for their online training. They collected feedback of the content with a survey but were not able to interview the participants. They also did a pilot with a master of psychology thesis worker who did research with real users and provided more qualitative feedback with open answers of a survey.

Startup SU4 had started by creating a **paper prototype** of their product that other startups could use in the common space the startups worked in. When they had a working prototype had made a campaign on betalist.com, a site for finding new startups. Through their campaign they got 500 signups for their beta version. Also startup SU6 had used paper prototypes to present their idea when interviewing potential business partners. Startups collected feedback from test users by email, surveys, Facebook page created for test users and informal discussions.

Log data and statistics collection was implemented in the product by startups SU1, SU4 and SU6. They all used Google analytics. Startups SU4 and SU6 used also Mixpanel. Analytics was used to understand from where people came to their site and how they interacted with the product. Startups SU4 and SU6 utilized data systematically during their product pilots. SU4 also followed how the behavior changed when the product version changed. SU6 had analyzed what kind of behavior lead to a positive feedback from users. Startup SU1 followed analytics occasionally.

Startup SU5 used **market research** to understand the target market and the expected users. They had read about statistics from other countries on services that were similar to theirs. The assumption was that Finland, as a market would be following the same trends. They did a survey with potential partners about the concept they had planned. They estimated the average user to be similar to whom it was in other countries' markets but did not conduct any user research. *"Until we have a working prototype of our product no-one is interested in us and we can't get useful feedback."* (H6)

Table 2. Practices used to gain user information and feedback

Practice or method	Startups utilizing the practice
User interviews	SU2, SU4, SU5, SU6, SU8
Surveys	SU4, SU6
Paper prototypes	SU4
Personal need for the product	SU1, SU3, SU4, SU6, SU8
Test users	SU3, SU4, SU8
Expert advice	SU6
Online user communities (eg. forums, Facebook groups)	SU7, SU8
Log data and analytics	SU1, SU4, SU6

Startup SU6 had strong background in research on interactive technology and online training from which the product idea had come from. They also had experts of psychology working part time in their team. Experts gave advice and reviewed the product from a non-technical viewpoint.

Startups SU1 and SU8 had people who were very interested in their product and wanted to help them in making it better. SU8 had recently created a Facebook page for these people to share ideas on features and give comments on design ideas. SU1 was planning how to connect with these people and make it possible for them to help improve the product but also market it.

Practices for Turning User Feedback to UX design. The roles of team members were mostly described to be vague and that they evolved. Tasks were divided among team members based on skills and personal interests. The product development processes were different and not systematic for the startups. Startups SU4 and SU6 described having a leader for the product development. Two startups described having two week sprints. Four startups (SU1, SU3, SU6, SU8) described using a backlog to collect their ideas and tasks. The startups did not have a specific process for making design decisions or transforming user feedback into design rationale.

Startup SU4 was the only startup that had clear UX goals. They had used the information gained from interviews to create user journey maps. They had defined emotions that the user should get from the product and design was made to meet those goals. Other startups could describe a vision for the UX they were aiming at but had not written them down. The common idea was to build something and then collect feedback or log data to see if the product was good. *"Now we try to only do the things that either totally make sense or that people are complaining about."* (H1) Startups SU1, SU2 and SU5 used UX designers from outside the startup to get feedback and ideas for the user interface. These UX designers were acquaintances of startup founders and helped them for free. *"We are such a homogenous team that we need to seek advice from people from other fields."* (H7) Interviewee H7 mentioned that even though not all the ideas from designers were realistic to implement they helped in thinking differently and in gaining new perspective.

All the startups had had a lot of ideas for the product they were developing. They needed to decide what they would be able to implement with the current resources. Prioritization of features was discussed with the whole team. Ideas and issues that were commented on repeatedly by users caused four of the startups (SU1, SU3, SU4, SU6) to modify the product. Interviewee H11 said that in the end he decided what was implemented to the product based on what was important to him as a user. Startups SU6 and SU8 described the qualitative data from interviews and surveys to be very valuable although they did not use it continuously when developing the product. They described returning to it occasionally.

Startups SU3 and SU4 were implementing in their pilot only the features that enabled the user to do two core actions while leaving everything else to later versions. Prioritization was done by intuition and not by systematically evaluating which features produce most value to users. *"Basically what we're working for now is the launch. And anything that gets us closer to that is our priority. Unless there's a fix or a fire we have to put out."* (H4)

4.2   Challenges with Gaining Feedback and Using It

All startups told they had had challenges in collecting meaningful information from users or customers. Interviewees from startup SU4 said that they would not know what to ask from people. Startup SU4 was receiving positive feedback from discussions with users but they were not gaining many new users. *"I don't know what data we need and I don't know how to ask questions. So I think there is a bit of challenge."*(H1) Interviewees from SU6 wondered if they were getting overly positive feedback since their product was the first one to help the users with the specific problem. They would have wanted constructive feedback to be able to improve the UX. Startups SU3, SU4 and SU5 said that they needed more users to be able to collect meaningful feedback and data about their current version of the product. SU8 told that they had gained 80 people signed up to be interested about their product but they were not prepared for it and could not utilize this user pool due to being so busy with other things. Limited resources affected all the startups and they needed to divide their time to balance between product development and business creation while still trying to learn if their focus was on the right product and market.

The product concept had changed for startups SU4 and SU6 after they had already conducted user research. The target market and end-users changed which resulted in them having user information that was not valid anymore.

Reaching the potential end-users in the planning phase was difficult for startups SU4, SU6 and SU7. Startups SU4 and SU7 were aiming to B2B markets so they were mainly discussing with customer representatives. Startup SU6 had problems to reach end-users because the product was targeted for people suffering from social anxieties and they did not want to be interviewed. Even though SU6 could not directly reach the end-users, they managed to get feedback with a survey and through people who worked with the people from the challenging target group.

Startup SU3 described having major technical challenges in getting test users to download their application. The tool they used to distribute the application that was not published required multiple steps from them and from users. The interviewee H4 estimated having lost hundreds of test users due to technical difficulties after having personally asked them to become test users. He also described that while some users gave in depth feedback with some test users he had to remind them to keep using the application and give feedback more than once. *"Especially the friends, they use it once and then I have to prompt them to try it again."* (H4) SU8 mentioned that if they had found the online forum where their users interacted earlier it would have saved a lot of time.

The use of log data and analytics was challenging for startups SU1 and SU6. They had implemented the collection of statistics but were not gaining as much insight from it as they would have wanted. Startup SU4 was using data systematically to evaluate the behavior of users but they still found it difficult sometimes. *"The most challenging part is finding the meaning of data when it does not explain the reasons [behind actions]. And if we make wrong guesses then we won't learn."* (H5)

The challenges included finding relevant users for user research and testing, and having the right methods to get meaningful information. The interviewees did not mention having special difficulties in the actual UX design. In user tests, the product and UX need to be good enough for people to get some value. Startups SU1, SU2, SU3 and SU4 needed users and user-generated content in their product or service for it to bring value to users. This proposed a problem on how to generate enough content for the launch so that even the early adopters would gain enough value to keep using the product or the service. When the product relies on user-generated content it makes user testing difficult since the users might not be patient enough to wait for content to be created. Startups may not have enough resources to drive the creation of such content in the early phases of product launch.

4.3   Needs for UX Work When Scaling Up

Startups that participated in the interviews were in different stages in their business and product development. When talking about the needs for UX work they would have in the future the answers varied. Startups SU3 and SU5 were preparing to launch the first public version of their product within a month and it was their first priority. They both mentioned that having perhaps one more person working on development and UX would be helpful but that they could also manage without one. They trusted that they would get enough user data after the launch which would then help them to improve the product. However, they did not have a clear plan on how to collect and analyze the feedback and data. *"The challenge with end-users might be that they just leave the site if they don't like it. We would need to know what made them leave."*(H6)

All the startups that currently did not collect log data and analytics (SU2, SU3, SU5, SU7) were planning to collect it from the upcoming versions of their product. They believed that it would enable them to understand users and react to it by improving the product. None of them had clear plans on how to gain insight from data but they trusted the tools available to help in it.

Startups SU4 and SU7 were preparing for a pilot with a B2B customer. They were expecting to get a better understanding of their customers and the user groups with the pilot. Since they had no direct contact to the end-users, the collection of usage data was seen as the best way to learn from the users. Startup SU7 hoped to build trust with customer so they could later be in contact with end-users.

Startup SU6 was next planning to build a product for a new market outside of Finland. They estimated needing more background information of their users to understand them in the new market. This information would be, for example, the socio-economic background, how they heard about the product and what motivated them to come to the site.

The most common future vision regarding understanding users was collecting log data and analytics. Primary reason to collect data for SU3 was creating revenue with it by selling the data. As for feedback channels, SU4 was planning to implement a user support portal. SU1, SU3 and SU8 wanted to better utilize the people interested in developing the product with them. None of the startups mentioned currently having plans to conduct end-user interviews. Surveys were seen as a possible way to collect feedback in the future but none of the startups had planned them for now. In general, the startups did not have a clear strategy for future UX work.

5   Discussion and Conclusions

The eight startups that were interviewed provided valuable insights of UX work practices that can be useful and feasible to conduct in the startup context. The startups that had human-centered-design knowledge used a variety of ways to collect information on end-users. Some of them had conducted interviews, surveys and experimented with paper prototypes. This is in line with Coleman's [4] observation of software development processes which concludes that the background of people inside the startup has the biggest influence on how processes are formatted. These startups sometimes felt that they were not using the information as systematically as they could have but it still provided them support when they needed it. According to the interviewees, going back and reading the qualitative data was a good way to find ideas. Startups with no knowledge of human-centered design reported having difficulties in collecting meaningful information about users due to not knowing what to ask from users. Since the developers in startups are empowered to affect the UX design, one option could be educating them to basic user research methods like in [14].

UX work in startups needs to balance with different aspects. On one side, user research and testing need to be done as early as possible while at the same time the product, users and market might still change. In addition, the product that is tested should be minimally implemented but have enough features and UX design to keep the test users motivated to use it. This is relevant especially in products that require many users or user-generated content to provide value.

The limited sample of startups in this study does not represent all kinds of startups. From the interviewed startups, four had an international team working for them but they were still operating from Finland. Also, all but one (SU3) were interacting and exchanging ideas with the same experts and investors within the local startup community. For more thorough understanding and generalization of the results, more startups should be investigated from different market sectors and locations. Further research with a larger number of startups over a longer period will help determining more profoundly what kind of UX practices best serve startups. Still, this study has provided new knowledge on how the startups approach different aspects of UX work and what challenges they face.

Startups should recognize the importance of UX when they are planning to enter markets with new, innovative products. Based on our research we suggest that startups would benefit from:

1. Having skills for user information gathering and analysis. This enables them to get more meaningful information and see past the generic feedback.
2. Applying lightweight methods for quick interviews, surveys and user tests that address questions arising in different stages of the startup's product development.
3. Putting effort in finding the right users for research and testing purposes, beyond the personal networks. This user base should be heterogeneous enough to present the user group and not just the early adopters. The size of the user base should be manageable to keep contact for a longer period of time and different product versions.
4. Preparing for the feedback and data that they will get. Log data and statistics might be challenging to analyze. Resources should be targeted in collecting what can be used afterwards, and for the analysis itself.
5. Creating UX strategy that would help keep focus and steer the product towards the wanted UX.

Addressing these issues from the very early phases of the product design and development will help startups create successful products with delightful user experience.

References

1. Ardito, C., Buono, P., Caivano, D., et al.: Investigating and Promoting UX Practice in Industry: An Experimental Study. International Journal of Human-Computer Studies **72**, 542–551 (2014)
2. Beck, K., Beedle, M., Van Bennekum, A., et al.: Manifesto for Agile Software Development (2001)
3. Blank, S.: Why the Lean Start-Up Changes Everything. Harv. Bus. Rev. **91**, 63–72 (2013)
4. Coleman, G., O'Connor, R.V.: An Investigation into Software Development Process Formation in Software Start-Ups. Journal of Enterprise Information Management **21**, 633–648 (2008)
5. Gasik, V., Lamas, D.: Lean design for good user experience. In: CHI 2013 Workshop "Made for Sharing: HCI Stories for Transfer, Triumph and Tragedy", p. 10 (2013)
6. Giardino, C., Unterkalmsteiner, M., Paternoster, N., et al.: What do we Know about Software Development in Startups? IEEE Software **31**, 28–32 (2014)
7. Giardino, C., Wang, X., Abrahamsson, P.: Why early-stage software startups fail: a behavioral framework. In: Lassenius, C., Smolander, K. (eds.) ICSOB 2014. LNBIP, vol. 182, pp. 27–41. Springer, Heidelberg (2014)

8. Gothelf, J.: Lean UX: Applying lean principles to improve user experience. O'Reilly Media, Inc. (2013)
9. Gulliksen, J., Boivie, I., Persson, J., et al.: Making a difference: a survey of the usability profession in sweden. In: Proc. of the Third Nordic Conference on HCI, pp. 207–215. ACM (2004)
10. ISO: 9241-210:2010. Ergonomics of Human System Interaction-Part 210: Human-Centred Design for Interactive Systems. International Standardization Organization (ISO), Switzerland (2009)
11. Jurca, G., Hellmann, T.D., Maurer, F.: Integrating agile and user-centered design: a systematic mapping and review of evaluation and validation studies of agile-ux. In: Agile Conference (AGILE), pp. 24–32. IEEE (2014)
12. Klein, L.: UX for lean startups: Faster, smarter user experience research and design. O'Reilly Media, Inc. (2013)
13. Kuusinen, K., Väänänen-Vainio-Mattila, K.: How to make agile UX work more efficient: management and sales perspectives. In: Proc. of the 7th Nordic Conference on HCI: Making Sense Through Design, pp. 139–148. ACM (2012)
14. Liikkanen, L.A., Kilpiö, H., Svan, L., et al.: Lean UX: the next generation of user-centered agile development?. In: Proc. of the 8th Nordic Conference on HCI: Fun, Fast, Foundational, pp. 1095–1100. ACM (2014)
15. May, B.: Applying lean startup: an experience report: lessons learned in creating & launching a complex consumer app. In: Agile Conference (AGILE), pp. 141–147. IEEE (2012)
16. Paternoster, N., Giardino, C., Unterkalmsteiner, M., et al.: Software Development in Startup Companies: A Systematic Mapping Study. Information and Software Technology (2014)
17. Ries, E.: The lean startup: How today's entrepreneurs use continuous innovation to create radically successful businesses. Random House LLC (2011)
18. Taipale, M.: Huitale – a story of a finnish lean startup. In: Abrahamsson, P., Oza, N. (eds.) LESS 2010. LNBIP, vol. 65, pp. 111–114. Springer, Heidelberg (2010)
19. Vivianto, A.: The Lean UX Manifesto: Principle-Driven Design. http://www.smashingmagazine.com/2014/01/08/lean-ux-manifesto-principle-driven-design/ (2014)
20. Vredenburg, K., Mao, J., Smith, P.W., et al.: A survey of user-centered design practice. In: Proc. of the SIGCHI Conference on Human Factors in Computing Systems, pp. 471–478. ACM (2002)

Why the Development Outcome Does Not Meet the Product Owners' Expectations?

Timo O.A. Lehtinen[(✉)], Risto Virtanen, Ville T. Heikkilä, and Juha Itkonen

Department of Computer Science, Aalto University School of Science,
P.O. BOX 15400 Fl-00076, Aalto, Finland
{timo.o.lehtinen,risto.virtanen,
ville.t.heikkila,juha.itkonen}@aalto.fi

Abstract. Many software development projects fail due to problems in requirements, scope, and collaboration. This paper presents a case study of the mismatch between the expectations of Product Owners and the outcome of the development in a large distributed Scrum organization. The data was collected in retrospective meetings involving a team of Product Owners and two software development teams. A focused root cause analysis of the problem "Why the expectations of Product Owners do not meet the outcome of development teams?" was conducted. The analysis aimed at explaining why the problem occurred and how the causes were related to one another. The outcomes were analyzed both quantitatively and qualitatively. Our results illustrate the challenges of implementing the Product Owner role in the context of complex, high-variability requirements and distributed development. We highlight the importance of true collaboration, effective requirements specification activities, and sufficient resources for the Product Owner role.

Keywords: Scrum · Product owner · Root cause analysis · Software process improvement · Requirements engineering · Global software development

1 Introduction

Matching the expectations of customers and software development outcomes is a fundamental business issue and research objective in the software engineering domain. The mismatch between customer expectations and software development outcomes has caused many software projects to fail, see e.g. [1].

The identified key factors of successful software product development [2] include the good requirements and flexible collaboration between the customers and developers. Respectively, the common factors of software project failures [3] include the difficulties with the customers, requirements specifications, and collaboration over the stakeholders. Most of the underlying causes of the success and failure have also been presented to be context dependent [3] and thus the in-depth analysis and dissemination of each new case is important in order to create generalizable knowledge of software engineering problem causes. Prior studies have mostly ignored the contextual differences in software projects [4].

© Springer International Publishing Switzerland 2015
C. Lassenius et al. (Eds.): XP 2015, LNBIP 212, pp. 93–104, 2015.
DOI: 10.1007/978-3-319-18612-2_8

This paper disseminates a case study on the problems in the collaboration between Product Owners (PO) and software development teams in a large distributed Scrum organization. The problems are analyzed from both the customer and development perspective. The main objective is to disseminate the causes of the mismatch between the software development outcomes and POs' expectations. In addition, the solutions to identified causes are proposed and evaluated. This study answers the following two research questions:

RQ1: Why the expectations of Product Owners do not meet the outcome of development work?

RQ2: What problems were perceived the most important to control in order to minimize the risk for a failure in the Product Owner expectations?

2   Background and Related Work

The way the expectations of a PO are communicated to the developers in a Scrum team is well-documented [5]. The PO creates and prioritizes the product backlog items. During the sprint planning meeting, the team creates a feasible sprint backlog for the following sprint. During the sprint, the team and the PO have a constant dialogue regarding the implementation of the backlog items. At the end of the sprint, the Scrum team and relevant stakeholders review the sprint outcome. Thus, the PO communicates her expectations to the team at the beginning, during and at the end of the sprint. Any mismatches are identified easily and amended quickly.

Although the PO is extremely important for the success of Scrum development, there has been little research on the causes of failed expectations in Scrum. Some studies exist on the topic of implementing Scrum in global software development. Lee and Yong [6] found that the distribution of development created misunderstandings between stakeholders and difficulties in adjusting priorities. They suggested on-site customer representatives as a solution for those problems. Paasivaara et al. [7] studied the challenges in scaling the PO role in globally distributed Scrum projects. They identified on-site PO representatives, teaming POs, frequent communication, and clearly communicated priorities as the means for a successful PO function in large distributed settings.

Moe et al. [8] studied teamwork in a Scrum project. They found that developers expected the PO to be able to provide answers to their questions on short notice. However, the PO lacked clear understanding of what the system was supposed to do and he was not always able to answer the developers' questions. Subsequently, the developers were often unsure of what they were supposed to do. The lack of planning and a rapidly changing environment were also identified as causes for the developers working on tasks that did not originate from the sprint backlog. Moe et al. identified the insufficient coordination of information dissemination and the lack of responsibility for the overall technical solution as the causes of failed PO expectations.

Strode et al. [9] propose that having an on-site customer representative leads to highly efficient coordination, but a team-external customer representative leads to more complex coordination needs. They suggest that a team member should take the role of an explicit coordinator if an on-site customer representative is not available.

According to Bjarnason et al. [10], overscoping refers to setting a larger iteration scope than the available resources allow. They identified the following causes of overscoping in large-scale software engineering [10]: Continuous requirements inflow from multiple channels, no overview of available resources, low development team involvement in the early planning phases, unclear vision of the overall goal and scope, and deadlines dictated by the management. They also found that overscoping caused failures to meet the customers' or clients' expectations.

3   Methodology

The overall research method was a case study [11]. Root cause analysis [12] was used in the data collection and analysis.

3.1   Case Company

The case company was a large distributed software development company which employed approximately 800 employees. The company developed complex systems that were integrated into customer specific systems with varying business logic. The company representatives reported that they had started to use the Scrum method [5] about a year prior to this study. The organization had 30 members who were software developers, Scrum Masters, or POs. The developers were split into two software development teams. Both teams developed independent sub-systems for the software product. The teams followed two-week development sprints, conducted daily stand-ups, sprint demonstrations and retrospectives.

Four POs conveyed the customer needs to the development teams. The organization was divided into three European countries, each having one local PO and members from both teams. The fourth PO was responsible for quality assurance. Both teams worked with all four POs. One reason for this was the regulatory localization: The product needed to fulfill country specific regulations and therefore it was useful to have multiple POs, each being responsible for a different set of regulations.

The case was purposively selected [13] as it was a rich source of data. It enabled us to accumulate understanding about the reasons for failed PO expectations in a large, distributed Scrum organization.

3.2   Data Collection with Root Cause Analysis

The data collection was made by focused retrospective meetings following the ARCA root cause analysis (RCA) method [14] and tool [12]. The organization had used such an approach in retrospectives preceding our case study, which enabled us to collect the data and observe the analysis in the real context of use.

The case study was based on on-going research collaboration including frequent knowledge sharing. The case study started with a 60-minute focus group meeting with one PO and one Scrum Master. The goal was to define the main problem in the software development activities. These discussions resulted in understanding that the expectations of POs did not meet the outcome of the development work.

The formal data was collected in three face-to-face retrospective meetings (3 x 60 minutes in total). Each retrospective meeting considered the following question: *"Why expectations of Product owners do not meet with the implemented functionality?"* The first and second retrospective meetings were conducted with a development team (three and five participants, respectively). The third meeting was conducted with the POs (four participants). One of the Scrum Masters chaired all of the retrospective meetings. All three retrospectives were conducted in succession during one day and the participants did not communicate between the retrospective meetings.

The teams used the RCA method and software tool in the retrospective meetings to detect the causes of the main problem and collaboratively create a cause-effect diagram that expresses the problem causes and their causal relationships in an electronic format. The method was used in the following way. First, the retrospective participants were given 5 minutes to individually write down causes related to the main problem. Thereafter, they presented their findings to others. Then, the participants were given another 5 minutes to add additional causes and sub-causes for the previously detected problems, followed by discussion. During the discussion, further additional causes were entered to the cause-effect diagram when detected. The participants also considered how the causes were related to one another. This helped them to express how the conflicts between the POs' expectations and the development work outcomes came to be. At the end of each retrospective, the participants voted on the causes that needed immediate corrective actions and were also feasible to solve.

The case analyses resulted in four corrective actions. These actions were evaluated by the organization members during the "improved" software development activities. In order to evaluate the process improvement impact, the company representatives conducted three 60 minutes interviews. One Product Owner and two developers, one from each team, were interviewed.

3.3 Data Analysis

The data analysis was conducted with the company representatives. The raw data from each retrospective meeting was analyzed separately first. The detected causes were classified applying the process area and problem type classifications proposed by Lehtinen et al. [3]. This made it possible to generalize the causes and map them to software development process areas, which helped to express what happened in the affected software processes.

After the detected causes were classified, the process interconnections were analyzed. A new modularized cause-effect diagram was made from each retrospective data separately. The diagram included process areas and cause types separated into "local causes" and "bridge causes" [3]. The bridge causes explain the external causal relationship between two process areas and the local causes explain the outcomes of a process area internally. The most controllable problems, voted by the retrospective participants, were also emphasized in the modularized diagram. This helped to communicate the analysis results to the members of the organization and decision makers, which was considered highly important because the aim of the company was to recognize feasible targets for process improvement, develop action proposals, and finally implement the corrective actions.

After the results from each retrospective were analyzed, the results were synthesized into a combined analysis. This made it possible to conclude the common problems and generalize the results to cover the whole organization. The reliability of the combined results was expected to be high because they were identified in each retrospective meeting separately. Corrective action interview results were analyzed by dividing the answers into "positive comments" and "comments why the corrective action should be improved".

4   Results

This section presents the results of the case study. First, the analysis outcomes from the retrospective meetings are presented. Thereafter, we describe the synthesis of the results analyzing similarities and differences between the outcomes of the different teams.

4.1   Retrospective Outcomes of Development Team 1

Development Team 1 (D1) concluded that the main problem was caused by insufficient requirements, which were not specific enough to be understood correctly. They were made with insufficient guidance from the customers. The requirements were also affected by the lack of collaboration, the lack of values and taking responsibility, and the lack of available resources.

D1 explicated causes from the development work. The team members did not communicate actively enough during the sprints. They did not ask for clarifications to unclear requirements. The team members also explained that they did not communicate enough directly with the POs, but too much thorough the Scrum Master. Additionally, the team members reported that development work usually included challenging tasks.

Furthermore, D1 presented that the software testing suffered from missed deadlines and insufficient requirements. Third parties provided test data for software testing activities. Occasionally, the third parties provide the data too late, which caused delays in the software testing. Insufficient requirements caused inaccurate workload estimates, which caused missed deadlines in software testing.

The lack of information flow between the sales & requirements and development work was identified as an important target for process improvement. Similarly, the collaboration practices were emphasized important to be solved.

4.2   Retrospective Outcomes of Development Team 2

Development Team 2 (D2) identified many similar causes than D1. D2 concluded that the main problem was affected by insufficient communication between POs and developers, which caused unclear specifications with vague priorities. The lack of knowledge, lack of values and taking responsibility, lack of collaboration between Product Owners and developers, lack of processes for communication, and lack of resources explained why the requirements were insufficient. In addition to D1 findings, D2 members explained that it was also the work practices of prioritizing everything as "must have" which caused the main problem.

The inactive communication between the POs and developers during the sprints was also elaborated as one of the important causes of the main problem. One team member found that "Dialogue might be missing during sprint", which was then explained by stating "No tradition in ongoing communication between POs and Developers" and "Product Owners [are] not involved as much as they should".

The lack of collaboration between the sales and requirements process and development work was concluded as an important target for process improvement. Furthermore, D2 proposed that the collaboration and development process needed to be improved.

4.3   Retrospective Outcomes of Product Owner Team

Similarly to both development teams, the POs concluded that the requirements were insufficient. They explained that the problems in the sales and requirements process were caused by the lack of knowledge, lack of values and taking responsibility, lack of collaboration, lack of work practices, lack of communication processes, and lack of resources. The POs thought that creating good requirements was difficult. The organization employed third parties to create the requirements and occasionally the POs could not understand those requirements.

The POs detected the causes of the main problem similar to the ones detected by the development teams. These included the lack of knowledge, lack of collaboration, and task difficulty. In contradiction, they explained that the quality of the development work outcome was occasionally insufficient. The POs emphasized that the lack of collaboration with the developers was the most important cause in explaining why the main problem occurred. They claimed that the organization members were inactive in collaboration. The POs stated that "Developers have not asked for meetings" and "No initiatives from POs or Scrum Masters to have meetings and discuss complex use cases". They also stated that the language barrier and geographical distances negatively affected the collaboration activity. The POs elaborated that the development work was not properly monitored during the sprints.

The POs stated that the main problem was also caused by management problems and the organization in general. They claimed that the knowledge of managers was limited and that the management suffered from the lack of collaboration, lack of communication processes, and lack of resources. The POs also identified problems in the whole organization. They claimed that the organization members did not know how to do Scrum. Finally, they explained that the complexity of the product caused problems for most members of the organization.

Insufficient requirements were identified as the most important targets for process improvement. Similarly, the lack of processes, insufficient task outcomes, the lack of taking responsibility, and the lack of resources in sales & requirements were important to be improved. The POs also emphasized organization-wide problems for process improvement activities. These included the lack of instructions and experience, and the complexity of the existing product.

4.4   Synthesis of the Individual Retrospective Results

Fig. 1 summarizes the causes that were identified in all retrospective meetings. It also shows the causes that were perceived as feasible targets for process improvement. The missing collaboration during the software development activities is one of the main problem causes in the organization. The output from the sales and requirements process was also found to be insufficient. Following from these causes, the developers did not know what to do and what to test. The members of the organization perceived that they did not receive enough instructions.

Furthermore, the participants presented that the lack of values and taking responsibility was a problem in the sales and requirements process area. The sales & requirements process area also suffered from the lack of resources. The feasible process improvement targets were mostly similar among the teams. Requirements understanding needed to be increased. The collaboration was also a feasible target for process improvement. A total of four corrective actions were finally developed. First, the POs were asked to participate in the teams' daily stand-up meetings. Second, the organization hired two new employees to work with the requirements specifications and usability designs. Third, the POs increased their mutual collaboration during the development sprints. Fourth, the POs started to regularly participate in sprint planning activities.

Only the first corrective action was not implemented. In the interviews, the impact of the other corrective actions was concluded as significant. On the other hand, it was noted that these corrective actions do not solve the main problem completely.

5   Discussion

This section answers our research questions and considers the implications for practitioners. At the end of the section, we also discuss the limitations of this case study.

5.1   Answers to the Research Questions

The main research objective of this case study was to conclude the problems between the outcome of Scrum teams and POs in large distributed Scrum organization. Table 1 summarizes the problems and detected causes including their solutions in relation to the related work.

RQ1: Why the expectations of Product Owners do not meet the outcome of development work? The first research question contributes to prior studies on software project failures by considering the problems to meet the expectations of customers. Regarding our results, the lack of collaboration between the customers and software development teams causes such failures. In the case organization, the POs had difficulties communicating and prioritizing the requirements to the development teams because the requirements were not clear for the POs themselves. This was caused by the lack of PO resources and the use of third parties in eliciting and defining the requirements. The geographical distance, language barriers, and inactive software developers exacerbated the problems. Clarifications for the requirements were neither requested during the development work.

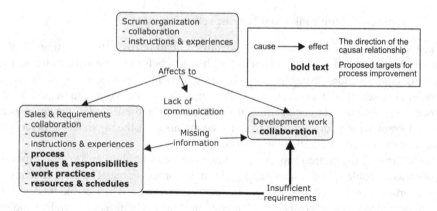

Fig. 1. Synthesis of the causes detected in the retrospective meetings

The problems of the case organization do not seem to be problems with the Scrum method, but problems in implementing it. The in-depth data analysis including the problems and corrective actions of the case revealed that the PO role was not fully implemented. The POs did not belong to the Scrum teams, but were isolated customer representatives occasionally participating in sprint planning and review meetings. They did not actively participate in the sprint planning, daily stand-up, and sprint retrospective meetings. These causes partially explain the failed PO expectations. The company representatives concluded that the POs were not parts of the development teams and subsequently the developers did not know which PO was responsible for which requirements.

RQ2: What problems were perceived the most important to control in order to minimize the risk for a failure in the Product Owner expectations? The second research question contributes to the research problem of how to successfully describe the requirements and communicate them to the Scrum teams. In our result, lacking instructions and experience, values and responsibility, collaboration, methodology, and resources and schedules are all important targets for process improvement.

The case organization members perceived that increasing the amount of collaboration between the POs and software developers would improve the outcome of the sales and requirements process. They also concluded that this would require changes in the methods used by the POs. The POs should have met with the development teams more often. Especially they should have actively participated in the sprint planning meetings, as was proposed in the corrective actions developed in the case. Additionally, the POs should have had frequent meetings together. This would have helped them to review the requirements before they were introduced to the development teams. Furthermore, sharing instructions and project experiences over the members of the organization were perceived as important for increasing the match-rate between the expectations of the POs and outcomes of the development teams.

Table 1. Comparison with the related work

Problem	Causes in this study	Causes in related work
Insufficient collaboration between the PO and the team(s).	• The distribution of development and heavy PO workload caused inactive collaboration during the sprints, which led to misunderstandings between the stakeholders.	• The distribution of development created communication misunderstandings between stakeholders [6]. • Low development team involvement in early planning phases [10] caused overscoping.
Challenges in adjusting the priorities.	• POs' heavy workload caused lack of resources to do prioritization. • POs' lack of knowledge caused unclear understanding in the development teams.	• Difficulties in adjusting priorities [6]. • The continuous requirements inflow from multiple channels [10]. • PO lack of understanding of product features [8]. • No overview of software development resource availability [10].
Developers working on the wrong tasks	• The development work was not properly monitored.	• Rapid change and lack of planning [8]. • Insufficient coordination of information dissemination and the lack of responsibility for the overall technical solution [8].
Lacking understanding of requirements.	• The third parties provided unclear requirements for the POs which caused problems reaching a consensus with the developers.	• Unclear vision of the overall goal, and scope and deadlines dictated by the management [10].
Solutions	**Solutions in this study**	**Solutions in related work**
Local customer representatives	• On-site customer representatives.	• On-site customer representatives [6], [7].
Product Owner resources	• A PO team. • PO meetings. • Increasing the number of POs. • Active PO participation in sprint planning.	• A PO team [7]. • Team internal coordinator if an on-site PO not available [7], [8]. • Frequent communication [7]. • Clearly communicated priorities [7]. • POs with technical background [7]. • PO pairwork [7].

Additionally, the organization needed more human resources. The POs were far too busy to handle the stream of all customer requirements and to communicate them in the large-scale distributed organization. Therefore, two new employees were acquired to the software organization. A new PO was hired to manage the product backlog, including the requirements elicitation, tracking, and prioritization. This was an improvement towards proper Scrum implementation. It also improved the software development outcomes. The organization members explained that the new PO had a positive effect on the clarity of requirements. The requirements were also provided well in time. Furthermore, a new employee was hired to ensure that the user interface was designed according to the requirements. This helped the organization to increase the match-rate between the implemented user interface and the customer expectations. This was a "great help" as was concluded in the post-interviews.

5.2   Implications for Practitioners

In a large distributed software organization, implementing Scrum successfully is challenging. It requires a fit between the customers and software development teams, which is highly dependent on the success of implementing the PO role. Scrum may also require heavy investments in collaboration, knowledge sharing, organization culture, and motivation.

We see that our analysis contributes to prior works on Scrum by considering the causes and possible solutions for the mismatch in the expectations of POs, proxies between the customers and development work. Our analysis studied why the expectations of POs did not meet the development work outcome, a gap in the existing studies. The prior works (see Table 1) have studied Scrum related problems, in general, and found that insufficient collaboration [6], [10], challenges adjusting priorities [6], [10], [8], developers working on the wrong tasks [8], and lacking understanding of requirements [10] are common challenges. Respectively, solutions to these problems have been presented, which include local customer representatives [6], [7] and PO resources [7], [8]. Our case organization suffered with similar problems and they also resulted in similar solutions. Therefore, our findings consolidate the prior works and make a contribution by showing how these problems and solutions are related to failed PO expectations.

We hypothesize that in a large distributed software organization, implementing Scrum is a longitudinal process which could be very time-consuming and difficult to implement fully. Our case organization had gone through an agile transformation about a year before our study was conducted. The Scrum roles were assigned to the employees and the Scrum rituals were conducted. However, despite the effort and time used to implement Scrum, our case analysis revealed that Scrum was not completely implemented. For example, the PO was not present at the daily stand-up meetings.

A PO needs to have both team-facing and business-facing expertise. Ideally, there is a single PO who works within one development team. This means that other human resources are needed when customer needs are highly variable and difficult due to, for example, complex country specific regulations. Scrum provides little help to increase the match between the highly variable expectations of multitude of customers and software development outcomes in a complex software engineering context. In addition to Scrum, effort in creating specific and clear requirements and in guiding the teams is required. POs cannot be solely responsible for the requirements elicitation. Instead, third parties, country specific experts, a lot of collaboration, and explicit prioritization decisions are needed in a domain such as in our case.

In our case, the POs were shared by the teams. This way the organization tried to manage the complexity of the country specific regulations and decrease the problems from the geographical distribution. It enabled the developers to communicate with at least one PO face-to-face during the development sprints. However, having a PO accessible was not enough. The POs did not have enough time to meet the developers during the development sprints because they had to work with highly varying customer requirements. This also caused insufficient requirements communication with the development teams. The case organization decided to increase the number of POs in order to solve these problems.

We also hypothesize that analyzing the causes of the match-rate between the PO expectations and development work outcome helps in adopting Scrum. Analyzing *"Why expectations of Product Owners do not meet with the implemented functionality?"* helped the case organization to understand what improvements are feasible for their needs. The root cause analysis approach was also well-liked in the case organization [12]. It helped them to develop corrective actions. They continued using it in their sprint retrospectives.

5.3   Limitations

The validity of the output of a root cause analysis method relates to human factors [15]. The problems and their underlying causes were detected in public retrospective meetings. Thus, our results may have been affected by group pressure and insufficient knowledge. The following measures were taken in order to mitigate these risks. First, our results are based on triangulation, the collective findings of three individual groups. Second, we asked the organization members to evaluate the "correctness" and "impact" of the detected problems, and both got good evaluations. Third, the main parts of the analysis were conducted by the company representatives who were experts of their domain. To mitigate the risk for reliability, the data was re-analyzed by the authors. All analyzers came to similar conclusions on the detected problems, their underlying causes, and the feasible targets for process improvement.

6   Conclusions and Future Work

Our results from a large-size distributed agile software organization, which claimed to follow the Scrum method, indicate that the lack of collaboration between the customer representatives and software development teams caused the mismatch of expectations between them. We found that the problems in the collaboration escalated during the software development activities. The outcome of the sales and requirements process was insufficient and caused the developers not knowing what to do and what to test. The members of the organization did not receive enough useful instructions for the customer collaboration and for the whole software organization.

Increasing the amount of collaboration between the customer representatives and software developers was perceived as a feasible target for process improvement. In the case organization, making an improvement to the collaboration required changes in the methodologies used by the customer representatives. Additionally, it required hiring more human resources. The customer representatives were far too busy to handle the stream of the customer requests and to communicate them in the large-scale distributed software organization.

In a large and distributed software organization working with a high number of country specific regulations and customers, converting the customer needs to satisfactory solutions is a complicated challenge. Scrum provides only a partial solution to this puzzle. In our case, the POs struggled with the heavy communication needs with the customers and the third parties. They had no time to participate in the daily stand-up meetings. Thus, we conclude the following research problem for future work:

"How to successfully improve the match between customer needs and Scrum development outcomes in the context of complex, high-variability requirements and distributed development?"

References

1. Verner, J.M., Abdullah, L.M.: Exploratory case study research: Outsourced project failure. Information and Software Technology **54**, 866–886 (2012)
2. Moløkken-Østvold, K., Jørgensen, M.: A comparison of software project overruns - flexible versus sequential development models. IEEE Transactions on Software Engineering **31**(9), 754–766 (2005)
3. Lehtinen, T.O.A., Mäntylä, M.V., Vanhanen, J., Lassenius, C., Itkonen, J.: Perceived Causes of Software Project Failures – An Analysis of their Relationships. Information and Software Technology **56**(6), 623–643 (2014)
4. McLeod, L., MacDonell, S.G.: Factors that affect Software Systems Development Project Outcomes: A Survey of Research. ACM Computing Surveys **43**, 24–55 (2011)
5. Schwaber, K., Sutherland, J.: Scrum guide. Scrum Alliance (2011)
6. Lee, S., Yong, H.: Distributed agile: project management in a global environment. Empirical Software Engineering **15**, 204–217 (2010)
7. Paasivaara, M., Heikkila, V.T., Lassenius, C.: Experiences in scaling the product owner role in large-scale globally distributed scrum. In: Seventh International Conference On Global Software Engineering (ICGSE), pp. 174–178. IEEE (2012)
8. Moe, N.B., Dingsøyr, T., Dybå, T.: A teamwork model for understanding an agile team: A case study of a Scrum project. Information and Software Technology **52**, 480–491 (2010)
9. Strode, D.E., Huff, S.L., Hope, B., Link, S.: Coordination in co-located agile software development projects. J. Syst. Software **85**, 1222–1238 (2012)
10. Bjarnason, E., Wnuk, K., Regnell, B.: Are you biting off more than you can chew? A case study on causes and effects of overscoping in large-scale software engineering. Information and Software Technology **54**, 1107–1124 (2012)
11. Yin, R.K. (ed.): Case Study Research: Design and Methods. SAGE Publications, United States of America (1994)
12. Lehtinen, T.O.A., Virtanen, R., Viljanen, J.O., Mäntylä, M.V., Lassenius, C.: A tool Supporting root cause analysis for synchronous retrospectives in distributed software teams. Information and Software Technology **56**(4), 408–437 (2014)
13. Patton, M.Q.: Qualitative Research. Sage (2002)
14. Lehtinen, T.O.A., Mäntylä, M.V., Vanhanen, J.: Development and evaluation of a lightweight root cause analysis method (ARCA method) – field studies at four software companies. Information and Software Technology **53**(10), 1045–1061 (2011)
15. Runeson, P., Höst, M.: Guidelines for conducting and reporting case study research in software engineering. Empirical Software Engineering **14**(2), 131–164 (2008)

Functional Size Measures and Effort Estimation in Agile Development: A Replicated Study

Valentina Lenarduzzi[1], Ilaria Lunesu[2], Martina Matta[2(✉)], and Davide Taibi[3]

[1] Università degli Studi dell'Insubria, 21100, Varese, Italy
valentina.lenarduzzi@gmail.com
[2] Università degli Studi di Cagliari, Piazza d'Armi 09123, Cagliari, Italy
{ilaria.lunesu,martina.matta}@diee.unica.it
[3] Free University of Bolzano, Piazza Domenicani 3 39100, Bolzano, Italy
davide.taibi@unibz.it

Abstract. To help developers during the Scrum planning poker, in our previous work we ran a case study on a Moonlight Scrum process to understand if it is possible to introduce functional size metrics to improve estimation accuracy and to measure the accuracy of expert-based estimation. The results of this original study showed that expert-based estimations are more accurate than those obtained by means of models, calculated with functional size measures. To validate the results and to extend them to plain Scrum processes, we replicated the original study twice, applying an exact replication to two plain Scrum development processes. The results of this replicated study show that the accuracy of the effort estimated by the developers is very accurate and higher than that obtained through functional size measures. In particular, SiFP and IFPUG Function Points, have low predictive power and are thus not help to improve the estimation accuracy in Scrum.

1   Introduction

In projects developed with Scrum [19], effort estimations are carried out at the beginning of each sprint, based on developer experience. However, as reported by several empirical studies, developers, involved in agile processes, usually underestimate their effort in agile processes [5, 6, 7, 8 and 13].

In order to understand if functional size measures allow for more accurate effort estimates, a case study on a Moonlight Scrum process was conducted in our previous work [1]. There we investigated whether functional size measures can help to improve the effort estimation accuracy of Scrum user stories and compared the accuracy of the resulting effort model with the developers estimated effort. The study shows that, in Moonlight Scrum, the estimation of developers is more accurate than estimation based on functional measurement and therefore functional measures do not help developers in improving the accuracy of effort estimation in Moonlight Scrum.

Since the case study was applied to a slightly modified version of Scrum, we expect that different results might be obtained when applying the approach to a plain Scrum process.

© Springer International Publishing Switzerland 2015
C. Lassenius et al. (Eds.): XP 2015, LNBIP 212, pp. 105–116, 2015.
DOI: 10.1007/978-3-319-18612-2_9

Thus, we investigate these two research questions:

RQ1: Can we extend the results obtained to the original case study to plain Scrum processes?

RQ2: Does IFPUG Function Points help to increase the effort estimation, compared to SiFP?

In order to answer to our research questions, in this work we performed two exact replications of the original case study [4], directly involving the original authors of the original case study, together with those responsible for the development of the new two development processes.

No changes to the original study design were applied, except for the context in which the study was executed. In this case, the development process changed from Moonlight Scrum to a plain Scrum process.

The result of this work will provide input for future research directions over than the validation of existing results.

The information reported in this paper is organized as suggested by the guidelines for replicating controlled experiments [3]. Section 2 describes the original case study. Section 3 presents the new study contexts and design, highlighting the similarities and differences with the original design. Section 4 presents the results of the study and compares them with the original study. Section 5 discusses results and describes the threats to validity and finally, Section 6 draws conclusions.

2   The Original Case Study

In this section, we will describe the original study [1], providing information on the study design and describing the research questions, the goal of the study, the measures identified, and the protocol adopted. Then we will describe the study context, highlighting the variables that affected the design of the study, and finally we will provide a brief overview of the major findings.

2.1   Study Design

The goal of the original study was formulated by means of the Goal Question Metric approach [2] as: *analyze* the development process *for the purpose of* evaluating the effectiveness of functional measures for effort estimation *from the viewpoint of* the developers *in the context of* a Scrum development process.

One of the most important requirements was that measures must be collected within a maximum of five minutes per user story at the end of the usual Scrum planning game, so as to not influence the normal execution of the required Scrum practices.

For this purpose, we identified a set of measures to be collected for each user story at the end of every sprint meeting.

To measure user stories, we first investigated the feasibility of existing functional size measures. Since standard Function Points such as IFPUG [15] or FISMA require a lot of effort to be collected, and most of the required information was not available in our context, we opted for Simplified Function Points (SiFP) [12]. We collected SiFP instead of IFPUG Function Points because SiFP provides an "agile", simplified and alternative measure that is compatible with IFPUG Function Points [15, 17].

SiFP are calculated as $SiFP = 7 * \#DF + 4.6 * \#TF$, where #DF is the number of data functions (also known as logic data files) and #TF is the number of elementary processes (also known as transactions). For this reason, we collected information for DF and TF separately. Moreover, we also split TF into two sub-processes: input processes iTF (data received from the server) and output processes oTF (data sent to the server). TF was finally calculated as (iTF+oTF)/2.

Then, before running this study, we asked our developers what information they take into account when estimating a user story. All developers answered that they consider four pieces of information, based on the complexity of implementing the GUI and the number of functionalities to be implemented. They usually consider each GUI component as a single functionality that requires sending or receiving information to/from the database. The complexity of the communication is related to the number of tables involved in the SQL query.

For these reasons, we also considered the following measures:

- GUI Impact: null, low, medium, high: complexity of the GUI implementation identified by the developers.
- # GUI components added: number of data fields added (e.g., HTML input fields)
- # GUI components modified: number of data fields modified.

Finally, we also collected some context information, such as the story type (new features or maintenance), so as to understand whether new development tasks should be estimated differently from maintenance tasks.

2.2   Study Context

The case study was applied in the context of the development of a web-based application [14] developed in C#/Asp.net with a simple 3-tier architecture that allows the development of independent features among developers.

The application developed is a relatively small application, composed of 12,500 effective lines of code developed using a Moonlight Scrum process [11], a special version of Scrum.

The development was carried out by four part-time developers (Master's students) with 2 to 3 years' of experience in software development and was organized as follows:

- The duration of each sprint is three weeks.
- Daily meetings are replaced by reporting on an online forum twice a week.
- Only one developer can work on a user story.
- Each developer works 8 hours per week.
- Every developer works in isolation during non-overlapping hours.
- The work is coordinated by the Scrum master via the weekly meetings.

2.3   Study Results

The project was analyzed for four months. A total of 136 user stories were examined, of which 65% were related to the development of new features, while only 35% were related to maintenance. Moreover, in this process, most of the user stories were related to the development of graphical features with high or medium complexity.

Functional measures were collected only for 55 user stories (40.4%) since the remaining user stories did not contain enough information for functional size measurement (e.g., GUI features that do not deal with data transactions).

The analysis of correlations between SiFP and effort reported in all user stories did not provide any statistically significant result showing very low goodness of fit. Even when we tried to cluster the user stories by story type and GUI impact, the results showed the same behavior.

A similar pattern was shown for the correlation between the number of GUI components added or modified and the multivariate correlations among GUI components added, GUI components modified and Data Files provided statistically significant results paired with low correlation.

The results finally showed that functional measures are not applicable to a Moonlight Scrum process.

Since the study focused on Moonlight Scrum, a slightly modified version of Scrum, we expected some variations in applying the same approach to a full-time development team working on a plain Scrum process.

3   Study Context and Design

Our studies are designed so as to accurately replicate the original study conducted in [1] by using the same research goals and study design as reported in Section 2.

In this section, we will describe the contexts of both studies. Then we will highlight similarities and differences of the context and the design of the new studies with, respectively to, the context of the original study.

The projects analyzed in the new study were developed at the Software Factory lab of the University of Cagliari (Italy).

The development process was Scrum, with the support of a Kanban board [16], without tight WIP limits, in order to visualize in each instant the work in flow.

The development processes were organized as follows:

- The duration of each sprint is two weeks.
- Daily meetings must last at most 10 minutes.
- Developers work two days per week for eight hours a day (16 hours per week).
- A user story can be developed only by one developer (no pair programming).
- Every developer works in the same room during the same hours in order to improve collaboration and communication.
- The development is coordinated by a coach with perfect knowledge of the project and the technologies, who is also involved in the development.
- All developers are actively involved in Sprint retrospectives, planning, and retrospective discussions, making important contributions in order to obtain a good final result.

As in the original case study, the project was developed using a 3-tier architecture, which allowed the development of independent features among developers.

3.1   Case Study 1: Matchall2

In the first case study, we monitored the development of a module for Matchall2, an industrial web-based application aimed at providing labeling facilities (namely a bookmarklet) that allow classifying and categorizing pictures and videos with custom tags. The project was developed from March 2013 to May 2013 for a total of nine weeks (4 sprints).

The team was composed of eight students participating in the course: two graduate students, four undergraduates, and two PhD students. One of the PhD students had a good level of knowledge of the project and all the relevant technologies. Therefore, he played the role of team coordinator/coach. A local entrepreneur played the role of the product owner.

3.2   Case Study 2: Serts

The Serts project aimed at implementing a semi-automatic tool, called SERTS (Software Engineering Research Tool Suite) with the goal of simplifying the analysis of data collected in software repositories such as Bugzilla, CVS, SVN, Git, and Jira. The project allowed navigating through versions and releases, storing the data in an internal database, so as to speed up subsequent analysis of the software, such as the calculation of metrics and the extraction of software graphs. The project was developed from September 2013 to November 2013 during a period of eight weeks (3 sprints).

The team was composed of six students, one undergraduate and five PhD students.

Like in the Matchall2 project, one of the PhD students had a good level of knowledge of the project and played the role of team coordinator/coach.

3.3   Commonalities and Differences to the Original Case Study

The original study design and procedure were strictly followed. The only difference of the new studies is related to the development processes applied and the development teams and the new measure investigated (IFPUG Function Points).

In the replicated studies, the process was plain Scrum instead of Moonlight Scrum. For this reason, developers in the original study worked in non-collocated spaces and during non-overlapping hours, whereas in these replications, the developers worked in the same space during the same timeframe.

A detailed comparison of the studies is available in Table 1.

Table 1. Context comparison among the three studies

	Original Case Study	Matchall2 Case Study	Serts Case Study
Development Process	Moonlight Scrum	Scrum	Scrum
Reporting	Online Forum	Kanban Board	Kanban Board
Developers' location	Distributed	Collocated	Collocated
Overlapping hours	No	Yes	Yes
Working hours/week	8	16	16
#developers	4	8	6
#weeks	18	9	8
#sprints	6	4	3
Project Type	Client-Server	Client-Server	Client-Server
	(web app.)	(web app.)	(desktop app.)

4   Results

In this section, we report the results of our two case studies. In both cases, we first analyzed the results for the functional measures (SiFP and IFPUG Function points). In order to understand if a different definition of SiFP can be adapted in our study to increase the accuracy of the effort estimation, we analyzed further correlations among the factors considered for the calculation of SiFP (#DF # iTF, and #oTF).

Then, we analyzed results of the correlations among the factors considered by our developers when they need to estimate a user story (GUI Components Added, Modified and Data Files).

Finally, we compared the accuracy of effort estimation predicted by our developers to the actual effort estimation.

Table 4, Table 5 and Table 6 in Appendix A report detailed results of the analysis.

4.1   Matchall2 Case Study Results

The Matchall2 project was composed of 81 user stories collected in 4 sprints in a total of 408 working hours. 75 user stories were related to the development of new features, five to refactoring, and one to bug fixing. All user stories had low GUI impact.

Since the number of user stories related to refactoring and bug fixing is not statistically relevant, and all user stories had the same GUI impact, we only analyzed the results for the new development user stories, without cluster results for story type or GUI impact.

After eliminating three outliers – identified according to Cook's distance [18], we reduced the number of user stories considered to 78. Table 2 shows descriptive statistics for the attributes analyzed in the Matchall2 case study.

The analysis of correlations between SiFP and effort does not provide any statistically significant result (see Fig. 1). A Pearson correlation coefficient of 0.121 (p-value =0.140 and r^2=0.015) was calculated for the 78 data pairs as presented in the scatter graph in Fig. 1. As a consequence of the low correlation, the accuracy is not acceptable (MMRE=66%, MdMRE=66%). The multivariate correlation analysis among the factors considered for the calculation of SiFP shows a similar trend as for the SiFP analysis, indicating that this information is also not significant for improving effort estimation in Scrum (see Table 5).

As expected, also the analysis of correlations among IFPUG Function Points and effort has a similar trend as these obtained with SiFP with no statistically significant results, as shown in Fig. 2 (Pearson=0.145, p-value =0.099 and r2=0.021). For this reason, the accuracy is also not acceptable (MMRE=116% and MdMRE=53%).

Taking into account the information considered by the developer to estimate the user stories, the univariate correlation between the sum of GUI Components Added and Modified and the effort, the correlation is very low and accuracy is not acceptable (Pearson= -0.017, p-value=0.440, r^2=0, MMRE=109% and MdMRE=76%). Moreover, also considering the results of the multivariate correlation among effort and GUI Components Added, GUI Components Modified, and DF, (Fig. 3) the results are still not statistically significant and accuracy is still not acceptable (MMRE=135% and MdMRE=93%).

Finally, as in our original study, we compared the accuracy of effort estimation predicted by our developers to the actual effort estimation (Fig. 4). The results show that expert-based effort estimation is much better than estimation predicted by means of functional size measurement, reporting an MMRE of 39% and an MdMRE of 25%.

Table 2. Descriptive statistics for the Matchall2 case study

Variable	Avg	Min	Max	Std. Dev.
Actual Effort (hours)	2.33	1	8	1.50
SiFP	6.11	4.6	7.20	0.64
IFPUG	13.64	6	60	17.23
GUI Components Added	0.55	0	3	0.69
GUI Components Modified	0.51	0	5	0.99
input Transactions (iTF)	1.32	0	8	2.84
output Transactions (oTF)	0.54	0	3	1.15
Data Files (DF)	0.87	0	3	1.26

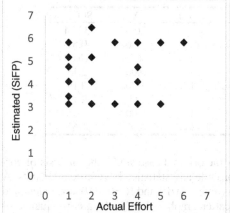

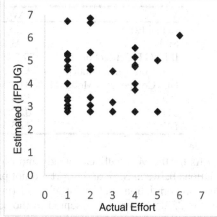

Fig. 1. Actual Effort vs Estimated Effort with SiFP

Fig. 2. Actual Effort vs Estimated Effort with IFPUG Function Points

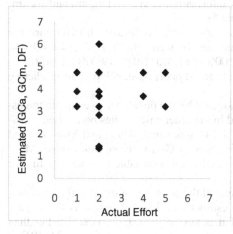

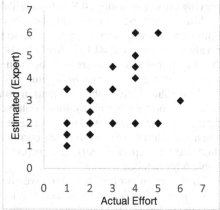

Fig. 3. GUI Components added, modified and DF

Fig. 4. Actual Effort vs Developers' estimated effort

4.2   Serts Case Study Results

The Serts project was composed of 25 user stories, collected in three sprints, for a total of 832 working hours. All stories are related to the development of new features. No stories were related to refactoring or bug fixing.

As for the Matchall2 project, GUI impact was always low for all user stories. Therefore, we do not cluster results for story type or GUI impact.

Table 3 reports descriptive statistics for the attributes analyzed in the Serts case study. In this case, no outliers have been identified by means of the Cook's distance.

Table 3. Descriptive statistics for the Serts case study

Variable	Avg	Min	Max	Std. Dev.
Actual Effort	33.28	1	120.00	33.74
SiFP	4.93	4.6	5.60	0.51
IFPUG Function Points	37.38	4	67	16.03
GUI ComponentsAdded	1.92	1	6.00	2.13
GUI Components Modified	0.04	1	1.00	0.19
iTF	1.88	1	6.00	2.17
oTF	0.77	1	6.00	1.36
DF	2.65	1	4.00	1.62

As for the Matchall2 case study and for the original case study, the analysis of correlations between SiFP and effort did not provide any statistically significant results. A Pearson correlation coefficient of 0.411 (p-value =0.019 and R^2=0.169) was calculated for the 25 data pairs as presented in the scatter graph in Fig. 5. As a consequence of low correlation, even though the p-value is within an acceptable range, accuracy is still not acceptable (MMRE=120.00%, MdMRE=76.00%). As for the Matchall2 case study, we analyzed further correlations among the factors considered for the calculation of SiFP. The results show a similar trend as for the previous data (MMRE=93.00% and MdMRE=54.00%), indicating that this information is also not significant for improving effort estimation in Scrum (see Table 5).

Also in this case, as expected, the analysis of correlations between IFPUG Function Points and effort reports a similar trend to the one obtained with SiFP (Pearson =0.444, p-value=0.013 and r^2=0.197, MMRE=145.00% and MdMRE=119.00%) confirming that functional size measures are not suitable for supporting developers in predicting the effort of the user stories in Scrum.

Taking into account the information considered by the developer to estimate the user stories, the results confirm those obtained in the other case studies both when considering the univariate correlation between GUI Components Added and Modified and when considering the multivariate correlation among GUI Components Added, Modified and DF, reporting very low correlation and a not acceptable goodness of fit (see Table 6 for detailed results).

Finally, as in our original study, we compared the accuracy of effort estimation predicted by our developers to the actual effort estimation (Fig. 8). The results show again that expert-based effort estimation, even if it is not very accurate, is still better than estimation predicted by means of functional size measurement, reporting an MMRE of 52% and an MdMRE of 58%.

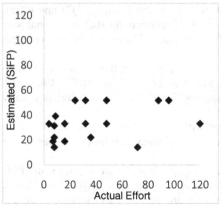

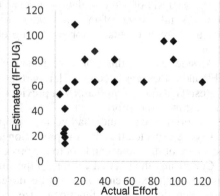

Fig. 5. Actual Effort vs Estimated Effort with SiFP

Fig. 6. Actual Effort vs Estimated Effort with IFPUG Function Points

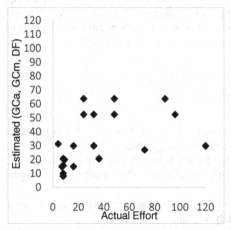

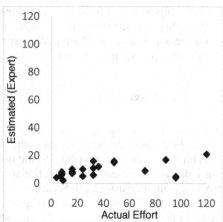

Fig. 7. GUI Components Added, Modified and DF

Fig. 8. Actual Effort vs Developers' Estimated Effort

5   Discussion

Based on the results obtained in the data analysis, we can answer our research questions.

As for the RQ1, on the extension of the results obtained to the original case study to plain Scrum, the analysis confirms the results obtained in our previous study. The main outcome of this replication is the confirmation of the low predictive power of SiFP in Scrum and that there are no correlations among the information considered by our developers and the actual effort. Moreover, also the analysis of the information needed to calculate SiFP do not help to improve the accuracy.

The analysis of the correlations among IFPUG Function Points (RQ2) and effort, show a similar trend of the one obtained with SiFP confirming that functional size measures are not suitable for predicting effort in either Moonlight Scrum or plain Scrum.

As side result of this work, we also confirm the accuracy of the conversion among SiFP and IFPUG reported in [17], reporting a MMRE= 27% and MdMRE=24%.

Results also confirm that, as in previous studies [5, 6, 7, 8, 13], developers usually underestimate the effort.

The original case study had been developed with a special version of Scrum, which is why we expected that the low prediction accuracy of functional measures was due to the nature of the project and not to the process.

Concerning the internal validity of the study, the developers were Master's and PhD students with experience in software development ranging from two to five years. Moreover, the identified functional size measures are designed to estimate complete projects or components while in this case studies we applied it to Scrum user stories and not to the whole project.

As for external validity, this study focused on two Scrum processes, with part-time developers who work only two days per week. We expect some variations in applying the same approach to a full-time development team working on a plain Scrum process.

Regarding the reliability of this study, the results are not dependent on the subjects or on the application developed. We expect similar results for the replication of this study with other Scrum processs.

6   Conclusions

In this work, we replicated a case study with the goal of understanding if it is possible to introduce functional size metrics to the Scrum planning game.

With this study, we contribute to the body of knowledge by providing an empirical study on the investigation of functional size measures for effort estimation in agile processes, and in particular in Scrum.

To achieve this purpose, we first gave an overview of the previous study and then we described the difference with the case study we ran.

The results of our study confirm that functional size measures, and in particular SiFP and IFPUG Function points, do not help to improve estimation accuracy in Scrum. Moreover, even trying to re-compute the formula for the calculation of SiFP does not help to improve the accuracy of effort estimation.

Accuracy does not increase when considering other measures usually considered by developers when they evaluate the effort required to develop a user story.

As side result of this work, we also confirm the accuracy of the conversion among SiFP and IFPUG reported in [17], with an MMRE= 27% and MdMRE=24%.

Future works will include studies to better understand the information considered by the developers when they estimate user stories and the replication of this study in another industrial context.

Acknowledgments. This research is supported by Regione Autonoma della Sardegna (RAS), Regional Law No. 7-2007, project CRP-17938 LEAN 2.0.

References

1. Lenarduzzi, V., Taibi, D.: Can functional size measure improve effort estimation in SCRUM?. In: ICSEA - International Conference on Software Engineering and Advances, Nice, France (2014)
2. Basili, V.R., Caldiera, G., Rombach, H.D.: The goal question metric approach. Encyclopedia of Software Engineering, 528–532 (1994)
3. Carver, J.: Towards reporting guidelines for experimental replications: a proposal. In: Proceedings of the 1st International Workshop on Replication in Empirical Software Engineering Research (RESER) (Held during ICSE 2010), Cape Town, South Africa, May 4, 2010
4. Shull, F., Carver, J., Vegas, S., Juristo, N.: The role of replications in empirical software engineering. Empirical Software Engineering 13(2), 211–218 (2008)
5. Jamieson, D., Vinsen, K., Callender, G.: Agile procurement to support agile software development. In: Proceedings of the 35th IEEE International Conference on Industrial Informatics, pp. 419–424 (2005)
6. Sulaiman, T., Barton, B., Blackburn, T.: AgileEVM - earned value management in SCRUM projects. In: Proceedings of AGILE Conference, pp. 10–16 (2006)
7. Haugen, N.C.: An empirical study of using planning poker for user story estimation. In: Proceedings of AGILE Conference, pp. 9–34 (2006)
8. Cao, L.: Estimating agile software project effort: an empirical study. In: Americas Conference on Information Systems (AMCIS), p. 401 (2008)
9. Basili, V.R., Caldiera, G., Rombach, H.D.: The goal question metric approach. Encyclopedia of Software Engineering, 528–532 (1994)
10. Buglione, L., Abran, A.: Improving estimations in agile projects: issues and avenues. In: Proceedings of the 4th Software Measurement European Forum (SMEF) Rome, Italy (2007)
11. Taibi, D., Diebold, P., Lampasona, C.: Moonlighting SCRUM: an agile method for distributed teams with part-time developers working during non-overlapping hours. In: Proceedings of the Eighth International Conference on Software Engineering (ICSEA), pp. 318–323 (2013)
12. Meli, R.: Simple function point: a new functional size measurement method fully compliant with IFPUG 4.x. In: Software Measurement European Forum (2011)
13. Mahnic, V.: A case study on agile estimating and planning using SCRUM. In: Americas Conference on Information Systems (AMCIS), pp 123–128 (2008)
14. Diebold, P., Dieudonné, L., Taibi, D.: Process configuration framework tool. In: Euromicro Conference on Software Engineering and Advanced Applications (2014)
15. International Function Point Users Group. Function Point Counting Practices Manual (2004)
16. Willeke, M.H.H.: Agile in academics: applying agile to instructional design. In: Agile Conference (AGILE). IEEE (2011)
17. Lavazza, L., Meli, R.: An evaluation of simple function point as a replacement of IFPUG function point. In: IWSM - Mensura 2014, Rotterdam, October 2014
18. Cook, R.D., Weisberg, S.: Residuals and Influence in Regression. Chapman and Hall, London (1982)
19. Schwaber, K., Sutherland, J.: The Scrum guide (2001). www.scrumguides.org
20. Huijgens, H., Solingen, R.V.: A replicated study on correlating agile team velocity measured in function and story points. In: Proceedings of the 5th International Workshop on Emerging Trends in Software Metrics (WETSoM 2014) (2014)

Appendix: Detailed Results

In this section we report detailed results of the correlation analysis carried out in both studies.

Table 4. Univariate Correlation Analysis Results

	Matchall2			Serts		
	SiFP	IFPUG	GUI (a+m)	SiFP	IFPUG	GUI (a+m)
Pearson	0.121	0.145	-0.017	0.411	0.444	0.422
p-value	0.140	0.099	0.440	0.019	0.013	0.016
r^2	0.015	0.021	0.000	0.169	0.197	0.178
MMRE	0.660	1.160	1.090	1.200	1.450	0.970
MdMRE	0.660	0.530	0.760	0.760	1.190	0.760

Table 5. Multivariate correlation between Actual Effort and iTF, oTF and DF

	Matchall2			Serts		
	iTF	oTF	DF	iTF	oTF	DF
Pearson	0.422	-0.063	-0.042	0.250	0.266	0.382
p-value	0.000	0.288	0.355	0.109	0.094	0.027
R^2		0.241			0.306	
MMRE		1.210			0.930	
MdMRE		0.580			0.540	

Table 6. Multivariate correlation between GUI Components Added, Modified and DF

	Matchall2			Serts		
	GUIa	GUIm	DF	GUIa	GUIm	DF
Pearson	0.114	-0.097	-0.042	0.438	-0.153	0.382
p-value	0.155	-0.423	0.033	0.013	0.228	0.027
R^2		0.018			0.265	
MMRE		1.350			0.950	
MdMRE		0.930			0.640	

Software Development as an Experiment System: A Qualitative Survey on the State of the Practice

Eveliina Lindgren[✉] and Jürgen Münch

Department of Computer Science, University of Helsinki,
P.O. Box 68 FI-00014, Helsinki, Finland
{eveliina.lindgren,juergen.muench}@cs.helsinki.fi

Abstract. An experiment-driven approach to software product and service development is gaining increasing attention as a way to channel limited resources to the efficient creation of customer value. In this approach, software functionalities are developed incrementally and validated in continuous experiments with stakeholders such as customers and users. The experiments provide factual feedback for guiding subsequent development. Although case studies on experimentation in industry exist, the understanding of the state of the practice and the encountered obstacles is incomplete. This paper presents an interview-based qualitative survey exploring the experimentation experiences of ten software development companies. The study found that although the principles of continuous experimentation resonated with industry practitioners, the state of the practice is not yet mature. In particular, experimentation is rarely systematic and continuous. Key challenges relate to changing organizational culture, accelerating development cycle speed, and measuring customer value and product success.

Keywords: Continuous experimentation · Experiment-driven software development · Customer feedback · Qualitative survey

1 Introduction

New possibilities to observe customers and collect customer feedback allow software-centric companies to shorten learning cycles and improve their understanding of customer value. A potential approach is to build software products and services (henceforth, products) by continuously deploying new versions to customers. Instead of relying on pre-defined requirements or opinion-based assumptions, the customer value of products, functionalities, and features is validated in their actual marketplace by conducting a constant series of experiments. This experiment-driven approach is currently most prevalent in the cloud computing environment, but it is beginning to affect the development of all Internet-connected software products [1].

Despite the recent interest in experimentation as an integral part of software development, industrial experimentation experiences have not been studied widely: most examples come from eminent web-facing companies. There has also been relatively little discussion about the obstacles faced by practitioners in this respect.

© Springer International Publishing Switzerland 2015
C. Lassenius et al. (Eds.): XP 2015, LNBIP 212, pp. 117–128, 2015.
DOI: 10.1007/978-3-319-18612-2_10

This paper presents an interview-based qualitative survey that aims at developing an understanding of the state of the practice of using an experiment system approach to software development. Key challenges related to the approach are also identified.

The paper is organized as follows. Section 2 presents the problem background and related work. Section 3 defines the research questions and describes how the study was designed and executed. The results of the study are presented in Section 4, followed by a discussion in Section 5. Finally, the paper is concluded in Section 6.

2   Background and Related Work

During the last decades, agile software development methods have permeated the industry [2]. Agile development has changed the way software is developed for instance by advocating iterative and incremental development, embracing changing requirements, and highlighting the importance of customer feedback. However, Holmström Olsson et al. [3] suggest that the application of agile methods within the research and development (R&D) organization is only one stage on the maturation path of companies' software engineering practices. The following stages are the continuous integration and deployment of R&D output, and finally, R&D as an experiment system. At this stage, development is based on rapid experiments that utilize instant customer feedback and product usage data to identify customer needs.

This final stage is further systematized by Bosch [1]. He emphasizes constantly generating new ideas to test with customers, suggesting that the approach is best described as an *innovation experiment system*. Bosch proposes using 2–4 week R&D iterations followed by exposing the product to customers in order to collect feedback either directly or implicitly by observing product usage. Various experiment techniques can be used throughout development. Experimentation does not necessarily require functioning software. Furthermore, the scope of experiment-driven development can vary from new products to new features and feature optimization.

Fagerholm et al. [4] combine the above-mentioned ideas with key elements from the lean startup methodology [5] and propose a framework for *continuous experimentation*. Continuous experimentation refers to the constant testing of the value of products as an integral part of the development process in order to evolve the products towards high-value creation. Consecutive iterations of the Build-Measure-Learn feedback loop structure the development process. Within each Build-Measure-Learn block, "assumptions for product and business development are derived from the business strategy, systematically tested, and the results used to inform further development of the strategy and product" [4]. This experiment-driven learning process is supported by a technical infrastructure that 1) enables the lightweight releasing of minimum viable products (MVP), 2) provides means for advanced product instrumentation, and 3) supports the design, execution, and analysis of experiments. Fagerholm et al. also provide a description of the roles, tasks, and information artefacts that are required to run a system of continuous experimentation.

Several case studies on companies' experimentation experiences have recently been published. Microsoft's experiences with systematic large-scale online controlled experiments have been recounted in numerous reports, for instance [6]. Google purports to experimentally evaluate almost every change that has the potential to affect user experience [7]. Supporting and fostering continuous innovation is a key element of the Google experiment system [8]. The Netflix "consumer data science" approach is two-staged [9]: experiments are first conducted offline, and if they succeed, an online customer experiment is executed to provide definitive validation.

Adobe's "Pipeline" innovation process attempts to maximize the learning about a given problem through rapid prototyping and frequent customer evaluation [10]. eBay uses a multitude of experimental techniques in addition to online controlled experiments, such as usability testing, focus groups, and diary studies [11]. The diverse experimentation practices of Intuit are described in [1].

The use of product usage data in the embedded systems domain is examined in [12,13]. The papers conclude that product usage data is not utilized efficiently as a basis for product improvements and innovations. Finally, examples of successful experimentation experiences in an academia-industry collaboration setting are described in [4], [14].

The above-mentioned studies portray different approaches to experimentation. In the context of this paper, the following criteria are used as requirements for *systematic experimentation*: 1) the business-driven definition of explicit assumptions, 2) the design and conducting of experiments to test those assumptions, 3) the analysis of experiment data, and 4) the use of experiment results as input for decision making and follow-up action. Continuous experimentation is achieved if these steps are a permanent part of the development process.

3   Study Approach

Research Questions. Based on the study goals, the following research questions were defined:

RQ1:   How is continuous experimentation applied in software development
          companies?
          RQ1.1: How is customer feedback concerning the software product collected?
          RQ1.2: How is the collected customer feedback used in the software product
                      development process?
RQ2:   What challenges are associated with continuous experimentation?

Study Design. The study was founded on a qualitative survey design, using interviews with industry practitioners to collect data [15,16]. Methodologically, qualitative surveys resemble multiple case studies [16,17]. However, while multiple case studies aim to produce an in-depth analysis of particular cases, the focus of qualitative surveys is less specific and more concerned with providing a multifaceted, diverse view of the topic of interest [15,16].

Semi-structured individual interviews were used to collect data, since they enable focusing on predefined research topics while also being highly flexible to allow for unforeseen information [18]. To structure the interviews, an interview guide was developed, outlining the key topics, questions, and prompts. Easy "warm up" and "cool down" questions were asked at the beginning and end of the interviews. The main topics of the interviews, along with example questions, are defined below (the complete interview guide is available in the Figshare repository [19]):

1. Current software development practices
    a.   What kind of software development process do you use?
2. Current practices of customer feedback elicitation and use
    a.   How do you make sure that you are building the right product?
    b.   How do you collect customer feedback?
    c.   Do you collect data about customer behavior, for example in the form of product usage data?
    d.   How do you use the collected customer feedback and other data?
3. Future practices of customer feedback elicitation and use
    a.   Do you think your current practices of customer feedback collection and customer involvement are adequate?
    b.   Are there any obstacles to obtaining deeper customer insights?

The interview data was examined through thematic coding analysis [18]. The analysis was based on an iterative coding process, during which a hierarchical codebook was developed inductively based on the interview data. Descriptive, analytic, or category marker codes were generated depending on the analytic needs. The codebook is also available in the Figshare repository [19]. The codes were then combined to identify common themes, or patterns, within the data.

A purposive, non-probability sample [15,16] was chosen for the study. Software development companies of various sizes, domains of operation, and stages of life cycle were sought to achieve a diverse set of participants. Furthermore, interviewees from different roles and with solid experience in the software industry were sought.

Study Execution. Study participants were recruited among the affiliates of the Need for Speed research program [20] and, outside the research program, through the professional contacts of the authors. Due to practical constraints, only companies operating in Finland were considered. Gatekeepers were contacted at each company, who either participated in the study themselves or suggested a suitable interviewee. In accordance with ethical guidelines [21], the purpose and procedures of the study were shared with the participants via an information sheet, in addition to which they were asked to give voluntary informed consent to partake in the study.

The recruitment resulted in the participation of ten software companies, represented by thirteen interviewees. The individual interviews were conducted in Finland between February and April 2014. The average length of the interviews was 48 minutes, with the range spanning between 36 and 64 minutes. All interviews were conducted in English and audio-recorded to allow for accurate, detailed data analysis. Eleven interviews were conducted by one researcher, and in the remaining two cases two researchers were present. Eleven interviews were performed face to face on the interviewees' company premises, one via video conferencing, and one as a VoIP call.

To facilitate data analysis, interview recordings were transcribed verbatim shortly after each interview. The transcripts were coded and analyzed using ATLAS.ti [22].

4   Results

This section first gives an overview of the study participants. It then outlines the software development practices of the participating companies. The companies' practices of eliciting and using customer feedback are considered next, after which the challenges with relation to continuous experimentation are presented.

4.1   Overview of Participants

Ten ICT companies operating in Finland participated in the study. The focus was on their software product development functions. Table 1 gives a characterization of the companies by size, domain, and product orientation (more details are not disclosed due to confidentiality reasons). Three of the companies can be described as startups.

Most interviewees held either senior management (31%) or middle management (54%) positions in their companies. Consultant and senior software architect roles were also represented (15%). The interviewees' length of employment in their current company varied between 1 and 26 years, with the average being 7.7 years.

Unlike the other companies who only had one representative, company C was represented by four interviewees. Their answers were merged together to form an overall impression of the company. As regards company E, their software development practices were not discussed during the interview since the interviewee was not actively involved in this part of the company's operations. Input from company E is therefore only included in the results presented in Section 4.4.

Table 1. Participating companies (size classification: small < 50, medium ≤ 250, large > 250)

Company	Company size by no. of employees	Company domain	Product orientation
A	Small	Gaming	B2C
B	Small	ICT services	B2B
C	Large	ICT services	B2B
D	Small	Sports	B2B, B2C
E	Medium	ICT services	B2B
F	Small	Software development tools	B2B
G	Medium	Software development tools	B2B, B2C
H	Large	Security	B2B, B2C
I	Large	Telecom	B2B
J	Small	Multimedia	B2B

4.2   Software Development Practices

All companies mentioned that they utilize agile methods such as Scrum, Kanban, and Lean. All companies also stated that they use continuous integration (CI) but, consistent with previous research [23], there was variability in how CI was interpreted and implemented. These findings are based on the interviewees' informal descriptions of their development approach rather than a formal questionnaire or definition provided by the researchers. The general impression of the companies' development practices was similar to a recent survey [2], although the prevalence of lean-inspired practices and CI appeared to be higher.

Release cycle length ranged from under one month (56%) to less than three months (33%) or more (11%). Interviewees often made remarks on constantly having a deployable product version available, working in a production-like environment to simplify deployments, and pursuing a DevOps mode of operation. The overall impression was that deployments were quite lightweight and flexible, except for on-premises installations in business-to-business (B2B) environments.

4.3   Practices of Eliciting and Using Customer Feedback

The companies used a wide array of techniques to learn about customer needs. Most techniques were based on eliciting direct customer feedback through familiar means such as stakeholder interviews and surveys, prototypes, usability and user experience testing, and other forms of user testing. Bug reports and feature voting were also used as a way to guide development.

Implicit customer feedback in the form of product usage data was collected by five companies (55%). In many cases the product instrumentation covered performance data and basic user demographics. However, some companies also had more sophisticated, feature-level instrumentation. Seven companies (78%) had plans either to begin collecting product usage data or to improve current practices in the future. The key motivation behind these plans was the possibility to assess customer value and enable data-driven decision making. Product usage data was considered *"an excellent tool [...] to see in which features to invest [and] how to improve them [...]. And also for [...] directly guid[ing] our development efforts."*

Despite the wealth of techniques used to collect customer feedback, their use in systematic, continuous experimentation with customers was rare. Experimentation based on explicit, business-driven assumptions only appeared to be an integral development practice in one (startup) company. Four companies (44%) used A/B or multi-variate testing, but most only used it occasionally and not necessarily in a systematic way. Additionally, three companies (33%) had plans to begin using A/B testing or to improve current practices. The unsystematic approach to experimentation was also acknowledged by some of the interviewees: *"Whether we are systematic and very good, I have some doubts. It's a little bit ad hoc. So 'Let's have a tagline like this, and maybe like that. Okay, let's put it up there [to production] and let's see'. [...] So[...] it is not very thorough and not very scientific."*

The collected customer feedback was typically analyzed to extract work items which were then prioritized into a product backlog. There was some variation in how the interviewees described their approach to feedback processing. Particularly the startup representatives emphasized the need to explore the feedback beyond face value in order to generate new ideas and innovations: *"The interesting thing is their [the customers'] complaint, not the solution that they are providing."*

The level of involvement of different stakeholders in analyzing customer feedback varied: in some cases, both management and the development team were heavily involved with analyzing the feedback and the responsibility was shared. In other cases, the responsibility was on management roles but all the feedback was reviewed together with the team. Lastly, particularly in the larger companies, the process was management-led and the development team mainly based their work on a ready-made product backlog. Some interviewees considered this problematic since it may lead to the loss of valuable insights: *"[T]here is still a lot [of room] for improvement in that area [sharing customer information with the development team]."*

Two divergent approaches emerged regarding the influence of customer feedback on business strategy and goals. First, some company representatives considered that the strategy is continuously being revised based on the feedback. This approach was predominant among the startup companies. As one interviewee said: *"Our strategy is to experiment."* In the second approach, business strategy and goals were considered more stable and therefore not directly influenced by the customer feedback. This approach appeared to be more typical to established companies.

4.4   Challenges with Respect to Continuous Experimentation

Fig. 1 gives an overview of the key domain-independent challenges that were identified in this study. Half of the company representatives considered organizational culture a major obstacle to moving towards an experimental mode of operation: *"I would say that the technical things are not [...] even close to the weight of the cultures' obstacles."* Another interviewee agreed that trouble in embracing experimentation *"has nothing to do with technology"*. The overarching issues with respect to organizational culture included a perceived lack of agility, proactivity, and transparency – either within the company or in relation to the company's customers. While cultural challenges were remarked upon by the representatives of both established and startup companies, the general impression was that the more fundamental issues were brought up by the established companies.

Concern over slow release cycles was one of the central themes in terms of product management. Reasons for this perceived sluggishness included R&D task overload and bottlenecks in the development process. Focusing on products and features that create the most customer value was seen as a way to speed up development: *"I don't think you can accelerate anything. What you can do is do less."*

Identifying the metrics to evaluate created customer value and product success was a challenge both in relation to dedicated experiments and to the general observation of product usage. In the words of one interviewee: *"To measure the right thing is the hard thing, to know [...] what is relevant. I think you can easily measure such a lot of things that you [...] lose sight of the forest for all the trees. And then you just optimize irrelevant things."* Particular challenges related to which metrics and techniques of customer feedback collection to use when scaling up a product: *"You can't throw big data analytics on this [product] with a few thousand people, but you can't really [...]interview each [...] one of them [...] either."*

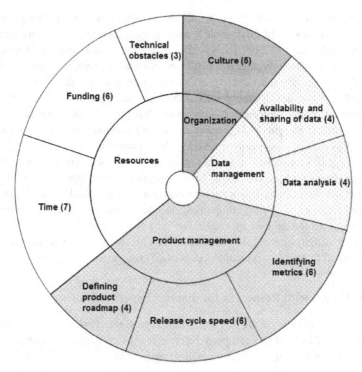

Fig. 1. The key domain-independent challenges with frequency of occurrence by participating company (outer circle) sorted by topic areas (inner circle).

A further set of issues was related to defining the product roadmap. Identifying a truly viable MVP was considered *"very easy to say, very hard to do."* As regards established products, one interviewee described formulating a product backlog as *"black magic"* as it could be so challenging to combine both the product vision and the requests and demands of various customer organizations.

Interviewees also expressed concern over deficiencies in the analysis of collected customer feedback and other data: *"There's too little analysis of available data, we should actually utilize [...] the existing data more in our decision making so that the element of gut feeling or some kind of intuition would be minimized."* Lack of time and analytic expertise emerged as possible reasons for inadequate data analysis. Obstacles were also encountered in the availability and sharing of data with all relevant stakeholders. As one interviewee said: *"The data is scattered all over the place. [...] [W]e are quite far from providing [a] really convenient, broad spectrum of data to all of the employees."*

Limited resources were a recurrent theme in the interviews. On the other hand, some interviewees emphasized the potential long-term benefits of investing in experimentation. Technical obstacles to experimentation were barely featured in the interviewees' commentaries; there were only three cases in which technical concerns restricted experimentation or had done so in the past. Moreover, these concerns appeared to be primarily linked to insufficient resources rather than insurmountable technical problems.

In addition to the domain-independent issues discussed above, obstacles specific to the B2B domain emerged. Five B2B company representatives considered the customer organizations' culture a challenge to experimentation. For instance, customers were not always able to give feedback or participate in development and experiments: *"[I]t's more like we pull the feedback from them, not that they push it to us. So people are very reluctant [...] [t]o give feedback."* Lack of time was the main supposed reason for the customers' disinclination to participate more. A second obstacle, cited by four companies, was limited access to end users. Some interviewees considered that improving product usage data collection would alleviate these challenges. However, customer consent could not be taken for granted: *"[I]t might be difficult to get some of the customers to agree that we can monitor their users and what they do."* This issue was mentioned by three B2B company representatives.

5   Discussion

The study found that the principles of continuous experimentation resonated well within the software industry: there was a wish to focus on customer value creation and data-driven decision making. Many of the contributing companies' current practices supported these aspirations: agile development was prevalent, continuous integration was utilized, and release cycles were reasonably short. Companies were attempting to further shorten release cycles for instance by focusing on key functionalities – a goal which experimentation may help to achieve.

Companies collected a wide range of direct customer feedback, but the collection of implicit customer feedback in the form of product usage data was not ubiquitous and was often hampered by insufficient product instrumentation. However, the potential in product usage data had been acknowledged and most companies had plans to develop their procedures in this respect. These findings are in line with [12,13], suggesting that there is untapped learning potential in product usage data. On a related note, identifying which product metrics to follow and how to analyze the results remained a major challenge.

The present study found experimentation to be systematic and continuous in only one startup company. In addition, several companies expressed interest in A/B testing. This suggests that many practitioners are aware of the possible benefits of embracing an experimental approach to software development. It is also noteworthy that besides controlled experiments, a wide array of customer feedback collection techniques can be used systematically (for examples, see [1], [12]).

The connection between product vision, business strategy, and technological product development is central to continuous experimentation [4] and business alignment [24]. Experiments integrate these aspects by providing empirical data to support both product-level and strategic decision making. This study found a highly flexible approach to business strategy management to only be typical of startups. As Fagerholm et al. [4] note, the continuous experimentation model is derived from a startup environment, and different variants of the model may be required to support other scenarios, possibly in a domain-specific manner.

Innovation is a key feature of a well-functioning experiment system [1]. The present results suggest that the collaboration between the R&D organization, product management, and customers is sometimes insufficient to fully support innovation. There were challenges in sharing and reviewing the collected customer feedback and product usage data with all necessary stakeholders. In particular, the development team was not always involved enough in the process. Furthermore, obtaining relevant customer and end user feedback was often a challenge in B2B environments. These factors may result in innovation potential being lost.

To summarize, it appears that although the majority of companies have not yet reached the stage of continuous experimentation, many are proceeding towards it as outlined by the "Stairway to Heaven" model [3]. Organizational culture has a major role in this transformation. Since an experiment-driven approach to software development is still relatively new [1], companies have had little time to transform their culture and practices accordingly. On the other hand, agile development is a well-established practice, but organizational culture is still cited as the key barrier to further agile adoption, as well as a leading cause of failed agile projects [2]. Similarly, the present study indicates that in many cases, further efforts are required to promote an experimental organizational culture.

Threats to Validity. In accordance with Easterbrook et al. [25], four commonly used criteria for validity are discussed below in the context of this study.

Construct validity was mainly threatened by possible misunderstandings between researchers and interviewees. To diminish this risk, the overall goals of the study and the central concept of continuous experimentation were shared with participants prior to the interviews. Furthermore, the use of semi-structured interviews enabled the asking of clarifying questions for all involved parties. Clarifications were also requested afterwards from the interviewees via email when necessary.

External validity in the sense of statistical generalizability is not the aim of qualitative surveys [15,16]. However, despite the limited scope of the study, a variety of companies represented by interviewees from different roles contributed to it. The authors therefore consider the results to be well grounded in actual practice.

Steps taken to improve the study's reliability included the development and review among the researchers of the interview guide and the analytic codebook. Finally, internal validity, with its focus on causal relationships, was not highly relevant to the present, mainly descriptive study.

6   Conclusions

This paper presented a qualitative survey on companies' experiences of software development as an experiment system. The study found that while many of the current development practices supported experimentation, the state of the practice is not yet mature. Although a broad array of techniques was employed to collect customer feedback, systematic experiments with customers are rare. Moreover, many companies do not use product usage data to learn about customer needs, and product instrumentation is often inadequate. Finally, the collaboration between the R&D organization, product management, and customers sometimes appear insufficient for supporting an innovative, experimental approach.

Key challenges in embracing experimentation are related to transforming organizational culture, achieving sufficiently rapid release cycles, identifying metrics for evaluating customer value and product success, and ensuring that the collected customer and product data is carefully analyzed by relevant stakeholders. Adequate resources also need to be secured. Additional challenges are faced by business-to-business companies.

Acknowledgements. We wish to thank the participants of the study for their time and contributions and the reviewers for their valuable comments. We would also like to thank the Finnish technology agency, Tekes, for funding the Cloud Software Factory project, and the Need for Speed program, under which the proposed study was undertaken. This paper is based on thesis work [26] completed at the University of Helsinki.

References

1. Bosch, J.: Building products as innovation experiment systems. In: Cusumano, M.A., Iyer, B., Venkatraman, N. (eds.) ICSOB 2012. LNBIP, vol. 114, pp. 27–39. Springer, Heidelberg (2012)
2. Version One: The 8th Annual "State of Agile" Survey. http://www.versionone.com/pdf/2013-state-of-agile-survey.pdf
3. Holmström Olsson, H., Alahyari, H., Bosch, J.: Climbing the "stairway to heaven": a multiple-case study exploring barriers in the transition from agile development towards continuous deployment of software. In: 38th EUROMICRO Conference on Software Engineering and Advanced Applications SEAA, pp. 392–399. IEEE Press (2012)
4. Fagerholm, F., Guinea, A.S., Mäenpää, H., Münch, J.: Building blocks for continuous experimentation. In: 1st International Workshop on Rapid Continuous Software Engineering, pp. 26–35. ACM, New York (2014)
5. Ries, E.: The Lean Startup: How Today's Entrepreneurs Use Continuous Innovation to Create Radically Successful Businesses. Crown Business, New York (2011)
6. Kohavi, R., Deng, A., Frasca, B., Walker, T., Xu, Y., Pohlmann, N.: Online controlled experiments at large scale. In: 19th ACM SIGKDD International Conference on Knowledge Discovery and Data Mining, pp. 1168–1176. ACM, New York (2013)
7. Tang, D., Agarwal, A., O'Brien, D., Meyer, M.: Overlapping experiment infrastructure: more, better, faster experimentation. In: 16th ACM SIGKDD International Conference on Knowledge Discovery and Data Mining, pp. 17–26. ACM, New York (2010)
8. Steiber, A., Alänge, S.: A Corporate System for Continuous Innovation: The Case of Google Inc. European Journal of Innovation Management 16(2), 243–264 (2013)
9. Amatriain, X.: beyond data: from user information to business value through personalized recommendations and consumer science. In: 22nd ACM International Conference on Information and Knowledge Management, pp. 2201–2208. ACM, New York (2013)
10. Adams, R.J., Evans, B., Brandt, J.: Creating small products at a big company: adobe's pipeline innovation process. In: CHI 2013 Extended Abstracts on Human Factors in Computing Systems, pp. 2331–2332. ACM, New York (2013)

11. Davenport, T.H.: How to Design Smart Business Experiments. Harvard Business Review 87(2), 68–77 (2009)
12. Holmström Olsson, H., Bosch, J.: Post-deployment data collection in software-intensive embedded products. In: Herzwurm, G., Margaria, T. (eds.) ICSOB 2013. LNBIP, vol. 150, pp. 79–89. Springer, Heidelberg (2013)
13. Holmström Olsson, H., Bosch, J.: Towards data-driven product development: a multiple case study on post-deployment data usage in software-intensive embedded systems. In: Fitzgerald, B., Conboy, K., Power, K., Valerdi, R., Morgan, L., Stol, K.-J. (eds.) LESS 2013. LNBIP, vol. 167, pp. 152–164. Springer, Heidelberg (2013)
14. Münch, J., Fagerholm, F., Johnson, P., Pirttilahti, J., Torkkel, J., Jäarvinen, J.: Creating minimum viable products in industry-academia collaborations. In: Fitzgerald, B., Conboy, K., Power, K., Valerdi, R., Morgan, L., Stol, K.-J. (eds.) LESS 2013. LNBIP, vol. 167, pp. 137–151. Springer, Heidelberg (2013)
15. Fink, A.: Analysis of qualitative surveys. In: Fink, A. (ed.) The survey handbook, pp. 61–78. SAGE Publications, California (2003)
16. Jansen, H.: The Logic of Qualitative Survey Research and its Position in the Field of Social Research Methods. Forum: Qualitative Social Research 11(2), 1–21 (2010)
17. Runeson, P., Höst, M.: Guidelines for Conducting and Reporting Case Study Research. Empirical Software Engineering 14(2), 131–164 (2009)
18. Robson, C.: Real World Research: A Resource for Users of Social Research Methods in Applied Settings. Wiley, Chichester (2011)
19. Lindgren, E., Münch, J.: Interview guide and codebook for the paper "Software Development as an Experiment System". http://dx.doi.org/10.6084/m9.figshare.1254619
20. Need for Speed research program (N4S). http://www.n4s.fi
21. Vinson, N., Singer, J.: A practical guide to ethical research involving humans. In: Shull, F., Singer, J., Sjøberg, D.I.K. (eds.) Guide to Advanced Empirical Software Engineering, pp. 229–256. Springer, London (2008)
22. ATLAS.ti Scientific Software Development GmbH, http://www.atlasti.com
23. Ståhl, D., Bosch, J.: Modeling Continuous Integration Practice Differences in Industry Software Development. Journal of Systems and Software 87, 48–59 (2014)
24. Basili, V., Heidrich, J., Lindvall, M., Münch, J., Regardie, M., Rombach, D., Seaman, C., Trendowicz, A.: GQM+Strategies: a comprehensive methodology for aligning business strategies with software measurement. In: DASMA Software Metric Congress (MetriKon 2007): Magdeburger Schriften Zum Empirischen Software Engineering, Kaiserslautern, Germany, pp. 253–266 (2007)
25. Easterbrook, S., Singer, J., Storey, M., Damian, D.: Selecting empirical methods for software engineering research. In: Shull, F., Singer, J., Sjøberg, D.I.K. (eds.) Guide to Advanced Empirical Software Engineering, pp. 285–311. Springer, London (2008)
26. Lindgren, E., Münch, J., Männistö, T.: Exploring Software Development as an Experiment System. Master's Thesis. University of Helsinki (2015)

Would You Mind Fixing This Issue?
An Empirical Analysis of Politeness and Attractiveness in Software Developed Using Agile Boards

Marco Ortu[1]([✉]), Giuseppe Destefanis[2], Mohamad Kassab[3], Steve Counsell[4], Michele Marchesi[1], and Roberto Tonelli[1]

[1] DIEE, University of Cagliari, Cagliari, Italy
{marco.ortu,michele,roberto.tonelli}@diee.unica.it
[2] CRIM, Computer Research Institute of Montreal, Montreal, Canada
giuseppe.destefanis@crim.ca
[3] The Pennsylvania State University, Penn State Great Valley, Malvern, PA, USA
muk36@psu.edu
[4] Brunel University, Kingston Lane, Uxbridge, UK
steve.counsell@brunel.ac.uk

Abstract. A successful software project is the result of a complex process involving, above all, people. Developers are the key factors for the success of a software development process and the Agile philosophy is developer-centred. Developers are not merely executors of tasks, but actually the protagonists and core of the whole development process. This paper aims to investigate social aspects among developers working together and the appeal of a software project developed with the support of Agile tools such as Agile boards. We studied 14 open source software projects developed using the Agile board of the JIRA repository. We analysed all the comments committed by the developers involved in the projects and we studied whether the politeness of the comments affected the number of developers involved over the years and the time required to fix any given issue. Our results show that the level of politeness in the communication process among developers does have an effect on the time required to fix issues and, in the majority of the analysed projects, it has a positive correlation with attractiveness of the project to both active and potential developers. The more polite developers were, the less time it took to fix an issue, and, in the majority of the analysed cases, the more the developers wanted to be part of project, the more they were willing to continue working on the project over time.

Keywords: Agile · Kanban board · Data mining · Social and human aspect

1 Introduction

According to the 8th Annual State of Agile survey report[1], "more people are recognising that agile development is beneficial to business, with an 11% increase

---

[1] http://www.versionone.com/pdf/2013-state-of-agile-survey.pdf

© Springer International Publishing Switzerland 2015
C. Lassenius et al. (Eds.): XP 2015, LNBIP 212, pp. 129–140, 2015.
DOI: 10.1007/978-3-319-18612-2_11

over the last 2 years in the number of people who say agile helps organisations complete projects faster." A main priority reported by users was to accelerate time to market, more easily manage changing priorities, and to better align IT and business objectives.

Agile project management tools and Kanban boards experienced the largest growth in popularity of all the agile tool categories, with use or planned use increasing by 6%. In addition, one of the top five ranked tools was Atlassian JIRA[2], with an 87% recommendation.

How does one classify a software as agile? The process of defining a software as "Agile" is not simple. Over the years, a variety of tools have been developed in order to help developers, team managers and other parties involved in the development process of a software system. These tools each constitute a specific aspect of the Agile world. The Agile boards, for example, represent the central aspect of communication in the Agile philosophy. As Perry wrote [7] "the task board is one of the most important radiators used by an agile team to track their progress." The communication aspect is central and is the key to fast development. When a new developer joins a development team, the better the communication process works, the faster the new developer can become productive and the learning curve can be reduced. The know-how and the shared-knowledge of a project should always be easily accessible for the development team during the development process. Fast releases, continuos integration and testing activities are directly connected to the knowledge of the system under development and hence the communication process is crucial.

Tools such as the JIRA board are a good solution to bridge the gap between open source software development and the Agile world. It is the view of many that agile development requires a physical aspect, i.e. developers working together in the same room or building, or at the same desk because the pair programming paradigm requires at least two people working simultaneously on the same piece of code, but can the developers work remotely? Is it possible to apply Agile methodologies even for open source software developed by a community which is spread out around the globe?

By using tools such as the JIRA board, it is indeed possible to apply the theoretical approach of the Agile board for a software project being developed by developers working in different physical places.

Working remotely, in different time zones and with different time schedules, with developers from around the world, requires coordination and communication. The communication process in this context becomes more difficult (if compared to the communication process used by developers sharing the same office) and the politeness, the mood and the social dynamics of the developers are important factors for the success of the project.

These days, even in the software development process, the social and human aspects of the development process are becoming more and more important. The Google style has become a model for many software start-ups. A pleasant work environment is important and affects the productivity of employees. Is politeness

---

important in a software development process? "Politeness is the practical application of good manners or etiquette. It is a culturally defined phenomenon and
therefore what is considered polite in one culture can sometimes be quite rude
or simply eccentric in another cultural context. The goal of politeness is to make
all of the parties relaxed and comfortable with one another."[3] The last part of
the definition is what we are considering in our analysis. In this specific work we
did not take different cultures into account (although developers involved in a
specific project could be from all around the world); we focused on the politeness
of the comment-messages written by the developers.

This paper aims to show how project management tools such as Agile boards
can directly affect the productivity of a software development team and the health
of a software project. We studied the relationship among global project metrics
(magnetism and stickiness) and affective metrics (politeness) by analysing the
communication among developers. We considered 14 open source projects from
the Apache Software Foundation's JIRA repositories.

This paper aims to answer the following research questions:

- **Does the politeness among developers affect the issues fixing time?**
- **Does the politeness among developers affect the attractiveness of
  a project?**

2   Related Works

Several researchers have analysed [6] [5] [10] [14] [11] the effect of politeness.
Gupta et al. [2] presented POLLy (Politeness for Language Learning), a system which combines a spoken language generator with an artificial intelligence
planner to model Brown and Levinson's theory of politeness in collaborative
task-oriented dialogue, with the ultimate goal of providing a fun and stimulating environment for learning English as a second language. An evaluation of
politeness perceptions of POLLy's output shows that: perceptions are generally
consistent with Brown and Levinson's predictions for choice of form and for dis-
course situation, i.e. utterances to strangers need to be much more polite than
those to friends; (2) our indirect strategies which should be the politest forms,
are seen as the rudest; and (3) English and Indian native speakers of English
have different perceptions of politeness.

Pikkarainen et al. [8] showed that agile practices improve both informal
and formal communication. The studies indicates that, in larger development
Situations involving multiple external stakeholders, a mismatch of adequate
communication mechanisms can sometimes even hinder communication. The
study highlights the fact that hurdles and improvements in the communication
process can both affect the feature requirements and task subtask dependencies as described in coordination theory. While the use of SCRUM and some
XP practices facilitate team and organizational communication of the dependencies between product features and working tasks, the use of agile practices

---

[3] en.wikipedia.org/wiki/Politeness

requires that the team and organization use also additional plan-driven practices to ensure the efficiency of external communication between all the actors of software development.

Korkala et al. [3] showed that effective communication and feedback are crucial in agile development. Extreme programming (XP) embraces both communication and feedback as interdependent process values which are essential for projects to achieve successful results. The research presents the empirical results from four different case studies. Three case studies had partial onsite customers and one had an onsite customer. The case studies used face-to-face communication to different extents along with email and telephone to manage customer-developer communication inside the development iterations. The results indicate that an increased reliance on less informative communication channels results in higher defect rates. These results suggest that the selection of communication methods, to be used inside development iterations, should be a factor of considerable importance to agile organizations working with partially available customers.

3   Experimental Setup

3.1   Dataset

We built our dataset collecting data from the Apache Software Foundation Issue Tracking system, JIRA[4]. An Issue Tracking System (ITS) is a repository used by software developers as a support for the software development process. It supports corrective maintenance activity like Bug Tracking systems, along with other types of maintenance requests. We mined the ITS of the Apache Software Foundation collecting issues from 2002 to December 2013. In order to create our dataset, since the focus of our study was about the usefulness of Agile boards, we selected projects for which the JIRA Agile board contained a significant amount of activity. Table 1 shows the corpus of 14 projects selected for our analysis, highlighting the number of comments recorded for each project and the number of developers involved. We selected projects with the highest number of comments.

3.2   Magnet and Sticky Metrics

Yamashita et al. [15] introduced the concepts of magnetism and stickiness for a software project. A project is classified as *Magnetic* if it has the ability to attract new developers over time. *Stickiness* is the ability of a project to keep its developers over time. We measured these two metrics by considering an observation time of one year. Figure 1 shows an example of the evaluation of Magnet and Sticky metrics. In this example, we were interested in calculating the value of Magnetism and Stickiness for 2011. From 2010 to 2012 we had a total of 10 *active*[5] developers. In 2011, there were 7 active developers and 2 of them

---

[4] https://www.atlassian.com/software/jira

[5] We consider active all developers that posted/commented/resolved/modified an issue during the observed time (from dev_1 to dev_10)

Table 1. Selected Projects Statistics

Project	# of comments	# of developers
HBase	91016	951
Hadoop Common	61958	1243
Derby	52668	675
Lucene Core	50152	1107
Hadoop HDFS	42208	757
Cassandra	41966	1177
Solr	41695	1590
Hive	39002	850
Hadoop Map/Reduce	34793	875
Harmony	28619	316
OFBiz	25694	578
Infrastructure	25439	1362
Camel	24109	908
ZooKeeper	16672	495

(highlighted with black heads) were new. Only 3 (highlighted with grey heads) of the 7 active developers in 2011 were also active in 2012. We can then calculate the Magnetism and Stickiness as follows:

- *Magnetism* is the portion of new active developers during the observed time interval, in our example 2/10 (*dev_6* and *dev_7* were active in 2011 but not in 2010).
- *Stickiness* is the portion of active developers that were also active during next time interval, in our example 3/7 (*dev_1*, *dev_2*, *dev_3* were active in 2011 and in 2012).

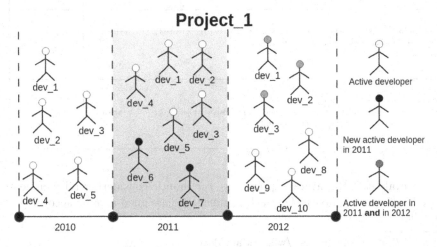

Fig. 1. Example of Magnet and Sticky in 2011

3.3 Politeness

Danescu et al. [1] proposed a machine learning approach for evaluating the politeness of a request posted in two different web applications: Wikipedia[6] and Stackoverflow[7]. Stackoverflow is well known in the software engineering field and is largely used by software practitioners; hence, the model that authors used in [1] was suitable for our domain based on Jira issues, where developers post and discuss about technical aspects of issues. The authors provide a Web application[8] and a library version of their tool.

Given some text, the tool calculates the politeness of its sentences providing as result one of two possible labels: *polite* or *impolite*. Along with the politeness label, the tool provides a level of confidence related to the probability of a politeness class being assigned. We thus considered comments whose level of confidence was less than 0.5 as neutral (namely the text did not convey either politeness or impoliteness). Table 2 and 3 show some examples of polite and impolite comments as classified by the tool[9].

Table 2. Examples of polite comments

Comment	Confidence Level
Hey <dev_name_a>, Would you be interested in contributing a fix and a test case for this as well? Thanks, <dev_name_b>	0.7236
<dev_name>, can you open a new JIRA for those suggestions? I'll be happy to review.	0.919
<dev_name>, the latest patch isn't applying cleanly to trunk — could you resubmit it please? Thanks.	0.806
<dev_name>, Since you can reproduce, do you still want the logs? I think I still have them if needed.	0.803

We evaluated the average politeness *per* month considering all comments posted in a certain month. For each comment we assigned a value according to the following rules:

---

[6] https:\/\/en.wikipedia.org\/wiki\/Main_Page
[7] http:\/\/stackoverflow.com
[8] http://www.mpi-sws.org/~cristian/Politeness.html
[9] User's names are reported as <dev_name_a> for the sake of privacy.

Table 3. Examples of impolite comments

Comment	Confidence Level
Why are you cloning tickets? Don't do that.	0.816
shouldnt it check for existence of tarball even before it tries to allocate and error out ???	0.701
<dev_name_a>, why no unit test? <dev_name_b>, why didn't you wait for +1 from Hudson???	0.942
> this isn't the forum to clarify Why not? The question is whether this is redundant with Cascading, so comparisons are certainly relevant, no?	0.950

- Value of +1 for those comments marked as polite by the tool;
- Value of 0 for those comments marked as neutral (confidence level<0.5);
- Value of -1 for those comments marked as impolite.

We finally averaged the assigned values for a certain month. We analyzed the politeness of about 500K comments.

4 Result and Discussion

4.1 Does the Politeness among Developers Affect the Issues Fixing Time?

Motivation. Murgia et al. [4] demonstrated the influence of maintenance type on the issue fixing time, while Zhang et al. [16] developed a prediction model for bug fixing time for commercial software. There are many factors able to influence the issues fixing time; in this case we were interested in finding out if politeness expressed by developers in comments had an influence on the issues fixing time.

Approach. In order to detect differences among the fixing time of polite and impolite issues, we used the Wilcoxon rank sum test. Such a test is non parametric and unpaired, and [9] [13] [12]. The test is non-parametric and can be used with no restrictions or hypotheses on the statistical distribution of the sample populations. The test is suitable for comparing differences among the averages or the medians of two populations when their distributions are not gaussian. For the analysis, we used the one-sided Wilcoxon rank sum test using the 5% significance level (i.e., p-value<0.05) and we compared issue fixing time between polite and impolite issues.

We grouped issues together as follows:

- we first divided comments in two sets: polite and impolite, ignoring neutral comments;

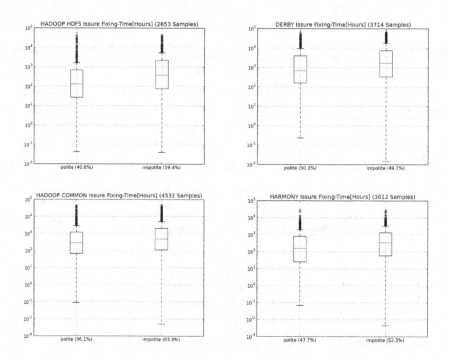

Fig. 2. Box-plot of the fixing-time expressed in Hours. The number in parenthesis next to polite/impolite indicates the percentage of impolite and polite issues.

- we divided issues in two sets: polite issues, commented only with polite comments, and impolite issues, commented only by impolite comments.
- we ignored issues with both polite and impolite comments, and ignored issues with neutral comments.

For each issue we evaluated the politeness expressed in its comments (removing neutral comments as discussed in section 3.3) and we then divided issues in two groups: polite issues containing polite comments and impolite issues containing impolite comments. For each of this two groups of issues we evaluated the issue fixing time as the difference between resolution and creation time. **Findings. Issue fixing time for polite issues is faster than issue fixing time for impolite issues for 10 out of 14 analysed projects.**

Figure 2 shows the box-plot of the issues fixing time for the two groups of issues considered (polite and impolite) in four projects *Harmony, Derby, Hadoop HDFS* and *Hadoop Common*. The issues fixing time is expressed in hours on a logarithmic scale. As we can see for the four projects in the example, the median of the issues fixing time for polite issues is smaller than that for impolite issues.

Table 4 shows the Wilcoxon test results. Test's column indicates if the median of the first group (group of polite issues containing polite comments) is greater or lesser than the second group (group of impolite issues containing impolite comments).

Table 4. Wilcoxon test results

Project	Test	p-value	effect size
ZooKeeper	lesser	***	0.14
Camel	greater	***	0.089
Infrastructure	lesser	0.67	0.007
OFBiz	lesser	***	0.15
Harmony	lesser	***	0.133
Hive	lesser	***	0.061
Solr	lesser	***	0.089
Cassandra	lesser	0.51	0.012
Hadoop HDFS	lesser	***	0.192
Lucene Core	lesser	0.492	0.01
Derby	lesser	***	0.15
Hadoop Common	lesser	***	0.11
HBase	lesser	***	0.144
Hadoop Map/Reduce	lesser	***	0.11

Table 4 shows that for 10 of the 14 projects analysed the issues fixing time of polite issues is faster than the issue fixing time of impolite issues. *Camel* behaved differently, in this case the issues fixing time for impolite issues is faster than the issues fixing time of polite issues. Furthermore for *Infrastructure, Lucene Core* and *Cassandra* projects the *Test* value indicates that polite issues fixing time is still lesser than the impolite issues fixing time but the *p-value* >0.05 and thus for these projects we cannot conclude that the two distribution are statistically different. We can see that the size effect is generally small with a maximum of 0.19 for Hadoop HDFS and a minimum of 0.007 for Infrastructure.

Figure 3 shows the the average politeness *per* month, calculated as described in section 3.3. We used the same four project depicted in Figure 2. It is interesting to note that there are variations in the average politeness over time. This is by no mean a representation of a time dynamics, but simply the representation of random variation of average politeness over time. In Hadoop HDFS for example, we can see how the average politeness is negative (namely majority of comments are impolite) for some time interval and positive of some others. As we have seen, for those projects polite issues are solved faster, so monitoring the average politeness over time can be helpful during software development. If there is a time period with a negative politeness, then the community may take action to drive the average politeness back to positive values.

4.2 Does the Politeness among Developers Affect the Attractiveness of a Project?

Motivation. Magnetism and Stickiness are two interesting metrics able to describe the general health of a project; namely, if a project is able to attract new developers and to keep them over time we can then conclude that the project is healthy. On the contrary, if a project is not magnetic and is not sticky we can

138   M. Ortu et al.

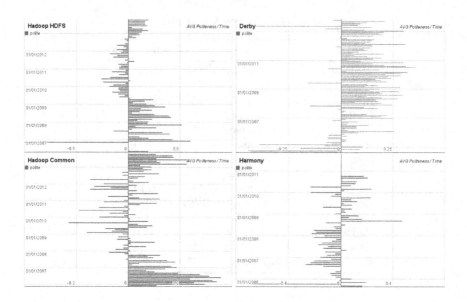

Fig. 3. Average Politeness per month

conclude that the project is losing developers and is not attracting new developers over time. Although there may be many factors influencing magnetism and stickiness, we were interested in analysing the correlation between politeness expressed by developers in their comments and these two metrics.

Approach. In order to detect if there was a direct correlation between magnetism and stickiness of a project and politeness, we considered an observation time of one year. During this time interval we measured magnetism, stickiness and percentage of comments classified as polite by the tool. Since we had no evidence that the politeness in the observed time could affect magnetism and stickiness in the same time interval or in the next observation time, we evaluated the Pearson's correlation coefficient and the cross-correlation coefficient.

Findings. In the majority of projects Magnet and Sticky are positively correlated with Politeness. Table 5 shows the Pearson's correlation and cross-correlation coefficient between the percentage of polite comments and magnetism and stickiness during an observation time of one year. The first two columns represent Pearson's correlation coefficient between Magnetism and Stickiness and the percentage of politeness comments during the same observation time (one year in our case). The second two columns represent the cross-correlation coefficient between the same metrics. The Pearson's correlation revealed that 9 out of 14 project have a positive correlation between Magnetism, Stickiness and Politeness. In the 5 projects where Pearson's correlation is negative we can see that when considering the cross correlation coefficient is positive in all cases. **Although Pearson's correlation is not always positive, we can conclude that Politeness is positively correlated with Magnetism and Stickiness metrics in the subsequent years.**

Table 5. Politeness Vs Magnet and Sticky Pearson's and Cross-Correlation Coefficient

Project	Pearson's Correlation		Cross-Correlation	
	Magnet	Sticky	Magnet	Sticky
HBase	0.672	0.667	0.581	0.667
Hadoop Common	0.848	0.641	0.848	0.641
Derby	-0.830	-0.804	0.126	0.240
Lucene Core	-0.399	0.705	0.494	0.705
Hadoop HDFS	0.716	0.526	0.716	0.627
Cassandra	0.876	0.631	0.876	0.631
Solr	0.602	0.773	0.602	0.773
Hive	0.372	0.802	0.714	0.802
Hadoop Map/Reduce	0.631	0.697	0.631	0.697
Harmony	-0.730	-0.784	0.142	0.372
OFBiz	0.692	0.498	0.692	0.498
Infrastructure	0.1	-0.112	0.479	0.610
Camel	-0.576	-0.67	0.120	0.293
ZooKeeper	-0.535	0	0.319	0.497

5   Threats to Validity

Threats to external validity are related to generalisation of our conclusions. With regard to the system studied in this work we considered only open source systems and this could affect the generality of the study; our results are not meant to be representative of all environments or programming languages. Commercial software is typically developed using different platforms and technologies, with strict deadlines and cost limitation and by developers with different experiences.

6   Conclusion

Software engineers have been trying to measure software to gain quantitative insights into its properties and quality since its inception. In this paper, we present the results about politeness and attractiveness on 14 open source software projects developed using the Agile board of the JIRA repository. Our results show that the level of politeness in the communication process among developers does have an effect on both the time required to fix issues and the attractiveness of the project to both active and potential developers. The more polite developers were, the less time it took to fix an issue and, in the majority of the analysed cases, the more the developers wanted to be part of project, the more they were willing to continue working on the project over time. This work is a starting point and further research on a larger number of projects is needed to prove and validate our findings especially considering proprietary software developed by companies. The takeaway message is that politeness can only have positive effect on a project and on the development process. Be polite!

References

1. Danescu-Niculescu-Mizil, C., Sudhof, M., Jurafsky, D., Leskovec, J., Potts., C.: A computational approach to politeness with application to social factors. In: Proceedings of ACL (2013)
2. Gupta, S., Walker, M.A., Romano, D.M.: How rude are you?: Evaluating politeness and affect in interaction, pp. 203–217 (2007)
3. Korkala, M., Abrahamsson, P., Kyllonen, P.: A case study on the impact of customer communication on defects in agile software development. In: Agile Conference, 2006, p. 11. IEEE (2006)
4. Murgia, A., Concas, G., Tonelli, R., Ortu, M., Demeyer, S., Marchesi, M.: On the influence of maintenance activity types on the issue resolution time. In: Proceedings of the 10th International Conference on Predictive Models in Software Engineering, pp. 12–21. ACM (2014)
5. Murgia, A., Tourani, P., Adams, B., Ortu, M.: Do developers feel emotions? an exploratory analysis of emotions in software artifacts. In: Proceedings of the 11th Working Conference on Mining Software Repositories, pp. 262–271. ACM (2014)
6. Novielli, N., Calefato, F., Lanubile, F.: Towards discovering the role of emotions in stack overflow. In: Proceedings of the 6th International Workshop on Social Software Engineering, pp. 33–36. ACM (2014)
7. Perry, T.: Drifting toward invisibility: The transition to the electronic task board. In: Agile Conference, AGILE 2008, pp. 496–500. IEEE (2008)
8. Pikkarainen, M., Haikara, J., Salo, O., Abrahamsson, P., Still, J.: The impact of agile practices on communication in software development. Empirical Software Engineering 13(3), 303–337 (2008)
9. Siegel, S.: Nonparametric statistics for the behavioral sciences (1956)
10. Tan S., Howard-Jones P.: Rude or polite: do personality and emotion in an artificial pedagogical agent affect task performance? In: 2014 Global Conference on Teaching and Learning with Technology (CTLT 2014) Conference Proceedings, p. 41 (2014)
11. Tsay, J., Dabbish, L., Herbsleb, J.: Lets talk about it: Evaluating contributions through discussion in: github. FSE. ACM (2014)
12. Weiss, C., Premraj, R., Zimmermann, T., Zeller, A.: How long will it take to fix this bug? In: Proceedings of the Fourth International Workshop on Mining Software Repositories, p. 1. IEEE Computer Society (2007)
13. Wilcoxon, F. Wilcox, R.A.: Some rapid approximate statistical procedures. Lederle Laboratories (1964)
14. Winschiers, H., Paterson, B.: Sustainable software development. In: Proceedings of the 2004 Annual Research Conference of the South African Institute of Computer Scientists and Information Technologists on IT Research in Developing Countries, pp. 274–278. South African Institute for Computer Scientists and Information Technologists (2004)
15. Yamashita, K., McIntosh, S., Kamei, Y., Ubayashi, N.: Magnet or sticky? an oss project-by-project typology. In: MSR, pp. 344–347 (2014)
16. Zhang, H, Gong, L., Versteeg, S.: Predicting bug-fixing time: an empirical study of commercial software projects. In: Proceedings of the 2013 International Conference on Software Engineering, pp. 1042–1051. IEEE Press (2013)

Coordinating Expertise Outside Agile Teams

Mawarny Md. Rejab(✉), James Noble(✉), and Stuart Marshall(✉)

School of Engineering and Computer Science, Victoria University of Wellington,
Wellington, New Zealand
{Mawarny.Md.Rejab,kjx,stuart.marshall}@ecs.vuw.ac.nz

Abstract. Agile software development projects depend upon roles located outside Agile teams such as User Experience Designers and Software Architects to support teams. As external specialists' expertise is valuable to Agile teams, further investigation is needed to explore the relationships between Agile teams and external specialists in coordinating external expertise. Through a Grounded Theory study involving 47 Agile practitioners and external specialists, we discovered five factors that Agile teams and external specialists need to consider when coordinating external expertise: *Availability, Agile Mindset, Stability, Knowledge Retention* and *Effective Communication*. We present strategies for each factor as a guideline for coordinating external expertise in teams. This study helps Agile teams to manage and utilize external expertise resources effectively.

Keywords: Expertise coordination · External specialists · Agile software development projects · Grounded theory

1 Introduction

An Agile team is intended to be a cross-functional team that includes all the expertise necessary for every phase involved in developing software [22]. In practice, it is not feasible for all the individuals with relevant expertise to be part of the team [20]. Agile teams normally consist of common Agile roles such as team lead, team members, and product owner [22], therefore, Agile teams often need to rely on other expertise which is located outside the team such as User Experience Designers, Database Administrators (DBAs), and Software Architects [11][20].

An external specialist is responsible for supporting Agile teams by bringing specialized skills into teams. There are various types of external specialists that support Agile teams: technical experts, domain experts and independent testers [11]. Each Agile project requires different types and numbers of external specialists depending on the project size and team composition.

Agile teams and external specialists depend on each other in managing and utilizing external expertise through external expertise coordination. External expertise coordination requires Agile teams to recognize external specialists, when and where the external specialists' expertise is needed, and how to access their expertise effectively [7].

© Springer International Publishing Switzerland 2015
C. Lassenius et al. (Eds.): XP 2015, LNBIP 212, pp. 141–153, 2015.
DOI: 10.1007/978-3-319-18612-2_12

According to Sharp and Robinson, further investigation is needed to explore the interaction between Agile teams and roles outside the teams [20]. Their study has motivated us to explore the interaction between Agile teams and external specialists in coordinating external expertise. Through a Grounded Theory study, we discovered how Agile teams and external specialists depend on each other to manage and utilize the external expertise. This paper aims to discuss factors of external expertise coordination in Agile teams. We also present several strategies for each factor to ensure Agile teams and external specialists take into account the emerging factors.

The rest of this paper is structured as follows: the next section describes Grounded Theory; the third section presents the findings of this study; the fourth section discusses these findings; and the last section puts forward conclusions.

2   Grounded Theory

Grounded Theory is an inductive research method that aims to infer new theories from observed data [9]. There are several reasons why Grounded Theory is applicable as a research method for this study. Firstly, Grounded Theory is appropriate for exploring human behaviour and social interactions [8]. This study focuses on how Agile teams and external specialists rely on each other in coordinating external expertise. Secondly, Grounded Theory is appropriate to be used in areas that are under-explored which require further investigation [2]. Further investigation is needed to conceptualize and theorise about the underpinnings of external expertise coordination in Agile teams. Finally, Grounded Theory is applicable for a study that emphasizes processes [4]. The aim of this study is to explore external expertise coordination in Agile software projects, which is aligned with the characteristic of Grounded Theory.

2.1   Data Collection

Semi-structured interviews have been carried out with 42 Agile practitioners and five external specialists from different software organizations mainly based in New Zealand and United States, as depicted in Table 1. Interviews provide reliable data sources because the researcher has direct contact with participants during data collection [4]. This situation enables us to gain a deeper understanding of participants' concerns.

This study requires a broad range of Agile roles including external specialists in order to enable the triangulation of findings. Theoretical sampling is a way to ensure the validity of this study by selecting subsequent participants for data collection based on existing data analysis [16]. Theoretical sampling should ensure that other perspectives are gained from the identified participants and drawn indirectly from a broad range of other participants [16]. Different roles provide different insights and perspectives toward external expertise coordination. We interviewed Agile team members as well as User Experience Designers, Software Architects, and DevOps (Development and Operation) as external

Table 1. Summary of Research Participants and Agile Projects

Person	Location	Agile Role	Agile Methods	Project Domain
P1	New Zealand	Developer	XP and Scrum	Mobile application
P2	New Zealand	Agile Coach	XP, Scrum, Kanban	Not disclosed
P3	Australia	Agile Consultant	Not disclosed	Not disclosed
P4	New Zealand	Agile Coach	Scrum and XP	Education
P5	New Zealand	Software Tester	Not disclosed	Printing
P6	Australia	Team leader	Not disclosed	Accounting
P7	New Zealand	Agile Consultant	Scrum and XP	Financial
P8	Australia	Agile Coach	Scrum, XP, Kanban, Lean	Human resources
P9	New Zealand	Business Analyst	Not disclosed	Insurance
P10	New Zealand	Software Tester	Scrum	Education
P11	New Zealand	Project Manager	Scrum	Education
P12	New Zealand	Agile Coach	Scrum and Kanban	Not disclosed
P13	New Zealand	Agile Coach	Scrum and Kanban	Government application
P14	New Zealand	Product Owner	Not disclosed	Not disclosed
P15	New Zealand	Agile Coach	Scrum and Kanban	Government application
P16	New Zealand	Agile Coach	Scrum and Kanban	Government application
P17	New Zealand	Tester	Scrum	Education
P18	New Zealand	Developer	Scrum	Education
P19	New Zealand	Business Analyst	Scrum	Education
P20	New Zealand	User Experience Designer	Scrum	Not disclosed
P21	New Zealand	Agile Coach	Scrum and Kanban	Mobile Application
P22	New Zealand	Scrum Master	Scrum, Kanban, XP	Web-based Application
P23	New Zealand	Developer	Scrum and XP	Dataware house
P24	New Zealand	Scrum Master	Scrum and Kanban	Banking
P25	New Zealand	Developer	Scrum and Kanban	Financial
P26	New Zealand	Team Leader	Scrum and XP	Goverment Application
P27	New Zealand	Developer	Scrum and XP	Fishery
P28	Sweden	Developer	Kanban	Telecommunication
P29	Denmark	Developer	Scrum	Medical
P30	India	Business Analyst	Scrum and Kanban	Not disclosed
P31	Malaysia	Scrum Master	Scrum and Kanban	Broadcast
P32	Malaysia	Scrum Master	Scrum, Kanban, XP	Enterprise
P33	Malaysia	Project Manager	Scrum and Kanban	Security Application
P34	United States	Agile Coach	Scrum	Financial
P35	United States	Developer	Scrum	Financial
P36	United States	Developer	Scrum	E-commerce
P37	United States	DevOps	Not disclosed	Not disclosed
P38	United States	User Experience Designer	Not disclosed	Not disclosed
P39	United States	Agile Coach	Scrum and XP	Not disclosed
P40	United States	Stakeholder	Not disclosed	Not disclosed
P41	United States	Agile Coach	Scrum and XP	Biotechnology
P42	United States	Tester	Scrum and XP	Retail
P43	Wellington	DevOps	Scrum	Not disclosed
P44	Wellington	Architect	Scrum	Oil Retail
P45	Wellington	Tester	Scrum and Kanban	Financial
P46	Wellington	Agile Coach	Scrum, Kanban and XP	E-commerce
P47	Wellington	Developer	Scrum, Kanban and XP	E-commerce

specialists. We will stop the data collection once we reached theoretical saturation, i.e when no new data emerged [9].

2.2 Data Analysis

Data analysis begins as soon as the first interview has been conducted and continues until the emergence of a core category [5]. We used key point coding to analyze the interview transcripts in detail. We collate the key points by examining phrases, words, and sentences from the interview transcripts [1]. Then, we construct codes by rephrasing key points with meaningful labels. In order to look for similarities and differences, we continuously compare every emerging code with the previous codes. We group together similar codes with common themes to form a concept. Many concepts emerge, and constant comparison is repeated until concepts form a category. A category is a group of similar concepts that is used to generate a theory. To date, several categories have emerged from our data analysis such as *"locating expertise"*[18] and *"distributing expertise"*[17]. This paper presents the category *"coordinating external expertise"* which is discussed in the next section.

3 Research Findings

The category *"Coordinating External Expertise"* describes how Agile teams and external specialists depend on each other to manage and utilize the external specialists' expertise in Agile teams. Our findings revealed five factors that Agile teams and external specialists need to consider in coordinating external expertise: *Availability (F1), Agile Mindset (F2), Knowledge Retention (F3), Stability (F4)* and *Effective Communication (F5)*. There are strategies for each factor in coordinating external expertise in Agile teams. The relationships between the

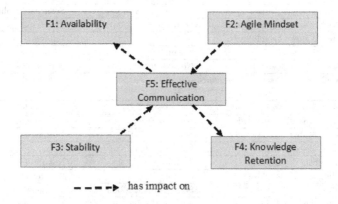

Fig. 1. The relationships between factors of external expertise coordination

factors of external expertise coordination are summarised in figure 1. The square shapes represent factors, and arrows represent relationships between factors.

3.1   Factor 1: Availability

Availability (F1) refers to the ability of external specialists to be present in Agile teams when their expertise is needed. The majority of our participants claimed that they had to rely on external specialists who were involved in multiple projects at one time. It was very hard for the external specialists to allocate their effort, responsibility, and time to the Agile teams. The external specialists were sometimes unable to present when their expertise was needed. Such delays caused bottlenecks that affected the performance of teams:

> *"We have difficulties such as the DBA is very busy and handles multiple projects. So to get his time can be more challenging."*- P33, Project Manager.

Strategy 1: Planning Ahead. Our findings revealed planning ahead is used by teams to address by *Availability (F1)*. Planning ahead is needed for external specialists to decide which project to be involved in at which time, without affecting other projects.

> *"Usually, what we do is we plan ahead of the release. For example, we needed a solution architect for 2 or 3 months. So we tried to get them involved before that. We told them earlier when we needed them to be involved. During planning, we get everyone to be involved."* - P33, Project Manager.

Planning ahead relies on prioritizing tasks. The value of the task should be the most important criterion when deciding which project needs to be worked on:

> *"Even they are outside resources that we depend on, they need to figure out what is the priority of the task compared to the other tasks."* - P36, Developer.

Figure 1 shows the relationship between *Availability (F1)* and *Effective Communication (F5)*. *Availability (F1)* depends on the *Effective Communication (F5)* between Agile teams and external specialists. This relationship is discussed in subsection 3.5.

3.2   Factor 2: Agile Mindset

Agile Mindset (F2) is one of the factors that external specialists need to consider when engaging in Agile teams. Agile teams depend on a variety of external specialists who have different software development backgrounds including Agile and non-Agile approaches. Some participants reported that they have to deal with external specialists who are unfamiliar with Agile methods. Indeed, some external specialists refused to learn and apply Agile practices. Presumably because they do not see the importance of Agile values. This leads to Agile teams facing many problems when dealing with non-Agile external specialists. For instance, external specialists were unable to align work with the sprints which required continuous value delivery at the end of each sprint. As a result, the external specialists failed to produce what they were expected to deliver for Agile teams on time:

> "They [external specialists] didn't go to the same Agile training that we went through. We started doing our project, and we called our Database Administrator. We need these tables to be set up. We need it to be done in two weeks. But it didn't go very well." - P35, Developer.

Consequently, external specialists had to carry over the unfinished tasks to the next sprint and this delayed the next tasks. This situation became worse when the Agile teams could not continue their work due to dependencies on external expertise. Therefore, the Agile teams faced a problem in managing and coordinating rescheduled tasks. Without proper organization of tasks, it was hard to keep track of the tasks progress:

> "Then, the way we receive the requirements is like a waterfall model. They won't accept iterative release for the product. We quite often postpone and move the current stuff to the next sprint. Sometimes we also couldn't believe what we had achieved or what we don't achieve for the last sprint. That's the problem of continuity." - P27, Developer.

User Experience Designers are another kind of external specialists that typically prefer to produce a comprehensive user interface design before implementation begins. As Agile practices undertake relatively little up-front design, this has a big impact on the Agile teams, particularly the lack of feedback from the development side in improving the design:

> "The User Experience Designer is the last batch of the waterfall approach [sic]. They don't know about the Agile method. They prefer the up-front [design] and not to share their work until it is finished [sic]. We have problems with that." - P12, Agile Coach.

Agile approaches are very personality driven and require particular personality traits in Agile teams. Several participants claimed that they struggled to deal with external specialists' misbehaviours, which very difficult to tolerate:

> "We invited one of the DBAs for our stand-up. But he just came once a week. It was because of personality of the guy, who was quite difficult to deal with." - P27, Developer.

Struggling with misbehaviours also happens the other way around. In certain circumstances, external specialists also have to deal with personality conflicts of Agile team members:

> "I can't stand some [Agile team members'] behaviours. There is a situation where a person holds a position for so long. There is no give and take."- P44, Architect.

External expertise coordination relies on the ability of Agile teams and external specialists to work in a cooperative manner. The progress of the project will suffer when the cooperation is disrupted. It is impossible to develop good cooperation between Agile teams and external specialists when personality conflicts happen in Agile projects.

Strategy 2: Understanding Agile Methods. *Agile Mindset (F2)* requires a strategy of being familiar with and understanding Agile values and practices helps external specialists to work with the expectation of Agile teams:

> "We discussed with them what and how we're doing in Agile [ways]. So they knew what they are responsible for and when it needs to be done. So once we started doing that, they got more ideas about the Agile (method)." - P44, Architect.

Educating external specialists to act in an Agile way requires a willingness from both parties, Agile teams and external specialists. The Agile teams need to understand the Agile method and behave in an Agile way. They also need to educate the external specialists about Agile values and practices. The Agile teams need to know and apply suitable methods for educating the external specialists about Agile methods. The perception and willingness of the external specialists to shift their paradigm into the Agile way, however, determines the success of educating external specialists about Agile methods.

As depicted in figure 1, *Agile Mindset (F2)* is interrelated with *Effective Communication(F5)* in coordinating external expertise. Failure to understand Agile values and practices hinders external specialists communicating and collaborating effectively with Agile teams. As a result, external specialists don't realize the importance of Agile meetings such as daily stand-up meetings or retrospectives in establishing effective communication and collaboration with Agile teams.

3.3 Factor 3: Stability

Stability (F3) refers to keeping Agile teams stable with a low rate of team members and external specialists turnover. *Stability (F3)* is an important factor that tends to affect expertise coordination in Agile teams. Many problems arise when there is high flunctuation in Agile teams composition, or in external specialists.

Some external specialists reported that they have to change to another team while they are still working on on-going Agile projects. They have had to adapt to a new environment with different specifications once they move to a new team. It takes time for them to cope with the new team and indirectly affects their progress:

> *"Changing teams happens all the time. Frequent changes in the (Agile) project requires me to be flexible."* - P38, User Experience Designer.

Involvement in unstable Agile teams has a negative impact on the external specialists. For instance, one of the participants, a software architect *(P44)* claimed that he didn't see the benefit of his presence in the Agile team. It was impossible to get support from Agile team members to accomplish his tasks while the team was struggling to solve their internal problems:

> *"People move to another team regularly. Teams need to recover from the changes. The team can't get stable. They are busy with other stuff, and they don't engage. So my role becomes irrelevant because [the project] it is not progressing well."* - P44,Software architect.

Strategy 3: Ensuring Consistency. Ensuring consistency is a way to establish *Stability (F3)* in Agile teams. Coping with frequent turnover of external specialists requires a consistent standard of work to enable external specialists to adapt easily to the new team and work:

> *"Frequent changes in the [Agile] project requires me to be very flexible. I have to familiarize myself as quickly as possible. So, we make sure that we do things more consistent. It is not difficult for someone to pick up the work."* - P38, User Experience Designer.

Figure 1 shows a relationship between *Stability (F3)* and *Effective Communication (F5)*. Communication will be disrupted when existing external specialists leave Agile teams and new specialists join teams.

3.4   Factor 4: Knowledge Retention

In coordinating external expertise, *Knowledge Retention (F4)* involves capturing external specialists' knowledge and preserving the knowledge in Agile teams. Knowledge retention should be extended to every segment of Agile teams, including external specialists:

> *"The things that got my bear there is a sustainability [sic]. How can the team learn from the person who comes in and then disappears? How can we extract the knowledge and learn from them?"* - P16, Agile Coach.

Retaining external specialists' expertise depends on the project's needs and requirements. Agile teams need to decide which external specialists' expertise has a significant impact on other roles. For instance, sharing software design ideas with developers assists developers to implement the software. This tends to speed up the development of software project:

> *"We help developers to understand the design principles and get them to sketch with us."* - P38, User Experience Designer.

Agile teams depend too much on external specialists when they are unable to retain external specialists' knowledge. Thus, it is essential to transfer external specialists' knowledge to Agile team members. If external specialists are unable to be available, at least someone in the teams can troubleshoot simple and routine problems.

Strategy 4: Sustaining External Expertise. External specialists' have several mechanisms for transferring and sustaining their knowledge to Agile teams such as collaboration, documentation, and coaching. The ideal mechanisms, however, depend on external specialists' roles and interactions between both parties:

> *"We have to make sure the knowledge can be passed to the team. We have person to person, pair-programming and peer review. They [also] pass the knowledge by mentoring and documentation."* - P27, Developer.

Figure 1 shows the relationship between *Knowledge Retention (F4)* and *Effective Communication (F5)*. *Knowledge Retention (F4)* depends on *Effective Communication (F5)* between Agile teams and external specialists. This relationship is discussed in subsection 3.5.

3.5 Factor 5: Effective Communication

In the context of this study, *Effective Communication (F5)* is defined as the activity of conveying sufficient information between Agile teams and external specialists through verbal and non-verbal mediums. Effective communication enables good cooperation between Agile teams and external specialists. Poor communication leads to failure in coordinating external expertise in Agile teams. Consequently, Agile teams and external specialists tend to point the finger and place blame on each other instead of finding solutions:

> *"The developer and the operation staff didn't talk to each other. This operation team did the deployment. Sometimes, there was failure, and we found that the development team blamed the operation team. The operation team blamed the development team."* - P15, Agile Coach.

It is difficult to coordinate external expertise when Agile teams convey incorrect and insufficient information to external specialists. Agile teams need to provide clear goals for the Agile software project at the beginning of the project. A lack of mutual goals drives the external specialists to work in their own direction without considering the whole project:

"It is hard because they have their ways and we have our ways in doing the tasks. We try to coordinate, but it is quite difficult." - P18, Developer.

Conveying insufficient information about task descriptions causes external specialists to be unable to align work with Agile teams' needs and expectations. External specialists fail to perform when they are not really clear about their roles and responsibilities:

"They didn't know what is happening if they don't have the project's visibility. They didn't know when they are needed, and they didn't have a feeling of being involved" - P16, Agile Coach.

Agile teams should provide sufficient information to external specialists verbally or in writing. On the other hand, external specialists also need to provide Agile teams with necessary information such as their availability, needs, and expectations when dealing with Agile teams.

Strategy 5: Keeping Everyone on the Same Page. As depicted in figure 1, our findings revealed keeping everyone on the same page is a strategy for establishing effective communication.

Through Agile meetings, Agile teams have opportunities to show their concerns, awareness and appreciation to external specialists. Indirectly, this could remind Agile teams of the value of the external specialists' expertise and their availability:

"For every project, we have a different databases and architecture. So we get somebody, and we pull them into a sprint. We make them a part of the team. Bringing them to the daily meetings, reinforcing them and making them realize 'Aah, this guy is true. He is waiting for me. That's why he keeps reminding me.'" - P35, Developer.

Working closely together depends on the workload that external specialists need to contribute to Agile teams. It is better for the external specialists to work closely with the Agile team if the workload is high. For a minimal workload, the external specialist needs to figure out how long they need to allocate their time with Agile teams:

"Depends on how much the work is [sic]. If there is a lot of work, we ask them to move their stuff and computer, and come over to us." - P12, Agile Coach.

Agile teams should provide necessary information without overwhelming the external specialists with an overload of information. Too much information may lead to more confusion than clarity and cause misunderstanding between external specialists and Agile teams.

Our findings indicated that *Effective Communication (F5)* is the centre of the factors' relationships. Figure 1 shows the relationships between *Effective*

Communication (F5) and other factors. *Effective Communication (F5)* tends to indirectly increase *Availability (F1)* and *Knowledge Retention (F4)*. Conveying sufficient information to external specialists assists them to bring the right and relevant expertise to teams in a timely manner. Effective communication also facilitates knowledge transfer from external specialists to Agile teams.

Effective Communication (F5) depends on *Agile Mindset (F2)* and *Stability (F3)*. Failure to understand Agile values and practices hinders *Effective Communication (F5)* between Agile teams and external specialists. Effective communication also affects the *Stability (F3)* because it is impossible to establish effective communication if Agile teams or external specialists change often.

4   Discussion

Availability (F1) is one of the factors that influence expertise coordination in Agile teams. Strode et al. [21] revealed that availability is a coordination strategy component in Agile teams. Engaging in multiple projects at a time causes coordination problems in Agile teams and affects the availability. Strode et al. [21] discussed coordination problems in general without specifying expertise coordination. Our findings, however, revealed the implications of external specialists' availability in coordinating expertise in Agile teams.

Adopting an *Agile Mindset (F2)* helps external specialists to work with the expectation of Agile teams. Our findings confirmed Kollmann and Sharp's study [10], when a good understanding of Agile is perceived to facilitate User Experience Designers' ability to work in an Agile context. Adopting an Agile mindset requires external specialists to believe the usefulness of Agile methods [10], so that they value the importance of Agile practices and principles in their work.

Stability (F3) also has impact on relationships between Agile teams and external specialists. Task reallocation and work disruption occur when there is a high rate of team member turnover [6][14]. Our finding indicated that unstable Agile teams hinder external specialists from allocating their expertise in teams. Thus, flexibility is essential for Agile teams and external specialists to adapt to new environments. Agile teams usually expect the new team member or external specialist to adapt to their fast-paced work [6]. In order to speed up the flexibility, the team members also need to quickly adapt to the new members or external specialists.

Knowledge Retention (F4) aligns with Moe et al.'s study [13] when they mentioned that knowledge retention requires identifying the location of external specialists and distributing their expertise. Our previous findings revealed how Agile team members locate and distribute expertise in teams [17][18]. Through our data analysis, we believe our previous findings are relevant as a basis to locate and distribute external expertise in Agile teams. Based on our findings here we now believe it is impossible to retain all external specialists' expertise in teams. This accords to Moe et al. [13] who claimed that there is a need to explore how to define which external specialists' knowledge needs to be retained in teams.

Effective Communication (F5) is the central factor for coordinating external expertise in Agile teams. As previously mentioned, our findings showed relationships between emerging factors. Much existing literature has discussed the relationships between these factors [15][12]. There is a paucity of studies, however, that focus on these factors in the context of interaction between Agile teams and external specialists.

There are possible factors' relationships which we did not find in our study. For instance, Melo and his colleagues [6] posited personality causes team members turnover in Agile teams. As Agile mindset is very personality driven [3][19], we classified personality under *Agile Mindset (F2)*. However, we did not find a relationship between *Agile Mindset (F2)* and *Stability (F3)*.

It is hard to avoid expertise dependencies in Agile teams, including dependencies on roles outside teams. This study has provided a positive insight into what factors Agile teams and external specialists need to consider when dealing with each other. These factors are basis of managing and utilizing the external expertise resources in Agile teams.

5   Conclusion

This paper presents five factors that Agile teams and external specialists need to consider when coordinating external expertise in Agile teams: *Availability (F1)*, *Agile Mindset (F2)*, *Stability (F3)*, *Knowledge Retention (F4)*, and *Effective Communication (F5)*. These factors require strategies to assist Agile teams and external specialists depend on each other to manage and utilize external expertise resources. In the future, we intend to determine the relationships between the category *"Coordinating External Expertise"* and other categories that have emerged from our study.

References

1. Allan, G.: A critique of using grounded theory as a research method. Electronic Journal of Business Research Methods **2**(1), 1–10 (2003)
2. Birks, M., Mills, J.: Grounded Theory: a Practical Guide. Sage Publications Limited (2011)
3. Chao, J., Atli, G.: Critical personality traits in successful pair programming. In: Agile Conference, p. 5. IEEE (2006)
4. Charmaz, K.: Constructing Grounded Theory: A Practical Guide Through Qualitative Analysis. Sage Publications Limited (2006)
5. Corbin, J.M., Strauss, A.: Grounded theory research: Procedures, canons, and evaluative criteria. Qualitative Sociology **13**(1), 3–21 (1990)
6. de O Melo, C., S Cruzes, D., Kon, F., Conradi, R.: Interpretative case studies on agile team productivity and management. Information and Software Technology **55**(2), 412–427 (2013)
7. Faraj, S., Sproull, L.: Coordinating expertise in software development teams. Management Science, 1554–1568 (2000)

8. Glaser, B.G.: Emergence vs Forcing: Basics of Grounded Theory Analysis. Sociology Press (1992)
9. Glaser, B.G., Strauss, A.L.: The Discovery of Grounded Theory: Strategies for Qualitative Research. Aldine de Gruyter (1967)
10. Kollmann, J., Sharp, H., Blandford, A.: The importance of identity and vision to user experience designers on agile projects. In: Agile Conference, pp. 11–18. IEEE (2009)
11. Martin, A., Biddle, R., Noble, J.: An ideal customer: a grounded theory of requirements elicitation, communication and acceptance on agile projects. In: Agile Software Development, pp. 111–141. Springer (2010)
12. Martini, A., Pareto, L., Bosch, J.: Teams interactions hindering short-term and long-term business goals. In: Continuous Software Engineering, pp. 51–65. Springer (2014)
13. Moe, N.B., Šmite, D., Šāblis, A., Börjesson, A.-L., Andréasson, P.: Networking in a large-scale distributed agile project. In: International Symposium on Empirical Software Engineering and Measurement. ACM (2014)
14. Narayanan, S., Balasubramanian, S., Swaminathan, J.M.: A matter of balance: Specialization, task variety, and individual learning in a software maintenance environment. Management Science 55(11), 1861–1876 (2009)
15. Nuwangi, S.M., Sedera, D., Murphy, G.: Multi-level knowledge transfer in software development outsourcing projects: the agency theory view. In: Proceedings of the 33rd International Conference Systems, Orlando, Florida (2012)
16. Parry, K.W.: Grounded theory and social process: A new direction for leadership research. The Leadership Quarterly 9(1), 85–105 (1998)
17. Rejab, M.M., Noble, J., Allan, G.: Distributing expertise in agile software development projects. In: Agile Conference, pp. 33–36. IEEE (2014)
18. Rejab, M.M., Noble, J., Allan, G.: Locating expertise in agile software development projects. In: Cantone, G., Marchesi, M. (eds.) XP 2014. LNBIP, vol. 179, pp. 260–268. Springer, Heidelberg (2014)
19. Salleh, N., Mendes, E., Grundy, J., Burch, G.S.J.: An empirical study of the effects of conscientiousness in pair programming using the five-factor personality model. In: Proceedings of the 32nd ACM/IEEE International Conference on Software Engineering-Volume 1, pp. 577–586. ACM (2010)
20. Sharp, H., Robinson, H.: Three 'C's of agile practice: collaboration, coordination and communication. In: Dingsyr, Torgeir and Dyb, Tore and Moe, Nils Brede, Agile Software Development: Current Research and Future Directions. Springer Publishing Company, Incorporated (2010)
21. Strode, D., Huff, S., Hope, B., Link, S.: Coordination in co-located agile software development projects. Journal of Systems and Software 85(6), 1222–1238 (2012)
22. Sutherland, J.: Scrum handbook. http://jeffsutherland.com/scrumhandbook.pdf(12-03-25) (2010)

Transitioning Towards Continuous Delivery in the B2B Domain: A Case Study

Olli Rissanen[1,2(✉)] and Jürgen Münch[1]

[1] Department of Computer Science, University of Helsinki, P.O. Box 68,
FI-00014 Helsinki, Finland
{olli.rissanen,juergen.muench}@cs.helsinki.fi
[2] Steeri Oy, Tammasaarenkatu 5, 00180 Helsinki, Finland

Abstract. Delivering value to customers in real-time requires companies to utilize real-time deployment of software to expose features to users faster, and to shorten the feedback loop. This allows for faster reaction and helps to ensure that the development is focused on features providing real value. Continuous delivery is a development practice where the software functionality is deployed continuously to customer environment. Although this practice has been established in some domains such as B2C mobile software, the B2B domain imposes specific challenges. This article presents a case study that is conducted in a medium-sized software company operating in the B2B domain. The objective of this study is to analyze the challenges and benefits of continuous delivery in this domain. The results suggest that technical challenges are only one part of the challenges a company encounters in this transition. The company must also address challenges related to the customer and procedures. The core challenges are caused by having multiple customers with diverse environments and unique properties, whose business depends on the software product. Some customers require to perform manual acceptance testing, while some are reluctant towards new versions. By utilizing continuous delivery, it is possible for the case company to shorten the feedback cycles, increase the reliability of new versions, and reduce the amount of resources required for deploying and testing new releases.

Keywords: Continuous delivery · Continuous deployment · Development process · B2B · Case study

1 Introduction

To deliver value fast and to cope with the increasingly active business environment, companies have to find solutions that improve efficiency and speed. Agile practices [10] have increased the ability of software companies to cope with changing customer requirements and changing market needs [9]. To even further increase the efficiency, shortening the feedback cycle enables faster customer feedback. Continuous delivery is a design practice that aims to shorten the delivery cycles by developing software in a way that it is always ready for releasing.

© Springer International Publishing Switzerland 2015
C. Lassenius et al. (Eds.): XP 2015, LNBIP 212, pp. 154–165, 2015.
DOI: 10.1007/978-3-319-18612-2_13

This study is an exploratory case study, which explores how continuous delivery can be applied in the case company that operates in the B2B domain. While existing studies of applying the practice exist [1,2], none of the studies focuses specifically in the B2B domain. This study specifically aims to identify the main requirements, problems and key success factors with regards to continuous delivery in this domain. Extending the development process towards continuous delivery requires a deep analysis of the current development and deployment process, seeking the current problems and strengths. Adopting continuous delivery also requires understanding the requirements of continuous delivery, and restrictions caused by the developed software products.

This study is organized as follows. The second chapter summarizes the relevant literature and theories to position the research and to educate the reader on the body of knowledge and where the contributions are intended. The third chapter presents the research design. The findings are then presented in the fourth chapter, organized according to the research questions. The fifth chapter interprets the main results, and discusses the limitations of the study. Finally, the sixth chapter summarizes the results of study and answers to the research question, discusses the limitations of the study and introduces further research avenues.

2 Background and Related Work

In the agile process software release is done in periodic intervals [10]. Compared to waterfall model it introduces multiple releases throughout the development. Continuous delivery, on the other hand, attempts to keep the software ready for release at all times during development process [4]. Continuous delivery is an extension to continuous integration, where the software functionality is kept in a state where it can be deployed to production immediately. Production deployments are manually triggered, but the entire deployment process is otherwise automated. While continuous integration defines a process where the work is automatically built, tested and frequently integrated to mainline [12], often multiple times a day, continuous delivery adds automated acceptance testing and deployment to a staging environment. The purpose of continuous delivery is that as the deployment process is automated, it reduces human error and documents required for the build, and increases confidence that the build works [4]. It therefore aims to solve the problem of how to deliver an idea to users as quickly as possible.

Continuous delivery differs from continuous deployment. Continuous deployment means that every change goes through the pipeline and automatically gets put into production, resulting in many production deployments every day. Continuous delivery just means that you are able to do frequent deployments but may choose not to do it, usually due to businesses preferring a slower rate of deployment [6]. An essential part of continuous delivery is the deployment pipeline, which is an automated implementation of an applications build, deploy, test and release process [5]. A deployment pipeline can be loosely defined as a consecutively executed set of validations that a software has to pass before it can be released. Common components of the deployment pipeline are a version control system and an automated test suite.

Challenges in adopting continuous delivery have been researched in multiple studies. Olsson et al. investigate the organization evolution path and the transition phase from continuous integration to continuous delivery [1]. The authors define continuous delivery as one of the final steps in the organization evolution path. The authors identify barriers that companies need to overcome to achieve the transition. One such barrier is the custom configuration at customer sites. Maintaining customized solutions and local configurations alongside the standard configurations creates issues. The second barrier is the internal verification loop, that has to be shortened not only to develop features faster but also to deploy fast. Finally, the lack of transparency and getting an overview of the status of development projects is seen as a barrier.

One of the largest technical challenges is the test automation required for rapid deployment [4,5]. Neely and Stolt found out that with a continuous flow, Sales and Marketing departments lost the track of when features are released [2]. Implementing the deployment infrastructure also requires knowledge from the development and operations team [5]. Another challenge is to sell the vision and reasoning behind continuous delivery to the executive and management level [2].

3   Case Study

To provide insight into extending the development process towards continuous delivery, the following research questions have been chosen:

RQ1: What are the B2B specific challenges of continuous delivery?

Software development practices and product characteristics vary based on the domain and delivery model. Typical B2C applications are hosted as Software as a Service (SaaS) applications, and accessed by users via a web browser. In the B2B domain, applications installed to customer environments are very common. The purpose of this research question is to identify the challenges faced in applying continuous delivery in the B2B environment. The research question is answered by conducting interviews to discover the current development process and its challenges in the case company, and using these findings and the available literature on continuous delivery to map the initial set of challenges these approaches will encounter in the case company. The available literature is used to provide a thorough understanding of continuous delivery as a whole, so that challenges can be identified in all aspects of the practice.

RQ2: How does continuous delivery benefit the case company?

To rationalize the decision to adopt continuous delivery in a company, the actual benefits to the business have to be identified. This research question aims to identify clear objectives for what is achieved by adopting continuous delivery.

Sections of the interview aim to identify the current perceived problems of the case company related to deployment, product development, collecting feedback and guiding the development process. These problems are then compared to the benefits of the approach found from the literature.

Research Design. In this research, the units under the study are two teams within the case company, and the two software products developed by these teams. By focusing on two different products, a broader view on the application and consequences of the development approach can be gained. The first product, a marketing automation called Dialog, is used through an extensive user interface. The second product under inspection is a Master Data Management [11] solution running as an integrated background application.

The primary source of information in this research are semi-structured interviews [8], performed within the two teams under study. The interview consists of pre-defined themes focusing on current development process, current deployment process, current interaction with customers, the software products and future ways with continuous delivery. Data is also collected through the product description documents and development process documents to verifying and supplementing the interview data.

The interview is a semi-structured interview with a standardized set of open-ended questions, which allows deep exploration of studied objects [8]. The interviews are performed once with every interviewee. There are a total of 12 interviewees: 6 in each team. The interviewees in the first team consist of 5 software designers and one team leader. In the second team, the interviewees consist of 3 software designers, a quality assurance engineer, a manager for commercialization and a team leader. Leading questions are avoided on purpose, and different probing techniques such as "What?"-questions are used. The interviews are performed in the native language of the interviewee if possible, otherwise in English, and are recorded in audio format. The audio files are then transcribed into text.

The data analysis is based on template analysis, which is a way of thematically analysing qualitative data [7]. The initial template was first formed by exploring the qualitative data for two themes: development process and deployment of software. Through multiple iterations of the data, multiple subthemes were then added to the two existing themes by further coding the data. Attention was paid to different roles of the interviewees.

4   Results

This section is structured according to the research questions. The challenges regarding continuous delivery are analyzed in three areas: technical, procedural and customer. Technical aspect includes the environmental challenges, configural challenges and other challenges related to the software product and its usage. Procedural aspect includes the challenges regarding the software development process. Customer aspect consists of the customer interaction process and customer commitment.

4.1   Technical Challenges

The technical challenges for continuous delivery are derived from the interviews. A part of the interview focuses on the current deployment process and customer interaction of the case company. The current deployment process, customer interaction and challenges related to them are then used as a basis for analysing challenges that influence continuous delivery.

Table 1. Technical challenges in continuous delivery

Specific problem
Downtime is critical for certain customers
Automated testing has to be built on top of a matured software product
Software is often integrated to multiple third party applications
Software is often accompanied by multiple external components
There exists multiple different configurations due to having multiple customers with different specifications
Transferring the software product to diverse customer-owned environments requires different deployment configurations

Downtime of the case company's products can be fatal. According to the Dialog product owner, downtime causes end-users being unable to perform their job. Downtime can also interrupt ongoing customer tasks, possibly losing critical data in the progress. Currently the deployment time for both projects is negotiated with the customer to prevent these cases, and the version deployments are done when the system can be closed for a short period of time.

The developers perceive automated testing and test environments to be the largest technical task. The developers state that building a sufficient test automation is a very laborious process especially due to the maturity of the software, and are concerned with the maintainability of the test suite. The management is not sure what to test with automatic acceptance testing to validate a version.

Both of the case company's software products are integrated to various third party applications and APIs. Changes to the interfaces communicating with these applications must be planned and discussed in advance. Based on the interview results, automatically updating the integrations requires an unduly amount of work considering the results.

It is also common for B2B applications to have external components that have to be configured when the software is installed or the APIs to these components changed. The configurations for these external components either have to be manually updated, or automated as well. One of the main differences between B2B and B2C domains is the production environment. Both of the case company's products are used in multiple different customer environments. This introduces a problem of managing different configurations per customer environment and software instance.

4.2   Procedural Challenges

The procedural challenges are analyzed based on the development process documentations of the company and the interviews. In the interviews, a section is dedicated to the current development process of the case company. The development process and its challenges are then used to analyse and identify challenges that influence continuous delivery.

Table 2. Procedural challenges in continuous delivery

Specific problem
User acceptance testing environment is a requisite for production release
The development process drifts towards small feature branches from long-lived feature branches
Triggering the compilation and deployment of a modular project to maintain integrity is hard
The software has to be deployed to multiple customers
Versioning is affected by having different customer profiles of the product
Responsibility of deploying moves towards developers
Management and sales loses track of versions

The basic deployment pipeline in the case company first includes a deploy to a user acceptance testing server, which is then tested manually by either the team or the customer. Only after the version has been acceptance tested and validated to work properly, can the production version be released. Continuous deployment to production is seen very risky due to the applications playing a major role in running the customers business.

Both of the case company's products are developed with a branching model, where feature branches are first thoroughly developed and then integrated to the master branch. With continuous delivery the long-lived feature branches should be changed to short-lived and relatively small feature branches to allow exposing new functionality faster to the customers, and receive feedback faster. While the small feature branches might be common for companies with a relatively new software products, companies that have been developing products for a long time might be more devoted to the practice of long-lived feature branches.

The software applications in B2B often are large and modular applications, as is the case in the case company. The point when a deployment is triggered has to be designed to maintain the integrity of the application. As the deployment process is currently manually triggered by first releasing a version, a suitable time can be chosen each time. When a production deployment is triggered in continuous delivery, each module has to be in the correct state in order to produce a coherent version.

Both of the case company's products are used by multiple customers, each having their own environments. As the deployments are currently done manually, the customers receiving each deployment can be manually chosen.However, with a continuous delivery process whenever a feature or a new release is ready to be delivered, it can either be deployed to a single customer or to every customer.

Multiple customer environments affects versioning of the software product. In the case company, each customer has a unique configuration of the product, with possibly different versions of certain components. According to Jan Bosch, in an Innovation Experiment System environment only a single version exists: the currently deployed one. Other versions are retired and play no role [3]. However, with multiple environments, multiple different versions of the software are necessary at least in the early phase.

Continuous delivery also drifts response towards the developer, and the developers decide what is ready to be released. Currently in the case company the product owners and team leaders are responsible for negotiating the deployment date with the customer, and they also inform the developers that a new version is required. If the developer can single-handedly deploy a feature, the management can quickly lose track on the features available to customers. This also requires the developers to deeply understand the details of the version control system and automated testing.

Due to increased developer responsibility and varying interval of version updates continuous delivery causes, a team leader expresses concern that the delivery process complicates tracking when deployments are performed, and when features are finished. This also concerns other parties working in the customer interface, such as sales.

4.3   Customer Challenges

The customer challenges are analyzed based on two sections of the interview: customer interaction and the deployment process.

Table 3. Customer challenges in continuous delivery

Specific problem
Some customers are reluctant towards new versions
Customers are trained to use a certain version, and modifications confuse the users
Changelogs are especially important, since as versions are released faster the customers become less aware on what has changed
Pilot customer is required for developing the continuous delivery process
Acceptance testing is performed by both the company and the customers, and requires a lot of resources from the customers
Production deployment schedule has to be negotiated with the customer
Ongoing critical tasks by users cannot be interrupted by downtime

Some customers of the case company are reluctant towards new releases. One of the reasons for this reluctancy is that new releases occasionally contain new bugs. In the case company, customers have been trained to perform certain tasks with a certain user interface. The customer might perform these tasks daily, once every two weeks or even less frequently. If the UI changes often, the customers feel lost and initially take more time to perform the tasks. This causes frustration in the users, and visible changes generally increases the reluctancy customers have towards new versions, unless the changes are significantly improving the user experience.

> "The user interface should be easy to use. Now it's relatively hard to learn. If customers have just learned to perform a task, and we change the UI, the feedback is terrible."
>
> Product owner

Listing the changed features in changelog entries is especially important when releases are made more often. While the changes become smaller the faster versions are released, customers become less aware of when the version will be updated and when features have changed. Currently the version deployments are negotiated with the customers, and when the deployments are made more often, discussions regarding version releases may be reduced or even ceased.

A way to identify the best practices in continuous delivery is to develop the continuous delivery process with a pilot customer. Pilot customer is a company willing to help the company to quickly learn what works and what needs to be improved. The interviewees expressed a desire to first test the continuous delivery process with a single customer that is willing to receive updates in a continuous manner, since the engagement model inevitably differs from the current model.

The acceptance testing is performed in varying ways. Some customers require to perform manual acceptance testing before the product can be deployed into production. Other customers trust the developers to perform the acceptance testing. The technical implementation therefore should make it possible to continuously deploy versions to the user acceptance testing environment, and by the push of a button to the production environment. However, if the versions are deployed to user acceptance testing environment very often, customers might feel encumbered by the amount of required testing. The customers also have to be informed whenever a new version is available to the user acceptance testing environment. Customers might be using the software when a new version is deployed, and the deployment process shouldn't interfere with ongoing usage.

4.4   Benefits of Continuous Delivery

A major problem found in the interviews is that currently the reliability towards new versions is low. The low reliability both increases customers reluctancy towards version updates, and increases the amount of user acceptance testing that is performed after version release. Versions are occasionally forgotten from the UAT phase due to the lack of comprehensive automated testing and the broad scale of features in both software products. These features can then remain broken or contain bugs when the users start using the new version. This is fundamentally caused by the lack of quality assurance before the release. Adopting a test automation solves this issue, as long as tests are written for every feature.

The case company has had problems with the human error factors in manual build processes. Essentially, every each deployment is a new error-prone experiment. This increases the duration required for deploying, and lessens both the reliability and confidence in builds. The human error factor is increased by lacking documentation and parts of the deployment being memorized by developers. With continuous delivery, only a handful of developers might have knowledge of the entire build deployment configuration, but everyone is able to trigger the deployment process.

The management considers improving the deployment process to be one of the most important improvements. According to the findings, continuous delivery mainly increases the speed, quality, and capacity of the development. Speed and capacity are ensured by automated deployment, while quality is increased by the automated testing and faster feedback. Smaller problems can be quickly fixed without spending unnecessary time on manually deploying a new version to the customer, and bigger changes only take as long as the implementation requires. After the initial investment, the practice will eventually allow the company to spend less money on management and operations, because unnecessary repetitive work and bugs caused by manual building can be eliminated.

5   Discussion

The results suggest that the challenges faced in continuous delivery in the B2B context are multidimensional, and related to the technical, procedural and customer aspects. The major difference a company operating in the B2B domain faces in the transition as compared to the B2C domain is that there are plenty of customers with unique properties, whose business relies on the software. The primary issues causing these challenges are the diverse customer owned environments and the importance of the software product for the customer.

Figure 1 visualizes the challenges the case company faces in transition towards continuous delivery. Multiple challenges are related to two or more aspects, and the problems affecting all aspects can be seen as the core challenges. Acceptance testing is related to all aspects, since customers want to perform acceptance testing with new versions, automated acceptance testing has to be implemented and the user acceptance testing is required before a production release can be made. Another challenge related to all aspects is the diversity of customer environments. It affects the technical implementation, as software has to be transferred to diverse environments. The procedural challenge is that the software has to be deployed to multiple customers, and it has to be decided whether each version is always released to every customer.

The issues into which the benefits are mapped were found by researching the current deployment process and challenges faced in the development process. An unexpectedly large part of the major issues stated by the interviewees are related to deploying the software, and it was identified as one of the major challenges in the current product development. The benefits found from continuous delivery, which were sought from existing literature [2,4,5], matched the challenges very well.

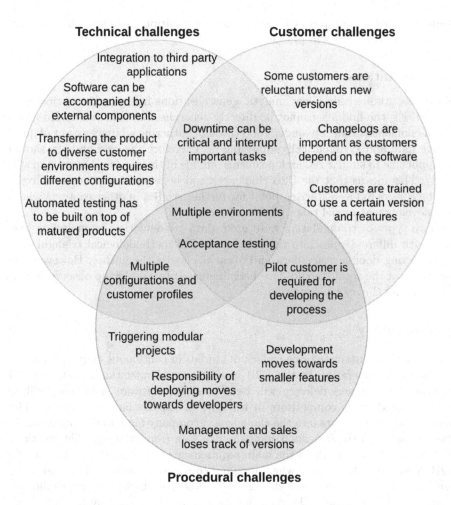

Fig. 1. Case company's challenges in continuous delivery

The study also suggests that continuous delivery corresponds to many of the case company's primary needs. The issues related to the deployment process are considered very important by both of the teams. The issues include low reliability of new versions, human error factors when performing version releases and deployments, and long feedback cycles. Additionally, a very large part of the case company's resources are spent on both deploying and testing new versions. One of the main benefits of continuous delivery is that the software is kept in a state where it is always ready for deployment [4], and that no manual work from the company is required to produce a new version.

The findings are in align with and could be considered as extending some of the theoretical contributions by Olsson et al. [1], who researched the transition towards continuous delivery. Identifying that transitioning towards continuous delivery requires a company to address issues in multiple aspects of the company also benefits companies in practice.

5.1 Limitations

Since case studies only allow analytic generalisations instead of statistical generalisations, the findings cannot be directly generalised to other cases. However, the phenomena was deeply understood through gathering a large amount of qualitative data and systematically analysing it. Therefore the core findings should be applicable to similar research problems outside of the empirical context of this study. This means that the B2B challenges and benefits of continuous delivery can be considered as a starting point for further studies in other contexts where this development model takes place.

Two types of triangulation were used: data triangulation by including persons with different roles into the interviews, and methodological triangulation by collecting documentary data and observations by the author. However, the reliability of the results could have been increased by employing observer triangulation and theory triangulation.

6 Summary

This study was motivated due to lack of studies in continuous delivery focusing on companies operating in the B2B environment. Understanding the central aspects of continuous delivery will be a must for software companies willing to stay ahead of its competitors in the current rapidly moving industry. The findings provide insights into the challenges a company faces in the transition in this domain, and the benefits a company can gain from adopting this practice.

This study has identified the main requirements a company operating in the B2B domain has to address when applying continuous delivery. The challenges can be divided into technical challenges, procedural challenges and challenges related to the customer. These challenges are mostly caused by having multiple customers with diverse environments and unique properties, whose business depends on the software product. While continuously deploying versions to a user acceptance testing environment requires a company to address multiple challenges, continuously deploying to production is even more difficult, since some customers want to perform manual acceptance testing before production releases can be made.

The benefits of continuous delivery matched to many business problems found in the case company, and a company operating in similar domain with similar products can use them as a basis when considering applying this practice. By utilizing continuous delivery, the case company can solve problems such as long feedback cycles, low reliability in new versions, human error factors and high amount of resources required for deploying and testing new releases.

Acknowledgments. We wish to thank the participants of the study for their time and contributions and the reviewers for their valuable comments. We also thank the

Finnish technology agency, Tekes, for funding the Cloud Software Factory project, and the Need for Speed program, under which the proposed study was undertaken. This paper is based on thesis work [13] completed at the University of Helsinki.

References

1. Olsson, H.H., Alahyari, H., Bosch, J.: Climbing the "stairway to heaven"-a multiple-case study exploring barriers in the transition from agile development towards continuous deployment of software. In: 2012 38th EUROMICRO Conference on Software Engineering and Advanced Applications (SEAA), pp. 392–399. IEEE, September 2012

2. Neely, S., Stolt, S.: Continuous delivery? easy! just change everything (well, maybe it is not that easy). In: Agile Conference (AGILE), pp. 121–128. IEEE, August 2013

3. Bosch, J.: Building products as innovation experiment systems. In: Cusumano, M.A., Iyer, B., Venkatraman, N. (eds.) ICSOB 2012. LNBIP, vol. 114, pp. 27–39. Springer, Heidelberg (2012)

4. Humble, J., Farley, D.: Continuous delivery: reliable software releases through build, test, and deployment automation. Pearson Education (2010)

5. Humble, J., Read, C., North, D.: The deployment production line. In: Agile Conference, p. 6. IEEE, July 2006

6. Fowler, M.: ContinuousDelivery (January 2015). http://martinfowler.com/bliki/ContinuousDelivery.html

7. King, N.: Template analysis. In: Qualitative Methods and Analysis in Organizational Research: A Practical Guide, pp. 118–134. Sage Publications Ltd (1998)

8. Runeson, P., Hst, M.: Guidelines for conducting and reporting case study research in software engineering. Empirical software engineering 14(2), 131–164 (2009)

9. Dzamashvili Fogelstrm, N., Gorschek, T., Svahnberg, M., Olsson, P.: The impact of agile principles on marketdriven software product development. Journal of Software Maintenance and Evolution: Research and Practice 22(1), 53–80 (2010)

10. Cockburn, A.: Agile software development. Cockburn* Highsmith Series Editor (2000)

11. Loshin, D.: Master data management. Morgan Kaufmann (2010)

12. Duvall, P. M., Matyas, S., Glover, A.: Continuous integration: improving software quality and reducing risk. Pearson Education (2007)

13. Rissanen, O., Münch, J., Männistö, T.: Extending the Development Process Towards Continuous Delivery and Continuous Experimentation in the B2B Domain: A Case Study. Master's Thesis. University of Helsinki (2015)

DevOps: A Definition and Perceived Adoption Impediments

Jens Smeds[(✉)], Kristian Nybom[(✉)], and Ivan Porres[(✉)]

Åbo Akademi University, Joukahaisenkatu 3-5 A, 20520, Turku, Finland
{jens.smeds,kristian.nybom,ivan.porres}@abo.fi

Abstract. As the interest in DevOps continues to grow, there is an increasing need for software organizations to understand how to adopt it successfully. This study has as objective to clarify the concept and provide insight into existing challenges of adopting DevOps. First, the existing literature is reviewed. A definition of DevOps is then formed based on the literature by breaking down the concept into its defining characteristics. We interview 13 subjects in a software company adopting DevOps and, finally, we present 11 impediments for the company's DevOps adoption that were identified based on the interviews.

1 Introduction

DevOps has become a vividly discussed phenomenon within software engineering during the recent years. DevOps addresses the challenge of what is often described as a gap between development and operations personnel. Reports (e.g. [18,19]) bring positive expectations of DevOps and organizations are becoming increasingly interested in the phenomenon and how to tap the potential benefits of it. Still, the term itself is surrounded by ambiguity. While the purpose is clear, "bridging the gap between development and operations" [28], there are still many interpretations of what DevOps actually means.

Adopting DevOps may not be an easy or straightforward task since it may require that an organization introduces process, personnel and technological changes and innovations. As in any software process improvement initiative, the path to a successful DevOps adoption is unique to each organization. Still, it is possible to learn from challenges experienced during DevOps adoptions in order to plan future DevOps adoption initiatives.

In this article, we tackle these two challenges as follows. We provide a definition of DevOps that can be used as a list of characteristics that an organization needs to adopt or exhibit in order to work according to the DevOps thinking. We continue by providing a list of possible impediments to the adoption of DevOps that can be helpful for other organizations when planning their adoption initiatives.

2 Research Questions and Study Design

The concept of DevOps has been claimed to be ambiguous and to lack a common definition [14,21]. The interest in DevOps, and how to adopt it, creates a need

© Springer International Publishing Switzerland 2015
C. Lassenius et al. (Eds.): XP 2015, LNBIP 212, pp. 166–177, 2015.
DOI: 10.1007/978-3-319-18612-2_14

for a clear definition of the concept. As the concept of DevOps is relatively new, not many studies on the challenges that organizations face when adopting DevOps exist yet. To clarify what adopting DevOps means and to provide some insight into what people perceive as impediments at the initial stage of adopting DevOps, this study addresses the following research questions:

RQ1: What are the main defining characteristics of DevOps?
RQ2: What are the perceived impediments to DevOps adoption?

To answer RQ1 we conducted a literature review, which presents what has been published about DevOps and how the term is used and defined. Based on the existing literature, we break down DevOps into a set of defining characteristics. As not much literature addressing RQ2 exists, we conducted an empirical study of our own. The social and organizational aspects of DevOps make qualitative interviews the preferred data collection method. Semi-structured interviews offer rich enough data without making the data handling too cumbersome. Therefore, we conducted semi-structured interviews for answering RQ2.

2.1 Threats to Validity

The main threat to the validity of our study of RQ1 is that the literature regarding DevOps is still scarce. A significant part of the available information about DevOps comes from blogs and other informal publication channels. To avoid the risk of missing important sources, we thus included publications that apparently are not peer reviewed but that we consider being of high enough quality or that have already been cited by peer reviewed publications. While this introduces a subjective quality assessment step that has the risk of being biased, it gives us the possibility to provide a definition of DevOps according to how the term is currently being used by multiple authors.

The validity of our study of RQ2 is threatened by limiting our study to one company. Including several companies could result in a more diverse list of impediments. Moreover, including only one company prevents us from studying the frequency of these impediments and from concluding how common they are. However, we consider our results valid and valuable to other organizations since we do not claim that the provided list of impediments is complete and we encourage each organization to assess how likely these impediments can become an actual problem in the adoption of DevOps in their particular case.

2.2 Conducting the Literature Review

A literature review was conducted to identify the main defining characteristics of DevOps. The following sources were used: ACM Digital Library, DBLP, EBSCO Academic Search Premier, Google Scholar, IEEE Explore, Springer Link and Web of Science. As a quality precaution, blog posts were deliberately not considered, although they do contain a significant amount of information related to DevOps. The word 'DevOps' was used as the search string. To filter out irrelevant results, the Springer Link search was limited to only articles and books, and the Google Scholar search was limited to work containing the search string in the title. The results were further filtered to only include English texts. Our inclusion criterion was that included literature must both refer to DevOps and provide a description of what DevOps is. Duplicates were excluded so that only the most comprehensive version of the text was included.

The search was performed on October 27, 2014 and resulted in 126 results. After excluding the duplicates, 99 unique results remained. The inclusion was then judged based on personal perception. Firstly, the decision was based on the abstract if one was available. If needed, the introduction and all sections containing the term 'DevOps' were read. We finally selected 27 publications.

The literature was categorized into five topic areas, as shown in Table 1. The first category contains only one article, a *literature review* of DevOps. *DevOps guidelines*, consists of five works that cover how to do DevOps. The third category, *DevOps success story*, consists of three studies describing how DevOps has been a success in certain organizations. The fourth category, *explaining DevOps*, consists of literature that discusses, focuses on describing, or explores new aspects of DevOps. It is the most popular category and comprises 11 publications. The last category, *specific DevOps practice(s)*, consists of 7 publications that present some specific technologies or practices that support DevOps. While a part of the literature discusses certain issues when adopting DevOps, perceived issues when adopting DevOps have not yet been the main subject of any study.

2.3 Conducting the Interviews

The selected organization is an international IT company with a long history and over 1000 employees. This study was carried out in a business unit that develops and operates in the cloud services area. At the time we conducted the interviews, their DevOps adoption process was at an initial stage. Motivations for the adoption were to make software deployments faster and more frequent and to share knowledge between development and operations.

Table 1. Publications selected in the literature review

Topic	n Author and Year
Literature review	1 Erich et al. [9]
DevOps guidelines	5 Hüttermann [14], Sacks [22], Swartout [24], Walls [26], Harvey [11]
DevOps success story	3 Cukier [5], Feitelson et al. [10], Yuhong et al. [30]
Explaining DevOps	11 DeGrandis [7], Humble and Molesky [13], Limoncelli and Hughes [15], Loukides [16], Bang et al. [2], Roche [21], Davis [6], Economou et al. [8], Preimesberger [17], Taft [25], Wettinger et al. [28]
Specific practice(s)	7 Azoff [1], Hosono and Shimomura [12], Spinellis [23], Wettinger [27], Ragan [20], Borgenholt et al. [3], Bruneo et al. [4]

A total of 13 experienced employees were selected by the company so they would represent different work areas, e.g. development, quality assurance, operations, and management. Their familiarity with DevOps prior to the interviews varied from understanding the basics of the concept to having previous professional experience of successfully adopting DevOps.

The interviews were conducted at the end of May 2014. Before the interviews, the participants were informed about the study, that the interviews will be recorded and that the answers will be handled anonymously. The interviews lasted roughly 45 minutes on average. An interview guide containing a broad field of questions was used. Many of the questions were open and the interview guide was not strictly followed. The recordings of the interviews were transcribed. Based on the transcriptions, the researchers individually identified what was perceived as challenges for adopting DevOps. The individual lists were then compared, discussed and merged into our final list of impediments.

3   What Is DevOps?

The retrieved DevOps literature clearly shows that providing a complete and clear definition of the term is a challenge. The definitions provided in the literature are usually vague or limited to a certain context.

What is DevOps? by [16] is an example of how difficult it is to define DevOps. Loukides tries to clarify the concept of DevOps by explaining the past and current nature of the work of IT operations. He describes how the work of IT operations has changed over the years and discusses challenges that IT operations face today. However, no final definition of DevOps is provided.

Roche [21] notes that, among blog posts, there are two stances on what DevOps means. Some bloggers support the notion of DevOps being a specific job position that requires both software development and IT operations skills. The other, opposing, stance is that DevOps cannot be summarized into a job description and that it is not a specific role. When browsing the current literature on DevOps, the second stance seems to be dominating. Hüttermann [14] is among those who strongly support the view of DevOps being more than a new job title and that you cannot hire a "DevOp". Hütterman also claims that the same applies not only on an individual scale, but also on an organizational scale: DevOps cannot be a department or a unit in the organizational structure.

Before listing what DevOps is not, Hütterman stresses the difficulty is to define DevOps and mentions that the term is multifaceted. He mentions four key aspects of DevOps described in a blog post by Willis [29]: *culture, automation, measurement* and *sharing*. Willis' blog post is also referred to in other studies (e.g. [2,13]) that use these four aspects as the defining characteristics of DevOps. Hütterman also states that "DevOps describes practices that streamline the software delivery process, emphasizing the learning by streaming feedback from production to development and improving the cycle time" [14]. This definition is, however, incomplete, since cultural aspects of DevOps are not mentioned, and it does not describe the actual DevOps practices.

DeGrandis [7] implies that adopting DevOps is an organizational revolution: "The 'revolution in the making' is a shift from a focus on separate departments working independently to an organization-wide collaboration – a 'systems thinking' approach." However, DevOps as such cannot be defined as a revolution, in the sense of a disruptive change, since it is a way of working. Adopting DevOps may still require a disruptive change in an organization.

Walls [26] looks at DevOps from a cultural perspective and states that DevOps is a "cultural movement combined with a number of software related practices that enable rapid development." Later in the book, Walls [26] describes the DevOps culture with the following four "key cultural characteristics": *open communication, incentive and responsibility alignment, respect*, and *trust*. He continues by describing how to reach the so-called DevOps culture. According to him, the term was introduced to define a desired culture that organizations can aim for. He presumes that the culture of an organization can be changed towards a target culture intentionally by following a set of steps. Walls [26] also notes that only the term itself is new, DevOps has been around before the term existed. The fact that only the term itself is new could be a reason for the different interpretations and vague definitions.

In our opinion, most of the existing literature focuses on the novel or differentiating aspects of DevOps. Cultural aspects of DevOps seem of key importance, but they cannot be defining aspects by themselves, since concepts such as *open communication, respect*, and *trust* can be applied to any kind of organization with people of different background or skills meet. Because of this, we feel that a definition of DevOps should not only be based on its cultural aspects but it should also include the engineering practices influenced by these cultural aspects.

3.1 DevOps Capabilities and Enablers

We define DevOps as a set of *engineering process capabilities* supported by certain cultural and technological *enablers*. Capabilities define processes that an organization should be able to carry out, while the enablers allow a fluent, flexible, and efficient way of working. Adopting DevOps in an organization requires an integration of the three core aspects of DevOps listed in Table 2.

The DevOps *capabilities* include the basic activities in software and service engineering: planning, development, testing, and deployment. These activities should be carried out continuously using feedback from the other activities.

In this context, the term *continuously* means in small increments and without delay. For example, the continuous deployment capability allows an organization to deploy new features in a service as soon as they have been integrated and tested successfully. For doing this efficiently, an organization should have automated its testing and deployment tool chain and streamlined the collaboration between the engineers creating new software releases and those deploying them.

According to DevOps, feedback is understood as using data collected from operating the service as input in the planning and development. The feedback data contains data on performance of the service infrastructure, and data on how and when the users interact with the service. This data collection is covered

Table 2. DevOps Capabilities and Enablers

Capabilities	Continuous planning Collaborative and continuous development Continuous integration and testing Continuous release and deployment Continuous infrastructure monitoring and optimization Continuous user behavior monitoring and feedback Service failure recovery without delay
Cultural Enablers	Shared goals, definition of success, incentives Shared ways of working, responsibility, collective ownership Shared values, respect and trust Constant, effortless communication Continuous experimentation and learning
Technological Enablers	Build automation Test automation Deployment automation Monitoring automation Recovery automation Infrastructure automation Configuration management for code and infrastructure

by the two capabilities of infrastructure monitoring and user behavior monitoring, which traditionally might not be considered within software development. These two capabilities provide feedback loops for the planning and development processes to improve and optimize the service. These feedback loops allow for true experimentation within the engineering process.

Finally, a DevOps organization should have the capability to recover from service failures without delay. Service failures can be caused by the service infrastructure or by software defects. The organization should have the necessary monitoring infrastructure to detect these failures immediately and there should be contingency plans for reacting to the failures.

The *cultural enablers* list traits that DevOps teams should exhibit. These behaviors will contribute to the DevOps-*capabilities* in a positive way. The *cultural enablers* mainly emphasize the need for extensive collaboration, a supportive working environment, a climate for learning, and awareness of the common goals among all teams and engineers. Accordingly, employees should work as a team of teams on the different work items while sharing responsibilities, communicating effortlessly, and being aware of both the entire software development system and the common goal of all teams. Blaming others for failures, showing disrespect towards fellow employees, and considering only personal work performance are examples of behaviors that contribute negatively to the DevOps model. Innovation is promoted by allowing both teams and individuals to experiment and learn from their successes and accept failures as a learning experience.

The *technological enablers* stress the need for automating tasks. As discussed in [19], automation does not only decrease the amount of errors in the system, but shifts the focus of the employees from manual error-prone repetitive tasks to creative and productive tasks. Automation additionally facilitates continuous delivery, especially when having automated infrastructure and configuration management, where custom programs or scripts configure and monitor the service infrastructure. Automation supports the DevOps-*capabilities* by making the software and service development process more streamlined and stable while allowing employees to be innovative and productive.

When comparing the three DevOps aspects, the *capabilities* can be seen as the main DevOps aspects. However, DevOps will only work efficiently when these capabilities are supported by the *cultural* and *technological enablers*. Establishing the *technological enablers* within an organization is a matter of tool choice, tool configuration, and tool design. Establishing the *cultural enablers* is a slow process, partially because people need time to adjust to changes, and partially because time and resources are needed for improvement work [19].

4   Impediments Hindering DevOps Adoption

Organizations adopting DevOps should enact the previously described capabilities in their engineering units. This is achieved by ensuring that the named cultural and technological enablers are in place. Adopting DevOps may not be trivial for large organizations with complex service requirements. Therefore, we have studied impediments, which can complicate the adoption of DevOps from the perspective of capabilities, cultural enablers, and technological enablers. As the list of impediments is based on an interview corpus collected at a single organization, it cannot be considered to be complete nor to apply to all types of organizations. Still, we believe that a study of the impediments found in an actual organization may help other organizations to plan a future adoption of DevOps. We emphasize that the impediments listed below are our analysis of concerns *as perceived by the employees*. We also emphasize that while some of the issues might not be real in the organization, if perceived as problematic, they will still negatively affect the adoption of DevOps.

4.1   Impediments Affecting Capabilities.

Unclear definition and Goals of Adopting DevOps As previously discussed, there is a need for a clear definition of DevOps. Ambiguity can lead to unclear goals and confusion in the direction of the DevOps adoption. If people have different understandings of what DevOps means, the understandings of the goals and of the actions needed to achieve these goals might also differ. Having a common understanding of the goals and agreeing on how to achieve the goals was mentioned during the interviews as essential contributors for a successful adaption of DevOps.

Organizational Structure. Adopting DevOps can be affected, both negatively and positively, by an organization's structure. The way an organization is structured was mentioned, for example when discussing communication, common goals and practices, decision making, and systems thinking within the organization. These topics are closely related to several of the *capabilities* and the *cultural enablers*.

Customers May Not Want DevOps. DevOps may not be suitable for all customers. Customers might, for example, require processes and practices including long testing periods or strict deployment procedures. Such processes and practices might in turn not be compatible with the processes and practices of DevOps. DevOps must be implemented in a manner that is compatible with the customers' processes and practices.

4.2 Impediments Affecting Cultural Enablers

Geographical Distribution. Geographical distribution of operations and development work was mentioned during the interviews. Geographical distribution can create challenges, for example, as communication cannot be done in person and as reaching people might be difficult due to different time zones. Social relationships and the environment are fundamental aspects of organizational culture. The cultural enablers, including not only communication but all other aspects as well, can thus be hindered by geographical distribution. The geographical distribution might also pose other, e.g. process related, challenges.

Buzzword Tiredness. When asking about how familiar DevOps is as a concept, or how to define it, a majority of the respondents mentioned the ambiguity of the term or something else regarding how the term is used. The lack of trust in DevOps as a concept was notable in certain answers. Many perceived it as a buzzword. As one person expressed it, what will be done in practice might actually not be that different from what was done before it was called DevOps. This suggests that even if people perceive at least a part of the aspects of DevOps as positive, the perception of DevOps as a concept is not always positive. A negative perception of DevOps might lead to a mindset of resisting change.

DevOps is More Work for Developers. Developers becoming overburdened by extra responsibilities related to operations was one of the most prominent concerns expressed in the interviews. The reason behind this fear was a perception that the workload of the developers might increase as the company adopts DevOps. Thus, the effort dedicated to pure development work would decrease, unless development resources are added. Another perceived concern was that added responsibilities related to operations would be intrusive and disrupt the development work, i.e. the added responsibilities might affect the capacity to focus and work productively. The concern of being overburdened and not as efficient due to more work can result in unwillingness to get involved, for example, in new collaborations and collective ownership. The concern might thus create a mindset that can act primarily as an impediment to the *cultural enablers*.

DevOps Requires Both Dev and ops skills and knowledge. Some answers in the interviews implies a concern of DevOps requiring development to have in-depth knowledge and skills of operations and vice versa. It was argued that people are not able to handle efficiently both development and operations as the areas differ so much in terms of skills and knowledge. Regarding what kind of new competence is needed on the development side, the examples include skills and knowledge regarding deployment of the different production environments. For the operations side, it was mentioned, for example, that the programming competence, not only limited to writing code, but also including knowledge of the development process, code reviewing etc., should be improved. The opinion that in-depth knowledge of both areas is needed and that it is better to focus on a narrower area of expertise can create a mindset where people are not open for the cultural traits of sharing, communicating, and collaborating.

Lack of interest in the "other side". The interviews also revealed concerns regarding the developers interest in operations work and vice versa. It was questioned whether the developers care about the operations work and vice versa. Especially the cultural aspects of DevOps rely on some level of interest in what other teams do. The reason behind this feeling of lacking interest in the other type of work was also discussed. It was explained that experts, by their own nature, are people who are interested only in their own area. It was also speculated if DevOps might be hindered by people feeling that doing DevOps means that you do not fully belong to a group, neither development, nor operations.

4.3   Impediments Affecting Technological Enablers

Monolithic architecture. The architecture of the system is closely coupled with how the system is developed, tested, and deployed for use. A monolithic architecture can be a bottleneck to rapid continuous build, test, and deployment. Transforming the architecture or improving the capability of the continuous deployment system is needed to overcome this impediment. It was mentioned during the interviews that a more modularized architecture allows for upgrading smaller parts of the system independently and, for example, shorter wait times for build, test, and deployment results. As the interviews suggest, overcoming this impediment can be particularly challenging if the value of such technical change is not evident. Without clear value in architectural improvements, these are easily postponed, for example, in favor of work on new software features.

Development and testing environments do not reflect production environments. Some interviewees perceived differences between development, testing, and production environments as a possible impediment. Difficulty to simulate production environments in testing environments create a risk that software is not properly validated before it is deployed to production. Differences between development, testing, and production environments can be problematic not only for continuous delivery and deployment, but also for sharing responsibilities. It was for example mentioned that if the development and test environments do not correspond to production, developers, who are accustomed to use the development and test environments, might face difficulty when in contact with production environments. This is mainly a potential impediment for *technological enablers*. However, as the differences also could complicate collaboration and having shared ways of working, this is also an impediment for the *capabilities* and *cultural enablers*.

Multiple production environments. Based on the perception of some of the interviewed people, multiple production environments and differences between them could be a possible impediment for continuous delivery. Different needs of environments cause complexity. Automating and having common tools and processes becomes challenging. Even different access rights can cause issues. In the interviews, it was for example stated that when fixing production problems, it is essential to have free enough access. The main perceived difficulties that multiple production environments cause are related to deployments and configurations. This is thus mainly an impediment for *technological enablers*. It was however noted that issues grounded in technical complexity might also make people feel limited in an unfair way, which in turn affect their mindset.

5 Conclusions

Despite the increased popularity of DevOps, what adopting DevOps means is still unclear. This article aims to clarify the concept and to provide some insight into what is perceived as impediments in the early stages of adopting DevOps.

To clarify the concept, the existing literature was first reviewed. Based on the existing literature, the concept of DevOps was defined by a set of defining characteristics. The characteristics were divided into three groups, *capabilities*, *cultural enablers*, and *technological enablers*. The second goal was to provide insight into what people perceive as impediments in the early stages of adopting DevOps, and 13 employees of a software company were interviewed. Based on the interviews, 11 potential impediments for adopting DevOps were identified.

We conclude that DevOps is a multifaceted concept and its definition still requires attention of the research community. We further conclude that adopting DevOps is not perceived as trivial but it can require overcoming several impediments. Analyzing which area impediments correlate to, shows that the impediments are complex and tend to affect several parts of DevOps. This supports the notion of DevOps being a cohesive but multifaceted phenomenon.

This study only exposes perceived impediments for one company in the starting stages of adopting DevOps. To fully understand and be able to make generalizable conclusions about the impediments of adopting DevOps, further research needs to include several organizations. Moreover, further research needs to be done on the later stages of the adoption process.

Acknowledgements This work has been partially supported by the Digile Need for Speed program and funded by Tekes, the Finnish Funding Agency for Technology and Innovation.

References

[1] Azoff, M.: Devops: Advances in release management and automation. Technical report, Ovum (2011)

[2] Bang, S.K., Chung, S., Choh, Y., Dupuis, M.: A grounded theory analysis of modern web applications: knowledge, skills, and abilities for devops. In: Proc. of the 2nd Annual Conference on Research in Information Technology, RIIT 2013, pp. 61–62. ACM, New York (2013)

[3] Borgenholt, G., Begnum, K., Engelstad, P.E.: Audition: a devops-oriented service optimization and testing framework for cloud environments. Norsk informatikkonferanse (NIK) (2013, 2014)

[4] Bruneo, D., Fritz, T., Keidar-Barner, S., Leitner, P., Longo, F., Marquezan, C., Metzger, A., Pohl, K., Puliafito, A., Raz, D., et al.: Cloudwave: where adaptive cloud management meets devops. In: Proc. of the Fourth Int. Workshop on Management of Cloud Systems (MoCS 2014) (2014)

[5] Cukier, D.: Devops patterns to scale web applications using cloud services. In: Proc. of the 2013 Companion Publication for Conference on Systems, Programming, & #38; Applications: Software for Humanity, SPLASH 2013, pp. 143–152. ACM, New York (2013)

[6] Davis, M.A.: Devops. Informationweek **1384**, 6–12 (2014)

[7] DeGrandis, D.: Devops: So you say you want a revolution? Cutter IT J. **24**(8), 34–39 (2011)

[8] Economou, F., Hoblitt, J.C., Norris, P.: Your data is your dogfood: Devops in the astronomical observatory (2014). arXiv preprint http://arxiv.org/abs/1407.6463

[9] Erich, F., Amrit, C., Daneva, M.: Cooperation between information system development and operations: a literature review. In: Proc. of the 8th Int. Symp. on Empirical Software Engineering and Measurement, ESEM 2014, pp. 69:1–69:1. ACM, New York (2014)

[10] Feitelson, D.G., Frachtenberg, E., Beck, K.L.: Development and deployment at facebook. IEEE Internet Computing **17**(4), 0008–17 (2013)

[11] Harvey, N.: Devops talent: Grow it internally. Informationweek **1393**, 7–8 (2014)

[12] Hosono, S., Shimomura, Y.: Application lifecycle kit for mass customization on paas platforms. In: 2012 IEEE Eighth World Congress on Services (SERVICES), pp. 397–398. IEEE (2012)

[13] Humble, J., Molesky, J.: Why enterprises must adopt devops to enable continuous delivery. Cutter IT J. **24**(8), 6–12 (2011)

[14] Hüttermann, M.: DevOps for Developers, vol. 1. Springer (2012)

[15] Limoncelli, T.A., Hughes, D.: Lisa11 themedevops: New challenges proven values. Login **36**(4), 46–48 (2011)

[16] Loukides, M.: What is DevOps? O'Reilly Media, Inc. (2012)

[17] Preimesberger, C.: 10 things you need to know about the hot devops trend. eWeek, p. 1 (2014)

[18] Puppet Labs and IT Revolution Press. 2013 state of devops report (2013). https://puppetlabs.com/wp-content/uploads/2013/03/2013-state-of-devops-report.pdf (Accessed 28 August 2013)

[19] Puppet Labs, IT Revolution Press, and Thoughtworks. 2014 state of devops report (2014). http://puppetlabs.com/sites/default/files/2014-state-of-devops-report.pdf (Accessed 28 August 2014)

[20] Ragan, T.: 21st-century devops-an end to the 20th-century practice of writing static build and deploy scripts. Linux J., 2013(230), June 2013

[21] Roche, J.: Adopting devops practices in quality assurance. Communications of the ACM 56(11), 38–43 (2013)

[22] Sacks, M.: Pro Website Development and Operations: Streamlining DevOps for Large-scale Websites. Apress (2012)

[23] Spinellis, D.: Don't install software by hand. IEEE Software 29(4), 86–87 (2012)

[24] Swartout, P.: Continuous Delivery and DevOps: A Quickstart Guide. Packt Publishing Ltd (2012)

[25] Taft, D.K.: Debunking the top myths about devops. eWeek, p. 3 (2014)

[26] Walls, M.: Building a DevOps Culture. O'Reilly Media, Inc. (2013)

[27] Wettinger, J.: Concepts for integrating devops methodologies with model-driven cloud management based on TOSCA. Master's thesis, U. of Stuttgart (2012)

[28] Wettinger, J., Breitenbücher, U., Leymann, F.: DevOpSlang – bridging the gap between development and operations. In: Villari, M., Zimmermann, W., Lau, K.-K. (eds.) ESOCC 2014. LNCS, vol. 8745, pp. 108–122. Springer, Heidelberg (2014)

[29] Willis, J.: What devops means to me, July 2010. http://www.getchef.com/blog/2010/07/16/what-devops-means-to-me/ (Accessed 3 December 2014)

[30] Yuhong, L., Chengbo, L., Wei, L.: Integrated solution for timely delivery of customer change requests: A case study of using devops approach. Int. J. of U- & E-Service. Science & Technology 7(2), 41–50 (2014)

Scaling Kanban for Software Development in a Multisite Organization: Challenges and Potential Solutions

Nirnaya Tripathi[✉], Pilar Rodríguez,
Muhammad Ovais Ahmad, and Markku Oivo

Department of Information Processing Science,
University of Oulu, P.O.Box 3000 FI-90014, Oulu, Finland
{nirnaya.tripathi,pilar.rodriguez,
muhammad.ahmad,markku.oivo}@oulu.fi

Abstract. In software development organizations, large-scale distributed projects pose many challenges, such as hierarchical requirements, large team size, and managing workflow. Agile methods, like Scrum, seem to have limitations in addressing those issues. Kanban offers an interesting alternative in this concern by setting work-in-progress (WIP) limits to manage flow and establishing visibility of requirements using a visual signaling system. However, only few empirical studies have investigated scaling Kanban for large organizations. To address this concern, a case study was conducted in a large multisite company to identify the challenges and possible solutions in scaling Kanban. During the study, defining WIP limits, coordinating with distributed teams, and dividing features between teams were found as major challenges. Setting WIP limits by common agreement between teams and visualizing product backlogs and teams on electronic board, with teams pulling features from the board, were found as possible solutions for overcoming the mentioned challenges.

Keywords: Software engineering · Large-scale scrum · Scaling kanban · Multisite software development

1 Introduction

The competition among companies in the high technology market is fierce. To gain a competitive edge, companies have made customer satisfaction their major goal and aim at achieving this goal by introducing new products and services [1, 2]. The globalization of the software industry has influenced software companies to develop software in a multisite environment to reduce costs and increase productivity [3]. For a multisite environment, companies have established several software development organizations in numerous geographical locations [4]. Within these organizations, research and development activities occur to create new product features among development teams. To improve team performance and increase customer interaction in development activities, agile methods such as Scrum and XP have been introduced [5–7]. Scrum, which has a positive impact on single team performance [8] and small projects, has been considered for large-scale projects to gain its advantages [9]. However, scaling Scrum in an organization in a multisite environment is a challenge

© Springer International Publishing Switzerland 2015
C. Lassenius et al. (Eds.): XP 2015, LNBIP 212, pp. 178–190, 2015.
DOI: 10.1007/978-3-319-18612-2_15

[10–12]. One barrier perceived during scaling Scrum is to manage dependencies between projects and teams [13]. In addition, collaboration and communication between product owners and development teams become increasingly challenging once a project begins to expand [10]. Thus, some authors have claimed that agile methods are not enough for large-scale development [14].

More recently, Lean thinking has appeared as a means to scale agile software development [15]. Lean thinking can help to bring the flow and pull principles, which are missing in agile methods [14]. One way to incorporate Lean thinking is through the use of Kanban [16]. The application of Kanban in software development projects has been proposed by previous studies [17]. For example, Anderson (2010) suggested the scaling of Kanban in large-scale projects to facilitate positive cultural changes in the organization and address the challenges faced during large-scale projects. Kniberg demonstrated the application of Kanban at the organizational level with three development teams in a co-located environment [18]. However, empirical evidence on scaling Kanban to an organizational level with operations in a multisite environment is limited [19]. There are some empirical studies conducted on Kanban software development projects [19, 20], but just few work in a large-scale context [12, 21].

With this paper, we aim to fill the above research gap by presenting an exploratory case study of using Kanban in a multisite environment of a large company. Our research goal is to explore the challenges faced when Kanban is scaled in a multisite organization and possible solutions to these challenges. In this case study, we took two software developing organizations of the same case company as units of analysis to reach our research goal.

The remainder of this paper is structured as follows. Section 2 reviews the related work on Lean thinking and scaling Kanban. Section 3 presents the research approach and data analysis method. Section 4 provides the empirical results. We conclude the paper in Section 5, briefly describing the limitations of our study and potential for future research.

2   Background and Related Work

The concept of Lean thinking first emerged in the 1940s from Toyota's car manufacturing process in Japan [22]. The basis of Lean focuses on the concepts of creating value and eliminating waste in organizations [22]. To bring Lean thinking to an organization, five principles were proposed: *value, value stream, flow, pull, and pursuit of perfection* [22]. In the context to software organization, Lean thinking can be introduced through the use of the Kanban method [16]. In 2004, David J. Anderson [16] introduced Kanban to a software development team at Microsoft. Kanban has five core principles: *visualize workflow, limit work in progress, measure and manage flow, make process policies explicit, and use models to recognize improvement and opportunities* [16]. The motivation to use Kanban was to visualize work, limit work in progress (WIP), and identify process constraints to achieve flow and focus on a single item at a given time [19]. Various studies [18–20, 23] have reported the benefits of using Kanban in software development, for example, better visibility and understanding of the entire process, improved transparency of work and communication, better control of flow and WIP, improved team communication and coordination with other stakeholders, and increased customer satisfaction.

To tackle the issues posed by large-scale projects, Anderson (2010) suggested the scaling of Kanban at the organizational level [16]. Few studies [18, 21] and a practitioner blog [24] also discussed the concept of large-scale Kanban. Kniberg in his book "Lean from the Trenches," [18] discussed scaling Kanban in a large-scale organization that had three development teams working in a collocated environment. Vallet describes of using explicit process policies and electronic board in distributed context [21]. However, although many companies are developing software products in multiple sites with distributed teams around the globe, the empirical evidence on scaling Kanban in large organizations with operate in multisite software development environments is very limited [19]. Therefore, this study aims to fill the above research gap by empirically exploring the challenges in scaling of Kanban in multisite large organizations, along with possible solutions.

3   Research Methodology

To address the research gap and reach our research goal, we define the following two exploratory descriptive research questions (RQ) [25].

RQ1: *What are the challenges in scaling Kanban in a multisite organization for software development?*

RQ2: *What are the possible solutions to these challenges when scaling Kanban in a multisite organization for software development?*

Therefore we focus on the challenges in the scaling phase of Kanban and recognize that the challenges may be different in organizations that have long experience in the use of Kanban in large multisite organizations. To attain valid answers for the two RQ's, we took a constructivist approach by focusing on how experts make sense of scaling Kanban rather than verifying theories. According to constructivist principles, we prefer methods that collect rich qualitative data on human activities [25]. As our study aims to explore and improve software development processes which usually involve human involvement, the constructivist approach is an appropriate standpoint for this study. Due to the nature of our research questions and constructivism as our standpoint, we chose an exploratory case study method in order to collect empirical evidence [26].

3.1   Case Study Design

Our context is multisite software development, and our research goal is to find challenges in scaling Kanban at multisite organizations while seeking possible solutions for those challenges. Therefore, we used embedded, single-case study where we took two software development organizations from the same company as two unit of analysis to reach our research goal [26, 27]. The case company under study offers products and services in the telecommunications sector. Most of the product development projects contain software development in a distributed context.

Unit of Analysis 1 (Organization A): The organization selected for the first unit was situated on site A, located in Northern Europe. It was a fairly large unit with around 50 people, containing five development teams and one area product owner. The product management team of the case company, situated at other site, was giving product area features to Organization A for development. For some features, teams within Organization A needed to coordinate with team of another organization (situated at Site C located in Western Europe) to develop features of the same product. Organization A was using Kanban at a team level for six months. After six months, Organization A is now scaling Kanban in their entire organization through training and coaching. Therefore, the first unit is appropriate for providing information on RQ1.

Unit of Analysis 2 (Organization B): Organization B is using Kanban at the organizational level for more than six months. Therefore, the Organization B was selected to understand how they scaled Kanban at the organizational level and provides possible solutions for the challenges found in the first unit. This organization was situated on site B in Northern Europe. Organization B had approximately 60 people and was comprised of six development teams and four area product owners working with a team at site D located in India. Therefore, Organization B was performing software development in a multisite environment and was appropriate for providing answer on RQ2.

3.2   Data Collection

Data were collected using thematic, semi-structured interviews and carried out from April to June 2012. These interviews were held face-to-face in English and were audio recorded. An interview guide was designed for the data collection [28]. As the interviews proceeded, our interview guide evolved to gain maximum coverage and depth for our study. For example, the guide for interviews in Organization B included questions based on challenges identified in Organization A. The interview guide can be made available by the author upon request. In addition, we employed the key informant technique for data collection, which is especially popular in social sciences [29].

Table 1. Details of interviews participants and duration

Interviewee (code)	Interviewee(s) profile	Software engineering experience (years)	Experience in Kanban (years)	Interview duration (minutes)
A1	Software Developer	8	1	55
A2	Scrum Master	8	1	51
A3	Software Developer	14	1	56
A4	Area Product owner	8	1	57
A5	Kanban Consultant	22	3	72
B1	Software Specialist	8	1	56
B2	Senior Manager	12	1	24

Key informants act as a natural expert observer of their surroundings and are able to provide deep insight into the concerned phenomena. The advantage of the key informant technique is the ability to acquire good quality expert information within a short period of time [29]. The authors and case company representatives discussed the criteria for suitable key informants. Seven interviewees were selected using the guidelines of the key informant approach. All the interviewees were proficient in the theoretical and practical aspects of Kanban at the organizational level. A brief descriptions of the interview participants and their roles are shown in Table 1. Participants A1–A5 are from Organization A and B1 and B2 represent Organization B.

3.3   Data Analysis

We used the constant comparison method, a classical theory developing technique used to analyze qualitative data [28]. The constant comparison method was performed using the software tool NVivo 10 to support the data analysis and synthesis. To code the data, we used an integrated method where we employed deductive and inductive approaches. In the deductive approach, we created pre-formed codes to reflect our research question and the goal of our study. During the analyses of the interview transcripts, pieces of text relevant to a particular pre-formed code were attached to it [28, 30]. In the inductive approach, post-formed codes were generated during open coding and were attached to specific portions of text from the transcript. The post-formed codes were constantly compared with each other until common themes emerged [28, 30].

3.4   Validity Discussion

This section discusses validity in terms of construct, internal validity, external validity, and reliability as described by Runeson and Höst [27]. Construct validity deals with taking the right measures to examine the phenomenon under study and taking complete precaution during data collection so that collected data align with given research questions. We designed our interview guide such that it focused on our research objective. During interview selection, experienced people within the organization were selected for interviews, keeping the following aspects in mind: knowledge in Kanban, software development process, and experience in multisite environments. In addition, we reviewed the interview guide along with a company representative in order to ensure that questions would be properly understood by the participants. Internal validity focuses on how to establish a causal relationship and is mainly used for explanatory and causal studies. As this study was of an exploratory nature, internal validity was not considered.

External validity refers to the extent findings can be generalized outside the investigated cases. The results of this paper are limited to two units conducted at the same company. However, for companies using similar large-scale framework in their software developing organization, results from this study can be applicable and useful in their context. Reliability is concerned on how data and the analysis depend on the specific researchers. During the initial phase of this study, the first author created a case study protocol as a means of rigorous preparation to conduct the case study.

Subsequently, the second and fourth authors reviewed the protocol. During data collection, the first and second authors designed the interview guide to discover challenges and possible solutions in scaling Kanban from various viewpoints. The fourth author audited and mentored the entire process. The summary of the findings were sent to interviewee via emails, who then validated the content. The findings were further reviewed by a company representative to validate the data found in both units.

4   Results

In this section, we first describe the context of our study. Next, we elaborate on the challenges in scaling Kanban in multi-site large organizations and possible solutions.

4.1   Context Description

Organization A Description: The Company's product management team specifies feature to Organization A. These features are internally analyzed in Organization A during a sprint planning meeting in the presence of the product owner and Scrum masters. The features are divided into product area based on their functionality and then put into an area backlog in the form of user stories. Larman and Vodde [9] suggest using area product owners for large-scale Scrum, a practice adopted by Organization A. The area product owner takes the user stories from the area backlog and gives them to the teams to work on at the start of the sprint. The team analyze the user story assigned by area product owner and then divides it into tasks. The teams visualize their workflow on physical boards and apply WIP limits on tasks. The team performs agile practices such as collective code ownership, pair programming, and test driven development during the implementation. For some features, teams at Organization A need to collaborate with team of another organization (situated at Site C located in Western Europe). After the tasks related to the user story are completed, the team give related demonstrations to other teams and the area product owner. After implementation, user stories are moved for system-level testing. Once the system-level testing is completed, the entire feature or release is tested before the final release.

Organization B Description: Figure 1 illustrates Organization B's workflow as visualized through the electronic Kanban board. The electronic Kanban board is used because it helps teams located at different sites (i.e., one at Site D, and the remaining at Site B) to collaborate efficiently. The product management team assigns features to Organization B. The features then move to Organization B where they are fine-tuned by the teams during product owner meetings. During meeting features are split into user stories that are sufficiently small. Each user story is then put into four different area backlogs. The senior manager creates a new card for each swim lane, which was created for each product area in the Order column on the electronic Kanban board. The senior manager picks the user story from the area backlog and puts its information on the card.

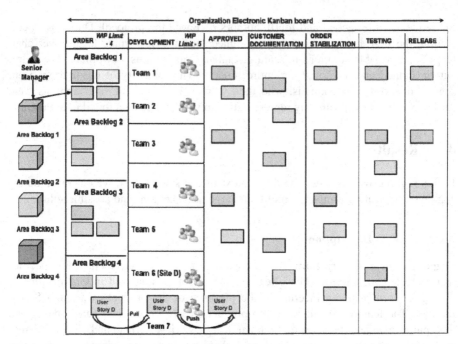

Fig. 1. Organization B workflow. On the left hand side, senior manager picks up a user story information from area backlog, and displays it on Order column. On the right hand side, organization workflow visualized in seven columns in which WIP limit is applied only to Order and Development column.

In this electronic Kanban board, the first column (Order) contains four swim lanes, one for each of the different area product backlogs. WIP limit is set for each area product backlog, which is defined by a common agreement between the area product owners and the team representative. The information on the card in the area backlog contains a description of the user story, area product owner name, release date, area backlog name, and the order date. Cards in the area backlog can be prioritized by the area product owner, with high-value items placed at the top. If a certain user story is very important, only that user story is made visible in the area backlog. Doing this will signal the teams and the organization that the user story is now very important and needs immediate attention. The WIP limit of four is noted on the area product backlog (i.e., a maximum of four user stories should be in each area backlog in the Order column at a given time). Next phase is the Development column. Seven teams are inserted in this column with their team's name. Each team has 5-9 members. Any team can pull a user story card from the first column (i.e., the Order column). Any member from a team can pull the user story card from the Order column, but what is chosen and who chooses it should be agreed upon beforehand within the team. The information on the cards in the Development column contains the description of the user story, the name of the team currently working on it, area product owner name, the planned release, the name of the area backlog from which it originated, the date on which it was ordered, and when the development started. A WIP limit of five is set on the Development column, as defined by a common agreement between teams. In order words, each team can pull a maximum of five user stories from any four different area backlogs.

At the team level, once a user story card is pulled into the Development column from an area backlog, a duplicate card is created on the development team task board (physical Kanban board). Team members then analyze the user story and divides it into tasks. Each member works on the task to prepare the user story. Once the user story is ready and has reached the 'Done' column on the task board, demonstrations with other teams and discussion with area product owners occur. During these discussions, if the area product owner agrees on a user story, the same user story currently in the Development column on the organizational electronic Kanban board is pushed to the Approved column. The next column is Customer Documentation, which is prepared by separate persons. These people pull the card from the Approved column, and once the customer documentation is created and completed, the card is pushed to the Order Stabilization column.

During stabilization iteration, the cards present in the Order Stabilization column are stabilized (i.e., that features are integrated and verified as a whole). After customer documentation and order stabilization, the cards pass through the Testing column at the point where a prerelease testing phase is done by the organization just before releasing the features to the customer. Finally, the cards reach the Release phase. For measuring the flow, average lead time is used at the organizational level. The organization works in two iteration phases: development and stabilization or testing and had three releases per year.

4.2   Challenges in Scaling Kanban and Possible Solutions

This section describes in detail the top five challenges most frequently mentioned during the interviews and presents possible solutions. A complete list of challenges and possible solutions with their reference are shown in Table 2.

Challenge 1: Distributed Teams: The first challenge relates to different product area teams located at various geographical sites. As an area product owner (A4) describes:

"I think that it's quite difficult to, at least in our program, to expand this Kanban from the level that we are now [currently at team level]. *So, in our system component, we are, all the teams are using Kanban. So, basically you could say that in our system component, we are using Kanban. But to expand that to the next level, I think it might be difficult. Well, for instance, because all the system components are located in different sites. So that makes it difficult . . ."*

The first challenge is connected to *Visualize and Manage Workflow*. In a large multisite organization, some program features are so big that they need to be split and distributed to various product areas situated at different sites (such as in this case, Northern Europe, Western Europe, and India). Therefore, teams within Organization A must coordinate with other site teams to develop such features. Thus, visualizing this type of interface on a Kanban board and managing it in a multisite context would be a challenge. An electronic board can be useful in this case because you can visualize the other site teams on the electronic Kanban board through swim lanes. This way, multisite teams working on common features can see each other work.

Table 2. List of challenges and possible solutions with their source

No	Challenge	Source	Possible solution	Source
1	*Distributed teams:* Product area teams located in different sites	A4, A2	Electronic Kanban board with team specific swim lanes can be useful in this case.	B1
2	*Feature division*: distribution of features across development teams	A4, A2, A3	Product owner team decides the allocation of prioritized features. Those prioritized features can be displayed on the Kanban board for the teams to pull work items.	B2, B1
3	*Defining WIP limits*: the setting of WIP limits for development teams	A2,	Estimate by common agreement between development teams must be provided during the initial phase of defining WIP limits.	B1
4	*Large features* may obstruct the flow for small features on the Kanban board	A5	The target size of one feature and the expected duration of implementation by an average team should be clearly communicated.	B2
5	*Product management* pushes too many features to the team. If there is a WIP limit based on their perspective, they might force more work	A4	Limit the number of features coming into the product backlog. This limit should be set by the product owners and development team representative.	B1
6	*Teams' visualization*: difficult for a team to know what other teams are doing in the organization	A1	Use the electronic Kanban board to create different swim lanes in the Development column for the teams. This way, each team can see the other team's work.	B1
7	*Feature preparation:* the preparing of features before forwarding them to teams in the organization	A4	The product owner team should fine-tune the features, and upcoming features should be visualized on the Kanban board for teams to pull.	B2, B1
8	*Loss of details of team-level work*: a possibility when using the organizational Kanban board	A4	At the organizational level, provide basic requirements (i.e., what is expected from the team).	B2
9	*Business pressure*: pressure to get the release ready can cause people to overlook the specified limits	A5	Product management or program management must conform to the WIP limit.	B2
10	*Fixed limit regarding feature size:* large features require small WIP limits, and the small features require larger WIP limits, thus, it is difficult to set a fixed limit	A4	A common goal regarding the average implementation time of the feature should be agreed upon.	B2

Challenge 2: Feature Division Across Development Teams: The second challenge is how the product owner team divides work among development teams. An area product owner (A4) adds:

"Well, of course there would be a kind of second layer, now that this quick Kanban process, they would somehow still have to give the tasks to these separate teams, right, so there's a kind of extra layer. Because, I think that now that phase is me, I'm dividing this work for these teams, but I guess it could work, it should just be decided that how this bigger team [product owner team] divides this work between the smaller Kanban team."

This challenge is also related to *Visualize Workflow and Manage Flow.* The features need to be distributed or given to teams for development. Visualizing how the feature division on a Kanban board could be done and continuously managing it with teams would be a challenge. This division problem can be resolved by visualizing product areas and teams on the Kanban board. Then, from the board, teams can pull the features for development. As a software specialist (B1) remarks:

"Is that even needed? Divided equally to the teams. I don't see that's even needed. Teams take that amount what they are able to take and what is kind of, what fits to that. ... I think it comes, everything comes from the team. It should be pull instead of push."

Challenge 3: Defining WIP Limits for Development Teams: The third challenge is with defining WIP limits for development teams at organization level. The challenge is related to *Limit WIP.* As a Software Developer (A3) states:

"I'm sure there would be some problems to.. When we scale up, there might be some problems with defining the work in progress limits. When you scale up, it takes some time to find the correct working practices to get the most out of the teams."

The challenge with defining WIP limit can be resolved by selecting an initial estimate on the basis of a common agreement between development teams. This way a suitable limit can be applied across development teams in the organization.

Challenge 4: Large Features May Obstruct the Flow: Another challenge identified in the first unit is if the features are too big, they will not move across the Kanban board. As a consultant (A5) from the first unit adds:

"Challenges in visualizing? Well, challenges are that, well, as I said, if there's too much things going on, it really doesn't tell how things are going. And if the features are, or subfeatures are too big, then there's nothing moving."

The possible reason for this challenge is that organizations usually develop large features, which may require several teams to complete. If this type of feature is visualized on the Kanban board, it is possible that other features may be queued for development. Such large features may obstruct the flow of other features on the board. To resolve this challenge, the target size of features must be clearly communicated (i.e., how long will it take to implement a large feature by an average team). The target size will enable the optimum splitting of a large feature into feasible user stories. These feasible user stories will not stay for long on the Kanban board. As a senior manager (B2) commented:

"It should be communicated clearly what is the target size of one user story, how long it will take to implement, by an average team. In our case, we are using the measurements of three

weeks in average, how long it can take to be implemented. Then it's only about the willingness of the teams and the product owners to do the work with the splitting."

Challenge 5: Product Management's Perspective of WIP Limits: A challenge with WIP limits emerges when product management team tries to force more features onto a team through a higher limit than teams can afford. As an area product owner (A4) describes:

"Well, the program is always trying to push more and more stuff for us, and if we have these limits, they might try to force us to take more than what we would like to get. So there's always this debate between the program and the teams, that we are trying to. They are trying to push a lot of things to us and we are trying to not take all, everything at once."

The possible factor causing this challenge is that if WIP limits are included on the organizational Kanban board based on the program perspective, a large limit could be indicated because the program wishes to give more features to teams than the teams can afford to take at a single time. It will be difficult for teams to take a large number of features when there are overly large WIP limits. This can be overcome by setting and honoring WIP limits for each area's backlogs and development teams. These limits should be specified by common agreement of the product owner team and development teams, not by the program. This way, appropriate limits can be applied.

5   Conclusion and Future Work

The research in this paper describes the scaling of Kanban in an organization involved in multisite software development. Various challenges, along with possible solutions, were identified when scaling Kanban within an organization. For a multisite environment, an electronic Kanban board appears to be a must for an organization to smoothly plan and execute software development. In addition, WIP limits can be set for product area backlog and development teams by mutual agreement. An average lead time would also be an appropriate metric to measure workflow at the organizational level. The contribution of this paper gives a description of challenges and possible solutions in scaling Kanban to a large distributed software developing organization. We hope the knowledge gained in this research could be useful for other organizations planning to scale Kanban in their environment. One of the limitations of this study was that most of the interviewees only have one year of experience with Kanban, which is very short. However, this is typical in any organization in the scaling phase, especially when scaling from (team level) agile development to large scale distributed Kanban.

Future Research. The results of this study are based on interviews conducted in two large software developing organizations. Insights on challenges and possible solutions identified when scaling Kanban should be validated in other organizations in future research. It would be interesting to do further empirical research on this topic in a situation with large amount of teams operating in a multisite environment to confirm or reject our findings in even larger organizations.

Acknowledgments. We would like to thank the case company and the interviewees for the opportunity to explore real-world transformation to large scale distributed Kanban. This research is supported by ICT SHOK N4S (Need for speed) program financed by the Finnish Funding Agency for Technology and Innovation (Tekes) and Digile OY.

References

1. Pleatsikas, C., Teece, D.: The analysis of market definition and market power in the context of rapid innovation. Int. J. Ind. Organ. **19**, 665–693 (2001)
2. Minderhoud, S., Fraser, P.: Shifting paradigms of product development in fast and dynamic markets (2005)
3. Herbsleb, J.D., Moitra, D.: Global software development. IEEE Softw. **18**, 16–20 (2001)
4. Gassmann, O., von Zedtwitz, M.: New concepts and trends in international R&D organization (1999)
5. Schwaber, K., Beedle, M.: Agile Software Development with Scrum (2001)
6. Beck, K.: Embracing change with extreme programming. Computer (Long. Beach. Calif) **32**, 70–77 (1999)
7. Rodríguez, P., Markkula, J., Oivo, M., Turula, K.: Survey on agile and lean usage in finnish software industry. In: Proceedings of the ACM-IEEE International Symposium on Empirical Software Engineering And Measurement - ESEM 2012, p. 139. ACM Press (2012)
8. Rising, L., Janoff, N.S.: The Scrum software development process for small teams. IEEE Softw. 17, (2000)
9. Larman, C., Vodde, B.: Practices for Scaling Lean & Agile Development: Large, Multisite, and Offshore Product Development with Large-Scale Scrum. Pearson Education (2010)
10. Paasivaara, M., Lassenius, C.: Scaling Scrum in a Large Distributed Project. 2011 Int. Symp. Empir. Softw. Eng. Meas, 363–367 (2011)
11. Schnitter, J., Mackert, O.: Large-Scale Agile Software Development at SAP AG. Commun. Comput. Inf. Sci. **230**, 209–220 (2011)
12. Sjøberg, D.I.K., Johnsen, A., Solberg, J.: Quantifying the effect of using Kanban versus scrum: A case study. IEEE Softw. **29**, 47–53 (2012)
13. Boehm, B., Turner, R.: Management challenges to implementing agile processes in traditional development organizations. Software, ieee. **22**, 30–39 (2005)
14. Vilkki, Kati: When agile is not enough. In: Abrahamsson, Pekka, Oza, Nilay (eds.) LESS 2010. LNBIP, vol. 65, pp. 44–47. Springer, Heidelberg (2010)
15. Rodríguez, P., Mikkonen, K., Kuvaja, P., Oivo, M., Garbajosa, J.: Building lean thinking in a telecom software development organization: strengths and challenges. In: Proceedings of the 2013 International Conference on Software and System Process, pp. 98–107 (2013)
16. Anderson, D.J.: Kanban. Blue Hole Press (2010)
17. Hiranabe, K.: Kanban Applied to Software Development: from Agile to Lean. http://www.infoq.com/articles/hiranabe-lean-agile-kanban
18. Kniberg, H.: Lean from the trenches: Managing large-scale projects with Kanban. Pragmatic Bookshelf (2011)
19. Ahmad, M.O., Markkula, J., Oivo, M.: Kanban in Software Development: A Systematic Literature Review (2013)
20. Ikonen, Marko: Leadership in Kanban software development projects: a quasi-controlled experiment. In: Abrahamsson, Pekka, Oza, Nilay (eds.) LESS 2010. LNBIP, vol. 65, pp. 85–98. Springer, Heidelberg (2010)

21. Vallet, B.: Kanban at Scale – A Siemens Success Story. http://www.infoq.com/articles/kanban-siemens-health-services
22. Womack, J.P., Jones, D.T.: Lean thinking: banish waste and create wealth in your corporation. Simon and Schuster (2010)
23. Ahmad, M.O., Markkula, J., Oivo, M., Kuvaja, P.: Usage of Kanban in software companies an empirical study on motivation, benefits and challenges. In: 9th International Conference on Software Engineering Advances (2014)
24. Klaus, L.: Scaling Kanban. http://www.klausleopold.com/2014/09/scaling-kanban.html
25. Easterbrook, S., Singer, J., Storey, M.-A., Damian, D.: Selecting empirical methods for software engineering research. In: Shull, F., Singer, J., Sjøberg, D.K. (eds.) Guide to Advanced Empirical Software Engineering, pp. 285–311. Springer, London (2008)
26. Yin, R.K.: Case Study Research: Design and Methods. Sage Publications (2009)
27. Runeson, P., Höst, M.: Guidelines for conducting and reporting case study research in software engineering. Empir. Softw. Eng. **14**, 131–164 (2008)
28. Seaman, C.B.: Qualitative methods in empirical studies of software engineering. IEEE Trans. Softw. Eng. 25 (1999)
29. Marshall, M.N.: The key informant technique. Fam. Pract. **13**, 92–97 (1996)
30. Cruzes, D.S., Dyba, T.: Recommended Steps for Thematic Synthesis in Software Engineering. 2011 Int. Symp. Empir. Softw. Eng. Meas, 275–284 (2011)

Short Papers

The Two Faces of Uncertainty: Threat vs Opportunity Management in Agile Software Development

Denniz Dönmez[(⊠)] and Gudela Grote

Department of Management, Technology and Economics,
ETH Zurich, Weinbergstr. 56-58, 8092 Zurich, Switzerland
{ddonmez,ggrote}@ethz.ch

Abstract. Uncertainty is an inevitable fact of software development that can determine success or failure of entire projects. Although often associated with risk or threat, uncertainty bears much overlooked qualities regarding market opportunities. Adopting a conceptualization of uncertainty that includes both threat and opportunity, we investigate different possibilities to manage the uncertainties preceding the creation of novel ideas and innovation. In this qualitative study, we empirically explore the concept of uncertainty beyond the focus on requirement uncertainty that prevails in the literature and explicitly emphasize its multidimensionality. We argue that the failure to distinguish between different dimensions of uncertainty can lead to their inadequate management at high cost. Our results show how teams exploit practices to manage different uncertainties in order to mitigate threats while remaining open to opportunities. We discuss the implications of our findings for product development teams as well as for the design of supportive organizational structures.

Keywords: Uncertainty · Risk management · Threat · Opportunity management

1 Introduction

The ability to manage uncertainty determines the success or failure of projects, and even entire companies, and has been established as a "core element" of performance [14]. In the face of high software project failure rates, uncertainty is naturally associated with risk and threats [16], whereas its qualities to enable business opportunities and competitive advantage are oftentimes overlooked.

In this paper, we explore the management of uncertainty and its role for innovation that may arise when teams deliberately do not strive to eliminate but rather work with uncertainty. Our perspective acknowledges the dual nature of uncertainty [14] that manifests in the possibility for positive and negative effects. On the one hand, no economic profit exists in a world without uncertainty [13]. On the other hand, large numbers of projects and even entire companies fail due to uncertainty [3] and, not surprisingly, the decisions that determine the course and outcome of a project are affected by uncertainty. From this paradox, the question arises how project teams can find ways to use uncertainty to their benefit instead of falling victim to it.

© Springer International Publishing Switzerland 2015
C. Lassenius et al. (Eds.): XP 2015, LNBIP 212, pp. 193–198, 2015.
DOI: 10.1007/978-3-319-18612-2_16

2   Uncertainty as a Multidimensional Concept

Because the "manifold nature of uncertainty" [8] includes aspects as distinct as risk, ambiguity, and equivocality, a number of scholars have put forward different definitions, the core of which is incomplete information [4]. Although uncertainty may seem similar to risk, scholars distinguish uncertainty from risk by acknowledging a fundamental difference between both; risk can be estimated, whereas uncertainty cannot [6]. A general definition establishes risk as the product of an event's probability multiplied by its impact [1], which theoretically is neither positive nor negative in its consequence. Yet, in the literature risk is often approached from a threat perspective [18] in an attempt to put forward mechanisms for its mitigation.

As benefits result from exploiting the potential of uncertainty without exposing oneself overly to it [5], a wider focus on uncertainty rather than risk [9] enhances project management research by "providing an important difference in perspective, including, but not limited to, an enhanced focus on opportunity management" [18]. To avoid confusion, we restrict the term 'risk', and use the terms 'threat' and 'opportunity' when referring to negative and positive outcomes, respectively, associated with uncertainty. According to the New Oxford American Dictionary, opportunity is "a set of circumstances that makes it possible to do something." We use the term to refer to any positive outcome associated with uncertainty that was not originally envisioned but only discovered during project work. We use the term 'threat' for negative outcomes that exist potentially, i.e. without certainty.

While there are different consequences of uncertainty, we must carefully study their origin and account for implications that result from different dimensions of uncertainty [2, 9]. In software development, such differences manifest in various forms. For example, software developers are often unsure about the best way to solve a problem, because the problem may be ill-defined, or because of lacking experience regarding the technology in use. In the literature the term task uncertainty is used when actors lack understanding of the problem or have insufficient information to complete a task [17]. Task uncertainty in software development can, for example, be caused by a lack of experience or knowledge concerning the technology in use [10].

Another source of uncertainty in development projects concerns the resources necessary to complete the work [15]. Resource uncertainty arises when the availability of either human resources or infrastructure including, e.g., software licenses or test user accounts, is unpredictable or unreliable.

A third and possibly the most prominent type of uncertainty in software development is requirement uncertainty, which refers to incomplete information or ambiguity regarding product functionality [12]. While investigations of requirement uncertainty exist in large numbers, other types of uncertainty in software development have not received similar attention. In order to remain wary of threats and opportunities at the same time, software developers need to increase their ability to distinguish different types of uncertainty and develop a portfolio of adequate approaches for their exploitation.

3   Data Collection and Analysis

We applied qualitative methods to capture how agile software developers manage different dimensions of uncertainty by conducting field observations, as well as 42 face-to-face interviews in 11 software development teams from five different companies in Switzerland. The interviews lasted between 20 and 90 minutes. All interviews were audio recorded and transcribed as soon as possible. In each team, we interviewed different functional roles, always including at least one person with managerial tasks, and at least two team members with software development tasks.

During the interviews, we asked team members how their teams had dealt with difficult situations in the past and encouraged them to share examples for incidents that had either positive or negative outcomes. Interview participants were informed about our goal to investigate the management of uncertainties that are faced in software development projects, and were subsequently asked about a number of situations in which they or their teams experienced related problems or difficulties. During the interviews, we could in some cases exploit information that we obtained during preceding interviews with different team members. This allowed us to triangulate data collection with descriptions of incidents from different perspectives.

Data analysis was performed iteratively and incrementally in parallel to late stages of the data collection. We let clues that we developed influence later interviews and included additional interesting aspects as far as possible during the interviews. We applied open coding until theoretical saturation was reached [11], after reading several times through the interview transcripts, and scanning for clues to our initial questions: How do teams deal with uncertainty, and how is information collected, analyzed, and systematically used to manage different uncertainties? To support the data analysis we relied on a software tool, HyperResearch. After the initial coding, we clustered similar codes and captured key ideas and concepts in memos in order to structure our data and uncover underlying approaches to uncertainty management. Finally, we verified our findings with the help of the study participants.

4   Results

Managing Task Uncertainty. Teams faced different situations in which insufficient information was available regarding the solution to a problem, and consequently regarding the tasks necessary to be performed. Several approaches to acquiring clarity included the use of so-called spikes (i.e., an investigative task), and the deliberate exploration of several solutions. While keeping options open requires redundancy to some extent, opportunities could be realized by selecting the most promising option under more information. In order to maintain these qualities, teams relied extensively on structures for knowledge sharing, e.g., in the form of regular internal workshops or techniques such as pair programming.

Once tasks are established, their estimation becomes important. Teams usually performed estimation meetings at the beginning of development iterations, but spent considerable time re-estimating the tasks once new information became available because estimations were often inaccurate in the beginning. To manage task uncertainty, teams generally kept task sizes as small as possible, splitting single tasks where possible, so that more precise estimates could be produced.

One team decided to split tasks and distribute them to separate sub-teams, making changes to the design of the project setup. This turned into an opportunity spotted by some of the developers: *"we split our projects up into different projects [...], and so we found [...] we can sell the [application programming interface], just the bare bones technical thing as a second product.' The developers thought of something and it turned into a product right away and we fond a customer [for it]."* Here, due to an opportunity arising from the separation of tasks, functionality that was originally intended for internal use only was transformed into a separate product.

Managing Requirement Uncertainty. Typically taxing development processes, requirement changes were met by teams with much acceptance under two conditions. The first is that change requests be limited to the points in time between two development iterations. The second condition demands that changes be buffered through the use of a managed product backlog in which tasks are assigned priorities in order to allow uninterrupted work during the development iterations. The use of short iterations was seen as positive because it allowed for more frequent feedback, thus reducing uncertainty: *"at some point we had like a change in the requirements, which was pretty disruptive and we had to [repeat] the Sprint. This shouldn't happen of course. [...] Having the shorter iterations helps you with doing that."*

Our data suggest that requirement uncertainty can be managed effectively through the close integration of diverse stakeholders into the development process. Development teams that engaged more frequently in communication with customers and suppliers often reported reduced uncertainty regarding requirements. For example, one developer remarked: *"in the old style waterfall system, you get a screenshot, you implement it, you don't understand it directly, you just do what's on the screenshot, and afterwards the customer says 'Well, that's not what I like'."*

In our data, the most reported incidents of opportunities were related to newly arising business possibilities based on added functionality, for example as requested by one client, which could be cross-sold to others. In one team for example, a new customer's feature request increased the value of an initially low priority feature. The development of this feature turned out to be valuable also for several other existing customers, increasing the product's attractiveness beyond the expectations of the team leader who now enjoyed an increased project budget. This example demonstrates the importance of the possibility to delay decisions (suspend judgment until more info is gathered). The flexibility to pursue emerging opportunities would have been excluded had the project scope and product functionality be specified when the sprint began.

Many mechanisms for the management of requirement uncertainty were adopted from the Scrum framework and complemented by communication practices of the teams that instructed team members to strive for transparency of problems regardless of their nature, and encouraged frequent feedback among all parties. A developer commented: *"you get a lot earlier feedback and can adapt [...] and change."*

Managing Resource Uncertainty. Teams frequently experienced difficulties and disruptions in their workflow due to unavailable input from stakeholders, e.g., when input from suppliers or contractors was delayed or of insufficient quality so that rework became necessary. One team experienced the threat of developer idleness resulting especially from their dependency on database specialists within the company, who repeatedly failed to supply the team. The lack of database support had threatened to delay the project at several times. The team's analysis of the issues revealed that no single person from the database team was responsible for any request, but rather incoming requests were shared so that amendments to requests became problematic. It was decided to approach the database department with a proposal to internalize one database specialist into the development team, which not only solved the problem but also led to the creation of a new business model inside the company; database specialists could henceforth be hired individually, which guaranteed that all of a team's requests would be processed by the same person. While this facilitated communication and scotched errors arising from ill-understood support requests, it also helped to eliminate a threat while creating an opportunity for the company (a new offering by the database team).

Effective management of resource uncertainty requires considerable freedom to explore solutions and tools that allow them to convince the customer to deviate from an original plan, e.g., in order to pursue technical solutions that are easier or faster available. One team explained to us their failure to convince a customer of such a deviation after several team members had become convinced of an alternative's superiority, but the customer did not want to allocate resources to the issue until a prototype was produced (at the team's own cost). A team member concluded that *"sometimes it's difficult to convince the customer if you can't show them something."*

The examples reveal the importance of allocating resources flexibly in order to explore emerging opportunities and minimize threats at the same time. Uncertainty is managed effectively when team structures can be modified flexibly in order to support external and internal collaboration.

5   Conclusion

We have detailed how a number of practices embedded in agile software development support teams in the management of uncertainty that can either turn into threat or opportunity. Our contribution distinguishes different dimensions of uncertainty linked to tasks, requirements, and resources, and provides a neglected perspective on uncertainty that includes negative as well as positive outcomes.

Our data show how both threat and opportunity are outcomes of ambiguous situations that have the potential to turn either way. Therefore, uncertainty must not be eliminated too early during a project. Instead, threats and opportunities that are related to different dimensions of uncertainty must be met by adequate mechanisms for their management. For example, teams addressed task uncertainty by designing small work packages that could be handled flexibly and measured with higher precision than larger ones. This resulted in better control of threats, and in some cases in the emergence of opportunities to create supplementary stand-alone product features. Requirement uncertainty was approached by the inclusion of different stakeholders, such as suppliers and customers based on frequent exchange in order to create and maintain a goal-oriented production process. Allowing deliberate opportunities for changes at specific points in time created possibilities to react to changing environments, and permitted uninterrupted focus on output during development iterations. Resource uncertainty was managed primarily by continuous activities of planning and re-planning in order to match the supply and demand of work. This was supported by the deliberate investment in redundant skills to some extent, which allowed teams to avoid bottlenecks in the production process as well as improve the search for innovative solutions.

One major difficulty for uncertainty management lies in distinguishing threats from opportunities. While many actors who face this task chose to disengage from a systematic approach to uncertainty management [7], our data underline the importance of systematic collection of information in combination with the delay of decisions that earns teams the possibility to prevent harm and allow benefit. One powerful approach offered by agile software developers lies in the incremental collection of information that turns uncertainty into probability and thus moves it closer to certainty. Despite the complexity of the uncertainty concept that can deter academics and practitioners, uncertainty management holds the potential to leverage large impacts on projects and deserves increased attention.

References

1. Bannerman, P.L.: Risk and risk management in software projects: A reassessment. Journal of Systems and Software (2008)
2. Bradley, R., Drechsler, M.: Types of Uncertainty. Erkenn. **79**(6), 1225–1248 (2013)
3. Flyvbjerg, B., Budzier, A.: Why Your IT Project Might Be Riskier than You Think. Harvard Business Review (2011)
4. Grote, G.: Management of Uncertainty - Theory and Application in the Design of Systems and Organizations. Springer, London (2009)
5. Holt, R.: Risk management: The talking cure. Organization. **11**(2), 251–270 (2004)
6. Knight, F.H.: Risk, Uncertainty and Profit. University of Chicago Press, Chicago (1921)
7. Kutsch, E., et al.: Does risk matter? European Journal of Information Systems (2012)
8. Lipshitz, R., Strauss, O.: Coping with Uncertainty: A Naturalistic Decision-Making Analysis. Organizational Behavior and Human Decision Processes (1997)
9. Madsen, S., Pries-Heje, J.: Conceptualizing Perceived Uncertainty in J. Pries-Heje (ed.) Project Management Multiplicity. Samfundslitteratur, Frederiksberg (2012)
10. McLeod, L., Smith, D.: Managing IT Projects. Boyd and Fraser Publishing (1996)
11. Miles, M.B., et al.: Qualitative data analysis. Sage Publications, Thousand Oaks (2013)
12. Nidumolu, S.: Standardization, requirements uncertainty and software project performance. Information & Management. **31**, 135–150 (1996)
13. Penrose, E.T.: The Theory of the Growth of the Firm. Blackwell, Oxford (1959)
14. Perminova, O., et al.: Defining uncertainty in projects – a new perspective. International Journal of Project Management. **26**, 73–79 (2008)
15. Sakthivel, S.: Managing risk in offshore systems development. Communications of the ACM. **50**(4), 69–75 (2007)
16. Song, M., Montoya-Weiss, M.M.: The Effect of Perceived Technological Uncertainty on Japanese New Product Development. AMJ **44**(1), 61–80 (2001)
17. Thompson, J.D.: Organizations in Action. Transaction Publishers (1967)
18. Ward, S., Chapman, C.: Transforming project risk management into project uncertainty management. International Journal of Project Management (2003)

Management Ambidexterity: A Clue for Maturing in Agile Software Development

Rafaela Mantovani Fontana[1,2]([⊠]), Victor Meyer Jr.[1], Sheila Reinehr[1], and Andreia Malucelli[1]

[1] Pontifical Catholic University of Paraná (PUCPR), R. Imaculada Conceição, 1155, 80215-901, Curitiba, PR, Brazil
rafaela.fontana@ufpr.br, victormeyerjr@gmail.com, sheila.reinehr@pucpr.br, malu@ppgia.pucpr.br
[2] Federal University of Paraná (UFPR), R. Dr. Alcides Vieira Arcoverde, 1225, 81520-260, Curitiba, PR, Brazil

Abstract. Organizational ambidexterity is the ability to be aligned and efficient in combining current resources and demands (exploitation) as well as adaptive and innovative due to changing conditions and demands (exploration). Maturity in software development is defined over exploitation – through processes definition and control. We argue in this study that mature agile software development is also exploratory – adaptive and innovative. Thus, our objective is to verify how ambidexterity occurs in mature agile software development. The research approach is a single case study with analysis of qualitative data. Our findings show how a mature team is managed by ambidextrous strategies.

Keywords: Ambidexterity · Maturity · Agile software development

1 Introduction

Organizational ambidexterity represents an essential ability in organizations that wish to prosper in high-velocity environments [1], and requires efficient management of current demands (exploitation) with simultaneous adaptation to a changing environment (exploration) [2], [3].

Our previous work shows evidence that an exploitative focus on process definition and control is not the means to mature in agile software development [4];[5]. However, solely focusing on exploratory practices may lead to "too many undeveloped new ideas and too little distinctive competence" [3, p. 71]). This is the reason we argue mature agile software development management presents ambidextrous abilities.

Our research question is therefore, the following: *How does ambidexterity occur in mature agile software development?* The research approach is a single case study with qualitative data collection and analysis. This study contributes to the research by integrating organizational theory and agile software development. For practitioners, our findings offer suggestions for strategic management actions that support maturing in agile software development.

© Springer International Publishing Switzerland 2015
C. Lassenius et al. (Eds.): XP 2015, LNBIP 212, pp. 199–204, 2015.
DOI: 10.1007/978-3-319-18612-2_17

This paper is organized as follows. Section 2 briefly presents the organizational ambidexterity concept. Section 3 describes the research approach. Section 4 presents the results and, finally, Section 5 discusses the findings and concludes the paper.

2   Organizational Ambidexterity

The ability to simultaneously pursue exploitation and exploration [3, p. 71] has currently been termed "organizational ambidexterity" [6]. Ambidextrous organizations are successful because they are aligned and efficient in their management of current demands while simultaneously adaptive to environmental change [2]. Alignment is characterized by the ability to maintain individuals working towards the same goals and adaptability refers to the ability to quickly adjust activities as a response to changes in the environment [7].

The challenge in describing ambidexterity is that organizations adopt idiosyncratic implementation strategies to become ambidextrous [7]. Gibson and Birkinshaw [7], for example, have identified contextually ambidextrous behavior by analyzing the ability of a business unit to be aligned and adaptable simultaneously. Tiwana [8] has identified ambidexterity in information flows among individuals, which can be "strong ties" or "bridging ties". Bridging ties lead to diversity of accessible knowledge, while strong ties lead to knowledge integration. Tiwana has also characterized ambidexterity as a combination of formal and informal (clan) controls [9].

Organizational ambidexterity is currently evolving as a research paradigm in organizational theory [2], is recognized as an adequate approach to the uncertainty of the software product market [10], and is verified in agile software development teams [11];[12]. It is relevant, then, to investigate how ambidexterity is accomplished in mature agile software development.

3   Research Design

The research question that drives this study is *"How does ambidexterity occur in mature agile software development?"*. We chose the single case study as research approach because it is an effective method to "understand the dynamics present within single settings" [14, p. 534].

The unit of analysis was an agile software development firm. We selected a Brazilian agile software development company, that developed and customizes a product which is currently used by a single big customer. This case is specifically interesting to study ambidexterity because company's manager has more than ten years of experience in managing agile teams (is one of the introducers of agile methods in Brazil). The firm has forty-five employees.

Our data collection and analysis were conducted in October/November, 2014 and guided by the proposition: *Management simultaneously combine formal and clan mechanisms in mature agile software development.*

To verify this proposition we applied a qualitative approach through interviews with three team members (a team leader, a functional analyst – named "feature owner" –, and a developer). The protocol for data collection was based on the study presented by Tiwana [9]. After the interviews had been conducted, they were transcribed and analyzed using thematic networks analysis [13]. With the objective to have descriptive statistics of the perception of maturity and ambidexterity, we also collected quantitative data through a questionnaire. It measured ambidexterity perception, based on [7] and [8], and maturity perception, based on [4].

The threats to validity in this study are internal and external. Internal validity is threatened by the interpretation of interviewees responses. To minimize this threat, we presented the results for evaluation by the manager of the firm, who did not participate in the interviews. The external validity is threatened by the findings from the single case study. In this case, we did not pursue statistical generalization, but analytical generalization instead [14].

4   Results

The measurement of maturity and ambidexterity showed that the majority of the respondents have a perception that the company is mature and that the management is ambidextrous. Twenty-one employees (46% of the total) responded the questionnaire. On average, 84% of the respondents agree with the agile maturity evidences in their work processes; 73% agree that management system encourages people to challenge outmoded traditions, is flexible and responds quickly to changes (exploration); and 95% agree that management works coherently to support the overall objectives of the organization (exploitation).

The analysis of the interviews resulted in a number of evidences that represent observations of firm ambidextrous behavior. In summary, we identified that ambidexterity is enabled by two main management strategies 1) exploiting enough to add value to the customer and the team; and 2) processes automation and results visibility. To accomplish the first initiative, we observed that management chases definition and execution (exploitation) in such a way that added value is realized by the customer (outcomes and estimates) and the team (definition of roles and estimates), but space is left for variety and discovery in estimates, in the relationship with the customer and within team. For the second initiative, we observed that management defined a few indicators concerning the process, and discussions and solutions are left to emerge from the informal interactions among team members.

Next subsections present the evidences for these management strategies.

4.1   Exploiting Enough to Add Value for the Customer and for the Team

Deliberate loose estimates. Estimates at this company are based on past data but are also deliberately loose: "... for example, nobody says that we have four or five hours to finish a task. We classify tasks as small, medium or big. There are some statistics that state the range of hours for small tasks, medium tasks and big tasks."(Developer, discussing loose estimates). Because deliveries are fixed every week, there are always features being delivered to customer. When required, long-term planning is made through milestones, leaving space for flexibility in the activities for each milestone. *We see here planning deriving from the combination of exploitation, through long-term milestones planning and estimates based on past data; and exploration from loose delivery dates, and considering individuals' experience on tasks classification.*

Customer care through people and perceived outcomes. The customer of this company is not significantly involved with the team, but the customer feels supported by a focal point, the feature owner: "We work a lot with the customer to define the requirements he needs." (Feature owner, about helping customer). The customer also receives weekly deliveries, which are validated and formally accepted. *In this relationship we see exploration evidenced by the customer sensing that the team assists in the processes, and exploitation from a defined process for deliveries, which provides the customer with a sense of outcome as a result of the team's work.*

Team atmosphere is friendly and established. The atmosphere among team members is pleasant. The team members do not typically perform overtime and, if they must, the overtime is planned and communicated. Whenever situations of concern occur in the team, the roles of the leaders able to assist in problem solving or decision making is clear. The teams under each feature owner are small, which facilitates informal communication and problem solving. *We see, then, exploration enabled through the close relationship between individuals and exploitation facilitated by well-defined problem-solving roles.*

4.2   Processes Automation and Status Visibility

Task work out with checkpoints and flexibility. This firm leads task accomplishment with a high level of automation. Repetitive and time-consuming development tasks are automated in an internally developed toolkit. Functional tests and code integration are also automated. The status of the repository, the tests suite, and other status in the environment are visible to the team through a number of dashboards on monitors distributed around the rooms. At the same time, tasks completion is flexible. Whenever problems occur with tasks execution, discussions for the solution are collective, and the decision to delay the task is also collective. *This extensive automation and status visibility aligns developers' work with processes, leading to exploitation. The discussions concerning the tasks and the status that is visible to all facilitate exploration in task work out.*

Process enduring through people and automation. The team members were highly involved in the definition of the process when the agile method was adopted. With the current established, stable process, people are encouraged to automate anything they consider may ease their work. The process is simple with few manual steps (coding, reviewing and testing). *Thus, we consider that* *automation retain exploitation in the process, while discussions and freedom to change guarantee exploration.*

Communication arena based on status visibility and conversation. All data concerning what needs to be done, what is being done, environment and tests status is shown in real time for everyone. This high visibility and the red indicators when something malfunctions stimulates people to discuss and engage in problem solving. *We find, then, that exploitation is derived from status visibility and exploration from intense, informal, and close communication.*

5 Discussion and Conclusions

This study aimed to identify how ambidexterity occurs in mature agile software development. We have qualitatively shown, based on a single case study, the management strategies used to allow ambidexterity in agile software development.

The benefits of combining exploitation and exploration have already been identified in agile software development. Boehm [15] emphasized the importance of combining plan-driven and agile approaches. Baskerville et al. [16] previewed the future of agility as the search for the dual objective of agility and alignment. These benefits and mechanisms have been empirically verified in globally distributed software projects [17].

Ramesh et al. [18] identified a number of balanced practices where exploitation and exploration (e.g., formal structures with flexibility, trust but verify etc) were simultaneously applied in agile software development. However, the research focus was on distributed development, which has an explicit need for discipline [18]. Our study adds to their findings showing that even a collocated team, when maturing, develops ambidextrous abilities – through deliberate management strategies – to maintain team work aligned and at the same time flexible and responding to changes.

This study also addresses a concern of the companies in the adoption of agile methods, which is the lack of managerial control [19]. We assume what companies fear loss of control based on processes exploitation, which leads to the search for stability. We demonstrated that management in agile methods remains exploitative, but is also exploratory.

Our findings are limited by the context of the studied firm, but may serve as a reference for practitioners that wish to improve management practices, and as a subject for further replication and validation for researchers that are interested in applying organizational theories to agile software development.

References

1. Tushman, M.L., O'Reilly III, C.A.: Ambidextrous organizations: Managing evolutionary and revolutionary change. California Manag. Review **38**, 8–30 (1996)
2. Raish, S., Birkinshaw, J.: Organizational Ambidexterity: Antecedents. Outcomes and Moderators. J. Manag. **34**, 375–409 (2008). doi:10.1177/0149206308316058

3. March, J.G.: Exploration and Exploitation in Organizational Learning. Organiz. Sci. **2** (1991)
4. Fontana, R.M., Fontana, I.M., Garbuio, P.A.R., Reinehr, S., Malucelli, A.: People over processes: how should agile software development be defined? J. Syst. Softw. **97**, 140–155 (2014). doi:10.1016/j.jss.2014.07.030
5. Fontana, R.M., Reinehr, S., Malucelli, A.: Maturing in agile: what is it about?. In: roceedings of the 15th International Conference, XP 2014, Rome, Italy, pp. 94–109, 26–30 May 2014. doi:10.1007/978-3-319-06862-6_7
6. Tuner, N., Swart, J., Maylor, H.: Mechanisms for Managing Ambidexterity: A Review and Research Agenda. Int. J. Manag. Reviews **15**, 317–332 (2013). doi:10.1111/j.1468-2370.2012.00343.x
7. Gibson, C., Birkinshaw, J.: The antecedents, consequences, and mediating role of organizational ambidexterity. Academy Manag. J. **47**, 209–226 (2004). doi:10.2307/20159573
8. Tiwana, A.: Do bridging ties complement strong ties? An empirical examination of alliance ambidexterity. Strat. Mgmt. J. **29**, 251–272 (2008). doi:10.1002/smj.666
9. Tiwana, A.: Systems Development Ambidexterity: Explaining the Complementary and Substitutive Roles of Formal and Informal Controls. J. Manag. Inf. Syst. **27**, 87–126 (2010). doi:10.2753/MIS0742-1222270203
10. Harris, M.L., Collins, R.W., Hevner, A.R.: Control of Flexible Software Development Under Uncertainty. Inf. Syst. Research **20**, 400–419 (2009). doi:10.1287/isre.1090.0240
11. Vidgen, R., Wang, X.: Coevolving Systems and the Organization of Agile Software Development. Inform Syst Res. **20**, 355–376 (2009). doi:10.1287/isre.1090.0237
12. Boehm, B.; Turner, R.: Balancing agility and discipline: evaluating and integrating agile and plan-driven methods. In: Proceedings of the 26th International Conference on Software Engineering, 23–28, 718–729 (2004). doi:10.1109/ICSE.2004.1317503
13. Attride-Sterling, J.: Thematic networks: an analytic tool for qualitative research. Qualitative Research **1**, 385–405 (2001). doi:10.1177/146879410100100307
14. Eisenhardt, K.: Building Theories from Case Study Research. Academy Manag. Review **14**, 532–550 (1989). doi:http://www.jstor.org/stable/258557
15. Boehm, B.: Get ready for agile methods, with care. IEEE Comp. **35**, 64–69 (2002). doi:10.1109/2.976920
16. Baskerville, R., Pries-Heje, J., Madsen, S.: Post-agility: What follows a decade of agility? Inf. Soft. Tech. **53**, 543–555 (2011). doi:10.1016/j.infsof.2010.10.010
17. Lee, G., Delone, W., Espinosa, J.A.: Ambidextrous Coping Strategies in Globally Distributed Software Development Projects: Strategies for enhancing flexibility and rigor. Comm. ACM **49**, 35–40 (2006). doi:10.1145/1164394.1164417
18. Ramesh, B., Mohan, K., Cao, L.: Ambidexterity in Agile Distributed Development: An Empirical Investigation. Inf. Syst. Research **23**, 323–339 (2012). doi:10.1287/isre.1110.0351
19. Melo, C.O., Cruzes, D.S., Kon, F., Conradi, R.: Interpretative case studies on agile team productivity and management. Inf. Soft. Tech. **55**, 412–427 (2013). doi:10.1016/j.infsof.2012.09.004

Towards Predictable B2B Customer Satisfaction and Experience Management with Continuous Improvement Assets and Rich Feedback

Petri Kettunen[1(✉)], Mikko Ämmälä[2], and Jari Partanen[2]

[1] Department of Computer Science, University of Helsinki,
P.O. Box 68 00014, Helsinki, Finland
petri.kettunen@cs.helsinki.fi
[2] Elektrobit Wireless Communications Ltd, Tutkijantie 8 90590, Oulu, Finland
{mikko.ammala,jari.partanen}@elektrobit.com

Abstract. Modern high-performing software product development organizations are nowadays more and more often transforming their operations towards continuous higher-level ends. In general, customer satisfaction (CS) is such a goal. This paper presents an approach of gauging and improving customer satisfaction in an industrial B2B product development project organization for continuous customer experience (CX) management. In order to do that, the Customer Satisfaction Index (CSI) used in the company was systematized with an applied impact analysis technique. The resulting artifact (called *CSI Impact Mapping Grid*) combines a set of satisfier improvement strategies derived from our initial work with the GQM⁺Strategies method coupled with the company assets (capabilities) and insights. It is furthermore aimed to be integrated with rich online measurement inputs for real-time predictive feedback. Such transparency across the whole organization enables employees to realize and insightfully support – even proactively in real time – the various cause-effect relationships of the CS/CX.

Keywords: Customer satisfaction · Customer experience · Business-to-business relationships · Performance indicators · Employee satisfaction

1 Introduction

In industrial business-to-business (B2B) product development projects customer satisfaction (CS) may be considered even with individual customers in longer-term relationships as a leading indicator to actually manage the product development projects to achieve the specific level of customer satisfaction with economical resource utilization. Existing research lacks such approaches. The objective of this paper is to address such a case in an industrial B2B R&D company. Elektrobit (later referred as the company), www.elektrobit.com, in the Wireless Business Segment offers products and product platforms for defense and public safety markets as well as for industrial use. The company has been measuring their project CS over the years with their in-house defined CS index. In this design scientific, constructive work, we have equipped the CS management and improvement by applying systems thinking methodologies following our initial studies with the GQM⁺Strategies method.

© Springer International Publishing Switzerland 2015
C. Lassenius et al. (Eds.): XP 2015, LNBIP 212, pp. 205–211, 2015.
DOI: 10.1007/978-3-319-18612-2_18

2   Customer Satisfaction in Industrial B2B Relationships

Traditionally, customer satisfaction has been treated differently in consumer businesses (B2C) than in industrial B2B organizations [1]. In the former settings, the product exchanges and interactions between the producers and customers are usually transaction-based while in the latter cases they are based more on longer-term relationships. Consequently, the sources and criteria for customer satisfaction are often more demanding in B2B when not only the actual product but also the delivery projects (e.g., schedule adherence, changes, risks) matter. The producer company and the customer cocreate value. The producer company may in turn engage in buyer-supplier relationships with different degrees of inter-company interdependences.

There are no specific universal standard CS measures defined, and even less for customer experience (CX) measurements. Some cues (e.g., # of customer incidents) could be applicable both in B2C and B2B. However, in industrial B2B relationships the customers are typically distinct companies with dedicated purchasing and project roles and individuals [2]. It is then often possible to actually ascertain their specific key satisfiers. There are available multiple general-purpose tools and scales, such as Net Promoter Score (NPS) and Customer Experience Maturity Model (CXMM) [3].

In sum, we see research needs to understand throughout the B2B organization how the CS is really judged and how each element affects it either directly or indirectly and collaboratively. The CS measures can then be systematically incorporated into the organizational performance management systems. Due to that, we take a holistic, systems thinking view of the customer satisfaction although the primary interest allies in the software development [4]. This work promotes transparency with continuous, rich feedback including "soft" factors (e.g., employee insights).

3   Research Case and Approach

Our industrial B2B case company has a longish history in applying agile software development and realizing Lean transformation. Overall, if predictability with the product development could be improved, the company could achieve better match with the satisfaction targets and therefore – ultimately – gain higher customer loyalty.

To begin with, we applied the GQM⁺Strategies [5]. In this paper, we continue and expand that to the full set of the company-specific Customer Satisfaction Index (CSI). The company has been measuring their project business feedback regularly over many years with their CSI comprising Project Management (CSI1), Solution Development (CSI2), Deliverables / Results / Quality (CSI3), and Motivation and Feeling (CSI4) elements (altogether with some 20 items).

We proceeded with the following research strategy (see Fig. 1):

1. The initial GQM⁺Strategies process produced a large set of strategies, which could directly be linked here to certain corresponding elements of the CSI goals (c.f., 'S1'). We proceeded by working systematically on the rest of the CSI items.
2. The company assets, resources, and competences (capabilities) were categorized systematically and linked to the CSI items as satisfiers, and to the strategy elements (e.g., 'S1') as realizations and improvements.

The research approach here is to see the B2B customer satisfaction as the result of the entire company project/product organization working as a system. Consequently, our research method is to apply systems thinking (hard and soft) to understand and improve it to develop an overall system for managing the customer satisfaction and project experience as measured by the CSI elements [6]. The rationale is the multifaceted nature of B2B CS in general, and the given compound composition of the company CSI in particular with the goal of improving overall customer satisfaction (c.f., 'G1' in Fig. 1).

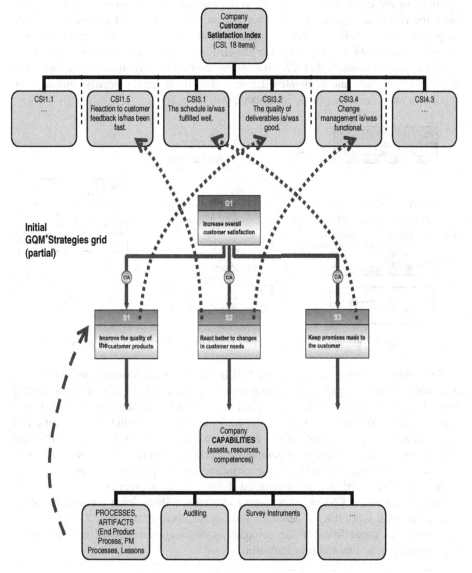

Fig. 1. Research and development approach

4   Results and Experiences

The main advancement of this research investigation stems from the insight that the elements in Fig. 1 as a combination can be comprehended as a causal relationship system like in Fig. 2. The target outcome of the system is managed overall customer satisfaction and experience. This addresses the following research gaps (c.f., Sect. 2): How to measure the customer satisfaction? What factors and capabilities impact it?

Considering the first question, in this research case we have reduced the problemacy by using the company-specific CSI as the measure. Furthermore, in order to estimate the real-time degree of CS during the project, we realized to utilize also rich employee insights as inputs. With respect to the second question, our key hindsight is the point that if we know *a priori*, how the customer will be satisfied, we can actively drive the project towards that CX goal. Many internal quality management activities (e.g., process audits and enchanted delivery maturity reviews) already provide such predictive indicators. Employee insights support them, too.

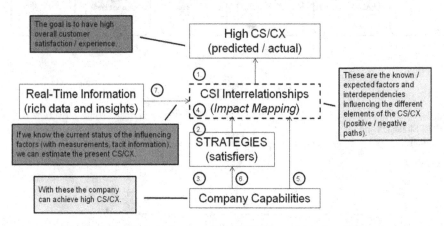

Fig. 2. Customer Satisfaction Index (CSI) Impact Mapping Grid system

Following that line of thinking, the CSI items (18) were analyzed as a system of potential (positive / negative) impact relationships between the different items starting from the project planning elements (CSI1) and ending with the deliverables (CSI3) that the project develops (CSI2) for the customer (success paths). The learning and motivational elements (CSI4) affect basically all those. The relations (hypotheses) were proposed based on the prior company experiences and lessons learned. Although all possible relationships between the elements[1] cannot probably be proved, many such intuitive connections can be assumed and confirmed in practice.

In addition to the CSI element impact interrelationships, each element has been augmented with supporting capabilities and improvement strategies (c.f., Fig. 1). Key developmental capabilities of the company were categorized based on the quality improvement activities and lessons learnt.

---

[1] Note that the total number of potential connections between 18 different items is huge.

In sum, the resulting design artifact illustrated in Fig. 2 forms a knowledge base what we call as the *CSI Impact Mapping Grid*. Currently it comprises the following pieces of information (corresponding tags 1-7 in Fig. 2): 1. CSI element goals (18 items); 2. Strategies for CSI goals achievement (~20, derived from the initial research phase [5]); 3. Company capability elements (~40); 4. CSI elements impact (positive / negative) relationships (hypotheses) (~80); 5. Capability dependencies for supporting the CSI elements and their (positive) interrelationships (~30); 6. Strategy realization capability element dependencies (~60); 7. Measurement information sources, links.

Of the CSI element impact relationships hypotheses (4. in Fig. 2), some 10 have been confirmed so far with company empirical evidence. Table 1 shows some examples of such positive and negative interrelationships. In practice, the B2B customer-specific CSI item priorities affect the actual weighting of the impacts.

Table 1. Impact Mapping Grid relationship validating

RELATIONSHIP	Impact Type	FROM	TO
Applied project tailored auditing ensures effective use of development tools by facilitating tool/process information.	**POSITIVE**	Capa-bilities	CSI2.1
Change information is propagated promptly.	**POSITIVE**	CSI1.3	CSI3.4
New requirements and information are recognized and processed systematically and promptly.	**POSITIVE**	CSI4.2	CSI3.4
Communication gaps cause wrong expectations about the maturity of unofficial deliverables.	**NEGATIVE**	CSI1.3	CSI3.3
Information overflow may distract and damp.	**NEGATIVE**	CSI1.3	CSI1.4
Communication may suffer from personnel changes (loss of knowledge, competence).	**NEGATIVE**	CSI2.2	CSI1.3

Taking into account the multifaceted nature of the CSI, it is reasonable expect that there may be even some cyclic relationships between different CSI items. We have discovered several such potential loops. Finally, for the measurement connections (7. in Fig. 2) there are already many company measurement data sources which could potentially be utilized in more real time, also softer ones such as employee surveys.

In sum, the results so far form a knowledge frame for understanding the company CS/CX and its various influencing factors, addressing the research objective (Sect. 1) of managing product development predictably to achieve projected satisfaction.

5   Discussion and Conclusion

This research work done together with the case company has produced as the outcome a system package realized as the *CSI Impact Mapping Grid*. There are two key resulting implications discovered. First, the company representatives have recognized the complexity of their various potential CS/CX interdependencies (also potentially adverse ones) illuminated by the large number of the hypothesized relationships in it (4.

in Fig. 2). Second, many existing company capability assets and ongoing quality improvement activities have been linked to its different strategy elements (2. in Fig. 2) according to their dependencies and aligned contributions (avoiding negative ones).

Notably the *CSI Impact Mapping Grid* has not been validated for prediction. Nevertheless, the project teams can use it as a relative local guideline and checklist to consider and prioritize the relationships of the CSI in their particular project case, and their specific responsibilities in its success / failure paths. Furthermore, it is an evolving, dynamic knowledge and experience base for continuous improvement.

One acknowledged potential limitation is that this research and development has been done in a single company based on their customized CSI. However, the items of CSI are not heavily company-specific, which lessens the generalization limitations.

In conclusion, the key idea of this research and improvement was to advance from traditional, backward-looking customer satisfaction measurements to more forward-oriented, proactive customer experience development and management in B2B projects. Based on the company-specific Customer Satisfaction Index (CSI), the approach developed here created a customer satisfaction improvement system realized as the *CSI Impact Mapping Grid* with initially applied GQM⁺Strategies method so that the company can consciously manage and improve their CX/CS related targets, capabilities and knowledge with holistic transparency to aligned CS strategies.

Our future research and development plans include the following:

1. Further evaluation and validation of the currently hypothesized parts of *CSI Impact Mapping Grid* in the company with the actual CS survey results
2. Connecting the *CSI Impact Mapping Grid* to the existing measurements for (real-time) feedback (7. in Fig 2) – in particular current KPIs and the Customer interface
3. Iterating with GQM⁺Strategies to elaborate the CSI strategies (e.g., 'S3' in Fig. 1)
4. Strengthening the overall CSI system modeling approach – potentially with system dynamics methods (causal loops) and structural equation modeling (path analysis)

Acknowledgements. This work was supported by TEKES as part of the Need 4 Speed Program of DIGILE (Finnish Strategic Centre for Science, Technology and Innovation in the field of ICT and digital business).

References

1. Tikkanen, H., Alajoutsijärvi, K., Tähtinen, J.: The Concept Of Satisfaction in Industrial Markets: A Contextual Perspective and a Case Study from the Software Industry. Industrial Marketing Management 29, 373–386 (2000)
2. Homburg, C., Rudolph, B.: Customer satisfaction in industrial markets: dimensional and multiple role issues. Journal of Business Research 52, 15–33 (2001)
3. Rossomme, J.: Customer satisfaction measurement in a business-to-business context: a conceptual framework. Journal of Business & Industrial Marketing 18(2), 179–195 (2003)

4. Kettunen, P.: Bringing total quality in to software teams: a frame for higher performance. In: Fitzgerald, B., Conboy, K., Power, K., Valerdi, R., Morgan, L., Stol, K.-J. (eds.) LESS 2013. LNBIP, vol. 167, pp. 48–64. Springer, Heidelberg (2013)

5. Münch, J., Fagerholm, F., Kettunen, P., Pagels, M., Partanen, J.: Experiences and insights from applying GQM+Strategies in a systems product development organisation. In: Demirors, O., Turetken, O. (eds.) 39th EUROMICRO Conference on Software Engineering and Advanced Applications (SEAA), pp. 70–77. IEEE (2013)

6. Lyneis, J.M., Ford, D.N.: System dynamics applied to project management: a survey, assessment, and directions for future research. Syst. Dyn. Rev. 23(2/3), 157–189 (2007)

Dimensions of DevOps

Lucy Ellen Lwakatare(✉), Pasi Kuvaja, and Markku Oivo

Department of Information Processing Science, University of Oulu, Oulu, Finland
{lucy.lwakatare,pasi.kuvaja,markku.oivo}@oulu.fi

Abstract. DevOps has been identified as an important aspect in the continuous deployment paradigm in practitioner communities and academic research circles. However, little has been presented to describe and formalize what it constitutes. The absence of such understanding means that the phenomenon will not be effectively communicated and its impact not understood in those two communities. This study investigates the elements that characterize the DevOps phenomenon using a literature survey and interviews with practitioners actively involved in the DevOps movement. Four main dimensions of DevOps are identified: collaboration, automation, measurement and monitoring. An initial conceptual framework is developed to communicate the phenomenon to practitioners and the scientific community as well as to facilitate input for future research.

Keywords: DevOps · Continuous deployment · Agile · Software deployment

1 Introduction

Companies offering Internet-based services like Facebook, are now deploying software functionality to customers on a daily basis [1]. This paradigm change towards continuous deployment of software functionality has brought opportunities as well as challenges for most companies [2]. DevOps, a blend of two words, Developers and Operations, is a new phenomenon that helps facilitate this change [2]. It builds a living bridge between development and operations and gives them an opportunity to work and collaborate effectively and seamlessly. Agile methods have improved the performance of software development teams by establishing cross-functional teams and providing closer collaboration with customers [3]. DevOps seeks to extend collaboration of development towards operations, which is responsible for deploying, managing and supporting systems' performance at the customer's site [2]. The continuous deployment paradigm requires software companies to increase communication amongst stakeholders, implement automation and improve agility in designing, delivering and operating software products and services. Erich et al. [4] identified the main concepts of DevOps as: culture, automation, measurement, sharing, services, quality assurance, structures and standards. Bang et al. [5] identified the DevOps perspectives to include: collaboration; automation of build deployment; testing; measurement of the process value, cost and technical metrics; and sharing of knowledge and tools.

© Springer International Publishing Switzerland 2015
C. Lassenius et al. (Eds.): XP 2015, LNBIP 212, pp. 212–217, 2015.
DOI: 10.1007/978-3-319-18612-2_19

Currently, there is lack of common understanding of what DevOps constitutes in academia and in the practitioners' communities. There is a need for research that investigates the DevOps phenomenon and examines how it impacts software development and operations. In this paper, the dimensions of DevOps are identified using relevant academic literature and interviews with practitioners actively involved in the DevOps movement. The main contribution of the study is the definition of the main elements that characterize the DevOps phenomenon and an initial conceptual framework that describes the phenomenon.

2   Research Approach

This study uses a literature review and interviews to investigate the DevOps phenomenon. To identify relevant academic literature, we followed the procedure proposed by Webster and Watson [6].

1. The search term, 'DevOps', was selected and, on 11.11.2014, it was used to retrieve a total of 187 studies from six databases: ACM Digital Library (34), ISI Web of Science (2), Science Direct (10), IEEE Xplore (13), Scopus (28) and Google Scholar (first 100).
2. Relevant studies were selected on the basis of: (a) relevance to the topic, (b) peer reviewed, (c) publication in a scientific journal or in conference proceedings
3. Snowballing was performed in Google Scholar to identify other studies (0).

Interviews. Interviews were conducted with four practitioners working at three companies (Table 1) and actively involved in the DevOps movement as organizers of DevOps Days[1] and DevOps Meetups[2].

Table 1. Description of interviewees

Company	Offering	Employees	Role of participants
A	ICT products and services	500	**P1**: Lead architect for cloud in Technology Strategy unit
B	ICT R&D services	80	**P2 & P3:** Senior consultants in a DevOps team consisting of developers and operations doing audits for software development process improvements
C	ICT R&D services	63	**P4:** Senior developer, DevOps expert and manager of a technology team

The collected data was imported to Nvivo[3] and analysed following the thematic synthesis approach [7]. The approach involved coding the problems addressed by DevOps, the actions taken (elements) and the impact of the actions taken.

---

[1] DevOps Days is a technical conference (*http://devopsdays.org/about/*).

[2] DevOps Meetups are face-to-face meetings taking place in different cities around the world.

[3] Qualitative data analysis software (http://www.qsrinternational.com/).

3   Dimensions of DevOps

This section presents the findings from a thorough literature analysis of 22 papers ([1,2], [4,5], [8-25]) and interviews with practitioners. Figure 1 presents an initial conceptual framework that depicts the dimensions that characterize DevOps, the problems that DevOps tries to address and the resulting outcomes.

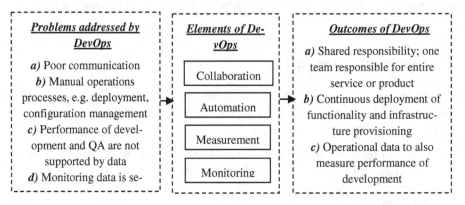

Fig. 1. Conceptual framework characterizing the DevOps phenomenon

3.1   Collaboration

There is consensus in the academic literature and among practitioners that the DevOps phenomenon encompasses a culture of collaboration between the software development organization and the operations organization [2], [8–11]. Other important stakeholders include testers and quality assurance [12]. According to practitioners, it is impossible to effectively transfer information about all releases between two separate organizations in continuous release mode. Other problems include: poor communication between developers and operations and systems designed without complete knowledge and visibility or support for their operational profile [1], [8], [13, 14].

Collaboration is enforced through information sharing, broadening of skillsets and shifting responsibilities between the two teams as well as instilling a sense of shared responsibility [1, 2], [15]. These approaches require changes in people's mind-set as well as changes in the organization's work culture. Collaboration impacts the team structure and the required skillsets of the software developers and operations personnel. The development team may become organized around an entire service taking full responsibility for developing and operating the software functionalities.

3.2   Automation

According to the literature and the practitioners, automation in DevOps is required in operations processes and increased test automation is necessary in the software development process [9], [15–17]. In order to keep up with the pace of Agile software development and continuous integration (CI) practices, operations processes need to be flexible, repeatable and fast by eliminating manual processes. In complex environments it is difficult and time consuming to manually deploy functionality and manage configurations of software functionality and infrastructure repeatedly and quickly [18, 19]. Additionally, test automation in the CI and customer acceptance phases need to be improved to ensure the quality of the deployed functionality.

One approach that DevOps uses to address the manual process is depicted in the concept of "Infrastructure as a Code" (IaC). The IaC concept is used to describe the idea that almost all actions performed to the infrastructure can be automated [19–21]. It emphasizes developing automation logic for deploying, configuring and upgrading software and infrastructure repeatedly and quickly, particularly in a cloud environment. This is observed through increased adoption of open source configuration tools, such as Chef, in companies (e.g. company A). In the literature, the studies that have contributed to this have focused on defining frameworks that help identify the limitations of the tools and test for their reliability and repeatability [17],[20],[22]. In a cloud environment, automation allows the infrastructure to be provisioned and the functionality to be deployed repeatedly and fast [8], [20].

3.3   Measurement

According to Roche [12], DevOps emphasizes "putting efficiency and process into perspective". This means the ability to measure the development process by incorporating different metrics that will help increase efficiency in product development. Claps [2] further described it as being able to go beyond Quality Assurance (QA) to the system's performance and usage data to seek insights about the quality and usefulness of software functionality.

Measurement in DevOps is achieved by measuring the effort of the software process beyond QA using real time performance and usage data of software functionality in the production environment. The impact is that software development efforts are effectively measured [10].

3.4   Monitoring

Operations personnel monitor systems and the underlying infrastructure to determine the appropriate resource assignment and to detect, report and correct problems that occur during or after system upgrades [13]. According to practitioners, operations personnel use monitoring tools and logs to obtain information regarding a system's health. However, in most cases the logs are voluminous causing developers and operations to spend an extensive amount of time locating the problems, especially when the systems are designed not to expose relevant information [23, 24]. Continuous deployment of functionality further challenges monitoring activities by requiring them to be effective and fast [14], [22]. Another problem addressed by DevOps is that the monitored data is not consolidated and effectively used [8].

DevOps addresses the challenges of effective monitoring by emphasizing collaboration between developers and operations so that the systems are designed to expose relevant information [13], [24, 25]. Additionally, analytics can be used to integrate the system and infrastructure performance data with customer usage behaviour [8]. The information is to be provided as feedback to developers and product management to use for product improvements and customization [2], [8, 9].

4 Conclusion

DevOps is a relatively a new phenomenon that lacks a common understanding and definition in academia and in the practitioners' communities. This study identifies four elements that characterize DevOps: collaboration, automation, measurement and monitoring. A conceptual framework is also presented to describe the phenomenon. This study contributes to previous research by confirming three elements of DevOps and it adds one new element. It also presents a conceptual framework to describe the phenomenon. There is still a need for empirical research that investigates the phenomenon in order to validate and enhance the presented conceptual framework.

References

1. Feitelson, D.G., Frachtenberg, E., Beck, K.L.: Development and Deployment at Facebook. IEEE Internet Computing 17, 8–17 (2013)
2. Claps, G.G., Berntsson Svensson, R., Aurum, A.: On the Journey to Continuous Deployment: Technical and Social Challenges Along the Way. Information and Software Technology 57, 21–31 (2015)
3. Rodríguez, P., Markkula, J., Oivo, M., Turula, K.: Survey on agile and lean usage in finnish software industry. In: ACM-IEEE International symposium on Empirical software engineering and measurement, p. 139. ACM Press, New York (2012)
4. Erich, F., Amrit, C., Daneva, M.: Cooperation between Information System Development and Operations. In: 8th International Symposium on Empirical Software Engineering and Measurement, p. 1. ACM Press, New York (2014)
5. Bang, S., Chung, S., Choh, Y., Dupuis, M.: A Grounded Theory Analysis of Modern Web Applications: Knowledge, Skills, and Abilities for DevOps. In: 2nd Annual Conference on Research in Information Technology, pp. 61–62. ACM, New York (2013)
6. Webster, J., Watson, R.: Analyzing the Past to Prepare for the Future: Writing a Literature Review. Management Information Systems Quarterly **26**, 13–19 (2002)
7. Cruzes, D.S., Dyba, T.: Recommended Steps for Thematic Synthesis in Software Engineering. In: International Symposium on Empirical Software Engineering and Measurement, pp. 275–284. IEEE Press, New York (2011)
8. Bruneo, D., Fritz, T., Keidar-Barner, S., Leitner, P., Longo, F., Marquezan, C., Metzger, A., Pohl, K., Puliafito, A., Raz, D., Roth, A., Salant, E., Segall, I., Villari, M., Wolfsthal, Y., Woods, C.: CloudWave: Where Adaptive Cloud Management Meets DevOps. In: IEEE Symposium on Computers and Communications, pp.1–6. IEEE Press, New York (2014)
9. Hosono, S., Shimomura, Y.: Application Lifecycle Kit for Mass Customization on PaaS Platforms. In: 8th IEEE World Congress on Services, pp. 397–398. IEEE Press, New York (2012)

10. Liu, Y., Li, C., Liu, W.: Integrated Solution for Timely Delivery of Customer Change Requests: A Case Study of Using DevOps Approach. International Journal of U-& E-Service, Science & Technology 7, 41–50 (2014)
11. Wettinger, J., Breitenbücher, U., Leymann, F.: DevOpSlang – Bridging the Gap between Development and Operations. In: Villari, M., Zimmermann, W., Lau, K.-K. (eds.) ESOCC 2014. LNCS, vol. 8745, pp. 108–122. Springer, Heidelberg (2014)
12. Roche, J.: Adopting DevOps Practices in Quality Assurance. Communications of the ACM 56, 38–43 (2013)
13. Bass, L.: Supporting Operations Personnel through Performance Engineering. In: International Conference on Performance Engineering, pp. 185–186. ACM Press, New York (2013)
14. Hosono, S., He, J., Liu, X., Li, L., Huang, H., Yoshino, S.: Fast Development Platforms and Methods for Cloud Applications. In: IEEE Asia-Pacific Services Computing Conference, pp. 94–101. IEEE Press, New York (2011)
15. Cook, N., Milojicic, D., Talwar, V.: Cloud Management. Journal of Internet Services and Applications 3, 67–75 (2012)
16. Spinellis, D.: Don't Install Software by Hand. IEEE Software 29, 86–87 (2012)
17. Wettinger, J., Andrikopoulos, V., Strauch, S., Leymann, F.: Characterizing and Evaluating Different Deployment Approaches for Cloud Applications. In: IEEE International Conference on Cloud Engineering, pp. 205–214. IEEE Press, New York (2014)
18. Borgenholt, G., Begnum, K., Engelstad, P.: Audition: A DevOps-oriented Service Optimization and Testing Framework for Cloud Environments. In: Conference of Norsk informatikkonferanse (NIK), pp. 146–157. Akademika Publishing, Trondheim (2013)
19. Harrer, S., Rock, C., Wirtz, G.: Automated and Isolated Tests for Complex Middleware Products: The Case of BPEL Engines. In: IEEE 7th International Conference on Software Testing, Verification and Validation Workshops, pp. 390–398. IEEE, New York (2014)
20. Hummer, W., Rosenberg, F., Oliveira, F., Eilam, T.: Testing Idempotence for Infrastructure as Code. In: Eyers, D., Schwan, K. (eds.) Middleware 2013. LNCS, vol. 8275, pp. 368–388. Springer, Heidelberg (2013)
21. Wettinger, J., Behrendt, M., Binz, T., Breitenbücher, U., Breiter, G., Leymann, F., Moser, S., Schwertle, I., Spatzier, T.: Integrating Configuration Management with Model-driven Cloud Management based on TOSCA. In: 3rd International Conference on Cloud Computing and Services Science, pp. 437–446. SciTePress (2013)
22. Zhu, L., Xu, D., Xu, S., Tran, A.B., Weber, I., Bass, L.: Challenges in Practicing High Frequency Releases in Cloud Environments. In: 2nd International Workshop on Release Engineering, Mountain View, USA, pp. 21–24 (2014)
23. Xu, X., Zhu, L., Weber, I., Bass, L., Sun, D.: POD-Diagnosis: Error Diagnosis of Sporadic Operations on Cloud Applications. In: 44th Annual IEEE/IFIP International Conference on Dependable Systems and Networks, pp. 252–263. IEEE Press, New York (2014)
24. Cukier, D.: DevOps Patterns to Scale Web Applications using Cloud Services. In: Companion Publication for Conference on Systems, Programming & Applications: Software for Humanity, pp. 143–152, ACM Press, New York (2013)
25. Shang, W.: Bridging the Divide between Software Developers and Operators using Logs. In: 34th International Conference on Software Engineering, pp. 1583–1586. IEEE Press, New York (2012)

Towards Introducing Agile Architecting in Large Companies: The CAFFEA Framework

Antonio Martini[✉], Lars Pareto, and Jan Bosch

Computer Science and Engineering, Chalmers University of Technology,
Hörselgången 5, 417 56, Göteborg, Sweden
{antonio.martini,jan.bosch}@chalmers.se

Abstract. To continuously deliver value both in short-term and long-term, a key goal for large product lines companies is to combine Agile Software Development with the continuous development and management of software architecture. We have conducted interviews involving several roles at 3 sites from 2 large companies employing Agile. We have identified current architect roles and gaps in the practices employed at the organizations. From such investigation, we have developed an organizational framework, CAFFEA, for Agile architecting, including roles, teams and practices.

Keywords: Agile architecture · Agile software development · Organizational framework · Architect roles · Software process improvement

1 Introduction

Large software industries strive to make their development processes fast and more responsive, minimizing the time between the identification of a customer need and the delivery of value. Short term responsiveness is given by Agile Software Development (ASD) [1]. A gap in the current Agile frameworks is the lack of activities to enhance agility in the task of developing and maintaining software architecture (*Agile architecting*), necessary for long-term responsiveness [1][2]. The role of architects becomes crucial, but there is a lack of knowledge, in literature, on how such roles are implemented in ASD. Therefore, the research questions that we want to inform are:

RQ1 What are the challenges in conducting architecture practices in Agile software development employed in large software product line organizations?

RQ2 Which roles and teams are needed in order to mitigate the challenges in conducting architecture practices in large product line organizations employing Agile?

We have combined literature review, interviews involving several roles in large product line companies employing Agile Software Development and a combination of structured inductive and deductive analysis in order to find the gaps in the architect roles and their activities. We have developed an organizational framework, *CAFFEA* (Continuous Architecting Framework For Embedded software and Agile), comprehending roles and teams to address the challenges related to the architecture practices in ASD.

© Springer International Publishing Switzerland 2015
C. Lassenius et al. (Eds.): XP 2015, LNBIP 212, pp. 218–223, 2015.
DOI: 10.1007/978-3-319-18612-2_20

2   Research Design

We have employed an embedded multiple-case study [3], where the unit of analysis is an (sub-part of the) organization: the unit needed to be large enough, developing 2 or more sub-systems involving at least 10 development teams. We selected, following a literal replication approach [4], 2 companies: A and B (3 sub-cases) large organizations developing software product lines, having adopted ASD and had extensive in-house embedded software development.

As for data collection, we selected [5] as an up-to-date (2008) and comprehensive categorization of *"what do software architects really do"*. From such classification, we conducted a literature review for each class of practices, selecting the articles containing condensed knowledge. Then we conducted 3 in-depth sets of interviews involving 3 of the cases, in particular A, B_1, and B_2. The interviews lasted 4 hours and involved developers, testers and architects responsible for different levels of architecture (from low level patterns to high level components). During the interviews we assessed if the architecture practices found in step 1 were carried out, who was responsible, and what challenges they were facing. With this step we identified the current gaps in ASD with respect to architecture management.

The interviews and workshops were recorded and transcribed. The analysis was done following an approach based on Grounded Theory [6], alternating structured inductive and deductive techniques (described below) and using a tool for qualitative analysis, to the trace the code to the quotations.

A preliminary evaluation of the framework is being carried out by the authors, but we could not report the data here for lack of space.

3   Results

First we show the identified architect roles in the companies, highlighting the challenges connected to such roles. We have divided the challenges in 4 main groups: *risk management, architectural decisions and changes, providing architectural knowledge* and *monitor the current status of the system*. Then we present the teams, the organizational mechanism to address the challenges involving more than one role. The overall components and framework CAFFEA is visible in Figure 1.

3.1   Architects

3.1.1   Chief Architect (CA)

The main role of the CA is to take high-level decisions and to drive the rest of the architects and the Agile teams in order to build an architecture able to support strategic business goals. In all the organizations that we have studied, the role of CA is present and well recognized, and there are few challenges related to ASD.

Risk management - The CA is usually not directly involved in the detailed development: however, in order to take decisions on feasibility and to assist the sales unit with technical expertize, the CA needs to elicit the information about the current status of the system. The current challenge is the lack of such reliable information and therefore the risk of taking business decisions based on wrong assumptions made on the system.

Monitoring the current status of the system (communication input) - As mentioned before, the current communication practices lack good mechanisms for providing input to the CAs to take informed decision and to address past erroneous decisions (e.g. tool chains not working as expected).

3.1.2   Governance Architect (GA)

We found that the key for the scalability of Agile architecting in a large setting is an intermediate role between the CA and the teams. Such role, (the Governance Architect, GA) functions as a coordinator and support, giving strategic directions for a group of Agile teams developing features within the same (sub-) system. Many architecture practices were mapped by the informants to this role as the main responsible, and we found many challenges in the current organizations. Such role is not always formally recognized: this causes lack of coordination among isolated teams, which favors the accumulation of architectural debt. Also, the non-recognition of this role leads to the lack of resources allocated for carrying out the needed architecture practices.

Risk management - The prioritization of short-term and long-term goals in the team is done by Product Owners through the backlog of the teams. However, such risk management activity usually leads to the down-prioritization of refactoring and architecture improvements, especially the long-term ones. A GA is needed to participate in prioritization to balance the focus between feature development and the long-term goals.

Managing decisions and changes - The architecture needs to support several features and the safe cooperation of the Agile teams. The investigation highlighted either the lack of such responsible for inter-feature architecting or the lack of communication and cooperation between the GA and the Agile teams.

Providing Architecture Knowledge (communication output) - With the shift to ASD, in some of the organizations (B_1 and B_2) the teams have changed from "component teams" to "generalized teams", free to change any part of the code given a feature to be implemented. However, such approach caused, in the teams, a lack of deep expertize about the components. The role of GA becomes therefore critical for assisting the teams and maintaining the architecture, both with face-to-face communication but also supported by documentation when the architecture knowledge is complex and extensive.

Monitoring the current status of the system (communication input) - One of the most emphasized challenges during data collection was the accumulation of architectural debt [7]: the implementation in the code quickly drifted away from the architecture defined and used for strategic decisions and risk management by the CA and other management activities. GAs need to monitor and react to architecture erosion and need for evolution, together with the support of TAs in the Agile teams.

3.1.3 Team Architect (TA)

The TA, the responsible for the architecture in the FT, is often present in the current organizations in the form of a technical leader or experienced developer. Such role is however not formally recognized, which bring the lack of responsibilities for the architecture practices in some of the teams.

Risk management - A challenge was the lack of participation of the team in risk management activities, such as tracking and reporting risky technical debt accumulated during the iterations (activity led by the TA) or to represent the interest of the teams in feasibility discussions with CA, GA and Product Owners (participation of TA).

Providing Architecture knowledge (communication output) - As mentioned for the CA and GA, the lack of capillary spread of architecture knowledge need to be mitigated by a peer in the team, which has been identified with the presence of TA, who would transfer the architectural knowledge from GAs.

Monitoring the current status of the system (communication input) - We found a lack of responsibilities, in the team, about tracking and reporting the status of technical debt that might affect other FTs. The TA would cover such responsibility, as well as lifting proposals for architecture evolution.

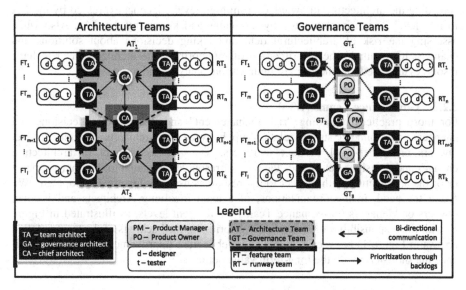

Fig. 1. The components of CAFFEA: teams, roles and their relationships

3.2 Teams

Analyzing the current gaps and the relationships among the architect roles previously mentioned, we found that most of the practices need the roles to coordinate and cooperate in order to mitigate the challenges. To achieve such coordination, suitable organizational mechanisms are non-permanent teams responsible for such practices visible in Figure 1. A special case is the Runway Team (RT), which involves a whole Agile team (see next section).

3.2.1   Runway Team (RT)

As mentioned about the GA and also confirmed by [7], a challenge in the studied companies is the down-prioritization of long-term refactorings or architecture improvements, causing the constant accumulation of architectural debt leading to responsiveness crisis. Such refactorings cannot be prioritized as stories in the backlog of the Agile teams, and therefore remains excluded from the development. In order to conduct such refactorings, a whole Agile team needs to be dedicated for one or more sprints to focus on the "architecture feature" rather than on customer-related features. The RT can be appointed dynamically by a team of Product Owners and architects (see "Governance Team") together, when a long-term refactoring is needed. RTs are visible on the right in Figure 1.

3.2.2   Architecture Teams (ATs)

Most of the architecture practices need coordination and collaboration among different architects in Architecture Teams (ATs in Figure 1): for example, in *monitoring the current status of the system*, no single architects can have all the information needed: the system might have different inconsistencies with architecture at different levels (e.g. low-level design and high-level components). Coordination is also important for spreading the architecture knowledge, from high level concepts expressed by the CA to low level design implemented by the teams and known by the TAs. Also when assessing the risk of architectural debt and taking decisions about solutions and changes, for example the prioritization of refactorings, the architects need to have resources allocated together for communication, analysis and tools.

3.2.3   Governance Teams (GTs)

For those practices regarding "risk management" and "architecture decisions and changes", we found a strong relationship between the architects and the Product Owners or higher-level Product managers. The risk assessment of architecture changes and decisions determines the ratio of resources allocated to the improvements or of the architecture with respect to the resources used for feature development. We found the need, in the organizations, of a team involving Architects and Product Owners or Managers (Governance Teams on different levels, as illustrated in Figure 1) with the responsibility of strategically prioritizing the backlogs of the teams (dotted arrows in Figure 1) between features and architecture improvements, in order to balance the short-term with the long-term value output.

3.3   Framework CAFFEA

The framework CAFFEA is the overall framework of roles, teams and practices. A representation is shown in Figure 1, which combines the visualization of different views: the relationships among the organizational components (architects, managers, teams) with respect to different perspectives (*Architecture* and *Governance*). Figure 1 shows also the communication needs by the architect roles (central area on the *Architecture Perspective*), between the roles and the Agile teams (left) and among the different GTs (*Governance Perspective*). Figure 1 shows the prioritization relationships among the roles and the teams (dotted arrows) and outlines, in both the perspectives, the RTs, our new concept for some of the Agile teams.

Several companies are adopting the CAFFEA framework in practice and we are currently evaluating its application through several case-studies.

4   Discussion and Conclusions

Our work takes inspiration from Leffingwell's work [8] and the concepts of architecture runway. However, the work done by Leffingwell is not supported by scientific investigation following a rigorous research process. Kructhen, in [5], defines several anti-patterns for software architects, based on several experiences in architecture teams. However, the anti-patterns are not specific for the context that we have studied.

The short-term responsiveness in delivering value offered by ASD needs to be enhanced, in large software organizations developing embedded software, by Agile architecting, the management of a software architecture supporting long-lasting responsiveness. We contribute by highlighting current challenges with respect to architectural practices (RQ1): such gaps point at the need for specific architect roles; Team architects, Chief architects and especially important is the Governance Architect, an intermediate key role for coordinating Agile architecting and scaling Agile in large organizations. Such architect roles need organizational mechanisms to cooperate, Architecture Teams, and to interface with Product Management for prioritization and decisions. We developed the CAFFEA framework, including roles, teams and practices, to give support for Agile architecting (RQ2). Such framework, given the current identified gaps, has a specific focus on architecture technical debt management and is being applied and evaluated in practice by several companies.

References

1. Dingsøyr, T., Nerur, S., Balijepally, V., Moe, N.B.: A decade of agile methodologies: Towards explaining agile software development. J. Syst. Softw. **85**(6), 1213–1221 (2012)
2. Daneva, M., van der Veen, E., Amrit, C., Ghaisas, S., Sikkel, K., Kumar, R., Ajmeri, N., Ramteerthkar, U., Wieringa, R.: Agile requirements prioritization in large-scale outsourced system projects: An empirical study. J. Syst. Softw. **86**(5), 1333–1353 (2013)
3. Runeson, P., Höst, M.: Guidelines for conducting and reporting case study research in software engineering. Empir. Softw. Eng. **14**(2), 131–164 (2008)
4. Yin, R. K.: Case Study Research: Design and Methods. SAGE (2009)
5. Kruchten, P.: What do software architects really do? J. Syst. Softw. **81**(12), 2413–2416 (2008)
6. Strauss, A., Corbin, J. M.: Grounded Theory in Practice. SAGE (1997)
7. Martini, A., Bosch, J., Chaudron, M.: Architecture Technical Debt: Understanding Causes and a Qualitative Model. In: 40th Euromicro Conference on Software Engineering and Advanced Applications, Verona, pp. 85–92 (2014)
8. Leffingwell, D.: *Scaling Software Agility: Best Practices for Large Enterprises*. Pearson Education (2007)

Optimal Refactoring

Susanne Siverland[1(✉)], Roger C.S. Wernersson[2], and Charlotte Sennersten[3]

[1] Sigma IT and Management, Östra Vittusgatan 36 SE-37133, Karlskrona, Sweden
susanne.siverland@sigma.se
[2] Ericsson AB, Ölandsgatan 1, Box 518 SE-37133, Karlskrona, Sweden
roger.wernersson@ericsson.com
[3] The Commonwealth Scientific and Industrial Research Organisation (CSIRO),
Digital Productivity Flagship, Autonomous Systems, College Road, Sandy Bay 7005, Australia
charlotte.sennersten@csiro.au

Abstract. This paper investigates if Code-Churn, Lines of Code (LoC), Duplicated Code, Complexity and Technical Debt (TD) can inform a coder where to prioritize refactoring. A mature code-base of 1 300 000 LoC in approximately 5000 files for a period of 20 months has been examined. The result is that code-churn is the strongest variable out of the studied variables followed by LoC and TD. Multiplying with code-churn strengthens LoC and TD even more, making them the strongest indicators of refactoring potential.

Keywords: Refactoring · Software maintenance · Qualitative research · Software quality · Industry · Return of investment

1 Introduction

With limited resources developers need to spend time refactoring ("...improving the design of the code after it has been written" [1]) where it makes the most difference. In order to be able to pick the most relevant files for refactoring this paper investigates a few commonly used code-quality-variables: Lines of Code (LoC), Complexity, Code Duplication as well as Technical Debt (TD) and Code-Churn. The research questions are:

Is LoC, complexity, code duplication, TD or code-churn a significant variable in finding refactoring-candidates to increase maintainability?

*Is LoC, complexity, code duplication or TD **multiplied with** code-churn a significant variable in finding refactoring-candidates to increase maintainability?*

The hypothesis is that one of the studied variables or the variable multiplied with code-churn will be more significant than the other variables in finding refactoring-candidates. Code-churn means how often a file is changed; the average frequency. As a proxy for Maintainability we have used the Total Defect Resolution Time (TDRT) of a file. There are several different approaches in finding refactoring-candidates [1] [2][3][4]. Feathers [5] has looked at finding refactoring-candidates with high complexity and high code-churn.

© Springer International Publishing Switzerland 2015
C. Lassenius et al. (Eds.): XP 2015, LNBIP 212, pp. 224–229, 2015.
DOI: 10.1007/978-3-319-18612-2_21

1.1   The Refactoring Variables and the Analysis

This study used and measured historical data from a mature code-base combined with data from the company's bug-reporting system to find out what files would be more beneficial to refactor. The *rows* in the illustration in figure 1 represent the four maintainability characteristics according to ISO 9126. The *columns* represent code-level properties.

		volume	complexity per unit	duplication	unit size	unit testing
	analysability	x		x	x	x
	changeability		x	x		
	stability					x
	testability		x		x	x

Fig. 1. The SIG-mm 'Mapping system characteristics onto source code properties' (ISO 9126)

The Software Improvement Group maintainability model (SIG-mm) acts as a bridge between the characteristics and the variables and hence how to change the code in practice. In table 1 we show how we bridge the variables to code following ISO standard 9126.

Table 1. From ISO standard 9126 with defined variables to code

SIG-mm	Bridging the Gap	Making use of in this study
Volume	The total number of LoC.	
Complexity/Unit	Cyclomatic complexity per unit (in Java a unit is a method).	As "complexity"
Duplication of Code	Duplicated blocks over 6 lines	As "duplicated lines"
LoC	File size	As "LoC"
Unit testing	Unit test coverage	

Code-churn - Zazworka et al. [3] is using change-prone files which are "indicators of problematic code". They use change-proneness (code-churn) to measure the result. This gives us a basis for being able to use it as a variable.

TD - TD has yet to be defined [6] but is commonly used as an indicator of code quality. We have used SonarQube's [7] calculation model.

Maintainability – Defect Resolution Time (DRT) is the time from when the defect was reported to when it was resolved and approved in the company's bug-tracking system. Total DRT (TDRT) for a file indicates Maintainability, an approach drawn from "Faster Defect Resolution with Higher Technical Quality of Software" [8].

The result is validated in two steps:
- Firstly by Spearman's Rank Correlation Coefficient [9] (SRCC) that will rank each individual file.
- Secondly by choosing the ten files with the highest TDRT in relation to our chosen categories: LoC, Duplication, TD, Complexity and code-churn. The coder can only refactor a limited part of the code-base. There is never a situation where the entire code-base can be refactored.

2   Methodology

The main method is data-mining. This study used and measured historical data from a mature code-base combined with data from the company's bug-tracking system to find out what files would be more beneficial to refactor.

3   Experiment Design

All gathered values were so called snapshots of existing code that had undergone change during the chosen time interval. For each file the collected data for the chosen variables were compared and also multiplied with code-churn against the TDRT of that particular file. Table 2 presents the tools being used in this study and how the variables were retrospectively calculated.

Table 2. Tools used to measure or calculate the variables

Variable	Tool
LoC	SourceMonitor is used to get the 'Lines of code' value where all but blank lines and leading and trailing comments are counted.
Duplication	In SourceMonitor duplication is defined as at least six duplicated lines of code. The entire code-base is scanned. If ten common lines in two files are found, the number will be added to both files. It makes it possible to see the total per file.
TD	SonarQube's TD-plugin is used. TD is measured in time (or money). For how this time (or money) is constructed, see SonarQube's documentation [10].
Complexity	SourceMonitor is used (as Feathers) to get a Complexity value. The maximum method complexity is used which calculates the most complex method in the file.
Code-churn	A mean value of number of changes per month is calculated, based on data from the Git repository [11].

4   Analysis

4.1   Baseline: Time Spent on Defects in the 'Top-ten' Files

To be able to say anything in relation to cause and effect via refactoring we have to create some kind of baseline. Analysis of the "top-ten" files consisted of the following steps 1) find the ten files with the highest TDRT; 2) sum up the TDRT for these files and; 3) in the rest of the paper the sum will be referred as the 'baseline', time spent on these files.

4.2   'Top-ten' Files per Variable

Now we continue by looking at the 'top-ten' worst files on a variable level (LoC, Duplication, TD, Complexity and Code-churn) to find the ten files with highest values for each variable and find the TDRT for these files.

4.3   Spearman's Rank Correlation Coefficient (SRCC)

We will use SRCC [9][12] which is a statistical measure between 1 and -1 of the strength of a monotonic relationship between paired data where 1 mean absolute correlation, -1 means reversed correlation, and 0 means no correlation.

5   Results

The SRCC shows best result for TD (0.616, strong), see Table 3. In column three all values are evened out by the multiplication with Code-churn (Variable* Code Churn SRCC). Column four shows what the impact would have been if the 'top-ten' files would have been refactored. Column five shows that all variables are strengthened when multiplied by code-churn.

Table 3. Summary of SRCC and % of baseline affected

Variable	SRCC	Variable* Code-Churn SRCC	Top-ten worst files (% of baseline)	Variable* Code-churn top-ten worst files (% of baseline)
LoC	0.435	0.558	38	50
Complexity	0.353	0.525	18	26
Duplicated lines	0.111	0.446	<1	36
TD	0.616	0.571	16	50
Code-churn		0.576		49

5.1   Summary TDRT 'Top-ten' Paired with the Results for Each Variable

Table 4 shows the ten files with the highest TDRT, and their rank when sorted using the other variables. This is to find out whether any of the files with the highest TDRT would have been refactored if the 'top-ten' files for each variable had been selected for refactoring. The time is relative. TDRT 1 is the file with the highest TDRT.

Table 4. Summary TDRT 'top-ten' paired with the results for each variable

File	Relative TDRT	Churn n (pos)	LoC (pos)	LoC* churn (pos)	TD (pos)	TD * Churn (pos)	Com-plexity (pos)	Complex * churn (pos)	Duplicat (pos)	Duplicat * churn (pos)
A	1	3	1	1	2	2	307	13	290,5	3
B	0,738	20	58	15	18	29	271	28	582,5	29
C	0,599	355	313	223	183	159	707	282	908	338
D	0,525	213	407	187	124	85	410	151,5	411,5	88
E	0,507	59	142	64	45	57	83	21	not ind.	not ind.
F	0,488	48	41	23	37	31	178	33	not ind.	not ind.
G	0,471	587	565	440	264	325	1524	652	660	331,5
H	0,464	587	569	443	265	326	1524	652	549,5	282,5
I	0,444	538	377	251	244	208	512	604,5	813	391
J	0,444	491,5	242	337	220	193	1524	305,5	1577,5	878,5

Only one of the 'top-ten' TDRT files is indicated among the 'top-ten' using any of the above variables. The marked boxes shows which position that one file got. The variables are TD, TD*Churn, LoC, LoC*Churn, Churn and Duplicated Lines*Churn. They all indicate the same file, File A. The other variables would not have indicated any of the 'top-ten' TDRT files.

This means that if a programmer decides to refactor the 'top-ten' files based on any indicator above s/he would have missed nine of the 'top-ten' TDRT files.

5.2   Result on Research-Questions

Is refactoring/code-churn a significant variable in finding refactoring-candidates to increase maintainability?

Yes, code-churn is one of the strongest variables investigated in this paper.

Further on we can ask: *How can a programmer be informed what to refactor to raise maintainability by using the variable, or the variable multiplied with code-churn?*

A programmer can select files ripe for refactoring if using code-churn. When Code-churn is taken into account the strongest variables are LoC*Churn and TD*Churn when the result is based on SRCC. However if a coder wanted to refactor the ten files with the highest Maintainability none of the ingoing variables would be suitable.

6   Discussion and Implication

We have not looked into whether longer files had higher TDRT per LoC than shorter files. All the files are not changed.

7   Conclusion

Code-churn is very useful in optimizing refactoring when used to select which files to refactor, when using TDRT as a proxy for maintenance. After code-churn, LoC is the most promising variable to use, followed by TD. (It is always wisest to refactor a file when you modify its function, because it is fresh in memory.)

References

1. Fowler, M.: Refactoring: improving the design of existing code. Addison-Wesley Professional (1999)
2. Tsantalis, N., Chatzigeorgiou, A.: Ranking refactoring suggestions based on historical volatility. In: 2011 15th European Conference on Software Maintenance and Reengineering (CSMR), pp. 25–34. IEEE (2011)
3. Zazworka, N., Vetro', A., Izurieta, C., Wong, S., Cai, Y., Seaman, C., Shull, F.: Comparing four approaches for technical debt identification. Software Quality Journal, 1–24 (2013) (article in press)
4. Feathers, M.: Working effectively with legacy code. Prentice Hall Professional (2004)
5. Feathers, M.: On Churn and Complexity. http://www.stickyminds.com/sitewide.asp?Function=edetail&ObjectType=COL&ObjectId=16679&tth=DYN&tt=siteemail&iDyn=2 (visited May 21, 2013)
6. Tom, E., Aurum, A., Vidgen, R.: An exploration of technical debt. Journal of Systems and Software (2013) (article in press)
7. http://www.sonarqube.org/ (visited October 2, 2014)
8. Luijten, B., Visser, J., Zaidman, A.: Faster defect resolution with higher technical quality of software. In: 4th International Workshop on Software Quality and Maintainability (SQM 2010).(March 2010)
9. How to calculate Spearman's rank correlation coefficient. http://en.wikipedia.org/wiki/Spearman%27s_rank_correlation_coefficient(visited June 20, 2013)
10. Technical Debt Calculation http://docs.codehaus.org/display/SONAR/Technical+Debt+Calculation(visited August 23, 2013)
11. http://git-scm.com/(visited October 24, 2014)
12. What the Spearman's rank correlation coefficient result meanshttp://www.statstutor.ac.uk/resources/uploaded/spearmans.pdf(visited June 20, 2013)

Agile and the Global Software Leaders: A Perfect Match?

Stavros Stavru[✉] and Sylvia Ilieva

Sofia University "St. Kliment Ohridski",
5, James Bouchier Str., P.B. 48 1164, Sofia, Bulgaria
{stavross,sylvia}@fmi.uni-sofia.bg

Abstract. The presented study examines the prevailing espoused values of some of the most successful software organizations and evaluates the extent to which they are promoted in the agile ideology. Its objective is to determine the level of value congruence and whether it could be used to further explain the widespread adoption of agile software development. Its findings reveal a perfect match between the prevailing espoused values of the examined global software leaders and the agile ideology, and suggest that the popularity of the agile methods might be explained through their capability to increase customer value, facilitate collaboration and teamwork, secure continuous improvement and ensure high quality of delivered products and services.

Keywords: Agile software development · Espoused values · Software industry

1 Introduction

Agile is ideology[1]. It systematizes concrete experience and knowledge, forms a set of values and principles, and defines rules and standards that must be followed. The specifics of this ideology had led agile software development to be strongly associated with the iterative and incremental development of new software systems by small, co-located and cohesive teams of highly-skilled and collaborative professionals. As result it is often believed that agile methods could hardly scale to fit various organizational, project and team contexts. Some of the most challenging scaling issues are related to team size, geographical distribution, system and management complexity, legacy systems, compliance with regulations, organizational culture, etc. [1, 2] Many of these challenges are expected to be even greater for large multi-national software organizations. However the majority of the global software leaders are successfully using various agile methods and techniques today (e.g. IBM, Microsoft, SAP, Symantec, Google, etc.) [3]. Having such a discrepancy between the expected limitations of scaling agile and the increasing number of success stories from the large-scale software industry is motivating the presented study.

Organizational values are long-lasting constructs which have emerged from the collective beliefs, experience and vision of a group or all members of the organization

---

[1] http://www.agilemanifesto.org/

© Springer International Publishing Switzerland 2015
C. Lassenius et al. (Eds.): XP 2015, LNBIP 212, pp. 230–235, 2015.
DOI: 10.1007/978-3-319-18612-2_22

on what the organization should holds of intrinsic worth and which influence (explicitly or implicitly) the decision making and evaluation of individuals and organizations in terms of their modes, actions and end states [4]. As such they could be defined as the ideology of the organization. Organizational values have been extensively studied in recent years and are often used to explain various organizational and industrial phenomena [4]. Following this trend of research the presented study examines the prevailing organizational values of some of the most successful software organizations and evaluates the extent to which they are reflected in the agile ideology. Its objective is to determine whether there is value congruence and whether it could be used to explain the widespread adoption of agile methods among the largest organizations in the software industry [3].

2   Methodology

The examined organizations were taken from PricewaterhouseCoopers's Global 100 Software Leaders [5]. The list ranks one hundred of the most successful organizations in the software industry in regard to their annual revenues. On the top are corporate giants as Microsoft, IBM, Oracle, SAP and Ericsson. The espoused values of these organizations were manually extracted from official corporate websites and then translated into a common terminology using the taxonomy of organizational values proposed by the authors in [4]. The taxonomy is briefly presented in Table 1.

Table 1. Agent and operational values

Category	Description
Agent values	
Customer values	Organizational values associated with stakeholders who are recipients of the products, services, etc. delivered by the organization.
Partner values	Organizational values associated with stakeholders on whom the "raw" input of the organization relies on.
Shareholder values	Organizational values associated with stakeholders who legally own part of the organizational share.
Employee values	Organizational values associated with stakeholders who are contributing labor and expertise to the organization.
Society values	Organizational values associated with the environment and the communities in the region, country or worldwide.
Operational values	
Process values	Organizational values which describe the desired characteristics of all sets of interrelated activities and tasks that transform organizational resources (inputs) into concrete products and services (outputs).
Product values	Organizational values which describe the desired characteristics of delivered products and services.

The taxonomy consists of 39 organizational values classified into agent and operational values. Agent values describe desired end states of various organizational stakeholders and rationalize the existence of the organization. Operational values on the other hand define the desired way of organizational functioning as well as the desired characteristics of delivered products and services. Therefore they are the conditions securing the fulfillment of agent values.

3   What's Valued Most by Global Software Leaders?

Almost all of the examined global software leaders with espoused values have organizational values associated with employees. This makes employee values the leading category and suggests that successful software organizations tend to highly appreciate their employees and acknowledge their great importance. The values associated with processes take a second place, followed by customer and product values. On the bottom of the list are partners, shareholders and society values. The distribution of these value categories is presented on Figure 1.

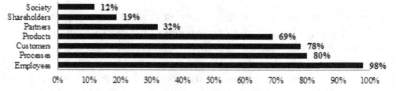

Fig. 1. Value categories and their distribution among the examined organizations

Figure 2 further shows the distribution of the organizational values. In regard to employees - discipline seems to be the most prominent one. This is not a surprise as all the examined organizations are highly recognizable by the public and their reputation is quite sensitive to corporate scandals, fraud trials, etc. The second most favorable employee value is cooperation, followed by accountability, creativity and competency. Continuous improvement is the top value in terms of processes. Other prevailing process values are resources utilization, communication and flexibility. In respect to customers, improving customer's financial and marketing positioning is the greatest concern. Customer's satisfaction, trust and loyalty, although important, are much less favorable. This could be explained with the specifics of the software industry where speed and cost are often crucial for customer's success despite that it might result in compromising the quality (thus satisfaction) and/or customer relationships (thus trust and loyalty). The distribution of product values shows that innovation is undoubtedly the prevailing value in this category. This is quite expected as global software leaders have to continuously deliver new and valuable products and services, and further improve existing ones in order to sustain their leadership status. Quality seems to be of much less importance. Trust and equity are among the top partner values. This is understandable as modern software organizations might heavily rely on many suppliers, contractors, etc. and the overall success of the business is determined by the fair play of all competitors. In regard to shareholders - the greatest concern is improving their financial well-being, as well as the reputation of their shareholders and the corporate image. Society values are the least preferred organizational values. This raises some concerns as global software leaders are expected to be much more engaged with ecological and social sustainability and serve as a role model in this regard.

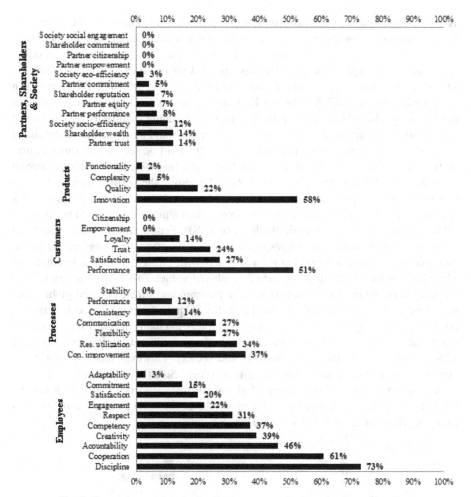

Fig. 2. Org. values and their distribution among the examined organizations

4 Is There a Perfect Match?

The first value of the agile manifesto is related to individuals and their interactions. More specifically it emphasizes the crucial role software engineers have for the successful software development and the need for continuous and effective cooperation and teamwork. This could be associated with employee values - the leading value category among the examined organizations. Moreover cooperation is the second most favorable value in this regard. Other top values are discipline and accountability which are also strongly advocated in the agile ideology. Respect and commitment seem to be of less importance although they could be found as value statements in various agile methods (XP and Scrum). In addition to individuals and their interactions, the first value of the agile manifesto emphasizes the need of processes and tools

as well. When applied cautiously they might provide empowering working environments. Process values are the second most favorable value category among the examined organization. On top is continuous improvement – a value which is strongly
emphasized in the agile ideology. The same is valid for resource utilization, flexibility
and communication. Consistency is the only process value which could be found in
many agile methods (XP, Scrum and Kanban) but seems to be of less importance to
the business. The second and the third values of the agile manifesto are associated
with customers. They state that the primary concern should be to maximize the added
value to the customers. As such the agile ideology could be seen as customer-centric
in its very nature. Customer values are the third most favorable value category among
the examined global software leaders as well. Moreover the performance of the customers is on the top of list, followed by satisfaction, trust and loyalty. Customer's
empowerment and citizenship seem to be overlooked although they could be found as
value statements in various agile methods (e.g. XP, Scrum and Kanban). The forth
value of the agile manifesto relates to change and its effective management. In the
used taxonomy there are two values associated with change. The first is employee
adaptability which is the least preferred employee value. This reveals a serious discrepancy between the agile ideology and the preferences of the examined global software leaders. However organizational flexibility is quite favorable value in terms of
processes which suggests that responding effectively to change is still valuable for the
top business. The four values of the agile manifesto could not be directly associated
with the products, partners, shareholders and society. However this does not mean
that they are entirely absent from the agile ideology. Still they play a secondary role
(as are the preferences of the examined global software leaders). Figure 3 shows the
extent to which the value categories are advocated in the agile ideology and distributed among the examined global software leaders.

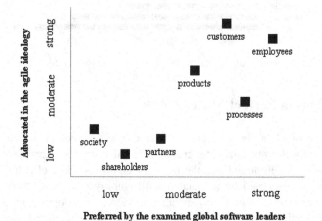

Fig. 3. Value categories and the extent to which they are advocated in the agile ideology and
distributed among the examined global software leaders.

5   Conclusions

The findings of the presented study reveal that the agile ideology reflects very well the prevailing espoused values of the examined organizations (all value categories in Figure 3 follow the 45-degree line). Similar to these global software leaders, the agile ideology is employee- and customer-centric and advocates important values associated with processes and products. This could further explain the widespread adoption of agile methods and reason why they have become the mainstream in software engineering.

The presented study has its recognized limitations. The first is related to its external validity. The findings of the study could not be generalized to the entire software industry neither to all successful software organizations. This is because its sample is limited to PricewaterhouseCoopers's Global 100 Software Leaders and therefore is non-probalistic. The second limitation comes from the extraction of the espoused values and their translation into the organizational values from the used taxonomy. The latter was hampered by the fact that many of the espoused values were defined vaguely which might have caused misinterpretation. In order to mitigate this threat to internal validity both authors did the translation independently from each other and the translation was repeated in one month interval. Yet another limitation comes from the mapping between the values bedded in the agile ideology and the values from the used taxonomy. As it is based on authors' interpretation of the agile manifesto one could argument the presence of research bias.

The presented study could be further extended. Its target population might be narrowed down to include software organizations from specific business or application domains, occupation, size, organizational life-cycle, etc. This could be used to evaluate whether the agile ideology reflects the prevailing espoused values in these particular contexts. Moreover the analysis could be narrowed down to specific agile methods or extended to include traditional software development methods.

References

1. Ambler, S.W.: Agile Software Development at Scale. In: Meyer, B., Nawrocki, J.R., Walter, B. (eds.) CEE-SET 2007. LNCS, vol. 5082, pp. 1–12. Springer, Heidelberg (2008)
2. Senapathi, M., Srinivasan, A.: Sustained agile usage: a systematic literature review. In: Proceedings of the 17th International Conference on Evaluation and Assessment in Software Engineering, pp. 119–124 ACM, Porto de Galinhas (2013)
3. Stavru, S.: A critical examination of recent industrial surveys on agile method usage. Journal of Systems and Software **94**, 87–97 (2014)
4. Stavru, S.: What do we know about Organizational Values? – A Systematic Review. Sofia University "St. Kliment Ohridski" (2013)
5. McCaffrey, M.: PwC Global 100 Software Leaders. PricewaterhouseCoopers (2013)

Experience Reports

High Level Test Driven Development – Shift Left

Kristian Bjerke-Gulstuen[1], Emil Wiik Larsen[1],
Tor Stålhane[2], and Torgeir Dingsøyr[2,3(✉)]

[1] Accenture, Rolfsbuktveien 2, Oslo, Norway
{k.bjerke-gulstuen,emil.wiik.larsen}@accenture.com
[2] Department of Computer and Information Science,
Norwegian University of Science and Technology, Trondheim, Norway
{stalhane,dingsoyr}@idi.ntnu.no
[3] SINTEF, 7465, Trondheim, Norway

Abstract. Agile development methods are increasingly used in large projects, with many development teams. Because acceptance testing can require a large chain of features to be completed, testing is often carried out late in such projects. In this experience report, we describe a large project where 11 development teams delivered a system in 12 three week iterations. We also describe how the focus of test activities was shifted towards the earlier phases of development, what we call "shift left". This involved shifting the focus both within the iterations, and in how the overall testing work was organized. We describe the results of this change, and provide recommendations for how to organize test work in future large-scale development projects.

Keywords: Large-scale agile development · Scrum · Test · Software engineering · Agile methods · Inter-team coordination · Test organization

1   Introduction

When agile development methods appeared, they were believed to "best suit collocated *teams* of about *50 people or less* who have easy access to user and business experts and are developing projects that are not life-critical" [1]. Today, agile methods are increasingly used in other contexts such as large-scale development projects. The application of agile methods in large-scale development raises a number of new challenges [2], including how test activities should be organized.

Large-scale projects typically involve high complexity both with respect to existing software systems and client organizations. Large projects are often run in large organizations with high expectations for quality and efficiency. Testing is expected to be an integrated and clearly defined component of the development method. A challenge in large development projects can be that test efforts are introduced late in the development, which may cause delays in delivery to the client. One reason for late testing is that there is often a large chain of user stories that needs to be implemented before the client can acceptance test the system.

© Springer International Publishing Switzerland 2015
C. Lassenius et al. (Eds.): XP 2015, LNBIP 212, pp. 239–247, 2015.
DOI: 10.1007/978-3-319-18612-2_23

In this experience report we describe Accenture's experience from one of the major development projects to date in Norway, which made extensive use of agile methods. Kristian Bjerke-Gulstuen and Emil Wiik Larsen are experienced test managers in Accenture. They have been responsible for planning and executing testing in several large-scale projects, using both traditional and agile development methods. Their experience from the project was discussed with researchers Tor Stålhane who has a focus on testing and quality assurance and Torgeir Dingsøyr who has a focus on agile methods and large-scale development.

We describe our experience with shifting the focus of test activities to the early phases of development, what we will refer to as the "shift left"-approach, or high-level test-driven development. We believe these experiences can be of interest to test managers, testers, project managers, Scrum masters and other participants in large-scale agile development projects.

We start by describing the project, the shift left-approach and two main implications before concluding with advice relevant for other large-scale projects.

2   Background: A Large-Scale Project to Meet a Political Decision

This large-scale IT development project was run by a client within the Norwegian public sector, and the delivery date was set by a political decision. The system was considered critical to the Norwegian society and the system-of-systems concerned was developed as an extension of an existing and mature system-of-systems for processing of payments. Therefore, both time and quality were critical factors.

The system covers information gathering, processing of data, decisions and calculation of payments. It is one part of a complex IT system including web services, automated processes, 200 GUIs, 70 batch services and integration services.

The project consisted of several vendors, developing systems connected via a service-oriented architecture. This experience reported is related to the core part of the system, which in this release involved more than 100 000 hours of development and testing. The vendor work spanned 12 three week-sprints, and a final six week system test following the last sprint. Faced with a fixed delivery date and therefore limited time to implement the functionality in scope, an existing maintenance project of three Scrum teams was scaled up to 11 teams during a four month period.

The Scrum teams included the following roles: Scrum master, developer, tester / QA resource, functional and technical architect. There were no client resources represented in the Scrum teams. The vendors were responsible for detailed design and development including unit, integration and sprint system testing of their deliverables. The client was responsible for sprint acceptance testing after every sprint, system integration testing running in parallel with the vendor's sprint system tests and a user acceptance testing (UAT).

3   High Level Test Driven Development – Shift Left

Test first or test-driven development is one of the agile practices that has received the most attention. The focus of testing has moved from unit testing to acceptance testing, with focus on achieving similar benefits at unit level [3].

More than half of all defects are introduced not due to coding errors but to requirements and design decisions according to Jones [4]. Since (1) more than half of the defects are introduced early in the development process and (2) the cost of defect removal increases during project life time, it makes sense to start test development as early as possible – i.e. shift testing leftwards in the process. In an agile setting, this has two main implications: Shifting test activities towards the early sprints and towards the start of each sprint.

In the following, we will describe our experience with high level test driven development, focusing on two main aspects: First, shift left during sprint work which involves early and high focus on testing in each development iteration. Second, how testing was organized to achieve this.

3.1   Shift Left During Sprint Work

Motivation. Design documentation delivered to the Scrum teams sometimes included information that could be interpreted differently depending on the team's previous experience with the system. This, in combination with the lack of access to client resources as part of the Scrum teams, made it clear that the teams had to extend their responsibility in making clarifications to unclear or ambiguous requirements and design. Also, the highly interconnected nature of the system and the number of Scrum teams working on interdependent tasks in parallel proved a challenge to testing.

Execution. To ensure that each team had an efficient approach to testing and quality assurance, a dedicated QA resource/tester was assigned to each Scrum team. This person would continuously work with quality assurance of design documentation, decide whether the implementation was testable, prepare the test model and test data and work closely with the developers and Scrum master to ensure high quality code. The tester also ensured that all test activities were performed as early as possible. The tester helped the team and facilitated involvement of the client during the sprints to ensure that the necessary clarifications were provided. The client was invited to walk-through-meetings in addition to reviewing the sprint test plans and test approach. During sprint closure the clients side resources were invited to sprint demos. These demos were arranged with the purpose of demonstrating the new parts of the system, providing information on how the testing was performed and what issues the teams had encountered in testing the implemented functionality.

Our test strategy described a clear definition of done prior to sprint system testing, and, more importantly, it described the expectations to the developer with regards to test. The following are some examples of these expectations:

- "Test expects and demands that code is not checked in without unit tests. Unit tests shall always be in the same check in."
- "Test expects and demands that peer review of the code is completed before the task can be set to finished and that the peer review covers the unit and integration tests and the quality of these tests"

These expectations provided a clear guideline for the tasks to be performed before the build was released to the test environment. It also demonstrated that testing is an integral part of the development process and established expectations to the quality of work within all activities and test phases, from unit test to integration and sprint system test. In order for the expectations to be accepted, and not be forced upon the developers, they were developed in collaboration with senior developers on the project. These senior developers were part of the Scrum teams and made sure the demands were known and followed. By being committed to the expectations the senior developers acted as ambassadors for testing and helped the project establish a mutual understanding for the level of quality expected in the development phase; we established a clear and visible culture for quality.

Functional areas were usually divided into several epics and numerous user stories, involving several application components/modules. User stories completing each functional area were often delivered by several Scrum teams, making them dependent on each other to complete development in the sprints. As part of the sprint planning, the Scrum teams created user story dependency maps (Figure 1) and used these to make sure that development was planned and completed in a correct sequence both within the Scrum team and cross teams. The purpose was to complete development in a timely fashion so that sprint system testing of complete areas could start as early as possible. The dependency map also included a map of module dependencies for each user story. In addition, the dependency maps were used in status and progress reporting in Scrum and Scrum of Scrum meetings as well as in informal cross-team communication.

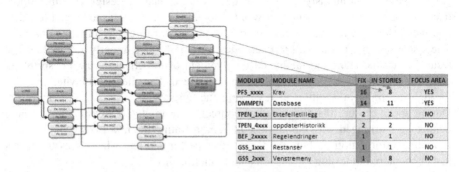

MODULUID	MODULE NAME	FIX	IN STORIES	FOCUS AREA
PFS_xxxx	Krav	16	8	YES
DMMPEN	Database	14	11	YES
TPEN_1xxx	Ektefelletillegg	2	2	NO
TPEN_4xxx	oppdaterHistorikk	2	2	NO
BEF_2xxxx	Regelendringer	1	1	NO
GSS_1xxx	Restanser	1	1	NO
GSS_2xxx	Venstremeny	1	8	NO

Fig. 1. Dependency maps and link to identified high risk modules

To ensure the necessary prioritization and focus during development and testing, we developed a risk-based approach that identified the high risk modules. I.e., modules were defined as high risk if

- previous experience with the module suggested that it was complex to change and test, both during development and in production
- the module was used in several contexts (i.e. a web service used by both batch and GUI modules)

The resulting list of high risk modules was merged with a list of modules involved in multiple user stories, as highlighted by the dependency maps (Figure 1). This was done to obtain an overview of what high risk modules the Scrum teams were making code changes to. Since we were working with an existing system we could also collect statistics from the production environment on modules with several defects reported and fixed (defect history). When we merged the defect statistics with the list of high risk modules, we developed a good overview and basis for prioritization in the development and test planning.

Result. We experienced that the *dedicated QA resource/tester* became one of the most central resources within the teams. We relate this to the lack of availability of the client resources as part of the Scrum team, thus allowing the tester to become the resource with extensive (cross) functional knowledge.

Client side involvement facilitated by the Scrum teams enabled direct feedback from the client early on in the sprints, helping the team to obtain a correct understanding of the functionality to be implemented. The insight gained by the client helped them in planning and effectively executing their own sprint acceptance test. The client also became a more active part in the development process than the original organization model allowed. Another positive effect was that the involvement ensured a transparent test approach and test process. This proved to be valuable in gaining trust in our development, quality assurance and testing process

Dependency maps and a *risk based approach* helped the Scrum teams plan their development and testing so that code was delivered in a way that allowed sprint system testing of the complete functionality within the sprint. We believe we were more accurate and reliable in our sprint deliverables, and achieved a higher degree of completeness in the sprint deliverables when using this tool. The results from the client side sprint acceptance test support this. The chart (Figure 2) summarizes the stories committed and approved after each sprint. It also shows the number of defects fixed in the sprint acceptance test.

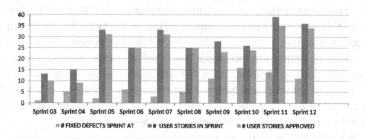

Fig. 2. Sprint status, defects and user stories

Sprint 10 to 12 consisted of implementation of the most complex functionality and more of the system was integrated to other systems. This caused a rise in defects being detected and fixed during the sprint acceptance testing.

3.2   Organizing the Testing to Achieve a Shift Left Focus

Motivation. Due to scope, risk, complexity and the fact that we were implementing changes in an existing system, the system needed a large amount of testing and regression testing. To reduce the demand on testing in later project phases it was important that the Scrum teams completed all planned test activities. This meant the Scrum teams also had to implement the concepts of "shift left" when organizing their testing.

Execution. Our test execution model consisted of both sprint system tests and a final system test (Figure 3). This model aimed at delivering a working system to the client every third week, a thoroughly regression tested system after the final system test, and to reduce the demand for testing in later project phases.

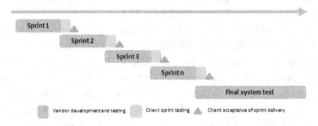

Fig. 3. Sprint development and test execution model

Within the sprint we focused on separate testing of each committed user story, followed by testing them in context of the complete functionality they were part of. However, due to the many dependencies we were not always able to test all functionality without stubs or mocks of integrated systems. Therefore, we had to repeat testing of complete areas after all user stories were developed. This final system test aimed at re-testing the essence in the delivery from all sprints as well as regression testing of selected critical functionality. For the final system test the testers were moved from the Scrum teams and organized as a separate team.

The test execution model aimed at dedicating most of the third week of each sprint to system testing and fixing defects. However, due to many of the development tasks being complex and time consuming, this was not always possible to achieve. To ensure that sufficient testing was performed we decided to rely on exploratory testing in addition to the structured testing. For our exploratory testing we teamed developers, designers, client side testers and Scrum team testers, and arranged sessions where the teams competed in detecting the most defects. These teams organized themselves in regards to what area to test and their strategy for identifying defects.

In the first week of the sprint each team was required to deliver a test plan for each user story. At the end of each sprint the client demanded a test report for every user story covering what we had tested and input for the next test phase. On average the 11 teams delivered three to four user stories in each sprint. This meant 30 to 40 test plans and test reports to be produced manually every sprint, hence both testers and managers spent a considerable amount of time producing reports rather than doing testing. This challenge was solved by including the test plan and test report with the development tasks already tracked and managed in a project tracking tool, and automating the process of presenting the reports to the client.

Result. The final system test was essential in demonstrating a complete and high quality system prior to the user acceptance testing (UAT). By being able to test larger units of functionality, the Scrum teams identified a large amount of changes due to unclear requirements before the UAT.

The exploratory testing had several positive effects. It became an important activity for facilitating collaboration across teams, roles, levels and vendor/client, which resulted in easier communication across "borders". Also, we found it valuable to include the developers in these exploratory test teams. We experienced that the developers enjoyed the activity and even fixed the defects identified before the defects were registered in the defect management system and assigned for correction.

We found the reporting automation strategy valuable as it helped us to present all plans and reports to the client in a timely fashion and freed up time for the testers to focus on the actual testing tasks. Also, this allowed the test manager to spend more time coaching the teams, helping them to complete all sprint testing.

3.3   Was It an Agile Project?

To deal with the challenges experienced and the size of the project, we needed to balance agility with processes and routines that gave us more control up front and a stricter management behavior towards the teams. We found these actions necessary to meet the goals of the project, but how did the project actually deviate from the principles in the Agile Manifesto?[1]

The Scrum teams did not have a client resource as an integrated part of the team, but they had a dedicated role within the team (QA/tester) and facilitated proactive involvement of the client side throughout the sprint.

The Scrum teams were planned to be self-managing and to organize their own work towards their Scrum team goals. However, to cope with the strict time schedule we had to develop a management, team and organizational culture that enabled the management to interfere with the teams if risks for delays were identified. Actions were taken to make sure all committed user stories were delivered on time and that testing was done according to the approach and plans. This included putting in extra effort, often demanded by the management. This was necessary to make sure we did not produce an unwanted backlog and technical and functional debt.

Having the testers organized as a separate team during the final system test is not compliant to the manifesto. However, we considered it necessary to meet the deadlines for our complete delivery to the next project phase.

---

[1] http://www.agilemanifesto.org/

The project also implemented a common set of guidelines and rules to aid the change request process in deciding if a change request was to be implemented or not. This process got stricter towards the later sprints and finally only changes critical for the political decision were accepted. Other changes were registered as technical and functional debt and deferred for evaluation to later releases.

4   Conclusion

Agile development methods are increasingly used in large development projects characterized by high complexity, interdependent tasks, fixed scope, fixed delivery date and a professional client with high demands and expectations for quality.

The key learning point from organizing testing in this project was to shift the test activities left towards the earlier phases of development. This shift ensured that test and QA activities were given the attention they needed. This helped us to detect defects in both design and code early on, and made it possible to deliver working software to the client by the end of every sprint. To achieve this, the organization must be mature and accept test as a vital part of the development process.

A second key learning point was that when the necessary conditions and expectations are clearly communicated and understood by the Scrum teams, a mindset and attitude is naturally developed saying "we plan, implement and deliver this software together". If the management and senior developers introduce concepts, expectations and tools through cooperation, these aids will not be perceived as being forced upon the teams. The result will be early test and high level test driven development as natural and integrated parts of the projects agile development process.

To conclude, projects need to find a balance between actions that increases the level of control and management while preserving the benefits gained by using agile development methods. However, the actions need to be implemented in a way that ensures that they are supported and agreed upon by the Scrum teams. Test management and project management should therefore be creative and bold in challenging the way agile is implemented; with the main goal to continuously improve the delivery models, and to deliverer working and high quality software to the client on a regular basis.

Acknowledgements. We are grateful to Ville Heikkilä for helpful comments on earlier versions of this experience report.

References

1. Williams, L., Cockburn, A.: Agile Software Development: It's about Feedback and Change. IEEE Computer **36**, 39–43 (2003)

2. Dingsøyr, T., Moe, N.B.: Towards Principles of Large-Scale Agile Development. In: Dingsøyr, T., Moe, N.B., Tonelli, R., Counsell, S., Gencel, C., Petersen, K. (eds.) XP 2014. LNBIP, vol. 199, pp. 1–8. Springer, Heidelberg (2014)
3. Haugset, B., Hanssen, G.K.: Automated acceptance testing: A literature review and an industrial case study. Presented at the Agile 2008, Proceedings, Toronto (2008)
4. Jones, C.: Software Quality in 2012: A Survey of State of the Art, presentation by Namcook Analytics LLC. www.namcook.com

Shorter Feedback Loops by Means of Continuous Deployment

Arjan Claassen[✉] and Laurens Boekhorst

Royal Philips, Amsterdam, Netherlands
{arjan.claassen,laurens.boekhorst}@philips.com

Abstract. Gathering early feedback on features is critical to many projects. Many Agile methodologies define feedback loops. Often, the feedback loop for completed features only closes after the iteration finishes. In this paper we will introduce a way of closing this feedback loop early, by means of continuous deployment. This also lowers the deployment effort for developers, increasing their happiness.

Keywords: Short feedback loops · Testing · TDD · BDD · Continuous integration · Continuous deployment · Hot compatibility · Zero downtime deployment

1 Introduction

The authors of this paper, Arjan Claassen and Laurens Boekhorst, are web developers at the Software department of Philips Innovation Services, an innovation service provider within Royal Philips. It is our aim to accelerate the innovation of our customers, from start-up to multinational. The Software department is comprised of five groups dedicated to web, mobile, device, and application development and a group that focuses on systems engineering. The Software department has adopted the eXtreme Programming (XP) principles and the Scrum way of project organization from the start in 2001, and has been supporting Philips Research for about 15 years, implementing research prototypes. Over the past few years we have been supporting Philips product divisions, such as Consumer Lifestyle and Healthcare, as well.

Historically, Philips has been a product organization. Nowadays, more and more projects are shifting from just product development and desktop software towards mobile application development and web services and applications. Therefore, the request for service solutions has increased. The authors have been developing for both research and innovation projects. The web development projects were initially small, sometimes only two people. These small sized project teams resulted in more responsibilities on the developers. Besides the development and test work they were also responsible for setting up and maintaining the infrastructure and deployment of the web services and applications. The developers responsibilities gave them also the opportunity to implement changes in their projects. With the projects' sizes increasing the same way

© Springer International Publishing Switzerland 2015
C. Lassenius et al. (Eds.): XP 2015, LNBIP 212, pp. 248–253, 2015.
DOI: 10.1007/978-3-319-18612-2_24

of working is applied, giving the developers the responsibilities they need to implement changes.

In the autumn of 2012, Laurens joined the web development team. Since then the authors have been working together on three major projects, running for several years, and about ten smaller projects, generally running for just a few weeks or months. The changes we talk about in this paper were instigated by the authors, solving a problem that was causing a waste of time. A bottom-up approach was adopted, spreading the knowledge through technical talks within the department without forming a special committee. This approach persists today. In this paper, we describe the process we went through in the past two-and-a-half years and the challenges that still lie ahead.

2   Test Automation

Testing is in the DNA of the developers in the Software department. From the start, Test Driven Development (TDD) has been taught as one of the important principles of XP. By writing the tests upfront the developers are encouraged to make the system testable.

During the early days, when we were still learning to do proper web development we already wrote tests. This was not as easy as we were used in other technologies. We built up experience in testing web services and web applications over a couple of months. Today, we are still learning new ways of defining tests in new technologies.

At the beginning, the test suite was rather basic, testing the functional classes and methods. We did not focus on testing the database schema or the class properties. We ran the test suite locally on the development machines. Even though a test suite was in place, we could not guarantee that the web service would function as specified. We did not have full coverage of all functionality. Since web development was rather new to us and we were not yet able to test everything as we wanted, we had to do manual testing to prevent the application from failing once deployed into production.

During the first few months we had been building up experience. This allowed us to define better tests and create a more rigid and elaborate test suite, both on unit level and integration level. The test suite covered more and more of the features and use cases. We started to gain more confidence in our test suite.

Having a solid test suite covering all use cases enables you to verify that the application does what it should do. Although this is standard practice in Agile development, in several projects we observed a manual verification and validation test phase was defined before releasing a product or application in production. We started defining verification tests in scenarios, following the Behaviour Driven Development (BDD) development process, using Gherkin syntax for the scenarios. These scenarios describe the systems behaviour from the user point of view. We chose to start verification testing just underneath the user interface. The main reason is that we wanted to define a stable API for the functional part of the system, independent of the user interface. The user interface built on top of the system was treated as a separate application, tested in separation.

Writing these scenarios afterwards has proven to be difficult. We learned that we should start writing these scenarios from the beginning. Testing your code base on different levels should be done from day one. BDD should drive the development, similar to TDD. Test automation and confidence in your test suite are *the* enablers for continuous deployment.

3   Deployment Automation

Until two years ago the deployment process was completely manual. We would upload our code and log in to the server remotely to install missing dependencies, compile assets, and migrate the database. Depending on the changes, this would take anywhere from minutes to hours and the application had to be stopped in order to do so. Rolling back was also difficult since the new code had overwritten the old code. Developers had to revert changes locally and upload them again. In some cases, this would happen on the server directly. Since the process was very error prone, feature deployments were postponed until the end of an iteration, deploying everything at once. The amount of time lost in this process drove us to investigate alternatives to manual deployment. Postponing the deployments also caused customer feedback to arrive too late to take into account during the next iteration.

Then we were introduced to Capistrano: a deployment automation tool for Ruby on Rails. Capistrano scripts contain instructions (comparable to tasks in Ant or make files) on how to install dependencies, migrate the database and restart the application. Deployments are done in isolation, not touching the application currently running in production and allowing an erroneous deployment be rolled back instantly. This requires basic knowledge of the application that is being deployed. The responsibility to write and maintain these Capistrano scripts rests on the developers responsible for development of the application itself.

With deployment scripts in place, the amount of time it took to deploy an application was reduced to seconds. The application was still inaccessible during deployment, but the time frame was much smaller. Human error that plagued the manual approach was also eliminated. The predictability of this solution instilled much confidence in the team. Deployments started happening on a far more regular basis and new features were demonstrated long before the end of an iteration. The shorter feedback loop enabled product owners to refine stories in the backlog before the next iteration started. The compounded time savings of these benefits were significant.

4   Continuous Integration

Integration and regression testing was done by the developers on their work stations. While developing, they regularly ran the test suite with unit and integration tests, as well as the behaviour scenarios. We encountered situations in which the tests ran on one development machine, but when running the same test suite on another development machine it generated errors. Not being able to run the test suite correctly on another machine was often caused by differences in the versions of the referenced libraries. This also happened on the production system resulting in the application not running correctly. Installing a newer version of the library by the developer for another project was often the root cause.

We started to set up a continuous integration (CI) server in order to have an independent machine verify the correctness of the code and its references. Continuous integration servers had been around for a long time in our department for the integration of the embedded software and desktop applications. However, for web development we did not have one in place. With the experience we had in setting up CI servers for other types of projects, setting it up for web development was rather straightforward.

The job in the CI server executed successfully if the test suite ran without problems and all the tests passed. After a successful job run, the project status on the build monitor would light up green. Any exception would fail the job and signal the development team to start an investigation. Failures rarely occur, except when developers didn't run the test suite on their development machine, or did not commit all the necessary project files. Another reason to have a continuous integration server was to prevent our customers from committing erroneous code, ignoring the test suite.

Even with the continuous integration server in place and writing tests as well as scenarios, the application would cause exceptions in production. In many cases these errors were caused by corner cases that were not under test. Occasionally, the authors were confronted with exceptions that should have been discovered by tests. Investigation revealed that the tests were excluded in order to make the suite pass. Since developers should never cut corners like this, we introduced additional failure criteria to the CI job.

Besides updating the build monitor, our continuous integration server reports statistics on the number of passed and failed tests, the duration of the build, code coverage, and more information. We started to add more failure criteria to the CI job, not only looking at the number of failed tests. Among others we started observing test duration to signal performance problems in a rudimentary way, covered classes to prevent untested classes to be introduced, and test exclusions to see whether tests are excluded. In this way we could see whether the code base quality was dropping.

5   Continuous Deployment[1]

At this point we were able to verify that our application was doing everything it was supposed to do. Development was still interrupted by the occasional deployment. We considered continuous deployment by the continuous integration server as a solution to this interruption. With deployment automation in

---

[1] Note: we do not employ continuous deployment for commercial applications or services.

place, implementing continuous deployment was simply a matter of appending the deployment script to the build process. Developers now no longer have to interrupt development to deploy the application. The maintenance burden is further reduced as developers do not need to have their access to the server administered either.

We were now deploying over ten times per day, but the application was still inaccessible during deployment. As the traffic to our applications increased, we could no longer afford to have them inaccessible this often. We considered configuring the continuous integration server to deploy nightly. This would however lengthen our feedback loops, while significant effort had been put in shortening them. It felt like a step back and that is why we opted for eliminating downtime instead.

In our case this meant we had to figure out a way of migrating the database in production without having the code that was still running on it to cause exceptions. The solution to this problem is referred to as hot compatibility. The goal is to ensure that each deployment is compatible with the previous. In order to achieve this goal, changes to the database schema happen in two distinct deployments. The first deployment deals with additions to the schema, possibly duplicating any functionality that is currently deployed. The second deployment deals with deleting any functionality that was duplicated in the previous deployment. By splitting up changes to be as small as possible, this approach will scale to big architectural changes as well.

Finally we needed to deal with downtime caused by restarting the web server. We adopted Passenger as a module to run Ruby-on-Rails applications within the Apache web server. Fortunately, Passenger was already capable of reloading the application without dropping connections. Instead of restarting Apache, we changed our deployment script to instruct Passenger to reload the application. It does so by finishing any outstanding requests and queuing any new connections, serving them as soon as the application has been reloaded.

6   Open Issues

Sometimes, even with our stringent testing process, an application will fail in production. By adopting Capistrano we already have the capability to perform automatic rollbacks to earlier deployments. Capistrano does not keep track of how many migrations are in a deployment however, and as such it is unable to downgrade the database. This is a process currently left up to the developer, although it is prone to error. We wish to automate it at some point, however it does not rank high on our priority list since it happens very rarely.

More important is the ability to deploy any number of branches simultaneously. Quite often a customer is interested in seeing a feature evolve during an iteration. This is valuable since it allows us further shorten our feedback loop. Deploying a different branch overwrites the deployed mainline however. This is highly undesirable due to the fact that a development branch may be unstable, or introduce database migrations that need to be rolled back when rolling back to the mainline. Ideally, we have a completely separate environment, dedicated solely to the branch that is being deployed. At this point it is mostly an infrastructural challenge as we already have test and deployment automation in place in order to enable branch deployment.

7   Conclusion

Continuous deployment has allowed us to significantly shorten our feedback loops. Product owners evaluate the application shortly after the developers finish a feature. Confidence in your test suite is *the* enabler for continuous deployment. Gradually moving forward from test automation to deployment automation, continuous integration and deployment has proven to be a sustainable approach. The burden on developers to perform system administration has been greatly reduced leading to significant time savings as well as increased developer happiness.

On a Different Level of Team

Johanna Hunt[(⊠)]

Aptivate, Swanns Road, Cambridge, Cambridgeshire, UK
johh@aptivate.org

Abstract. This experience report summarises the decision-making process used at Aptivate, focusing on the decision to create 'standing teams' with delegated authority to plan the distribution of their own work across multiple projects. The paper presents the company approach to consensus decision-making, and how this has supported company culture and values as well as enabled this change with full participation. This experience report covers the time period from September 2014 to March 2015.

Keywords: Team · Multi-project · Decision-making · Consensus · Consent · Culture

1 Introduction and Background

Aptivate is currently considering options for change, including experimenting with teams. This is not to 'become more agile', but to open up options for improvement; such as delivering greater value to their clients and increasing empowerment for staff. This has been handled using a consensus decision-making approach.

Aptivate (originally founded as Aidworld Humanitarian ICT in 2003) is a not-for-profit company primarily focussed on providing support for international development ICT initiatives. Aptivate works with other non-profits, charities, and NGOs as web / software developers and technical consultants.

There are 18 general members of staff in the company. Staff are distributed across two main sites in the UK (Brighton and Cambridge), with further colleagues in Europe and USA. Projects are primarily run as distributed remote projects, but some are run collocated in the relevant country to ensure participation and input from users.

Aptivate embraced agile approaches from their beginning in 2003, and consensus for organisational coordination and decision-making in 2009. From late 2013 it was recognised that the organisation was facing coordination challenges from the growth in numbers, reducing effectiveness of decision-making and communication. To address this the organisation started delegating consent for internal coordination.

2 Teams in Software Development

This section details three distinguishing categories when talking about teams in software development; responsibility and capability, size, and duration.

© Springer International Publishing Switzerland 2015
C. Lassenius et al. (Eds.): XP 2015, LNBIP 212, pp. 254–261, 2015.
DOI: 10.1007/978-3-319-18612-2_25

2.1   Responsibility and Capability

In the agile community there has been a lot of focus on feature teams as opposed to component teams. This is most commonly defined as the difference between responsibility focussed on a layer or layers of an application (most commonly an architectural or technological divide) versus end-to-end delivery of working (tested) features. The latter is typically espoused in agile organisations, with cross-functional teams of generalising specialists able to collaborate on an end-to-end or vertical slice of value. It is common for feature teams to include testing and quality capability.

2.2   Size

Team size varies significantly. While the standard presented scrum team size is 5-9 people, effective teams can be smaller or larger depending on context. With fewer people there can be less knowledge distribution and skill coverage, whereas with more there is a rapidly increasing cost of communication, coordination and alignment.

2.3   Duration

Over time a team will form; aligning around values, ways of working, processes and improvements. Project teams by definition end with the project the team was formed for, whereas product teams continue for the duration of a product's funding. In the former this is normally marked by project end (by having met project goals or by cancellation), whereas for the latter the end point is normally when a product is either retired or when there is no longer a business case for adding new features.

In both cases there is a clear end point to the team, at which it is disbanded. Much of the learning around effective collaboration is lost when the team disbands – as this relates to how individuals work with each other in an effective manner, understanding strengths, capabilities, weaknesses.

For long projects, and long running products or clients, the impact may not be so apparent as the end matches the end of the overall goal. However, for shorter projects (up to three months) the abbreviated lifecycle of the project team becomes increasingly visible, with an increased overhead for ramp up and kick off.

An alternative is that of standing teams which continue indefinitely. Such teams are without a defined end-point, and with continued existence across multiple projects or even products, gain the advantage of experience and unity of identity. This may be a team that moves from one project to the next, or one that handles multiple concurrent incoming streams of work depending on the organisational setup. In time they develop their own rituals, values and ways of working which can be considered a team culture. The risk with such teams is the possibility that they might eventually become insular and less open to outsiders or new ideas.

3   Teams and Projects at Aptivate

Due to the comparatively small size of the organisation and the nature of the work, projects typically involve 1-2 developers over periods of two weeks to three months. In the majority of cases a designer will be involved for part of the time and there will be a project manager supporting the client communications.

Projects are assigned to individuals through a traditional 'resource management' style of coordination; sales people responsible for bringing in the new work coordinate with a person responsible for planning, assigning projects tentatively to people based on their skills, interests and availability. As client timeframes change, or individuals are needed elsewhere, so the overall plan is adjusted.

Projects are sold to clients in 10 'developer day' blocks of value delivery (for example, 5 days each of two developers, or one person for 10 days). These tend to be consecutive, but may be split depending on client and need.

Project teams all use digital boards to coordinate their work and visualise to clients. There is normally a unique board per client. A typical project will involve daily check-in calls with a client representative as Product Owner for the work. There are frequent demos and retrospectives, although these are often not on a regular cadence due to project planning and time limitations. Project managers coordinate the outward facing communications, often across multiple projects at any time.

This approach had worked well for Aptivate for several reasons, but as the numbers in the company have grown, this has become unwieldy, with a large overhead of moving 'people pieces'. Where repeat work on an existing site occurs it may or may not be the same people involved, leading to inconsistencies in approach to both development and coordination.

4   Company as Team at Aptivate

One reason that the approach as described above has worked for Aptivate is because the company itself has been functioning as a single team. The values and ways of working that one might find within a project team are distributed across the whole organisation, rather than at the delivery level. There are a number of unifying values and practices across the organisation which support this.

4.1   Organisational Practices

- The whole organisation, across all locations, attends a daily video call standup or 'Morning Meeting' (MM). In cases where timezones prohibit attendance these meetings are recorded for later consumption.
- Lunch is taken at the same time across the UK offices – with each site preparing a shared lunch and sitting down to eat together every day.
- The entire company meets for a full day 'Monthly Management Meeting' (MMM) on a regular cycle. Where possible this involves having everyone in the same room for the full day – any staff who cannot attend in person attend as remote participants. This includes a monthly organisation-wide retrospective.

4.2   Organisational Values

The following are a set of perceived organisational values that support unity of focus.

Everybody is equal and has a voice

- o There is a commitment to equal empowerment and ownership for all staff. Ownership is not just reflective of empowerment, but also of responsibility. Everyone is considered equally responsible.
- o There is a company ideal of equal pay and benefits for all, no matter length of time or experience. Where there are exceptions these are reviewed by the full company and considered limited term.
- o Any member of staff can be involved and have a voice in any company decision. Any member of staff can propose a change that could affect the entire company.
- o The job title for *all* employees is 'General Member of Staff.'

Everybody will share and be transparent

- o Within legal and ethical constraints, all workings of the company are transparent to anyone within the company.
- o There is a commitment to sharing back to the community both through speaking at, and running, open events and making code Open Source where possible.

Work has value

- o A societal or ethical benefit or impact should be identifiable in any project picked up. Normally this is for international development, but can also include local communities and organisations.
- o An initial check goes out to the company before a project is accepted – anyone can question a project on ethical or impact grounds to ensure this value is sustained.

Participation is key

- o Participation with clients and users to ensure that the right people are involved is considered vital. Where possible clients are expected to act as Product Owners, collaborating directly with the teams on a daily basis. Clients and users will typically be engaged in participatory workshops to ensure the best value for all is identified.
- o Everyone is expected to participate and contribute to the running of the company as a whole however they choose (from washing up, to facilitating meetings, to doing the accounts).

5   Culture of Consensus

The values presented previously are held across the entire organisation – alignment at this level supports trust and collaboration in project groups. The company itself functions as a single self-organising entity. A major supporting aspect of this is the culture of consensus.

From the start Aptivate had a strong value of consultation and participation. Practices from Formal Consensus decision-making [1] were adopted in 2009 as a more structured approach to current practice. Rather than being added as a new company value, this was formalised primarily to improve the approach to decision-making, which had been tending toward long and occasionally adversarial meetings.

Consensus was seen as a way to improve self-governance in keeping with existing approaches and values - a way to ensure everyone had a voice and would be heard. The style of discussion in meetings swiftly shifted from adversarial to calm and co-constructive. This in turn gave space for the quieter voices to participate.

While decision-making is delegated for day-to-day operations, the MMM is the primary venue for assessment of ongoing work, review of individual performance, and policy and strategy decision-making. This is achieved through 'proposals' that anyone can create. The aim is not to get everyone to agree, but to collaboratively produce the best possible decisions. The consensus approach nurtured the key values, as it encouraged everybody to participate, have a voice, and collaboratively own decision-making, thus also enabling transparency.

5.1   Consensus at Aptivate

Anyone can raise a proposal for change. The test for a proposal is this: "Does anyone have a Critical Concern about the proposal at hand?"

Any proposal is considered accepted unless there is an unresolved Critical Concern, and will not progress unless this is resolved. A Critical Concern may be an issue that presents unacceptable danger to Aptivate's ability to deliver, or it may mean that the person raising the concern would be unable to participate in the company effectively. If a Critical Concern is raised, it is owned by the whole group until resolved. The proposal will be reconsidered and altered until all concerns are met - usually making the first step less expensive or risky. As a result, affordable experiments are made to the company and its operation.

As part of the process people can raise issues, risks or non-critical concerns which are incorporated into the proposal for monitoring. These are cases where the proposal is not stopped from progressing, but is considered to carry additional risk that would need to be tracked or monitored. Thus any proposal will be modified through the decision-making process until all concerns have been resolved or are considered mitigated or affordable risks.

Consensus, as practiced at Aptivate, thus produces good solutions, often as interim 'experiments' with organisational buy-in from the point of acceptance and the majority of risks and underlying issues addressed. Solutions are cooperatively created, and not owned by the original proposer. Everyone works to make it the best decision for the group. All involved are responsible for expressing concerns.

This has resulted in a high level of staff engagement within the company. As every member of the organisation has a role in making policy, there is a sense of owning "the rules" with everyone bought in and focussed on making them work. The majority of proposals are considered and adjusted at the Monthly Management Meeting (MMM). There is normally preparation work completed in advance to ensure that the facilitated discussion at the MMM is effective. Proposals will often be shared in advance.

Consensus decision-making may appear to take longer, but decisions are not the end state. Any change starts with an idea, and ends with the implementation of that change. While more time is spent elaborating an idea and cooperatively agreeing on it, the end result is a decision that is fully understood and comes with full buy-in from all involved. Reaching consensus does not mean that everyone is in complete agreement. No proposal is agreed until all concerns have been resolved whether by adding monitoring or by adjusting the proposal.

Open questioning and non-violent conflict is encouraged for consensus to produce effective proposals. One of the challenges with everybody having a voice in all decisions is that this can lead to a natural and positive tendency to question, which could be perceived as "culture of criticism" or as risk-aversion. If a proposal gets pushed back for later discussion, the proposer may get discouraged.

While discussions of proposals are best had face-to-face, not every discussion could or needed to be held at the MMM. The discussions prior to a proposal, whilst valuable, can be time-consuming. A tool has been developed by Aptivate (http://www.econsensus.org) to enable digital discussion and tracking of responses. This is especially useful where topics need initial discussion, or a decision outside of the monthly cycle.

5.2   Delegated Consent and Working Groups

A challenge with consensus is the implied expectation that everyone provides input to everything. For many groups using consensus, all members of a group make all policy decisions. As Aptivate numbers grew, the MMM became unwieldy and less effective. While everyone being able to contribute is vital for alignment and transparency, not everyone needed or wanted to be involved in all proposal discussions and decisions.

This led to an organisational change which started in late 2013. Working Groups (WGs) or 'circles' with delegated authority for an aspect of the organisation were created – such as finance, people, output (delivery), marketing. These act as incubators for proposals, providing clearer accountability as well as taking many organisational decisions.

Anybody can contribute to any working group at any time. These WGs provide a service to the MMM and all individuals in the company, by enabling those who are not interested in certain areas to delegate the decision-making to a smaller group. Each WG has an elected product owner and project manager.

Where proposals are considered to affect multiple WGs, have a large delivery impact, financial implication, or high organisational risk these are brought back to the MMM. While this rule is not explicit there is a tacit agreement around the types of proposals this covers. Everyone has a right to be involved in decisions that affect them. The MMM retains the right to withdraw delegated consent.

Delegated consent is a pattern of practice which appears in both Formal Consensus [1] and Sociocratic Consent [2]. Participants in a group using these methods choose people to serve in empowered decision-making roles; where the group is too large, multiple teams may each receive delegated authority in a specific domain. Consent differs from many folk practices of consensus in that it has a clearly defined test for when a decision is made. For the MMM to withdraw consent, someone would need to clearly identify a risk that could negatively affect the organisation as a whole. Within the framework of delegated consent, WGs function as empowered domain-focussed teams, enabling distributed policy-making.

One of the reasons that this approach was able to succeed, was that the shared values within and across the organisation (despite covering many locations) had led to a high level of trust. Everyone is trusted to want the right thing for Aptivate as a whole. This meant that delegated consent to the Working Groups was possible - acknowledging that not everyone can be involved in everything enabled groups to be empowered and effective.

6   Moving to Standing Teams

While, WGs function as organisational teams with delegated consent for decision-making, Aptivate continues to have challenges at the delivery level with individuals assigned to projects. While individuals may function or cooperate as short-term sub-teams, there are organisational challenges:

- Low ownership of code
- Inconsistent quality and testing approaches
- Variable working practices
- Inconsistent ways of working with clients
- Late engagement of staff with project (often starting on day of project, rather than ramping up or involved in up-front discussions)
- Low knowledge sharing across projects (innovation, improvements and new techniques may be made, but not carried forward to other projects)
- Increasing levels of project-specific specialist knowledge
- Lack of visibility of upcoming work for individuals
- Increasing feeling of being constrained to a role (e.g. 'developer')
- No consistently used predictive planning approaches across projects (due to variation in staff combinations, estimation approaches, and client needs)
- Hard to ensure sustainable pace for individuals across projects
- Low ongoing improvement at the delivery level

Rather than have the 'company as team' with ad-hoc sub-team groupings, a proposal was made to take the key people who worked on projects (seven 'developers', two 'project managers', and two 'designers') and form two teams equally balanced by capability with delegated authority for their ways of working. The move was thus from multiple small ad-hoc groups, towards two larger teams.

The decision for this change could not sit within just one working group. A collaborative proposal document was created and discussed/shared out for questions, comments, risks and concerns with all who would be directly affected by this proposal. Some areas were agreed to be monitored as part of the proposal, for example the impact to 'company as team'. Modifications to the proposal included the explicit consideration that teams would be reviewed and members exchanged every few months, to ensure that the teams did not become silos. As the Working Groups are cross-cutting, alignment is expected to be retained across the company.

This proposal document was revised over the course of three weeks, eventually growing to seven pages, until all immediate points and concerns were met. It was then presented at the January 2015 MMM, as a two month experiment before review, and fully accepted with no Critical Concerns.

The final proposal included delegating authority for short term planning to each team. The newly formed teams would take delegated responsibility for planning and distribution of work within each team by whatever route they decide, normally focussing on the forthcoming two weeks, but with an awareness of future projects. Teams may still continue to work on multiple projects, but the decision for how to coordinate this can sit with them, thus retaining a sense of empowerment for how that work will be shared and how it can best be achieved within the team. Each team can develop its own ways of working. Future projects will be considered by a 'planning' working group, containing representatives from each team, to ensure that these are planned to the appropriate team.

7   Conclusion

Without standing teams and with many projects typically being planned to only require one or two people, it is hard to share responsibility for quality and make shared agreements about technical practices. It is also difficult to use any 'normal' measures to predict, schedule and manage early expectations on projects let alone assess whether pace is sustainable. While the organisation can reflect and improve, there is no team to reflect and improve for the longer term. This can cause projects to become short-sighted. Innovation, improvements and new techniques may still be made, but may not be carried forward to other projects.

The model of shared ownership and 'company as team' supported by Aptivate's consensus model has alleviated the impact of this, but as the company has grown it is moving towards clearer delegation of authority and accountability.

This experience report has summarised the approach to decision-making at Aptivate, in which I participated as a member of staff, focussing on the proposal to change to 'standing teams'. This proposal was put into effect from March 2015 and will be reviewed in May 2015.

Acknowledgements. Thanks to everyone at Aptivate, this report is the culmination of an experience including everyone there. Particular thanks to Alan Jackson, Hamish Downer, Kavita Rajah, Nathaniel Whitestone and Tom Lord for their clarifications and comments. Finally, incredible thanks to Jutta Eckstein for all her hard work keeping me on track and shepherding this paper into its final form.

References

1. Butler, C.T., Rothstein, A.: On Conflict and Consensus: A Handbook for Formal Consensus decisionmaking, 3rd edn. Food Not Bombs, Tacoma Park Maryland (2007)
2. Buck, J., Villines, S.: We the People: Consenting to a Deeper Democracy - A Guide to Sociocratic Principles and Methods. Sociocracy.info Press, Washington DC (2007)

Applying Agile and Lean Elements to Accelerate Innovation Culture in a Large Organization – Key Learnings After One Year Journey

Jari Partanen[1] and Mari Matinlassi[2(✉)]

[1] Elektrobit Wireless Communications Ltd, Oulu, Finland
`jari.partanen@elektrobit.com`
[2] Neone, Ii, Finland
`mari.matinlassi@neone.fi`

Abstract. This paper describes how lean elements have been applied in a large company to change existing agilean culture towards innovation culture. Innovation concentrates on radical, new business innovations but covers product and process innovations as well. The main motivation and need to build the innovation culture was an assumption that the company has a lot of competence and innovation potential not utilized. The final goal is to measure if the actions taken really have an impact to the amount and quality of new, radical innovations and business growth of the company. This paper is limited to the intermediary results achieved after the first year being (1) ideas-to-innovations value stream established (2) idea flow and positive pull created among personnel and (3) group of perfection practices has been stabilized for continuous improvement. We plan to describe, measure and analyze concrete examples of radical innovations in the future.

Keywords: Idea management · Radical innovation · Incremental innovation · Acceleration · Lean · Cultural change · Experimental culture

1 Introduction

Companies compete in being innovative through successful idea harvesting, optimizing the impact of critical experts and stimulating innovation culture. Herein, we define ideas as exploration items or concepts that potentially will be new features, products or services. Ideas may turn into innovations when there is a proof that, those ideas have succeeded in creating new business and therefore provided value to the users or end users. Radical innovations [1] create new products or even completely new business ecosystems.

According to Farsi et al. [2] "organizations need different stimuli and driving forces in order to implement and execute innovation". This paper describes one possible approach and key learnings on stimulating innovation culture in the wireless segment of a large, international company, Elektrobit (EB) (www.elektrobit.com), who specializes in demanding embedded software and hardware solutions for the automo-

© Springer International Publishing Switzerland 2015
C. Lassenius et al. (Eds.): XP 2015, LNBIP 212, pp. 262–269, 2015.
DOI: 10.1007/978-3-319-18612-2_26

tive industry and wireless technologies. Company has previously applied lean and agile methods widely in the company [3, 4] for example on R&D activities, human resources management (e.g. transparent goal setting) and finance (e.g. beyond budgeting) as well as continuous strategy and planning [5], however applying lean principles to innovation culture creation has not been experimented before.

One of the main motivations to build the innovation culture was assumption that the company has a lot of competence and unutilized innovation potential. That is, tacit ideas that have value but lack a forum to make them noticed by describing them and sharing them among personnel. This unmined human capacity to create new and combine existing things in a new way is one of the main valuable assets of a company [6]. Therefore the goal was to promote lean startup thinking inside the company [7] and build a growing organizational culture of innovation by further utilizing lean and agile approaches.

In the beginning of this journey the organizational barrier for innovation in the company was seen generally quite high. The existing methods and tools, as well as the process for innovation, were considered to be too heavy. Further, the existing processes focused on inventions and patenting and did not cover other types of ideas such as process ideas, new features ideas or new product ideas efficiently enough.

In order to utilize the full innovation potential of the company we wanted to apply lean thinking [4] also to the cultural change. Lean thinking means creating a "pull", aiming for "less waste" in ways of working and processing, emphasizing transparency, openness and collaborative development together with the people.

Both the authors are involved in the creation of the ideas-to-innovations change. We created a systematic way to (1) collect, grow and scale ideas and (2) visualize ideas early as lightweight demos to collect early phase of market or internal expert feedback. Further, we created a (3) flow and pull of ideas among personnel starting from business management to experts and implementation teams. Last but not least we stabilized perfection practices to (4) continuously iterate and improve the way the cultural change was applied itself.

In this paper we will first describe the background and motivation for cultural development and general status of innovation processes and culture in the beginning of journey. Then we introduce the lean principles applied and timeline of the case. A set of particular methods and tools was applied to support the stimulation of innovation culture. Detailed description of the tools and methods is out of the scope of this paper, however. In the end of this paper we represent the early phase results, current key progress indicators and retrospectives as well as lessons learned so far. Future plans and conclusions are included in the paper at the end.

2   The Case Company, Background and Motivation

EB is a business-to-business provider of embedded systems for the wireless and automotive industry with more than 1600 employees in seven countries. EB´s wireless segment offers wireless technologies in the state of the art products, services or solutions and employs approximately 500 people distributed mainly in Finland and the United States.

Company has used a stage gate based invention and patenting process for a long time, roughly 13 years, during which much more than 50 patents or patent families have been established. However focusing on patenting merely has not been enough in order to create also flow of potential business ideas, inventions or demos to be experimented in short time frame. Or, for example, utilizing open sourced innovations or even ideas outsourcing. Due to authority requirements patenting process can take up to two years to be completed.

Company has also had business – decision based process for new solutions or products for several years'. Therein, the first step proposal already requires many aspects to be fulfilled for a business potential of product or solution innovation, so the requirements for this are quite demanding.

Collecting ideas has not been systematic enough and therefore has not reached its full potential to capture new business ideas. Collecting ideas also needed to be lightweight and apply new experimental or exploratory ways of working.

Based on studies, findings have evidenced numerous compatibilities between Lean and Agile, also called Agilean [8]. Also EB´s Wireless Segment has utilized Agile methods since 2007 and began to adopt Lean principles in 2010. Adopted methods include e.g. Scrum and Kanban, which have been increasingly applied not just to software development but to embedded systems and hardware development as well.

3   Elements for Cultural Change

According to Rodriquez et al. [4], creating a "pull" and reducing "waste", putting stronger emphasis on transparency and collaborative development have been driving forces in the company during the past years. Same authors found 5 lean principles and 2 supporting aspects to be the main elements characterizing EB's Wireless Segment Agile and Lean way of working: value, value stream, flow, pull and perfection complemented with transparency and people oriented development. Below, we define what these elements mean in the context of innovation culture acceleration.

Value and value stream i.e. ideas and the idea-to-innovation chain of actions. All ideas potentially provide value to the company or to the customer. Tacit ideas do not provide value and therefore are waste. The goal is to turn tacit ideas into visible, valuable ideas. After that, into visual demonstrations and finally into real customer leads, products and projects i.e. innovations. Example of applying this element is introducing JIRA based "idea collection tool and process" (see Fig. 1) as a system which represents the value.

Flow and Pull means that the idea-to-innovation stream does not have bottle necks but ideas steadily grow towards innovations. Management does not have to demand or force ideation but, it rather reflects natural, human need to create ideas and innovations. Selected tool well supports the flow of ideas. It provides a visible backlog of new ideas, ideas in progress and closing as well as definition of done. Review of all new ideas is done weekly with concurrent team, delegating ideas to further processing and implementation. Team does not make decision, it supports the ideation.

Perfection means continuous improvement practices in order to keep cultural change progressing and growing and ensure long term results. Long term change of a large organization is a lot of work. From method development point of view, we wanted to keep things progressing by creating the first concept of a method/process quickly and started iterating and continuously learning from our experiences and users feedback. That is why lightweight retrospectives are done every week during idea reviews in order to capture continuous improvement initiatives for the ideation. We simply talk within team about what works and what does not work and what we can do to improve things. Larger scale retrospectives were organized twice during the first year (Retrospectives 1and 2 in Fig. 1) in order to reflect the general status of change and agree on future directions. From the point of view of idea processing, it is equally important to keep things progressing i.e. ideas shall not pile up in any phase and the feedback loop must be relatively short. Coaching team ensured this by having the 1st processing of new ideas every week on Friday since April 2014.

Transparency means valuating good communication, visibility and openness. That is, transparency and openness of ideas that are in the process as well as intranet news and publications of ideation success stories. Sartori & Scalco [9] define clear communication and open information sharing as extra important competences for innovation.

Involving people throughout the company. Key idea of the approach was to provide a low threshold for anyone to participate. Therefore, since the official internal launch of the ideation tool (at Q1/2014 in Fig. 1), anyone could submit an idea anytime. In addition to that, a couple of ideation campaigns were organized later to boost ideation on specifically targeted business domains defined by business management.

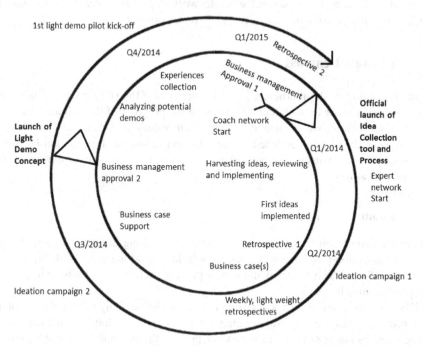

Fig. 1. Timeline of the cultural change during 2014 – early 2015

According to Sartori & Scalco [9], "the higher the degree of communications and the larger the employees social network, the better the context for the occurrence of innovation". Therefore, in parallel, a "coach network" (Fig. 1) was established. Coach network is a small group of personnel specially trained with knowledge about idea submission, review and demonstrations. These experts work in daily projects and provide their expertise to idea submitters whenever needed. "Expert network" (Fig. 1) is a larger group of people that takes care of taking ideas further and implementing them. Expert network consist of small cross competence teams wherein idea submitters are the core of teams complemented with supporting experts. Further, because involving business management into the innovation activities can have a positive impact on the efficiency and performance of innovation activities [10] as well as on the company economic performance [6], we also wanted to have business management commitment.

Business management commitment means company-wide communication of they support to the innovation activities and commitment to the change. Business management approval was applied for the overall change decision in the beginning ("Business Management Approval 1" in Fig. 1) but, also for each individual method and tool introduced along the journey e.g. "Lightweight Demo Concept" (Fig. 1). Further, a 7 person review team (i.e. coach network) has involved business management and key stakeholders to participate in idea processing by directing discovered new ideas weekly. That is, reviewing of all business ideas with the help of idea management tool. In addition, several separate workshops have been held for business reviews e.g. for one area of ideas series of 5 workshops in total.

4   Lessons Learned

In the beginning of the journey, a limited number of KPIs (Key progress indicators) was defined in order to quantitatively measure the progress of the cultural change. In the sections below, we present the KPIs, their values in December 2014 i.e. ten months after the change launched as well as comparison to the situation before the change. Further, we discuss the gained experiences and retrospectives during the first year of the journey.

4.1   Results

In the prior approach there was only process for handling inventions. Now, we still have the invention process complemented with idea handling process. Table 1 shows selected KPIs and their values with the new process. Below we describe situation with the prior approach.

The number of all ideas has not been measured before. Only the number of invention proposals has been measured being 5-10 in a year previously. All these can be categorized as business ideas. In the earlier process the inventions were submitted by mostly the experts, representing much less than 5 % of the personnel. In the earlier invention process, a very limited amount of experts and technology management representatives have been handling invention proposals. This is due to legal aspects of invention process. In the earlier invention process the cycle time for the first processing was not measured but instead, invention proposal total processing time was measured. It took up to 60 days before the processing of inventions was completed.

Table 1. Key progress indicators and their values

KPI	Value	Details
# of idea submissions	>100	40% started, 30% in progress, 30% done
# of potential invention submissions (may turn as technological idea)	10	2 completed, 8 in progress
% of potentially new business ideas	25%	Categorized as "business idea"
% of personnel submitting ideas	10%	
# of people participated in idea processing	>100	20 teams, 3-15 people in each team
Cycle time to the 1st processing	<1week	
Cycle time total	12 weeks	From idea submission to a demo
# of ideation campaigns	2	Focus in specific business topic
% of potentially new business ideas from the campaigns	50%	Categorized as "business idea" and selected for further studying

4.2 Gained Experience

Based on both large-scale and lightweight retrospectives there seems to be two main factors that have affected the results above. First, in idea submission, it was created as simple as possible idea submission form that makes it easy to get started. This was done in order to lower the burden to submit ideas. Second, in idea screening, it was not made go/no-go decisions but rather a coaching and shepherding guidance. This was done in order to scale and grow the ideas and to create a safe environment for ideation.

Lead time of the ideas handling i.e. the latency between the submission and implementation of an idea, have been improved all the time. Especially our experience is that focused ideation campaigns can shorten the total lead time of individual ideas however the lead time still being in large, international company around 12 weeks (from idea to demo). Relatively long sounding lead time is, however, not a problem if things keep progressing all the time and the status of the idea is open and visible to the personnel.

Further, it seems that focused ideation campaigns lead to more promising and beneficial ideas, based on first experiences. Even though final results are not yet there i.e. no radical innovations implemented on the market, this experimental approach based on Lean and Agile principles seems to be a solution for developing a large ideation environment. Transparency of the approach is important for the people to see the progress of ideas and to understand how they could contribute to the ideation leading into innovations.

5   Discussion

This section discusses the impact of the cultural change to the company and limitations of the study.

5.1   Impact of the Cultural Change on the Company

To see the final impact of the change needs patience. So far, it is already the first sign that the change has had some impact when people discuss, create and share ideas continously. Further, it seems that people have learned how to create ideas and how to present them. Also, the more the ideation culture has progressed in the company, the more business potential the ideas start to have as for example the first focused ideation campaign lead up to 50% share of potentially relevant ideas for business. This impact already shows initial cultural change within the organization.

This might also be considered if we see this as a problem in the future – will there be invasion of ideas and not enough resources to process and implement them all. The goal has been to prevent this by making small steps and put the minimum necessary effort to proof and grow the business value of the idea step by step – not as a big bang. Current lean and agile way of working involves idea submitters always in the idea processing and implementation team i.e. same people create ideas and implement them.

5.2   Limitations

Changing culture in a large organization is a process that seems to take years. The first year journey shows limited early results. The first focused ideas already show business relevance however the business volume impact remains to be seen. As the very first demos (2 of them) have just emerged within the first 3 months, it is too early to measure if they are radical innovations or innovations and, whether they contribute to the business growth of the company.

The presented way of working is fundamentally established based on lean and agile principles as well as tools utilized in the practical implementation. Therefore the presented acceleration approach requires agilean culture and way of working as a starting point for adopting the approach.

The business environment is continuously evolving due to multiple markets and therefore, the results achieved in this kind of B2B environment may be limited to this case only and not easily applied to other kind of companies working on other kind or markets.

The KPIs that were in use before the change are not completely same as after the change. Further, we plan to introduce some new KPIs during 2015 as well. For example, earlier we measured only inventions and now we measure all kinds of ideas - even process improvement ideas. Therefore the improvement from 5-10 inventions leading into patents per year compared to 108 ideation items in 10 months are not directly comparable.

6   Conclusion

At the time of writing this paper, it has been approximately one year since the process was launched within the organization. The early results show that the number of ideas, number of people submitting ideas and participating in idea handling has increased. At the same time, the lead time of idea processing has decreased. Therefore, it may be concluded that experimental approach based on Lean and Agile principles seems to be a solution for developing a large ideation environment. Management commitment and continuous sharing of the results for the people and their supervisors is also seen essential to promote the experiment Way of Working and building the culture of innovation.

Changing the culture is a long term process and we plan to continue and actively promote the change during the - at least - next two years. An interesting future research area is to measure business growth of the company in the light of concrete ideation and innovation examples.

Acknowledgments. This work was supported by TEKES as part of the Accelerate project of ITEA 2 and has also interfaces to Need 4 Speed Program of DIGILE.

References

1. Ledwidth, A., Martin, A., Nicholas, J., Nosella, A.: Exploring Radical Innovation Search Practices. Int. J. Tech. Intell. Plann. 8(4), 389–403 (2012)
2. Farsi, J.Y., Rezazadeh, A., Najmabadi, A.D.: Social Capital and Organizational Innovation: The Mediating Effect of Entrepreneurial Orientation. J. Comm. Pos. Pract. 2, 22–40 (2013)
3. Heidenberg, J., Matinlassi, M., Pikkarainen, M., Hirkman, P., Partanen, J.: Systematic piloting of agile methods in the large: two cases in embedded systems development. In: Ali Babar, M., Vierimaa, M., Oivo, M. (eds.) PROFES 2010. LNCS, vol. 6156, pp. 47–61. Springer, Heidelberg (2010)
4. Rodriguez, P., Partanen, J., Kuvaja, P., Oivo, M.: Combining lean thinking and agile methods for software development: a case study of a finnish provider of wireless embedded systems detailed. In: Sprague Jr., R.H. (ed.) HICSS 2014, pp. 4770–4779. IEEE, Los Alamitos (2014)
5. Suominen, T., Kuusela, R., Tihinen, M.: Continuous Planning - An Important Aspect of Agile and Lean Development. J. Agile Syst. Mgmt., 23
6. Antonioli, D.: Industrial Relations, Techno-Organizational Innovation and Firm Economic Performance. J. Econ. Pol. 1, 21–52 (2009)
7. Blank, S.: Why Lean Start-Up Changes Everything. Harvard Business Review, 9, May 2013
8. Azevedo, S.A., Govindan, K., Carvalho, H., Cruz-Machado, V.: An Integrated Model to Assess the Leanness and Agility of the Automotive Industry. Resources, Conservation and Recycling 66, 85–94 (2012)
9. Sartori, R., Scalco, A.: Managing Organizational Innovation through Human Resources, Human Capital and Psychological Capital. European J. Mgmt. 14(2), 63–70 (2014)
10. Spalanzani, A., Zait, D., Zait, A.: Organizational Innovation – Significant Factorial Connections. Scientific Annals of the "Alexandru Ioan Cuza" University of Iasi – Economic Sciences Section, pp. 159–169 (2011)

It Has Been a Long Journey, and It Is Not Over Yet

Avraham Poupko[✉]

Cisco, SPVSS, Shlomo Halevi 5, Jerusalem, Israel
apoupko@cisco.com

Abstract. This paper tells the story of my Agile Journey over the last 15 years. It is neither exceptionally rosy nor excessively pessimistic. It is an attempt to give an honest experience report.

Keywords: Experience · Journey · Extreme programming · XP

1 Introduction

> "If you are going through hell, keep going."
>
> *Winston Churchill*

I have been in the industry for over 20 years, and I have been practicing some or another form of Agile from the very early days. I have seen myself mature, I have seen the industry grow and mature, and in particular, I have seen my organization mature. This paper tells that story. It tells about challenges, hopes, frustrations and accomplishments. I then offer some retrospective.

2 Background

Since 1994 I have been working for NDS that was acquired by Cisco in 2012. I write code and design systems. I take great pride in a job well done. Having fun is a major objective.

My current role is defined as Senior System's Architect. I am expected to be deeply familiar with the core products, to understand the customer's needs, and to lead the task of building something that meets the customer's expectations, while remaining in line with the company's technical and business objectives.

I work directly both with customers and with developers and development leads. As a senior person within the organization, I am also expected to provide technical guidance and inspiration. Currently I do not have any direct reports, but I influence the work of several dozen engineers.

© Springer International Publishing Switzerland 2015
C. Lassenius et al. (Eds.): XP 2015, LNBIP 212, pp. 270–278, 2015.
DOI: 10.1007/978-3-319-18612-2_27

3   The Pre-agile Days

In the early days of my career (1995-1998), the company I worked for (NDS) and myself were heavily invested in Object Oriented Design as a design paradigm and in C++ as an implementation language. We strongly believed that OOD allows the close modeling of the real world. We would often argue: "The world is made of objects, not functions or procedures", and that if done correctly, OOD would make code development much easier. Most importantly we believed that OOD would allow us to "get it right." All you needed to do was understand the domain, map the domain to a class hierarchy, and go implement. Of course you had to make sure that the domain was clear, because if not, you would misunderstand it, and create a wrong hierarchy. That would be painful to fix. But that was an error left to amateurs. Professional programmers and designers would get it right, and once done right, adding or changing requirements would be a piece of cake. Personally, I strongly believed that as I got better at my job, I would be able to design Object Oriented systems that are robust.

4   The Journey Begins

4.1   Getting Started

My personal journey with Agile began in May 1999. This is when I read an article by Kent Beck in C++ report on something called "Extreme Programming." The name caught me. If programming is fun, then extreme programming must be extremely fun. The article started with a discussion of. "How does the cost of changing software change over time?" I knew by then, from painful experience, that the later a mistake is discovered, the more costly it is to fix. That was the reason that upfront design is so important. I knew that the reason we make mistake in upfront design was that we did not design enough. All we needed to do was design more.

The direction the article took surprised me. The article said that we design *too much*. If we designed less, we would make fewer mistakes. The article went on to explain the idea that in extreme programing we do not plan for the future, rather we develop for the known. Less design is better.

I showed the article to my boss, and had a chat with him. He read it and said, "I am not sure if this is naïve, or really smart. Does he mean that we are all doing it wrong?" I did not have the experience or internal conviction to aggressively push this. I needed to learn more.

I started reading up on Extreme Programming, and I tried to convince my boss to let me just try it out. He was not willing to take the risk. He was not willing to forgo code reviews, he was not willing to forgo upfront design, and he was not willing to allow shared owner ship of code. I think I know why he refused to take the risk. My boss was a very moderate, thorough and levelheaded guy. He believed in deep deliberation, and considering all options. Even the name "Extreme Programming" rubbed him the wrong way. At the time "extreme sports" were becoming popular. The participants in these sports came across as thrill seeking, risk takers. Another part of the problem was that I came across as too enthusiastic, and too dismissive of current practice. In hindsight I realize that this was a tone I had picked up from articles written by the likes of Kent Beck. The XP people are sometimes too enthusiastic, and too optimistic. This can frighten some people.

4.2   The Conference

The first break came when I was invited to the first XP conference that took place in Sardinia in late June 2000. At this conference I met lots of people that were already well known in the field of software development.

I met Ron Jeffries, Kent Beck, Robert Martin, Martin Fowler, Alistair Cockburn and others. I remember feeling that these are all people that are truly passionate about their job. They firmly believe that they can do better, and they want to do better. I attended workshops and lectures, and had great informal conversations with lots of people. I remember that conference as the best I have ever attended. I felt that XP is a real methodology that can solve real problems. I felt inspired to learn more about XP

I came back from the conference deeply inspired. I felt that something very significant was about to take place, and that the software development world is about to undergo a change. I felt challenged, and resolved to do more to get the organization to accept Extreme Programming.

I started rethinking my position that the problems with OOD were due to lack of expertise. I had a particular case where a class hierarchy that I was rather pleased with, contained a structural problem that was only discovered a year too late, and parts of the framework needed to be rewritten. Rewriting the code was long and painful, and in our effort to preserve as much work as possible, and not rewrite everything, we ended up with classes and member functions, with names that no longer represented the actual meaning of those classes. I knew that this code would forever be hard to maintain, and there was little I could do about it. The timing was perfect.

4.3   Trying Harder

I decided that I would try harder to make the company adopt XP. (Spoiler Alert – I failed, but I did succeed in getting some people to adopt some good behaviors). Since then I have learned many times that change in the organization can only happen if there is an individual, or individuals, that are able to drive a change forward. A non-Agile company will only convert to Agile, if there is someone actively pushing.

I decided to start with Test Driven Programming. I knew that Test Driven Programming has value that is independent of any other XP behavior.

First of all, I took aside a senior developer, whom I have a lot of respect for, and I showed him how to do Test Driven Programming. This is a guy that had been programming in many languages for many more years than I had, and who was significantly senior to me in the company hierarchy. I showed him JUnit and CUnit, and I showed him the example that Martin Fowler had shown in his workshop. To my delight, *he got it*. He understood exactly what test driven programming could do for him, and he has been doing test driven programming ever since.

Lesson Learned: If you are going to promote an idea in an organization, try to convince one person. One person is a great start.

Unfortunately, TDD is still as widely accepted within our company as it should be. We have discovered some major problems with it, but basically it works and its value is recognized.

One bizarre effect of TDD was the following. Sometimes a new behavior is required of a function, and the developer has a choice, whether to add a control variable, or just create a new function. For example there is a function: `f(int x);` that does something, but we sometimes need the function to do something else g, so we have two options:

1. Extend the function to `f(int x, bool do_also_g = false);`
2. Create a new function `f_and_g(int x);`

The decision whether to go for option 1 or option 2 depends on all sorts of considerations. The ease of reading and writing the *program* are certainly legitimate considerations. However, the programmers discovered that option 1 makes writing the *tests* easier. So people were extending the signatures of the function with more and more control parameters, not because that is what made programmatic sense, but because that is what allowed the developer to avoid writing a whole new set of tests.

Where is the fallacy here? By adding more parameters, *proper* test coverage grows combinatorically. That means, in the above example, the entire set of tests needs to be copied, with the control variable set to true.

In general, I noticed that people often treated test writing as sort of an "overhead," something to be avoided. This can be a big problem. I might go as far as saying that if you treat tests as overhead, and not as part of the code to be delivered, you might as well not write them.

Also, people only wrote tests for *new* functions. Writing tests for the thousands of existing functions seemed to be too daunting a task and was never done. So even though all the tests had passed, it was only those tests that we had written. Thus we never really had test coverage.

I tried to introduce pair programming. I took a friend, and we started programming together. That was a miserable failure. It failed because we did not adopt supporting behaviors. For example, the programming was done at my PC, and I left the email client on. Whenever an email popped up, I would take a look to see if it was urgent, and if it was urgent or short, I would take care of it. This is bad behavior even when programming alone, but it is absolutely devastating when working in pairs. While I was checking my email, my partner went to check his. By the time we got back together, 20 minutes had gone by, and we had lost the flow.

4.4   Not Really Agile

Over the next ten years, people within the organization started becoming more and more exposed to Agile methodologies. We adopted some practices, but not others. We never really became a truly Agile organization. The following paragraphs outline that.

Pair programming never really picked up. There might be cultural reasons for that, or issues to do with ego. I tried to do my part in educating people on the value of pair programming, but I was not very good at it myself, and thus had a hard time convincing others.

Shared ownership never really picked up either.

I know why "shared ownership" did not work. Some people took "ownership" to mean everyone can change any code anywhere, but the *real* "owner" of the code will clean it up if there is a problem. They did not really internalize the idea that with "ownership" anyone that touches the code is responsible to leave it in as good or better condition than it was before he started it. Ownership does not give you a right to break things.

Daily build and Test Driven Programming did pick up a bit. However, we cheated a little, and as a consequence we never really got the full advantage of those two great ideas.

For example, if there was some code that did not pass all the tests, we just commented it out. We did not want to break the daily build. We would start in the morning, uncomment our code, and start writing. At the end of the day, if we did not pass all tests, we would comment out the code again, and do our daily build. So over a few days we ended up having quite a bit of code that did not fit into the daily build.

4.5   Retrospective

Looking back at the early days, I realize several things. First and foremost, in order to do XP, you must do more than just follow the rules. You must follow the spirit, and understand how to apply the rules. Also, in order to push XP within the organization, you need a champion that gets what it is about and believes in it. He needs to be technically excellent and able to show results rather quickly. The champion needs to be passionate, charismatic and convincing. This is true about any change, but XP involves so many changes at once that this is much more significant. Not enough thought was given by the initial pioneers of XP as to how to migrate code that was written in a non-XP environment to become "XP friendly".

5   Where We Are Today

5.1   Growth

Over the following ten years, the company was growing, fast. Our branch of the company had grown from 200 people to over 1000. Some parts of the company adopted Agile practices, mainly Scrum, and others did not.

Personally, I was becoming more involved in design and less in the day-to-day coding.[1] As I got into more and more of a design and architecture role, I became more proficient at "lightweight design." I resisted making the design flexible in support of requirements that might one day come along. But design was never refactored, so

---

[1] At the time, the company encouraged that separation. Architects design, and Coders implement.

when we made bad design based on wrong assumptions, the bad design often stuck even after our assumptions were corrected.

In 2012 our company was acquired by Cisco. Cisco was a whole new ball game. Cicso is a large company, by any standard, that puts a huge emphasis on optimal performance. Cisco is very aware of the cost of developing and maintaining software, and will go to lengths in order to reduce costs and keep them down.

One of the things that our new mother company was concerned about was that even though our customers were getting most of their requirements met, the cost of developing software was on the rise. Our systems were large and complex and brittle.[2] One day, management of the newly created division prescribed the following: "From now on, we will be an Agile organization. We will all do Agile 'by the book'."

Everyone wanted to be part of the Agile transformation. The particular form of Agile chosen was Scrum. So people started training as Scrum Masters, and Product Owners. We were supposed to transform from a company that exhibits some Agile practices in some places, to a company that was fully Agile. My personal reaction was one of "reserved optimism". On the one hand, I was excited that we were now going "fully Agile" and I was hoping to play a significant role in that transformation. On the other, I was not really sure what "fully Agile" means, and if being "fully" anything was a good idea.

Over time, I noticed the following phases. Not every part of our unit went through the phases in the exact same way, but all parts of the organization certainly went through some variant of them.

5.2   Phase 1 - Optimism

Agile is great. If it is Agile, it is good. In this phase, people were going around touting Agile as the solution to all problems. There were people from other parts of the company going around telling these great Agile stories of how if we would only adopt Agile, many of our problems would be solved. Everyone wanted to become a scrum master or product owner, and everyone was attending workshops. I was delighted. More than 10 years after having attending the first XP conference, it seemed that the company I worked for was willing to fully commit to being Agile. I volunteered to mentor, to teach, to coach, to preach and guide on anything and everything that had to do with Agile.

---

[2] While the two often go together, it is worth explaining the difference between "complex" and "brittle".

"Complex" means "Many parts with many interactions". This goes together with high coupling, where the knowledge to implement requirements requires knowledge of lots of "neighboring" components. This makes the cost of change high.

"Brittle" or fragile is when the design is precarious, in the sense that every small change, force changes to the design.

5.3   Phase 2 - The Problems

Not everyone understood Agile, but almost everyone liked it. Once in a while something really troubling would come up. For instance Agile was occasionally used as an excuse for laziness, but it was hard to tell when. I myself, when asked for a detailed design of some particular aspect would often say: "Oh, we are Agile now, we don't need that." But deep inside, I was not sure if I was being Agile, or being lazy. The YAGNI (You Ain't Gonna Need It) principle can give easy rise to procrastination. I do not like doing very tedious detailed work, and the YAGNI principle was too convenient. After seeing this behavior in others, and myself I started to try to articulate "Patterns" of Agile design. I tried to define heuristics and rules to help us identify which elements need to be done up front, and what can be deferred. One activity I found particularly productive was to review the relationships between the real world entities and to have a discussion as to which relationship is intrinsic and which is not ("incidental"). More important than the actual architecture was this common understanding. I tried to make sure that everyone involved in the coding, understood these underlying assumptions so that the design decisions that were taken every day accounted for them.

Another example of the misunderstanding of Agile is in the way people understood user stories. I often heard people say, "Stories?? They are just requirements. Take all the requirements and translate them into user stories (As an X I need Y so that Z)."

They simply missed the point that stories are meant to first be *told*, and only then captured as user stories. The *telling* of a user story shifts the emphasis from the formal and context free description of what the system does, to the highly contextual. I later came to learn that this is an extremely common misunderstanding in the world of Agile. A lot of people really don't get user stories. As a consequence, people often would just read the user story, but never had the story told to them, and sometimes missed important information, that would have been conveyed had they actually been told the story. This is certainly a battle worth fighting and whenever we use Rally or some other tool, I also make sure that before the story is written, it is *told*.

While we were quickly adopting some Agile behaviors, the core values of "Agile" were took longer to sink in. I realized that a value such as "prefer individuals over process" must come from deep within the individual and within the organization. And if you do not believe in the values, then it is very difficult to really be Agile.

A typical example might help illustrate. I once spent quite a bit of time at a customer site to learn about the customer's needs and business. I came back from that customer, gathered the team, and told them the story. I told in dramatic detail, how the operator (Fredrik) gets his instructions, and how he configures the system on a daily basis. I told about how frustrated Fredrik gets with the current system, and how some modifications would make his life much easier. I then wrote some "place holder" stories such as "When adding a channel, Fredrik needs to be able to easily copy a configuration from an already configured channel. This allows Fredrik to save time, and to make fewer configuration errors." I thought that the story was clear, and so did the developers. We entered the story into Rally, and expected that whenever people read the story, they would remember what I told them in detail, and would know how to implement. Yet, one of the PMs objected, "How can you put a first name in a requirement? And you must follow form. This is what the story should say – 'As an operator, I need to copy configuration from an already configured service, to a newly defined service, so that the correct specification of the service parameters is ensured'." He went on to explain that since they are the basis of acceptance, the user stories must be properly formal, and have full detail.

I chose not to fight this particular battle, and just complied. But since then, I have been campaigning to craft user stories that explain what the system must do to bring value to the users, and acceptance criteria that explain what the system must do so that we get paid.

5.4   Maturity

It seems like at the moment, we are reaching some sort of equilibrium. We are figuring out what Agile practices work for which groups and which parts of the organization. We are not yet a fully "Agile organization" (does such a thing exist?), and we might never become one, but we are doing much better.

A lot of the effort is focused on process training. There is also technical training, in the use of tools and languages. What I find lacking most is training in proper design. I am currently working on creating a community of analysts and architects that train and mentor each other in good design. Because design is in the grey area between skill and art, it is not an easy thing to teach, but we are trying.

Over the last year I have noticed that some of the very good developers are not properly trained or skilled in analysis and design. This is a shortcoming that I think can and must be fixed. If we claim that everyone is responsible for the overall quality of the final product, then everyone is responsible for the design.

6   Retrospective

It has been a very long journey, and I learned a lot along the way. Here are some of the main takes that I would like to share.

Legacy is an extremely powerful force. If we have a large organization that has been around for a long time and thus has lots of legacy software and behaviors, it will require a great deal of force to change the organizational behavior. Whenever we discuss adopting Agile behavior, we need to discuss how we get there.

Adopting behaviors is not enough. In order for Agile to be successful, you need to believe in the values.

The evolution from extreme programming to Agile shows a great deal of maturity. Extreme programing preached that you must follow all the rules in order to be an extreme programmer. Agile preaches only core values, and lets the individual or organization, blaze their own trial.

The process of going from waterfall or partially Agile to Agile, is an important process. We are not yet done, and it will not be easy. It will probably continue to be a very bumpy ride.

Acknowledgements. Special thanks to all my friends and most of my managers in NDS and then Cisco, who patiently listened to all my ideas. Your feedback was not always kind, generous, or even welcome. But it was always honest, and after a while – appreciated.

Thanks to Rebecca Wirfs-Brock for great comments and insights.

Organizational Culture Aspects
of an Agile Transformation

Shlomi Rosenberg[✉]

Cisco Systems, Service Provider Video Software and Solutions, Jerusalem, Israel
shrosenb@cisco.com

Abstract. For an organization wishing to be more agile after working waterfall for years, it is not enough to just start learning and implementing new ways of working. There must be a parallel activity, at least equally important, of dealing with the organizational culture changes required to support this transformation. In Cisco I deal with those on a daily basis. An organizational culture is much harder to change than work methods. It involves feelings, perceptions and fears, so it is advisable to be aware of the importance and invest in dealing with it. This experience report details examples of these culture aspects, how we deal with them and some tips that can help make such transformation successful.

Keywords: Organizational culture · Agile transformation · Management · Leadership

1 Introduction

I am a senior development manager and part of the leadership of an organization with a staff of over 200 people, which is part of a much larger multinational engineering organization. This paper shares insights from my experience in being an active part of an amazing agile transformation that we have gone through and are still making progress with. I will focus on the organizational culture aspects of an agile transformation of this scale, which in the beginning I wasn't aware of as relevant. I came to realize their importance to success in the transformation and that it is at least as important as the agile practices themselves.

2 Background

For the past twelve years I have been an engineering manager at various levels, managing teams and activities related to development, integration and testing of complex systems in the digital TV industry. The entire development process was completely waterfall based. Our organization has always been structured in a way that is tightly coupled to clear functions. These domains can be based on job roles such as integrators, developers, QC engineers, etc.

They can also be based on components, projects, customers, etc. and all of these were divided between multiple sites worldwide. This type of organizational structure

© Springer International Publishing Switzerland 2015
C. Lassenius et al. (Eds.): XP 2015, LNBIP 212, pp. 279–286, 2015.
DOI: 10.1007/978-3-319-18612-2_28

nourished an organizational culture that exhibited some underlying problematic characteristics such as ownership, territorialism, lack of trust, over-management and so forth. Actually, it was sometimes hard to believe that these domains were part of the same company or even that they were all working on the same project, a situation that is clearly harmful to efficiency and productivity. These aspects of organizational culture and various behaviors deriving from them not only make it difficult to improve effectiveness, but also need to be dealt with, specifically when considering such a large-scale transformation to Agile.

3   Ownership

Ownership in general doesn't indicate something negative. After all, when engineers feel ownership, they also feel responsible and it is clear who to go to with questions, support, and bug fixes required. These are things managers actually like and need. The question is what to build the ownership around?

3.1   The Culture Issue

The problem in our organization starts from the fact we develop complex end-to-end systems, which are built from numerous stacks running on various machines at different physical locations and each built from tens of components. Our organization was heavily based around component ownership i.e. Managers and their teams owned code.

When I refer to code ownership I refer to a culture of "no one but the component team is allowed to modify our code". It also nourished a management culture of focusing around what they own "physically", which allowed them to get some materialistic measure of their "power".

This direct correlation between code and teams was drastic and it caused strong dependencies and obstacles in our ability to move fast. For example, different time zones of component owners caused delays in progressing integrations. Some component owners would not even expose their code, so integrators could not debug by themselves. These dependencies were a big contribution for our heaviness as a development organization.

When we decided to transform to become more agile, one of our key principles was to enable our teams to progress feature development in as self-sustained way as possible. We decided that instead of owning code, the teams should own features. For supporting them in doing so, it meant we must reduce the code/component ownership to a minimum so when developing an E2E feature they'll need to develop and integrate all involved components in the feature's vertical flow.

This code ownership was, and still is in few cases, one of the biggest obstacles to our full Agile transformation. Component teams, owners and managers in particular, were nervous about this change. This code ownership is what defined their organization in many ways for so many years. Code is something tangible and is something you can "fight" for. Also, for many engineers, it was comfortable and "encouraged" them to be narrowly focused. Rather than building fast velocity feature development capabilities, they got used to focus on their narrow component domains. They could raise dependencies and have someone to "blame" for not progressing.

Also for those not owning components, specifically the integration teams, it nurtured frustration of not being able to progress effectively as they were constantly dependent on others. For others it was a comfortable situation, as their job was just to perform builds and report back if what they got is sufficient based various level investigations. This integration dynamic was comfortable for the owners and some of the integration teams.

For most people, something comfortable shouldn't be changed, and they will fight for it. They focus on rationalizing this way of work by pointing the problems to other places and by focusing on the importance of people being experts in their function or component. They would also convince each regarding his role that "it's too complex for anyone to do it or no one has the knowledge or experience to do what they do". All valid points, but all can also change.

3.2 How We Dealt with It

The described situation impacts effectiveness as it virtually causes formation of teams within teams, limiting their agility. If not dealt with, it cripples the enablement and self-sustainability of the functional scrum teams turning them practically in to a semi-waterfall integration teams.

As a start, from team structuring perspective, as mentioned above, we defined vertical teams. These teams' mission is to deliver end-to-end user stories and features. That is what they are measured by. We tried to limit as much as possible the number of horizontal (component centric) teams. The reason it's limiting the number and not eliminating is because after all there are areas where it makes a lot of sense to remain horizontal (such as point products within the solution which are used by other solutions also, third party component porting, etc.).

To compliment that, decision wise, we made a decision and communicated to all teams, that components can be branched by vertical teams if they need to do so for progressing. This mainly disconnected the "only owners can modify code" from the component ownership. At the beginning we experimented with a vertical team to prove this increases velocity. We were proved right and use the concept more widely in other teams. Also, we are pressuring vertical teams not to be intimidated by new unfamiliar code. We are communicating clearly that we are not happy with them opening impediments for each bug they find in Horizontal components, but rather push to fix them.

3.3 Culture Tip

At early stages and continuously after, identify engineers in vertical teams who are both technically strong and willing to enthusiastically try the change. These engineers together will prove it is doable. This is quicker than depending on external parties. Success stories with results will be your best proof and motivator for others.

4   Territorialism

It's the most trivial thing to have different job roles in a development organization. We have architects, developers, integrators and QC engineers. Our organization was built according to these roles i.e. each of the above roles was grouped also organizational-wise. So we had an architecture department, a development department, an integration department and a QC department. The flow of development was that architects defined a work-package, the development teams involved developed their part of it, the integration team integrated the components and then the QC teams tested it. Sounds reasonable, but it developed an underlying engineering culture that doesn't go with agile development.

4.1   The Culture Issue

The underlying culture around our previous structure came mainly from prestige related reasons. It's simple. Some of these roles subjectively have better reputation than others. Few examples:

- Developers want to develop code, they don't want to do integration nor QC work.
- Integrators feel it's beneath them to test.
- Developers don't want integrators to find fixes for their bugs.
- Integrators feel threatened by QC engineers investigating the bugs they find.

For these reasons and more, people guarded their domains carefully. The engineers were territorial about their engineering function and would usually stay away from other functions.

One of our major goals of the transformation was building vertically enabled teams, who deliver end-to-end tested features. This was not a trivial change for many of our engineers. Suddenly an engineer is responsible to deliver an end to end feature. Together with his team, he is required to do much more than just write code, just integrate it or just test it. He needs to be involved and aware of all aspects of delivering the end-to-end user story. That is part of the new Definition of Done for the team's user stories. This is a major change to engineering mindset.

4.2   How We Dealt with It

This proved to be a difficult change. It's not easy for someone who always used to writing code and passing it to someone for integrating and then testing, to start delivering end-to-end working features.

First, we invest a lot in training to understand this concept and its importance as a key to our success. We are also pushing POs to minimize defining user stories, which correlate to these different functions as there was a tendency to define user stories such as "Write tests for functionality X" coming from pressure from within some of the teams. We constantly monitor to see we don't have single task type engineers in the teams, even on the expense of in the short term sometimes slowing down some activities. Naturally, some engineers are stronger or more experienced in some functions than the others, which is a positive thing.

4.3   Culture Tip

Be persistent on this and work closely with the engineers to explain and convince them that the new way of work is better. Also acknowledge and praise high quality rather that high pace.

5   Managers vs. Leadership

Our command and control driven waterfall organization structure had a heavy management structure of roughly one manager to six employees.

The team responsibilities at the majority of cases were narrow related to the product the organization delivered. Also these team managers were responsible to all aspects of their team. This caused a lot of silos, which was slowing us down and limiting the variety of influence sources to the wide organization product perspective. The culture was also that only managers can lead or influence.

When we began our transformation we didn't focus on organization restructuring, we focused on activity restructuring. We didn't even discuss the organization structuring until we were confident with our program structure.

This proved to be a smart approach as it instantly eliminated all silos, which contributed greatly to the senior leadership to cooperate amazingly. This was crucial for leading the transformation. The leadership team literally didn't have anything to fight about in terms of private interests as with all the scrum teams' buildup it so happened that each manager had his reporting engineers spread between different teams, so teams were not associated with managers. Later, when we were confident with our program structure, the management organization restructuring was much clearer in terms of needs. We could restructure to fit our activities rather than organizing activities to fit a reporting structure. We divided the classical management role into three main categories, namely People, Activity & Technical:

- The people manager role is now focused on taking care of the Engineers and staffing the program teams rather than "interfering" with the teams work - **this is the reporting structure**.
- The activity management is done by the scrum teams and their PO (not a reporting structure).
- The technical management is a tech lead type network that continuously mentor, advise and lead technically the teams (not a reporting structure).

5.1   The Culture Issue

For an organization with such an embedded command & control mindset and culture, the strongest source of influence, power and leadership came from the reporting structure. The common perception was that leadership equals management.

The downside that started building up slowly was that our people managers, which until transitioning to working agile had clear responsibility, didn't find their place in the system. The activities and team management was provided by the scrum teams themselves and the program management, so "all" that was left for them is the people management, which was unclear. The perception was that being a people manager is just a bureaucracy role. It started causing tension and insecurity, specifically for the first line managers. On the other hand, the engineers also gradually showed signs of confusion not understanding who to go to for what kind of issues. This situation alerted us, the leadership team, that we needed to move forward with the reorganization in order to fill all these gaps.

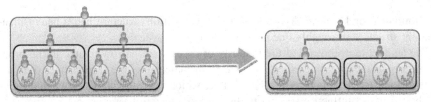

Fig. 1. Alignment of organization structure to support agile

When starting to communicate the structure change shown in Fig. 1, managers, (mainly first line managers) got nervous. At first look and considering the management culture we were coming from, it looks like are eliminating a level of seniority. If they are not chosen as people managers they perceived it to mean they are demoted and they are not part of our leadership anymore. It could be perceived as limiting for carrier development. Although I am confident in that structure, it's not that easy to make people understand that. Many people who were managers in the old organization structure are no longer managers. It doesn't mean they can't be leaders.

5.2 How We Dealt with It

There are actually many more influential positions available at this structure once you understand people manager is not the only way to develop your carrier. It is also not necessarily always the most visible leadership position in terms of the program day-to-day performance.

Saying all that, it's not that trivial to explain, specifically to a mature organization with such different organizational culture. One of the main actions we took is to consider scrum masters, product owners and architects (we try to assign an architect for each team) as part of the organization leadership. They take an active part in shaping our way forward. As senior leaders, we respect and keep the well-defined boundaries between people management issues, which will be dealt with people managers, and scrum team management, which is dealt with the scrum masters or product owners.

There is a continuous learning and improvement process for shaping the different leadership roles, empowering the different roles to lead their domain.

5.3 Culture Tip

From early stage start communicating the difference between functional management and people management. Also focus on the importance of the different roles in an agile organization. These things take time to absorb and it will drastically reduce frustrations when you apply your reorganization.

6   The Buzzword Trap

My last topic involves a communication related aspect to our agile transformation. Anything new usually involves a lot of buzzwords. Agile is no different and as the name implies, they do indeed create a buzz. In a large scale transformation such as we went through, you must create a buzz, or a sense of excitement, in order to pull everybody on board. However, if you don't walk the walk at the same pace you talk the talk, it is easy to achieve the opposite effect. What my experience showed me is that you can't answer questions or give guidance with buzzwords if you want them to transform the way people work. You must focus on the methodology and only afterwards relate it to its name if you want. Another issue related to this is that I observed people actually turning agile to be their goal rather than the means to achieve their goal.

6.1   The Culture Issue

As agile methodologies are so different in so many ways from waterfall, mentioning words such as sprint, scrum, agile and retrospective as the solution for all the problems we face is far from being enough to motivate a large organization to change. For someone taken out of their comfort zone by such change, specifically many engineers, buzzwords are not comforting. In fact, overloading people with new terminology can be quite intimidating and cause the opposite effect of contempt.

At the start of our transformation, anyone who wanted to sound like he is fully agile "compatible" used a lot of agile buzzwords. However, it became clear that different people have different interpretations of the different words. This can easily cause damage to what you want to achieve as it causes misalignment. For example, you show up for a demo and find that the team was working on it for three days rather than showing their current raw state. Another example is teams being managed by their scrum master by him asking for status at each standup, commenting on it and giving directions for next day. The problem with these behaviors is that it is easy to derail from what we try to achieve as these are command and control behaviors masked by agile structure and neglecting those can easily regress the work culture back to what you originally want to change.

6.2   How We Dealt with It

This requires a lot of self-discipline. We started being aware, mainly when guiding the teams not to use these words. E.g., many times we actually ban the word agile from our discussions. We focus on the methodology and what we want to achieve.

The focus is on understanding the problems we want to solve and discussing the way we believe it can be solved. We don't focus on coupling our solutions with an agile framework. We created a culture, which is open for improvement and feedback. We invest in agile coaching. We continually conduct classes and to complement these, we have coaches joining the teams, even the more experienced teams and providing feedback on what to do more of, what to do less of and what to change. We focus on continuous improvement rather than on achieving some ultimate goal.

6.3   Culture Tip

When going agile and passing the messages needed for this transformation, don't focus on agile related buzz words it is not sufficient to achieve a real transformation. Focus on the characteristics and qualities that come with it and why you need them.

7   What did I Learn from This Experience

My agile transformation experience has shown me the importance of the culture aspects involved in such a deep change to the way we work. It also proves to me and makes me confident that being aware to it and addressing it, is an absolute key factor to a sustainable culture change. I think the following should be an integral part of any leadership team's agenda when transforming to agile.

- Your organization's culture aspects are equally important to succeeding with your transformation. They are more difficult to deal with.
- Be persistent on explaining the advantages of multidiscipline engineering within the teams and value high quality over fast pace.
- Communicate the difference between functional management and people management. Focus on the leadership aspects of different roles
- Focus on the characteristics and qualities that you believe are important for your culture, not on agile buzzwords.
- Choose the right leadership to lead your transformation. Make sure they trust each other, work well together, and understand that organization success is their success.
- Your leadership at all levels must encourage change and support change.

Acknowledgements. I'd like to thank Cisco for the opportunity to be part in leading such an agile transformation. I would also like to thank my colleagues at the leadership team running this transformation.

Lastly, I would really like to thank my experience report shepherd Ken Power for encouraging and really helping bringing this paper together. *Thanks Ken for all the help. It probably wouldn't come together without you!*

The Guide Board, an Artefact to Support the Continuous Improvement of an Agile Team's Culture

Matti Schneider[(✉)]

Université de Nice Sophia-Antipolis, Nice, France
`agile@mattischneider.fr`

Abstract. The Guide Board is an artefact that supports continuous improvement of practices and interactions within a team, with the same materials as classical agile artefacts. It represents the conclusions of a team's retrospectives as "guides" to make them tangible. By specifying how these guides are visualised and handled depending on their actual application, the Guide Board improves the production system efficiency by increasing the critical reuse of previous conclusions. A successful application substantially increases the team's self-awareness of its culture, and makes its habits more visible to other stakeholders, thus improving communication. Finally, it improves the readability of its social rules to newcomers, thus supporting integration of new hires and therefore growth.

Keywords: Guide Board · Agile · Artefact · Continuous improvement · Retrospective

1 Introduction

A few years ago, I started a highly constrained software project with a small team that had a strong agile potential. The team members were lacking most of the theory, but were eager to learn. I decided to gradually introduce concepts while development started. After presenting the bare minimum of Scrum to get a working Sprint 0 came the first retrospective. Along with it came the following question: how will I give my motivated but newbie team a feeling of tangible outcomes from this first occurrence of the most important ritual? How can I make them feel the crucial nature of this opportunity to reflect upon how they work and interact? How can I give the team a hint that this long-term investment will pay off, and that it is paving the way towards a better version of itself?

This is how the first version of the Guide Board came to be: by a simple facilitator's reflex of writing down the answers the team had given to its own questions on sticky notes, with a little playfulness in illustrating them. What made it more specific than a simple "reflection workshop output" [2] artefact was the column grouping under a sprint number card (Fig. 1), to give an idea that others would follow.

© Springer International Publishing Switzerland 2015
C. Lassenius et al. (Eds.): XP 2015, LNBIP 212, pp. 287–293, 2015.
DOI: 10.1007/978-3-319-18612-2_29

Fig. 1. The "guides" of the first sprint (*top*), defining the expected times of the standup (*middle*) and lunch (*bottom*), as an answer to the waste the team members felt in waiting for each other

Most agile teams rely on physical artefacts to help them visualise, inspect and improve their processes. Burndown charts provide input for continuous improvement. Happiness indexes increase the salience of its need. On the contrary, if there is a common ritual for the team to "reflect on how to become more effective", there is no common way to help it "then tune and adjust its behaviour accordingly" [7].

The first role of the Guide Board is to help with formalising the retrospective decisions that have long-term effects. These decisions are crucial to continuous improvement, yet are hard to respect consistently enough[1] to yield the expected results, leading to the same type of problems being detected again and again. By offering a simple, well-defined format, the Guide Board decreases the barrier to entry to take such decisions and eases their inspection and adaptation in later retrospectives. More importantly, by making these decisions tangible and visible enough to influence day-to-day situations, the board nudges team members in respecting the decisions they took, even when they are focused on production rather than improvement.

Over months, the Guide Board truly became what allowed us to achieve the cultural changes we needed to overcome the obstacles that kept coming.

2   The Board and Its Making

2.1   Overview

From its original first column, our Guide Board kept on growing to the right, always as a repository of retrospective conclusions. It quickly took enough space to grant a specific place. Considering its use, it was obvious it had to be visible from everywhere. The large paper sheets covered in stickies ended up at the top of a wall, overlooking the workstations (Fig. 2).

---

[1] Especially without external coaching.

This position felt right[2], but it brought a few readability issues. This is why, from iteration 23 on, most sticky notes are pasted sticky side down (Fig. 3), which makes them lean downwards and thus more readable from below.

2.2   Opening a Guide

After each retrospective, a column is added to the board, materialised by sticky notes of different colours (Fig. 4). On the first line, a red sticky note mentions the iteration number. The team then creates a new "guide" for every rule that it decides to adopt to enhance its strengths and reduce its weaknesses. These guides are represented by a green sticky note covered by a few words accompanied by schematic drawings. After a discussion leading to a precise characterisation of the rule, the guide is added below the number of the current iteration. A guide is therefore the reification of a debate conclusion, *a reminder that a discussion took place*. These keywords and drawings are here to recall the agreement to participants, as a tangible trace of the decision.

We stopped drawing illustrations at some point. However, after a few weeks usage, it became clear that the illustrated guides were easier to

Fig. 2. Our Guide Board, at the top of a wall

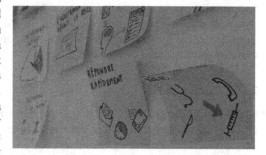

Fig. 3. Sticky notes should be pasted upside-down

Fig. 4. Top left corner of the Guide Board

memorise, and much easier to identify when glancing at the board. By starting to use them again, we realised that they were even more important than expected.

Indeed, agreeing on an illustration led to much deeper debates than agreeing on a sentence[3]. Upon observing this improvement, we opened a guide stating that "The illustration defines the rule": agree on the drawing first. The team will define the expected impact much more precisely, and the textual description will be obvious.

---

[2] It actually has very good reasons for being there, one of them being friction isomorphism [5].
[3] That may sound counterintuitive, but makes sense if you consider how much information can be encoded through drawings, as opposed to words, on a single sticky note.

Interestingly, cognitive psychology confirms images strongly help in constructing mental models of processes [4], which is exactly what we are after here. Empirical evidence confirms this: illustrated guides were closed much less often than pure texts.

To avoid overload, we quickly had to define what was allowed on the board and what was to be kept as oral conclusions, or stored otherwise.

The first criteria is *actionability*. A guide defines an action, or refines how one should be done. For example, the guide "Describe bugs from the point of view of the user" defines the way the team considers most efficient to describe bugs. Simply stating "Bugs are not properly described", while an acceptable retrospective conclusion if the team cannot come up with a solution yet, is not an acceptable guide.

The second criteria is *durability*. Anything that was to change durably our habits was in, any non-recurring or experimental action was out. Experiments are a good thing, but only the successful ones are stored as guides, once they have proven benefits. For example, "No story over 10 points in the backlog" is eligible, while "Split all stories over 10 points currently in the backlog" is not[4]. The distinction is simple to grasp by remembering that a guide embodies a course of action the team wants to follow for the foreseeable future.

2.3   Using Guides

One usage of the guides is individual. A team member unsure about how to handle a given situation may first turn to the Guide Board as a repository of common agreed-upon policies before turning to colleagues.

For example, we observed far less rushed deliveries after opening the guide "Deliver and prepare the demonstration the day before the sprint ends", as each team member knew what to focus on without waiting for others to be available to take a collective decision: the collective decision on priorities had *already be taken*.

Another usage is collective. When a team member believes that a debate has already happened earlier, she may simply point to a guide to end the discussion. This closes the debate without generating frustration, since it simply reminds a point that had already been agreed upon by all team members.

For example, our mean daily standup duration went down from 13'42" to 5'55" after opening the guide "Keep the stand-up under 6 minutes" [5]. The tangibility of the guide allowed team members to discretely point at it rather than interrupting a colleague being inadvertently too long.

Objectification of the collective decision decreases social risks on both the giving and receiving ends of a reminder: you are not accusing me, and I don't have to justify myself; you are simply reminding me something we all agreed on, and I had simply temporarily forgotten; now I remember, and have the opportunity to adjust my behaviour to be consistent with my own choices.

2.4   Closing a Guide

Obviously, even rules enacted with the best observations and intentions may fail on delivering value over time, would it be only because of external context changes.

---

[4] Even though adding the new rule implies the one-shot action, the latter is not added to the Guide Board but handled on its own.

There is thus a need to stop observing obsolete rules. Yet, simple removal is a waste, as these modifications are also opportunities. Opportunities to improve decision-taking on later rules by observing the ones that failed. Opportunities to better characterise external pressures by observing their impact on our system. Opportunities to ensure external stakeholders are aware of a change in our processes.

The Guide Board defines a way to "close" past guides while maximising the value of such events. You may have noticed some of the guides are covered by blue sticky notes. These guides are closed, and they have been through the process that follows.

The team may decide to put a guide "under observation" if it considers, in a retrospective, that it failed to respect the embodied decision. The last line of the board is headed by a large exclamation mark, and includes all guides that are under observation for the current iteration (Fig. 5). These guides will be reinstated in their previous place at the end of the iteration if the team believes it finally respected them. Otherwise, they will be closed. Closure is achieved by covering the guide with a blue sticky note on which the closure iteration number is written. In such a case, repeating the mistake is avoided by also writing down the reasons for inadequacy of the guide to the current situation on the back of the sticky.

The closure iteration number has two roles. On one hand, it allows measurement of the time between opening and closure, and thus to check that a guide is not closed right after having been enacted, which would mean that guides are adopted too quickly. On the other hand, the iteration numbers are a reference to a set of experiences shared within the team. Therefore, reading that index often allows a team member to recontextualise the closure without consulting the reminder on the back.

This full reminder comes in handy to help the team grow over failing habits. When confronted with a specific type of problem, a human group often has a specific type of response. By having a tangible anchor for a past solution that failed, the team is able to spot similarities with a solution it could come up with to face a new problem. It is much easier to design a solution that learns from a past failure by reading the reasons identified at the time of closure than by trying to remember what went wrong later on.

3   Limitations and Open Questions

3.1   Team Maturity

Empirical evidence shows that theoretical knowledge of agile practices is not necessary to experience benefits from using a Guide Board. However, since its inputs are decisions taken collectively during retrospectives, the rewards are directly proportional to the quality and regularity of said retrospectives.

This means that the prerequisites for a return on investment in a Guide Board are the same as those for retrospectives. Goodwill, collective responsibility, personal safety [2] and regular inspection-and-adaptation are required. Only then can the benefits of objectification of collectiveness through an artefact be felt[5].

---

[5] More accurately, the prerequisite is system entanglement [5]: the ability of the team to modify its artefacts combined with the ability for the artefacts to prescribe members' behaviour.

3.2   Adoption in Existing Projects

Teams that tried to adopt this artefact mentioned that it would probably be most efficient when used from the beginning of a project. This hypothesis is based on the idea that an already-formed team may not benefit from a partial representation of its culture, as only the latest additions to it are made visible.

The representation of a team's practices will always be partial, as what is made tangible is only what the team deemed valuable enough to explicitly try preserving, and what it struggled with enough to discuss and try solving. Elements that don't emerge through discussion will stay invisible anyway, so those missing because they emerged before the board's presence should not bring specific problems. If an important element is not treated, it will come back in retrospectives until a decision is taken, and thus a matching guide is opened.

One team had success filling a Guide Board a posteriori upon adoption, highlighting important recent decisions, both that they struggled with and that were a success.

Starting with the latest retrospectives rather than an empty board could be good practice for existing projects, but this has to be done with the whole team. Otherwise, the guides will be only one member's understanding and fail to embody agreement.

3.3   Project Duration

I have often heard that due to its long-term benefits, the Guide Board is probably only worth using in projects that will be longer than a certain amount of iterations. If there is such a minimal investment number, it is not characterised yet. I can tell that we felt immediate improvement with the first, trivial guides that eased synchronisation for team-wide events, as they were what the retrospective made emerge as a priority.

Since the basis of a Guide Board is retrospectives and that its aim is to increase their impact, the question of whether it is worth using it in a specific project can probably be reduced to whether it is worth doing retrospectives at all for that project.

A question that is still open, though, is how much a board is specific to a *team* or to a *project*, which may change the phrasing to how much you want to invest in a team rather than in a project.

4   Conclusion

One may see the Guide Board as a generalisation of the Kanban principles [1] to the culture: make practices visible, reflect upon them regularly, characterise and measure failure. However, one must keep in mind that "guides" are not simply moving parts in a meta-production system that would make the best praxis emerge. A Guide Board is not a driving wheel, it has to be owned by a team willing to improve if it is to deliver any improvement [5].

We like to think of it more as a "production style guide": a growing set of parameters defining how software is to be produced, according to experience in how to avoid common failures (and bits of personal preference), collectively owned, maintained and enforced. It does not dictate end goals, nor is it a golden, immutable law that may never be transgressed. It is a style guide that does not address only code, but critical parts of software engineering too often forgotten [3]: the interactions between the people, machines and software that form the production system.

Acknowledgments. Nicolas Dupont, Thomas De Bona, Paul Percier, Thibault Vigouroux, Sallyan Freudenberg, Alistair Cockburn, Anouchka Labonne.

References

1. Anderson, D.: Kanban — Successful Evolutionary Change for your Technology Business. Blue Hole Press (2010)
2. Cockburn, A.: Crystal Clear: a human-powered methodology for small teams. Pearson Education (2004)
3. Curran, B.: What is software engineering? ACM Ubiquity (2005)
4. Glenberg, A.M., Langston, W.E.: Comprehension of illustrated text: Pictures help to build mental models. Journal of memory and language 31(2), 129–151 (1992)
5. Schneider, M: Partage de représentations et ritualisation au sein d'une équipe de développement logiciel agile. Université de Nice Sophia-Antipolis (2014)
6. Schneider, M: L'approche centrée artefacts. In: Agile France Conference (2014)
7. Signatories of the Agile Manifesto: Principles behind the agile manifesto (2001)
8. Wells, D.: Daily Stand Up Meeting. Extreme Programming (1999)

Testing Modtalk

Josh Fridstrom, Adam Jacques, Kurt Kilpela, and John Sarkela[✉]

Northern Michigan University, Marquette, MI 49855, USA
jsarkela@nmu.edu

Abstract. The Modtalk project is an effort to create a production ready tool chain for compiling Smalltalk programs into standalone executables. This development project entailed writing and testing code in a cross development environment, in a target executable environment, and a C based runtime that supports the compiled executable. We discovered that test-driven development supported team communication, focused design efforts, and produced code artifacts that documented the system. In the process, we also discovered that tests were often brittle and would break for a variety of reasons. We identify why some of our tests were brittle and ways in which we responded when tests failed.

Keywords: Test driven development · Compiler · IDE · Smalltalk

1 Introduction

The Modtalk project is an extra-curricular software development project that has been under development at Northern Michigan University since January 2013. A pedagogical goal of the project is to allow undergraduate students to have the opportunity to experience team development of a software project of significant scope and complexity. The project goal is to develop a set of developer tools for production Smalltalk development. This report covers the experience of the first two teams to contribute to this multi-year project. The first team was a pair consisting of a student, Steve Jarvis, and instructor, John Sarkela. The second team included three additional students who were entering their senior year, Josh Fridstrom, Adam Jacques, and Kurt Kilpela.

Why Smalltalk? Smalltalk introduced the term object oriented. The original usage of this term implied much more than a language that supported classes and polymorphic message sends. Object orientation implied a development process that entailed direct manipulation of objects. The Smalltalk environment was at once an operating system and a programming environment. In this environment, everything was an object. This even included the implementation of the compiler, debugger, classes, compiled methods, processes, and method activations. To create a new subclass, the developer sent a message to the proposed superclass requesting that subclass be created. To add behavior, the compiler was sent a message with a class and some source text to compile. This source was transformed into a compiled method object, and added to the method dictionary of that class. In this environment, the program, the operating system, the

© Springer International Publishing Switzerland 2015
C. Lassenius et al. (Eds.): XP 2015, LNBIP 212, pp. 294–301, 2015.
DOI: 10.1007/978-3-319-18612-2_30

language implementation, the developer tools were all represented with a very large object graph known as the virtual image. The virtual image was brought to life by a virtual machine that animated the object graph implementing message sends that modified the object graph.

This environment was extraordinarily productive for a single developer. However, because the activity of coding was a process of incremental modification of a running program, sharing developed software was problematic. Further, there was no clear distinction between the development tools, the program under development, the language implementation, or the operating system, making the deployment of a standalone application difficult.

The Modtalk project seeks to address these issues by taking a radically different approach to Smalltalk development. Modtalk stores source code in files. It has an integrated development environment that compiles that source code into a mix of C and assembler that can be compiled with a standard C compiler tool chain into a standalone executable. In this paper, we will be reporting on our experiences testing this system into existence and evolving it over the first two years of project development.

The scope of the work involves three distinct domains of execution. The cross development environment, Pharo Smalltalk, in which the tools are being developed, C in which the runtime support libraries are implemented, and actual programs created by the cross development tools. Therefore, we had unit tests that needed to run in each of these three domains.

As is often the case, as test cases accumulated, they started to become a burden on progress. There is a natural tension between keeping tests passing and the principle of continuous design improvement. Tests that break because of an improvement to the code base, we call brittle. Imagine a plate of glass. If you attempt to bend or deform that plate of glass, the expected outcome is many shards of broken glass. Similarly the deformation of an interface often leads to test failures. Sometimes these changes can be foreseen; other times they take us by surprise. Note that we do not believe that brittle tests are inherently bad. For example, tests for key system interfaces should be brittle and complain loudly when an implementation is out of conformance. However, in our case, we were in the process of attempting to not only define these interfaces, but also to determine on which boundaries they lived.

2   The Project

2.1   Project Release Plans

We identified goals for the first two release cycles of the project. The first release cycle was six months long and had the objective of being able to compile a simple program that allocated objects and sent messages. The tests for this phase of the project were written in the Pharo cross development environment and in our C language runtime environment.

The second cycle was eighteen months long targeted a system with sufficient functionality to compile standard benchmarks such as the delta blue constraint solver. This second cycle introduced tests running in the context of a program compiled by the Modtalk compiler.

The traditional unit of compilation for Smalltalk is a method, so we initially envisioned a compiler that first loaded all of the global definitions into a model of the program, and then it compiled the method definitions in the context of that program model. Modtalk introduces the notion of source code modules to Smalltalk. Program and subsystem modules define global namespaces. Packages hold the actual source code definitions and clusters provide views on those packages. Modtalk does not change the syntax of Smalltalk, but does add a higher order language for expressing how packages are composed to define subsystems, and how subsystems are composed to define a program.

We wanted all of this to be under source control, so we had the further requirement of a framework for loading versions of source modules into memory so that they could be semantically validated and decorated as a full model of the program. Our initial subsystem break down looked like this.

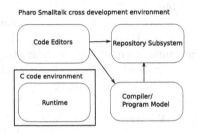

Fig. 1. The initial rough breakdown of subsystems

We would not need to begin work on the runtime until we had the ability to create and load a program, so work on the runtime was deferred. Our repository subsystem was to be responsible for saving a module object as source text in an external repository as well as later retrieving a version of the source and producing a module object. We wanted to be able to support svn or git as a backend, and settled on git for the first implementation. At the time, the simplest course of action seemed to be to use the FSGit framework on SqueakSource. We created a bridge class that delegated to the implementation class. FSGit supported memory based repositories, which made it very easy to create and destroy repositories when testing.

We created classes to model all of the Smalltalk source code definition types defined in the ANSI standard. Most of these objects were simple information holders and we did not write tests for them. Next up was the module system. Modules are the unit of persistence for source code in Modtalk. We had not settled on an external syntax for our source code modules, and chose to use a concrete syntax that was easy to generate and parse, but not particularly easy for a human to read or write directly. We knew that we would be replacing the module syntax at least once before this phase of development was over.

We designed abstract module reader and module writer tests. The tests were all of the form: given a module, produce the corresponding source; or given source, produce the corresponding module. We implemented the test methods for the readers and writers in the abstract test case. This abstract test case included concrete methods that returned instances of modules required by the tests. We declared abstract accessing methods responsible for returning what the corresponding external source strings should be. Creating a concrete test case for the module readers and writers entailed writing an accessing method that returned the appropriate source string for that version of the module syntax. We subsequently changed the syntax for modules twice, in each case, the readers, writers, and their test cases were all completed in a day of work.

Once we could save and restore software modules from the repository, we needed to start the process of decorating these modules to produce the program model used during compilation. We identified two key objects, a module manager and a definition manager. The module manager was to be responsible for ensuring the referential integrity of the module structure. The definition manager was responsible for managing program scopes and program model artifacts as definitions were loaded into a program model. We implemented the module manager and definition manager by sequentially writing tests for everything we could identify they needed to do. The level of complexity of this part of the system caused us to implement a bulk whole program loader, rather than an incremental loader. We wrote tests to ensure we could recognize and record global program errors. Unfortunately, the resulting code had all of the structure and elegance of a big ball of mud. On the positive side, we did design a fairly stable and complete interface for the module manager. A very important aspect of writing tests first, is that it is an effective way to scope design activities. By focusing all of ones attention on the task of writing tests, one is forced to consider what the component under test needs to do, not how it does it. The consequence of this is that just enough design gets done.

The method scanner, parser, and abstract syntax tree nodes were easy to test into existence and had a very stable specification. We wrote tests for each type of token, and each production of the method grammar. These were well understood, and implemented in a week.

At this point, we could load a program, build global scopes for name spaces in the program, and we could compile methods. We were four months into the first cycle of development. The ability to generate code was next in our queue. We defined a low-level stack/register machine that would serve as the model for the Modtalk code generator for this purpose. At this point, we welcomed Josh, Kurt, and Adam to the team. They were given documentation of the Modtalk machine register architecture and op code set, as well as the types and memory formats for objects in memory. They were initially tasked with implementing a direct threaded interpreter for this abstract machine, as well as implementing the object allocator.

There was a big learning curve to get up to speed on the work that had been done to this point. Once again, tests helped to focus effort as new team members

were being on boarded to the project. We built the simplest possible C based
test runner, wrote tests for byte and pointer object allocations and tests for the
op code set. While the new team members were busying themselves with getting
runtime tests to pass, Steve and John tested a code generator into existence.

Shortly thereafter, we could compile a program that created an object and
sent some messages. We could not yet handle method arguments, or temporary
variables, but we could send messages. This completed our first release cycle.

2.2 Refining the Design

At the beginning of the second release cycle, we had 27 test cases in the Pharo
cross-development environment with 149 test methods. The runtime had 6 object
allocation tests, 20 interpreter tests, and 3 method lookup tests. We needed to
get enough Modtalk classes written so that we could compile a working SUnit
test framework. This was important, as we did not have debugging tools for
the generated program beyond gdb and lldb. They are great debuggers, but the
wrong level of abstraction for debugging our generated code. To get an adequate
library of classes compiled, we needed to get a garbage collector, more primitives,
full block closures with non-local returns, and exceptions working.

In our retrospective of the first release of the project, we noticed that no one
had contributed to the FSGit project in over a year. This caused some concern,
and we decided to fork a shell and run standard git commands instead. While
this change did not break any tests directly, the performance characteristics were
profoundly different. So much so, that running all the tests became problematic.
We ran the tests and assured that they behaved the same as the old implementation. After that, we stopped running the repository tests as written for a number
of months. Over time, we rewrote the tests to be less file system intensive.

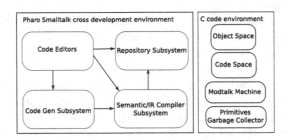

Fig. 2. A more refined understanding of the system

Upon revisiting our block diagram of the system, we discovered that we
needed to refine our Compiler subsystem into a Semantic subsystem and a Code
Generation subsystem. To do this would require an extensive rework of the compilation subsystem. All of our compiler tests were testing actual generated code
sequences produced from abstract syntax trees. To expose the new Semantic

subsystem interface, we needed to compile up to an intermediate representation in the Semantic subsystem and generate the actual runtime code in the Code Generation subsystem from intermediate representation. Our strategy was to introduce intermediate representation in the existing implementation and a threaded code generator. We validated the intermediate representation and code generator by ensuring that the existing compiler tests all green lighted. The next step was to cleave the code generation subsystem from the semantic subsystem. This action broke every compiler test, and was a needed design refinement. Knowing that the compiler tests green lighted prior to this shattering of the compiler tests gave us the courage to proceed.

We now faced a big problem. Modtalk library development needed to proceed at a break neck speed. At the same time, we needed to radically restructure the underlying implementation of the semantic subsystem. Both of these activities needed to happen simultaneously. Our solution was to introduce two new facade objects: one for the repository subsystem, and one for the semantic subsystem. All of the tools were refactored to use these objects. In this way, library construction could proceed using the big ball of mud implementation, while the refactored module manager and definition manager were developed. We were able to get a version of SUnit ported in about one month of effort. We focused testing of the new semantic subsystem on the edge cases of the new implementation, as the main paths of execution were implicitly covered by other tests.

Meanwhile, work on the new primitives and garbage collector proceeded as quickly as possible. Our simplest of C based test runners was rapidly becoming inadequate. The garbage collector stress tests malloced gigabytes of memory. In order to isolate interactions between tests, it was necessary to extend the C test runner to fork each test in its own process. Running each test in its own process allowed us to record tests that crashed the test process as errors and continue running the rest of the tests. The garbage collector was written over a two-week period, and has been stable and reliable. It is certainly the case that having tests for the closure operations and traversal operations performed by the garbage collector contributed to this stability. We also took the time to add support for test suites in the C test runner. This way, when we worked on a runtime component, we were able to simply run just the tests relevant for the component on which we were working.

2.3   The Process of Processes

In order to implement asynchronous IO in a portable way, it was necessary to implement the Smalltalk process class and a process scheduler. Host OS signals are converted into program interrupts. Interrupt handlers are dispatched by a highest priority interrupt process. We had to get this working in our compiled programs.

The Smalltalk Blue Book specifies the interface for the process scheduler, process, and semaphore. Tests for much of the behavior could be generated directly from the specification with the use of an Interpreter mock object.

A big problem arises when one tries to actually test the occurrence of a process switch. It is possible to write tests that infer whether or not process switches have occurred, actually observing and testing this is somewhat problematic. The problem of debugging the process scheduler given the status of our debugger further compounded the problem.

Our solution was to follow the advice of Fredrick Brooks in The Mythical Man-month.

> If the target computer is new, one needs a logical simulator for it. This gives a debugging vehicle long before the real target exists. Equally important, it gives access to a dependable debugging vehicle even after one has a target machine available. Dependable is not the same as accurate. The simulator will surely fail in some respect to be a faithful and accurate implementation of the new machines architecture. But it will be the same implementation from one day to the next, and new hardware will not.[1]

We built out our mock interpreter until it could execute a major subset of our ANSI tester. This allowed us to use the Pharo Smalltalk debugging tools to ensure that the process scheduler was working correctly. When this work was done, we were near the end of our release cycle, and settled for hand testing the scheduler. To compensate for this lack of testing, we did build a number of tests that heavily exercised the process scheduler. The interesting thing is that we were able to run the process scheduler in a runtime that was embedded within the context in which the test itself was running. Given a bit more schedule time, we could actually have a test that reflects on a program running in an interpreted runtime environment.

Another curious consequence of this activity is that we had a major insight into how the code generator should be structured. We would have been well advised to take Mr. Brooks advice about planning to throw out the first two implementations. The task of retargeting our code generator to a Smalltalk-based interpreter helped us to distinguish the deep abstractions that characterized the design of the code generator, from the particulars of our code generation strategies. From this test driven exploration we made a major design discovery that gave us pluggable object writers and code writers.

When the process code was merged with the development branch, every runtime interpreter test broke. In this case, the problem was not with the tests themselves, but rather with the naive assumptions we made at the end of the first release cycle when most of these tests were written. When these tests were written, we had no clear understanding of the order in which the runtime process of a compiled program was initialized. The fix was straightforward, and identified an aspect of the runtime we had overlooked in our original design.

3   What We Learned

Tests serve a number of distinct purposes on a complex project:

- Tests may be used to inform team members.
- Tests focus and scope design activities.
- Tests prioritize implementation activities.
- Tests define boundaries of major components. When using a test for this purpose it is wise to define a facade and write the tests against that object.
- Tests validate implementation semantics.
- Tests can facilitate porting. In our case supporting new target architectures.

Tests often tend to be brittle, and if one is not careful, that can be an impediment to rapid development. Tests can be brittle for a number of reasons:

- Changing technical architectures can reveal hidden performance assumptions in the implementation of the tests.
- Changing specifications or requirements can lead to broken tests. If you know how the specification will be changing, you can capture common test structure in an abstract test case.
- Evolution of system boundaries can lead to broken tests.
- Tests written with incomplete understanding.

Brittle tests must be managed lest they burden development and halt the forward progress of the project. It is useful to consider that some tests are forever and should be maintained. Some tests are used to drive an implementation trajectory and may not be needed forever. Many tests are brittle because they depend on details of representation. Many of our early tests became obsolete because the representation of code sequences changed. Many of these tests are not strictly necessary because the semantics of our ANSI tester program validates the semantics of the generated code. We have also become aware that the intention of a set of tests can change over time.

Originally, the runtime interpreter tests were used to instruct and inform students. Now they document the garbage collector and primitives. We have spiked an implementation of a native x64 based target, and are looking at ARM64 as a future native platform. In support of that, we are considering the possibility of generating Modtalk machine validation tests. These would replace the hand written interpreter tests with machine generated tests for each platform to which we port.

Students working on the next release are developing a native debugger, and GUI support. Other students are looking into support for optimization and project configuration. We hope to make Modtalk an environment in which undergraduates can explore the implementation of a dynamic language and get experience of agile development outside of the classroom.

Acknowledgments. Our special thanks go out to Rebecca and Allen Wirfs-Brock. Rebecca for her insight and advice, and Allen for his insightful work on Modular Smalltalk in the mid 1980s which inspired much of this project.

References

1. Brooks, F.: The Mythical Man-Month (20th Anniversary Edition). Addison-Wesley (1995)

Building Learning Organization Through Peer Hands-on Support Community and Gamification

Tomáš Tureček$^{(\boxtimes)}$, Martin Chmelař, Roman Šmiřák, and Jan Krchňák

RainFellows.s.r.o., Bohumín, Czech Republic
tomas.turecek@rainfellows.com
http://www.rainfellows.com

Abstract. The story is about how we decided to activate potential of the teams in a product portfolio with 21 products and more than 400 people in 5 countries and started to build a learning organization where product teams share experience and knowledge with each other and improve. And this all driven by their own motivation. How? By organizing a community a bit different way, using peer hands-on support in between community sessions and by gamifying personal growth. This paper describes how we designed the community, piloted it for 3 months and summarizes the results. Teams are now much more connected cross team/product borders and they actively help each other to improve.

Keywords: Learning organization · Leadership · Community · Experiment · Pilot · PDCA · Mentoring · Coaching · Growth · Gamification · Business for breakfast

1 Context

We, RainFellows, are a team of coaches and mentors who help leaders to build, develop and efficiently lead teams and companies. Our main focus is to help the leaders to involve and engage employees into the changes they need to make to become more successful in their business and to teach the employees how to continually improve their way of working together. Our experience comes from hundreds of teams and companies supported in past 10 years.

In 2009 we helped to outsource development of Tieto Energy products from Scandinavia to Ostrava, Czech Republic. The biggest challenge of the service ramp-up was also the change of way of working from traditional to an Agile one. In XP2010 paper [1] we published all the constraints we were fighting with together with all the lessons learnt. Long story short, we managed to stabilize new way of working quickly and later on rolled this Agile way of working out to other products as well. There has been established so called **Lean office of coaches and mentors,** which we RainFellows are still part of, in order to help the teams to stabilize the situation after the radical changes they went through and at the same time to continually improve the way of working to meet challenging business goals. This went very well but one thing. It is currently 28 cross-functional Agile teams of various sizes working on 21 products in 5 countries and they got used to the Lean office mentors being drivers of continuous improvement and gave over this responsibility to them. From external perspective it

© Springer International Publishing Switzerland 2015
C. Lassenius et al. (Eds.): XP 2015, LNBIP 212, pp. 302–309, 2015.
DOI: 10.1007/978-3-319-18612-2_31

seems that most of the team leaders (TL) got used to their comfort zones of routine and do not feel the need to work on their leadership skills. We applied many of Agile and Lean principles but we failed in maybe the most important one - activate the people potential in the organization. Finally, we (the mentors and the management) decided to change this and to do it in an Agile/incremental way.

2   Motivation

TLs did a great job with their cross-functional teams while applying Agile rituals and they were very well aligned with the product and portfolio vision. But there was a **huge opportunity to improve in the area of innovation and collaboration**. Retrospectives were kind of dull, not bringing much improvement, mostly pointing outside (to the management) and missing actions in most cases. At the same time most TLs, as former developers, admitted they actually lack soft skills to efficiently lead their teams. Last but not least, it was clearly visible the teams within one product and also between the products were living in silos with little motivation to change their way of working. The teams gladly shared outside what they were doing and how they had done it but almost no one was willing to ask for help or feedback to improve their own "silo".

Vision of a Truly Learning Organization

We dreamt of something more lively and energetic. Of people being more engaged and willing to share with and offer help to their peers in other teams in the portfolio. Of people challenging themselves and being proud of what they do. And of leaders growing their skills and helping their teams to grow as well.

This **change of the mindset** of all the people in the organization is definitely an **evolutionary thing,** it cannot be fixed by just sending all the people to a training course or get them certified and hope for the best. After a visioning we, the mentors and the management, agreed to focus on three cornerstones:

- **Focus on TLs** and through them **change the mindset of their teams** as well
- Set up a **TLs community** to regularly meet, share, inspire, cheer up, ask for help and most important to **provide hands-on peer support** to each other
- Activate and boost TLs' interest in **personal growth** through inspiration, success stories of their peers and **gamification**

3   Proposed Solution - Community and Gamified Growth

We already had a chance to organize communities couple of times before. Having done so, over the course of time **we identified community patterns helping us to create a positive reinforcement loop** [3] to create and keep the momentum of our communities and thus increase their chance to blossom further.

- **Attractive vision and purpose** - a common goal, a reason to meet, share and do something together.
- **High value delivered** - a value coming from attending has to be much higher than the comfort zone of not attending. A cake helps :-)
- **Minimal overhead** - joining has to be as easy as possible, from organizing sessions in suitable time and place to high efficiency of the meetings.
- **Charismatic community leaders** - people follow leaders having and loving their strong vision who are able to inspire people and make them cooperate
- **Management support** - people have to have slack time to meet and the community activities have to be prioritized among other things to be done.

Having previous experience of working as TLs and Scrum Masters (SMs) and knowing the drill pretty well we **designed the community the way we believed would be the best to serve the purpose of building a learning organization**. These were, of course, still hypotheses that **had to be validated**. Therefore we organized a **3 month pilot to validate the design and all the hypotheses** (see section 4). The sections below describe how we had designed the community - including all the mentioned patterns.

3.1   Attractive Vision and Purpose of the Community

The community has to provide TLs **practical help** with their daily challenges just in time when they need it. **Not just sharing and inspiring but also acting.** The community has to help TLs to make the change happen. Together with the community leaders we defined the following vision/purpose of the community:

> *"Enjoy working together through our growth*
> *and improving the environment around us."*

The vision is reflected in the practical arrangement of the community as a platform helping TLs to (1) **grow** as Leaders, (2) **support** each other, (3) **celebrate** their success and growth, (4) **get support** from skilled coaches and mentors and (5) **get support** from management.

3.2   Value and Minimal Overhead

As mentioned in section 3, we as former SMs and TLs defined what we would expect from the community as the following:

- "**Someone helps me** to deal with my challenges"
- "**I get inspired** by what my peers (or guests) work on and what they've achieved"
- "**I can share** with my peers what I have accomplished and get their **appreciation**"
- "**I learn what's going on** in general in our organization"

The whole community concept has been designed to fulfil these needs.

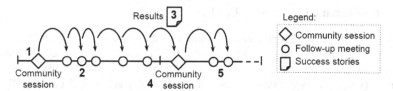

Fig. 1. Community activities

As depicted in Fig. 1 – a **Community session** (1) happens once a month and its main goal is to let TLs capture challenges and opportunities they have (either concrete issues to be solved or inspiration from someone else's success story) and **pair with other TLs** (or Agile/Lean mentors) who already experienced a similar situation in past. They immediately **plan hands-on Follow-up meeting/s** (2) focused on bringing the idea into life. This cooperation results either in a success story or at least in lessons learnt presented as **Results** (3) at the next Community session (4) which typically again yields new hands-on Follow-up meetings (5) – a **positive reinforcement loop** [3]. If TL does not want to wait for follow-ups or the topic is interesting to many others, then we continue with a **focused topic discussion**, where we have dedicated time to elaborate more on the topic and make everyone satisfied.

As can be seen from the community design, it clearly **covers all four TLs' needs** described at the beginning of this chapter.

Community meeting has to be perceived as very efficient. Therefore we got inspired by **Business for Breakfast (B4B) concept** [2] which we find **exceptionally effective** and we know it very well since we lead one of the B4B business clubs in Ostrava, Czech Republic. We adjusted B4B procedure to suit the community needs.

Community meeting agenda (2-4 hours)

1. Each attendee gives **one minute elevator** pitch to:

    a.   Introduce her/himself
    b.   Share **what s/he has done** great and **what s/he can help** others with
    c.   **Ask for help** with the challenge s/he's currently facing

After each pitch we, as moderators, **summarize** the key needs and offers mentioned and **encourage** attendees to request/offer practical hands-on support from/to this attendee (30m).

If any of other attendees is interested in learning more or wants to offer help s/he **writes it into so called Referral sheet** (RS) [2] and addresses it appropriately to reach the right attendee later on in step 3. RS is in paper form since people like tangible things, its physical passing to the respective addressee visualizes the connection and it also serves as a connection record for later use and statistics.

2. Attendees **share the success stories and lessons learnt** from the last month (1h)
3. The moderator **delivers** filled RSs to their addressees (**visualization**) and **makes attendees to plan follow-up meetings immediately** in their calendars (30m)
4. **The focused topic discussion** – topic gathering, voting and solving (up to 2h)

This way the meeting **is not just usual status reporting** but it **motivates everyone to be active** and results in **a tangible outcome in form of planned follow-up meetings**.

3.3   Charismatic Community Leaders

In order to attract enough community members, the community leaders have to possess a **strong passion** and put a lot of effort into organization of the community. Fortunately, we really believe in the idea of a learning organization and we organize each community session as a small conference. **We meet weekly and continually work on the next community session** to make it even more efficient than previous one and to have good success stories and new achievements (see section 3.5) there. Good refreshment helps too :-)

3.4   Management Support

The Management has been **fully supporting** the activity. We agreed on **3 month pilot** funding to see if the challenging goals mentioned in the Vision section would bring the fruits. The Management did not insist on any concrete evaluation criteria; we agreed we would collect the data and check the results and then decide whether to continue after the pilot period. We collected following data:

- Attendance
- Connections - how many times people connected for follow-up hands-on work
- Success stories - numbers and concrete impact (positive change)
- Feedback from participants

The 3 month pilot is over now; this was the original budget:

- 3x 8h/TL - 3x 4h for 3 community sessions and the rest as a slack time for follow-up activities. Hands-on work is part of their work time already
- 3x 2,5d/mentor (4) to organize community and provide hands-on support to TLs

3.5   Gamification of the Growth

TLs plan follow-up activities if they hear something interesting or have a challenge to tackle. **But what if they don't have one?** What else can encourage them to challenge themselves, step out of their comfort zone, try out new things, experiment and grow their skills? We came with such a concept. We identified 7 skills, based on identified gaps, and elaborated them into **Agile Team Leader Guru game**. TLs can **gather achievements** in form of sticky stars they can glue into the spots at particular skills in their own printed game plans in Fig. 2.

We defined **3 levels of achievements** for each skill and we **encourage TLs to aspire to gain them**. We tried our best to define tasks to be accomplished to get each achievement, but there's nothing like one-size-fits-all. Therefore we defined the tasks on general level and only when a TL aspires for an achievement **we tailor concrete tasks together** with her/him in order to do things that bring **as high value as possible**. Then we actively **support/pair TLs** in accomplishing these tasks. In the end the TL captures results and lessons learnt and **presents them in the next community session**. This way TLs get also **appreciation** for the work done. The stories also **inspire** others to challenge themselves and aspire for an achievement as well.

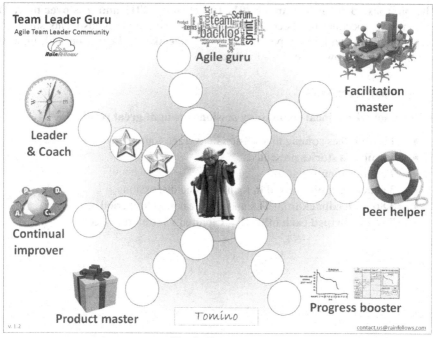

Fig. 2. Game plan

Leader and Coach Achievement Example

Goal: be able to coach and lead team members to help them grow

- Symptom when missing:
    - Team expects to be told what to do
    - Team members ask the TL to do things for them they can do themselves
    - Quiet and disconnected team members in meetings

- ☆ Give at least once positive and constructive negative or corrective feedback
- ☆ ☆ Coach one team member to help him improve himself (GROW model)
- ☆ ☆ ☆ Coach another coach in using the coaching model

As stated above, we always tailor these general tasks together with a concrete TL.

4   Experiment and Results

Since everything we designed was based on hypotheses, despite all our lessons learnt from the past communities, we needed to **pilot this approach** in a controlled environment. We agreed with the Management to pilot community activities for **3 months with 15 TLs and their teams that reside in Ostrava (one location only).**

We also agreed with the Management that the **attendance of the community must be strictly voluntary** and it will not be used for any kind of formal evaluation. Otherwise it would be difficult to distinguish whether attendees come because of the value they get or because of being evaluated better.

The pilot lasted from November 2014 to February 2015 and it is over now. The community procedure has been followed 3 times with slight adjustments since after each community session we performed a **retrospective** and came up with improvements. See the following sections for details.

4.1   What Went Well

- **The pilot with 3 local community sessions brought great results:**
    - **11 attendees** coming to a session in average (out of 15)
    - **11 success stories** presented
    - **7 achievements** gained
    - **3 concrete topics** solved in focused topic discussions
    - **3.86/4 - feedback** from TLs about the whole pilot period
    - **75x TLs helped each other!!!** – captured via Referral sheets

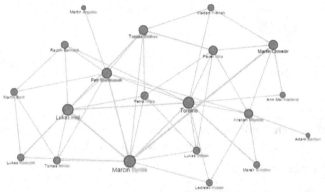

Fig. 3. Visualization of Referral sheets - pairing within the community

- As seen from the results the **concept really attracts people and generates follow-up activities**. Changes really happen in teams and generate success stories.
- We asked for feedback after each session and we also organized one anonymous feedback survey in the end of the pilot. These are the points mentioned the most:
    - "The community meeting produces concrete tangible results - follow-up hands-on work with peers and coaches helps to solve concrete challenges"
    - "Pairing and connecting during the community session (B4B concept)"
    - "Achievements game" and "Cake :-)"

- The roughly estimated time/budget for TLs and mentors was surprisingly accurate.
- The **hypothesis about success stories and achievements** working as a motivator for TL activation **has been proven true**. For example, one TL shared a success story about how mentors helped him to improve facilitation of an Iteration retrospective which yielded 3 aspirations for the same achievement (**ripple effect**).
- The chart of visualized connections in Fig. 3 seems to have gamification potential. Two TLs shared they were more active in generating connections to have more connection lines and have their bullets bigger.

4.2   What Can Be Improved

- The second part of the community session – the focused topic discussion – has been **less attended**. We are now processing community members' feedback to improve the situation.
- The community partially **duplicates the work of line management** in sense of challenging and helping TLs to grow. Line managers haven't been involved so far.
- Once, attendance was lower than before, and we found out there were some colliding mandatory management meetings – we agreed with the management to respect these community time slots.
- The community faces the **risk of eating all its topics** so we plan to introduce guests from other units but at this moment we have not decided yet how to sponsor their support if they ask for help as well.
- The **community depends very much on us and the community leaders** – we plan to focus more in next months on making community more self-sustaining.
- The **gamified growth (game) depends on us as mentors** – we plan to involve people who gained an achievement in helping their peers to get the same one.

5   Conclusion

In order to activate teams and build a truly learning organization we engaged their TLs into a community standing on two major pillars: practical hands-on peer support and gamified growth (see section 3.5). The 3 month **pilot has proven the approach we chose has worked** (see section 4). The **positive feedback** from both the community members and their management **resulted in approval of another 6 months of continuation** and an explicit **request to scale the community** concept up also to other parts of the Energy organization (other countries). The concept also attracted attention of the local HR department which asked us to **share it with other community leaders** in Ostrava to inspire them and to also to **build the concept into the local talent management programme**.

We have plenty of ideas how to improve the concept, e.g. how to gamify the attendance of the community members so they create a habit of joyfully coming to every community session and prioritize it over their other duties. **Feel free to contact us to get an update on new stories and the latest progress.**

References

1. Tureček, T., Šmiřák, R., Malík, T., Boháček, P.: Energy project story: from waterfall to distributed agile. In: Sillitti, A., Martin, A., Wang, X., Whitworth, E. (eds.) XP 2010. LNBIP, vol. 48, pp. 362–371. Springer, Heidelberg (2010)
2. Business for Breakfast meeting record. http://www.bforbfranchise.co.uk/work/ (June, 03, 2015)
3. Daniels, A.C.: Bringing Out the Best in People, pp. 53-63, McGraw-Hill, Inc. (2000) ISBN 0-07-135145-0

From Sprints to Lean Flow: Management Strategies for Agile Improvement

Marcelo Walter[1], Ramon Tramontini[1], Rafaela Mantovani Fontana[2,3(✉)],
Sheila Reinehr[2], and Andreia Malucelli[2]

[1] Objective Solutions, Av. Horacio Raccanelo Filho, 5355,
Maringá, PR 87020-035, Brazil
{mlwalter,ramon}@objective.com.br

[2] Pontifical Catholic University of Paraná (PUCPR), R. Imaculada Conceição, 1155,
Curitiba, PR 80215-901, Brazil
rafaela.fontana@ufpr.br, sheila.reinehr@pucpr.br,
malu@ppgia.pucpr.br

[3] Federal University of Paraná (UFPR), R. Dr. Alcides Vieira Arcoverde, 1225,
Curitiba, PR 81520-260, Brazil

Abstract. This paper describes management strategies for continuous improvement in agile software development teams. We have applied these strategies in a Brazilian team, which was born in 2009 and now grew into a headquarter of the company with ninety people. We have currently reached lean flow state with constant throughput, reduced lead time and enhanced quality by cutting bugs rate in half. In a continuous improvement cycle, our management strategies are based on looking at the situation, sensemaking the situation and providing simple responses. We describe how we applied these strategies to learn how to correctly limit work in progress (WIP) and to face challenges with coaching, estimates, team motivation, sprints and pair programming.

Keywords: Agile software development · Management · Improvement · Lean · Flow state

1 Introduction

As complex adaptive systems, agile teams present challenges to leaders on how to make space for innovation, flexibility and self-organization [1,2,3]. We experienced managing a Brazilian agile team from ground up to a ninety people headquarter, in a five-year journey. Throughout this journey we recognized the importance of the management actions to lead a successful agile adoption [5].

The management strategies we applied are based on looking, sensemaking and providing simple responses. As there is no silver-bullet in managing agile teams [6], we exemplify how these strategies guided continuous improvement from sprints – i.e. an adoption of Scrum "by the book" – to lean flow state. By lean flow state we mean having the work to flow through the system, removing waste and impediments [7,8].

© Springer International Publishing Switzerland 2015
C. Lassenius et al. (Eds.): XP 2015, LNBIP 212, pp. 310–318, 2015.
DOI: 10.1007/978-3-319-18612-2_32

2   The Case Organization

The management strategies described in this paper were developed in Objective Solutions's headquarter in Maringá, a small city in the South of Brazil. Our business is software development for big Brazilian telecommunication companies. Our main product is a Customer Relationship Management application that today has more than 4000 Java Classes, 1700 Oracle tables and around 33000 functional automated tests. We build on a daily basis and deliver a new version for all customers every month.

The activities in this headquarter started in 2009. Our set of initial practices was mainly based on Scrum and Extreme Programming: daily meetings, sprints, planning poker, calculating velocity, pair programming, task-board, move people around (M.P.A.) and retrospectives. In the continuous improvement endeavor, we faced challenges and implemented improvements, as described in Figure 1.

All these facts have been recorded throughout the journey. The first two authors were directly involved in day-to-day activities and faced all the challenges described here. The others are researchers who were responsible for analyzing and compiling the lessons learned.

3   Management Strategies

Our focus on continuous improvement has led us, since the beginning, to continuously analyze our practices and implement improvements by managing our team with a cycle, as Figure 2 summarizes. For each challenge we face, first, we understand what is happening based on *physical visibility*. This visibility makes us and the team *look* at symbols, colors and drawings to realize what is wrong. What is wrong bothers people and emergent *emotions* lead us to *make sense* of the situation. We then observe and create *simple measurements*. Our focus, then, is on *quickly* acting with *simple responses*. These actions should generate *physical visibility* so that the cycle restarts.

These strategies allow us to experiment solutions before making decisions, which is a reasonable way to manage agile teams as complex adaptive systems [2], [3]. The examples we present separately in next sections could all have been described as applications of the cycle: looking, sensemaking and providing simple responses. We actually chose to classify them according to each challenge's main topic and its applied strategy. Anyhow, they represent the continuous cycle of improvement we have faced throughout the journey, as shown in Figure 1.

3.1   Looking at and Building Emotions

Things that are shown to be wrong bother people. We have always worked on creating boards, processes written on the walls, colors and symbols. In Figure 2 we show that this visual information makes people feel emotions – either good or bad – and take more coherent and collaborative decisions.

Fig. 1. Challenges and improvements journey.

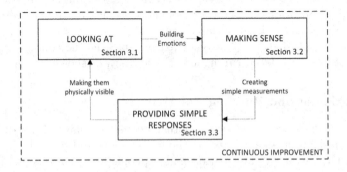

Fig. 2. Management strategies.

Confused Coach. When we had eleven pairs of programmers with only few months of experience, the team coach had a hard work guaranteeing tasks were delivered with quality and on time. We felt the need to create a means to see how much help was being required – we needed physical, concrete visibility. We created low-tech red flags for this purpose. Each pair had a flag they had to raise every time they got stuck on a task. The flags should remain up until help came.

These flags showed us how individuals in our team behaved and led us to realize we had to be more proactive on keeping up with the pairs. This is the reason we responded creating the Yellow Flags (other examples of simple responses are given in Section 3.3). Every pair had a yellow flag that should be raised first thing in the morning. The coach had to check all pairs with a raised yellow flag and problems were prevented before they happened. Besides, the number of yellow flags that were still up at the end of the day made us realize we had limitations and that we needed more coaches. We created, then the cross-pair review, in which pairs reviewed other pairs' work.

Unbalanced Task Board. As prescribed by Kanban, we have always worked with physical task boards, which provides itself physical visibility. One day we were looking at our task board and realized that our tasks were completely unbalanced. The column "Review" was full of tasks in queue. Besides it, there was a great amount of blocked tasks: activities that were waiting for a customer decision. With this problem that bothered us visually, we counted the tasks and identified that the amount of unfinished tasks was twice the WIP.

To gain more visibility, we changed our task board. In spite of having just columns-like layout such as "to do", "doing", "done", we created slots in the "doing" column for each pair. Each slot had three parts: in the top, one part in which was the current task; and, in the bottom, two parts where were the blocked tasks and tasks to review. This change enabled us to look at the board and make sense of what was happening. We identified WIP per pair and saw there was something wrong, as described next.

Disguised Pushing. We still had too much concurrent tasks, and it seemed that the only way to reach flow state was to reduce parallelism. In our process, we were still promoting parallelism because we allowed each pair to have a current task, a blocked task and a task waiting for review. Besides it, we observed that most developers were more prone to start a fresh, interesting task, instead of finishing a blocked and complicated one.

We saw, then, we were self-pushing tasks in our team because our WIP was not correctly limited. We changed the task board (again) to reduce the possibility to have more than one blocked task. In the first column, the backlog; in the second column, the pairs slots. In each slot, we had space for just one task. The blocked tasks remained behind the current task. When it was finished, the next blocked task was automatically assigned as the current. The third column was, then, the "to review" tasks.

This new restriction reduced parallelism. At this time we also created an application that automated our task board, providing us real time tasks status, assignees, time spent and other important data. To keep visibility, the virtual task board was projected on the wall.

These examples showed how physical visibility triggered emotions which led us to make sense of the facts. The following section shows other examples of how metrics and observation helped us providing simple responses.

3.2   Making Sense and Creating Simple Measurements

When we name this strategy as "making sense" we refer to Karl Weick's sense-making process, in which we develop "plausible images that rationalize what people are doing" [4, p. 409]. In this case emotions precede interpretation of facts, which sometimes require texts, numbers and explanations. Besides, the executive board in companies usually want these data. So, we usually work with automated and simple metrics. In this section we show examples of how simple data helped us making sense of the situation and implementing improvements.

Still Pushing. We had recently automated our task board and we noticed something was still wrong with our WIP. We had sixteen pairs and sixty-nine current tasks in our board... A simple measurement of our current tasks made us see that, yes, we were misapplying the concept of limited WIP.

We studied the concept and understood that all started tasks should be counted as WIP, even if they were blocked for reasons out of our control (e.g. a customer delay). As we could not simply reduce WIP from sixty-nine to sixteen tasks, we just prevented the seventieth task to start. Every time our WIP reduced, we reset WIP limit to the current WIP size. As the tasks board was virtual, developers could not even drag a new task from the backlog when WIP was reached!

Soon the team got used to this restriction and removing impediments in blocked tasks became a team effort. We realized the secret to reach the flow state was to control our WIP. By reducing the amount of tasks people could deal with simultaneously, we gained the flow state. We saw in practice that to do more, people tend to start several new tasks [1], in an attempt to make the process more efficient. It actually leads to an ineffective process. By measuring our WIP we could identify how many simultaneous things we were working on and make the decision to limit WIP.

Ineffective Estimates. At this time, we had already left sprints and were working with a continuous flow of tasks, as in Lean Software Development [8] (see Figure 1). With a history of comparisons between the tasks estimates and the real work – simple measurements, we realized that our developers were behaving as stated by the Parkinson's Law: "The work expands so as to fill the time available for its completion." [9]. While we noticed this behavior in some estimates, another issue bothered us. Once our team agreed with the task estimation and deadline, we still had to wait for the customer endorsement before working on the story. Most of the time, we had to wait several days to get it and, when we finally got it, sometimes the given solution was not applicable anymore.

We decided, thus, to dissociate the team from estimations. We kept an initial estimate to the customer, given by an experienced proxy we had in the team (the specifier), but our team stopped estimating.

We knew our velocity. It was calculated over past data: if a task estimated with 10 hours took us 15 hours to be accomplished, our velocity was 0.66 (10/15). We used this velocity factor to adjust every estimate the specifier did and this was the estimate told to our customer. The team got the first estimate, without the adjustment, to avoid the Parkinson's Law effect. No more planning poker, no more task estimates on the team.

Estimates Variance. We did a good job on knowing our velocity and using it to adjust estimates to customer. However, we are always looking for improvements and, observing our data, we saw that, on average we were fine, but standard deviation was still high: we had a lot of tasks with delay and a lot of tasks finishing earlier.

We decided, then, to implement the T-shirt sizes for estimation. Our tasks would be estimated in sizes: extra-small, small, medium, big, extra-big. Ok, but how much is a "small task"? The amount of hours in each size was calculated with historical data (usually last two months, based on the effort reported by developers), using a clustering algorithm. This algorithm calculated, as an example, that, in the past two months, a small task for this team was from eight to twelve hours. It gave us an estimation for each task, reducing standard deviation we had when we adjusted the estimates with the velocity average.

Bored Team. This is another example of sensemaking what was happening, but not related to measuring things but observing people. Suddenly we realized we were losing people motivation. It seemed that, when we got to a stabilized process, the days were always the same and the lack of novelty took away our "sparkling eyes". With a little study and based on the work by Daniel Pink [10] who poses that knowledge workers get motivated when they have purpose, autonomy and mastery, we implemented gamification in our team. We believe games stimulate purpose by creating short-term achievable objectives, autonomy by engaging people in technical goals they are capable of achieving, and mastery by the competition it stimulates.

Our endeavor was to create games to solve day-to-day issues, such as a big stack of broken automated tests. We were very successful with our games and started to promote them every week. We learned two lessons from frequent games: the first is that challenge is lost when games are too frequent; and the second is that awards may be in accordance with what really motivates the team (see [10] for knowledge workers motivation). Gamification is a powerful tool *if* games are well planned and used occasionally.

These examples showed that measurements and observation helped us making sense of the situation. Our focus on responding quickly and in a simple way were already shown in previous examples. Next section complements these examples with situations that present how simple responses may generate great outcomes.

3.3 Providing Simple Responses and Making them Physically Visible

Whenever working with complex adaptive systems, trying to predict what is going to happen is not the means to make decisions. There is a need to probe [3]: we take simple actions to observe the success (or not) of the practice and make our decisions based on what we observed.

Sprint Starvation. In the beginning of our journey (see Figure 1) we had a backlog of about 1500 hours and planning the tasks was a real challenge. We soon realized that the sprints-planning format was not adequate to our context. The way demands continuously arrived showed us that a continuous flow of stories would fit better to our needs. This was the end of our sprints – and a step towards Lean Software Development [8].

Not Every Pair Works Well. Since the creation of the team, we always believed that pair programming allows developers to do a better job than by themselves. However, we realized that different personalities and professional experiences lead to some issues with pairing. By observing, we identified that there were programmers that preferred to work alone; there were programmers that preferred not to code and just watch the other working. We thus developed a simple tool we called "Keyboard rotation alarm". It is a software that warns developers, from time to time, that they should shift positions. With this tool, pairs got used to shift positions several times during the day.

Biased Move People Around (M.P.A). When we established pair programming, we defined a fixed period for the M.P.A practice: once a week developers could change their pairs as they pleased. The issue with this practice was that people tended to keep their pairs. Therefore, with pairs that did not change we were loosing the benefits of knowledge sharing throughout the team. We developed, thus, a software to automatically create best M.P.A combinations based on parameters such as: skill levels, M.P.A. history, vacations, seniority etc.

Radical Pairing. Later, with almost ninety people in the team, we kept with 100% pair programming. We had good results, but we realized that some tasks actually could be performed with solo programming. As we had our limited-WIP culture established, we started to change WIP to allow stories to be implemented not in pairs. With time and maturity, we left each team to self-organize and set their own WIP size. It naturally remained on 70% or 80% of the size of the team.

These simple responses triggered important changes in our process. Creating physical visibility allows the cycle to restart and provide basis for the continuous improvement we always looked for.

4 Conclusions

This experience report described the management strategies applied to launch an agile team and lead it to a headquarter with ninety people. We have been working with a cycle that supports continuous improvement by looking at the situation, sensemaking it and providing simple responses. The strategy is based on physical visualization, building emotions and simple measurements. Our main result since the creation of the team was reaching flow state (constant throughput), with reduced lead time (around 70%) and enhanced quality (reduced bugs in around 50%). We also described challenges we faced with coaching, estimates, team motivation, sprints and pair programming. Our report complements the view by [7], which describes the impediments to flow in agile software development.

Considering that complex adaptive systems should be managed with simple rules [11], the take-home messages to conclude our paper are five simple rules: 1) always listen to your team, they have the best solutions; 2) try new approaches without fear: constant and small changes; 3) do not trust your intuition: measuring is essential, always; 4) you can measure everything [12]; and 5) motivation is a transitory state: a stable environment does not trigger stable motivation.

References

1. Denning, S.: The leader's guide to radical management. John Wiley & Sons, Inc., San Francisco (2010)
2. McDaniel Jr., R.R.: Management Strategies for Complex Adaptive Systems. Performance Improvement Quarterly **20**, 21–42 (2007)
3. Snowden, D.J., Boone, M.E.: A leader's framework for decision-making. Harvard Business Review, 68–76 (2007)
4. Weick, K.E., Sutcliffe, K.M., Obstfeld, D.: Organizing and the Process of Sensemaking **16**, 409–421 (2005). doi:10.1287/orsc.1050.0133
5. Melo, C., Cruzes, D., Kon, F., Conradi, R.: Interpretative case studies on agile team productivity and management. Inf. Soft. Tech. **55**, 412–427 (2013). doi:10.1016/j.infsof.2012.09.004
6. Bustard, D., Wilkie, G., Greer, D.: The maturation of agile software development principles and practice: observations on successive industrial studies in 2010 and 2012. In: 20th Annual IEEE International Conference and Workshops on the Engineering of Computer Based Systems (EBCS) (2013). doi:10.1109/ECBS.2013.11
7. Power, K., Conboy, K.: Impediments to flow: rethinking the lean concept of 'waste' in modern software development. In: Cantone, G., Marchesi, M. (eds.) XP 2014. LNBIP, vol. 179, pp. 203–217. Springer, Heidelberg (2014). doi:10.1007/978-3-319-06862-6_14

8. Wang, X., Conboy, K., Cawley, O.: "Leagile" software development: An experience report analysis of the application of lean approaches in agile software development. J. Syst. Soft. **85**, 1287–1299 (2012). doi:10.1016/j.jss.2012.01.061

9. Parkinson, C.N.: Parkinson''s Law and Other Studies in Administration. Random House Inc., New York (1957). http://sas2.elte.hu/tg/ptorv/Parkinson-s-Law.pdf

10. Pink, D.: The puzzle of motivation (2009). video available at http://www.ted.com/talks/dan_pink_on_motivation

11. Power, K.: Social contracts, simple rules and self-organization: a perspective on agile development. In: Cantone, G., Marchesi, M. (eds.) XP 2014. LNBIP, vol. 179, pp. 277–284. Springer, Heidelberg (2014). doi:10.1007/978-3-319-06862-6_21

12. Hubbard, D.W.: How to measure anything: finding the value of "intangibles" in business, 2nd edn. John Wiley and Sons, New Jersey (2010)

Mob Programming - What Works, What Doesn't

Alexander Wilson[✉]

Unruly, London, UK
alex.wilson@unrulymedia.com

Abstract. At Unruly we are constantly trying to turn up the dial on our XP practices, and in the second half of 2014 we started to take the step from Pair Programming on all production code to Mob Programming with the entire team. This report shares experiences that Unruly has gained in pushing the boundaries of Extreme Programming.

Keywords: Mob programming · XP · Extreme programming · Groupthink · Continuous delivery

1 Introduction

A company specialising in video ad technology, Unruly[2] was founded in 2006 with eXtreme Programming values baked in right from the start. While it has occasionally been an uphill battle to keep these aspects in place, we are still strong adherents to XP practices.

This paper explains how and why we adopted Mob Programming[6] at Unruly, how we started, what worked for us, what downsides we discovered, the response from the rest of the business, and where we are now.

2 Life at Unruly

As part of our application of XP, we maintain that all of our production code must be developed using pair programming. We have worked hard to encourage collective ownership across our 3 teams (of around 6/7 software developers each). The teams use frequent pair rotation to share knowledge within the team and we hold cross-team lightning talks and developer exchanges. This is made easy by co-locating all development teams in our London HQ.

Towards the end of 2014, some of us attended a talk by Woody Zuill at the annual JavaOne conference on the topic of Mob Programming[7]. Mob Programming, as Zuill describes, is "the whole team working on the same problem, at the same time, using the same workstation". It resembles the Randori[5] style of programming popular at Coding Dojos that we already use during sessions to learn new technologies.

© Springer International Publishing Switzerland 2015
C. Lassenius et al. (Eds.): XP 2015, LNBIP 212, pp. 319–325, 2015.
DOI: 10.1007/978-3-319-18612-2_33

At Unruly the product development teams are free to try new things that might improve our workflow. After an informal whiteboard discussion with the rest of the team about what Mob Programming consists of, we resolved to give Mob Programming a try to find out how useful it would be for us. We're accustomed to pairing every day, so the cognitive jump for us to experiment with Mob Programming seemed relatively small. It wasn't too hard to convince the rest of the team as we were about to embark on a particularly difficult piece of work - we had been suffering performance issues on one of our systems and had decided to re-architect it. The code in question was the worst kind to refactor/extract: old and business critical.

We decided mobbing could be useful for this piece of work because we wanted as many eyes on what we were doing as possible.

3   Our Mobbing Setup

Our team started by declaring that all Fridays were "Mob Fridays".

When Mob Programming it is essential that the whole team is able to read the code as it evolves. In his talk, Woody spoke about isolating the team from everyone else in a meeting room and we decided to adapt this tactic to our own existing setup. We placed a portable whiteboard as a screen between us and the rest of the development area, and used it to hold architecture discussions and team huddles.

Unruly has an open-plan development area with shared workstations. It was going to be hard for us to all crowd around one monitor. However we were loathe to leave our area for a meeting room (which would be hard to book for an entire day) and it would require us to move a workstation to somewhere else in the building.

Our solution was to supplement the large monitors on our paired workstations with an additional 50inch monitor that was a mirror of the workstation screen. This was placed at right angles to the actual monitor, with the intention that 1the team watches the large screen and the driver is able to look at both the screen and the rest of the team - see Figure 1.

The team felt our setup was more productive than having everyone looking at a single screen and passing a keyboard around. The arrangement emphasised the discussion-rooted relationship between the driver (who acted as "the hands of the team") and the observers (who were not just backseat passengers along for the ride).

Initially we used a large television that we borrowed from our internal Infra team, but this had a much lower resolution than the mirrored monitor and the team felt that the screen flickered too much. We fixed this by purchasing a larger, higher-resolution monitor out of our team's budget. One side effect of mobbing in an open work space is that other teams working in the same area saw us mobbing and decided to try it too.

Taking the piece of work with the highest priority already in progress - the team ran a Randori-style session until we completed it or the day was over.

Fig. 1. Running a 4-person mob. Driver in the background

A Randori session in the context of programming is the timed rotation of a single *driver* at the keyboard writing code, while the rest of the group either observes in silence or guides the driver. At the end of the allocated time period, elaborated on in section 6, the driver rejoins the group and is replaced by a different member of the group. This felt like a good format to start mobbing with.

4   Tracking Mob Work

As part of visualising the current state of our iteration, the team already used a whiteboard of "hieroglyphs" depicting different activities we worked on. These include (but aren't limited to) story work, maintenance tasks, meetings, and story research. We use them during standups to make sure that our efforts are allocated effectively (and the same people aren't always pairing or doing support). Additionally, they form part of our retrospectives as a way of keeping note of how we are spending our time and on what types of work over the course of an iteration.

(a) Mobbed story work is represented in red   (b) Key to hieroglyphs on our board

When we discussed how to reflect mobbing in this pre-existing tracking system the team consensus was the mobbing was a different way of accomplishing a task. As it was not a different task, mobbed activities were represented with the same symbols but in a different colour. This is one difference between our team and the other teams at Unruly who later adopted mobbing.

5   Mobbing on Critical Code

As mentioned, the team was in the middle of making some important performance improvements. The company has grown substantially over the last 2 years and we were beginning to experience issues with how much data our stats processing pipeline was able to handle. We resolved to extract functionality from our monolithic web application in order to both avoid resource contention and move towards a better architected system. However, these changes involved touching a lot of critical code in a lot of potentially dangerous places, including but not limited to payments. Any mistakes here that might lead to lost data would have translated into equivalent financial losses.

With 5+ pairs of eyes on this code during these changes, the team managed to make the hardest parts of the transition with relatively little stress and worry. The unanimous feeling from the team was that they felt more confident in the changes made over this period than if they had been paired on. We realised that Mob Programming is also beneficial as a form of Team Building, with everyone learning together.

6   First Observations

After mobbing once per week for a couple of months, our team made the following observations:

- We initially decided on 5 minute rotations in the driving seat which turned out to be near optimal for our team size. A mob of 4 to 6 developers meant only 15 to 25 minutes between the same person being in the driving seat again. This was just long enough to accomplish writing a failing test and making it pass, but not too long that the team (or any of its members) might lose focus.
- We noticed that operating as a mob does not work effectively without a well-maintained and fast test-suite. With our 5 minute rotation time, if our test suites went above 10 minutes then 2 or more people lost out on their turn in the driving seat. In the beginning this felt like a brutal approach but the XP spirit of "if it hurts, do it more" incentivised us to keep our test suites fast. The longer integration tests were still necessary, but these provided us opportunities to turn into a huddle and discuss where to go next, ensuring we were aligned at all steps on the way to the goal

- The ping-pong style of pair programming[3] that we were used to no longer applied. We started settling into a new style where the observing team guides the construction of the test, and the person in the driving seat makes the test pass as normal. In this sense, it evolved into something resembling one-with-many pairing style.

Overall the team was happy with these results, so we decided to take what we felt was the next logical step: mobbing on a story from beginning to end. We felt this would be a good test of some of the claims made by proponents of Mob Programming, namely the alleged increased productivity throughput resulting from One-Piece Flow[1]. Our application of XP and paired programming leads us to rarely having more than 2 pieces of work in progress at a time, so we already have a naturally enforced WIP (Work-in-Process) limit.

Before we started, we wanted to address some concerns that non-developer members of the team (such as our product manager) had. In particular, it can be hard to convince the business that having the whole team working on a single story or piece of work is more effective and productive than having pairs working on different stories. We also decided that if the team *as a whole* needed to be interrupted (e.g. if there was a group discussion that needed to happen) it could only happen after a complete rotation of the team. Since the team was situated in our open-plan working area, this was a hard change to become accustomed to instead of being able to interrupt people at any time to talk about stories or support issues.

7   The Risks of Mob Programming

Mob Programming is not the ultimate software development panacea - the majority of problems that arise in mob programming are very rarely of a technical nature and are much more likely to stem from people-oriented issues. We observed two such things over our period of mob programming - the effect of dominant personalities within the group and the emergence of Groupthink, a well-documented psychological phenomenon. Taken together, both of these problems have the potential to limit the effectiveness of the mob and undo its usefulness back to a level behind that of even pair programming.

According to the book of the same name, **GroupThink** is most likely to occur in groups with strong senses of group identity and refers to *the deterioration of mental-efficiency, reality testing, and moral judgement that results from in-group pressures*[4]. It is, in other words, the tendency to draw a skewed perception of the situation at hand due to the group's overconfidence in both its technical abilities and how well it can perceive future events.

We encourage developers to rotate into other teams for a week or the length of a story if they have expertise or interest in the work that another team is doing. During one such rotation, a developer from another team asked *"How are you not worried about the changes that you're making?"* and the team's conclusive response was that with the entire team there any issues would be easily solved.

We didn't know it but we were slowly slipping into a GroupThink mentality, although this was ameliorated by only having weekly sessions to start with. There was also the issue of "dominant personalities" in the team. This is not necessarily about who is the loudest, or who talks the most. A dominant personality is someone who the team will subconsciously or consciously defer to in an argument. Team members such as a sufficiently experienced developer with strong domain knowledge can be a focal point for this.

In these scenarios, the team is less likely to challenge ideas from one such person and due to the nature of the mob a dominant personality can exhibit influence over the team even when not driving. Ironically, dominant personalities tend to be less effective when they are driving, as the driver is frequently the hands of the team rather than engaging their own interests.

We tackled both issues by trying to nurture constructive dissent at all points during the software development process - it's encouraged to flag up potential issues and ask questions from the beginning of a story (and in fact whether a story is even needed) all the way through the code-writing process. In our experience there's no real recipe or process that promotes such counter-thinking but we try to lead by example.

We've also found it beneficial to have an external observer taking part in the Mob who isn't normally part of the team. Including non-developer specialists in the team had an additional positive effect of mitigating this problem - by acting as unofficial moderators, the specialists could (and did) inject criticism into the Mob's discussions and kept us from succumbing to both of the aforementioned issues.

8 The Cross-Team Response to Mob Programming

After 5 months of Mob Programming across all 3 teams, each team member filled out a small survey about their experiences with Mob Programming so far. The results were by and large what was expected, but a few surprising results came back:

- Almost no one would agree to use Mob Programming on all stories as a rule, and instead preferred to evaluate whether the story would benefit from it.
- The developers felt that Mob Programming was more beneficial for complex work (where there is still room for error) than for complicated work (where the solution is known but time-consuming), and that complicated work can be just as efficiently completed by a pair.
- A significant portion of the developers were in favour of a hybrid approach - running a Mob every day but being able to fluidly move in and out of other tasks, like a pair being able to join the Mob if they were waiting for customer feedback.
- Tasks that were dull, repetitive, or unclear were most likely to cause the Mob to dissolve.
- The ideal time limit for a Mob of 4-6 people seems to be 5 minutes, but for a Mob of 3 people we found that 10 minutes was more appropriate.

– Most teams drifted into having regimented breaks of around 15 minutes after 2 to 3 rounds of rotation. In practice this translated to a break every 1 to 2 hours, but members were able to break off if they needed to take short breaks due to meetings or other needs.
– All teams noticed a small decrease in cycle-time across stories, but no noticeable change in story throughput.

9   Conclusion

We adopted Mob Programming to solve the specific problem of making changes to critical code. Having experienced the results and perceived safety first-hand, we resolved to decide at the beginning of each story whether it was worth mobbing on it from start to finish, which yielded best results on complex pieces of work where the proliferation of operational knowledge is at its most valuable.

There are problems that need to be constantly guarded against such as GroupThink and defending against dominant personalities exerting too much influence on the team. Finally, given Unruly's unusual approach of making developers responsible for the entire software development process including research and operational support, we felt Mob Programming did not yield suffient gains to be worth mandating for every piece of work.

Our conclusion is that while Mob Programming is a useful tool in particular situations and to solve specific problems, it is but one of many tools available to us as a team, and not a new methodology to adopt across the board.

References

1. One-Piece Flow (2015). http://www.kaizenworld.com/kaizen/one-piece-flow.html
2. Unruly.co. (2015). http://unruly.co/
3. Hoover, D.: Ping-Pong Programming: Enhance Your TDD and Pair Programming Practices (2005). http://www.stickyminds.com/article/ping-pong-programming-enhance-your-tdd-and-pair-programming-practices
4. Janis, I.L.: Groupthink: psychological studies of policy decisions and fiascoes (1982)
5. Rooksby, J., Hunt, J., Wang, X.: The theory and practice of randori coding dojos. In: Cantone, G., Marchesi, M. (eds.) XP 2014. LNBIP, vol. 179, pp. 251–259. Springer, Heidelberg (2014)
6. Zuill, W.: Mob Programming (2012). http://mobprogramming.org/mob-programming-basics/
7. Zuill, W.: Mob Programming at JavaOne (2015). https://oracleus.activeevents.com/2014/connect/sessionDetail.ww?SESSION_ID=2181

Panels

Continuous Delivery – From Concept to Product: Trade-offs in Effectiveness and Efficiency?

Steven Fraser[1], Ismo Aro[2], Henri Kivioja[3], Erik Lundh[4],
Ken Power[5], Linda Rising[6], Werner Wild[7], and Rebecca Wirfs-Brock[8]

[1] Innoxec, CA, USA
sdfraser@acm.org
[2] Omenia, Finland
ismo.aro@omenia.fi
[3] Ericsson, Helsinki, Finland
henri.kivioja@ericsson.com
[4] Compelcom, Sweden
erik.l.lundh@gmail.com
[5] Cisco Systems, Galway, Ireland
ken.power@gmail.com
[6] Independent Consultant, TN, USA
risingl@tds.net
[7] University of Innsbruck, Austria
werner.wild@uibk.ac.at
[8] Wirfs-Brock Associates, OR, USA
rebecca@wirfs-brock.com

Abstract. The implementation and release of software products has progressed from a lengthy delivery cycle – the methodical sequential path of "big bang" waterfall product delivery – to the rapid iterative release cycle supported by agile practices. Recently, "continuous delivery" has emerged as a strategy to accelerate product availability. However, only a systematic automation of the build, test and deployment processes in concert with superbly coordinated teams of software practitioners and business partners makes make this possible. However, trade-offs in the optimization of process may act to limit the innovativeness of product output. This panel will discuss approaches, challenges, risks, and strategies for using continuous delivery to competitive advantage.

Keywords: Agile · Waterfall · Automation · Processes · Innovation · Delivery

1 Steven Fraser (*Panel Impresario*)

Steven Fraser is based in Silicon Valley California and has served as an innovation catalyst with global influence for three Fortune 500 Companies as: Director, Cisco Research Center; Senior Staff, Qualcomm Learning Center; and Senior Manager, Nortel Disruptive Technologies and Global External Research. In addition to a year spent as a Visiting Scientist at Carnegie Mellon University's Software Engineering

© Springer International Publishing Switzerland 2015
C. Lassenius et al. (Eds.): XP 2015, LNBIP 212, pp. 329–333, 2015.
DOI: 10.1007/978-3-319-18612-2

Institute (SEI) consulting on Domain Engineering (software reuse) processes and practices he has organized and delivered over 75 software engineering conferences, panels, keynotes, workshops, and tutorials.

Continuous delivery of software features, systems and services is a dream that may becoming reality. This panel will discuss challenges and results – observing and reporting on current best practices and pitfalls.

2   Ismo Aro

Ismo has an extensive track record in the corporate world as a change agent. He is enthusiastic to work with companies to improve their capability to produce customer value faster and drive them to be amazing places to work. Nowadays he works as an entrepreneur at Omenia.

Inventories are one of the biggest source of waste in software development. Companies that develop software accumulate immaterial inventories as feature requests in backlogs, in code waiting, in source control systems, or software packages waiting for deployment. We should systematically locate and reduce these inventories, by finding constraints and exploiting them.

3   Henri Kivioja

Henri has experienced and lived transformations in many corporations: moving from a two year release cycle to a more frequent delivery and deployment cadence. He has learned from experience with large telecom operators on what it means to move towards rapid value creation. Henri has been fortunate enough to be at the center of change as a project and program manager and more recently as a head coach. He has learned the fundamentals of large-scale change, feedback mechanisms and people. Henri is a popular public speaker in the Lean-Agile community.

Continuous Deployment should be based on market and business demand. Another dimension is that how (and if) we understand how it works. Conventional management treats this aspect as efficiency. In knowledge, work efficiency is a broader concept and sometimes misunderstood. We need to agree on some general terms and concepts. What is continuous? What is the purpose of R&D? How does the contractual situation affect value creation? How is culture impacting teamwork and way the work is improved? What is the relation between Continuous Integration, Continuous Delivery and Continuous Deployment? All in all the term "competitive advantage" needs to be rephrased in modern software and knowledge work, as tools and availability of different technologies is possible outside the industries' entry barriers (regulation, cost, availability). This implies that advantage is created through people and culture – not solely with tools and frameworks.

4   Erik Lundh

Erik Lundh has more than 30 years' experience in product-technical-software development beginning as an apprentice at an innovative design and engineering firm. Erik has worked in mature firms and start-ups, from small to large (Ericsson and ABB). Erik programmed industrial just-in-time (Lean) systems in the 1980's, was a "process-management guy" in the 1990's, and spent the fun part of the 2000's as an agile evangelist-coach. Erik facilitated his first (highly successful) agile project in 2000 and helped Sweden's top e-commerce brand go agile in 2006. Erik was invited to mentor Ericsson's first major agile transformation of 2,300 staff at 10 R&D sites in 5 countries 2006-08.

Continuous Delivery is the name of the game both for products and services. Do a feature, deliver it and get feedback as soon as possible. Either split-test or roll-out/roll back. But wait! Why are many organizations failing with – or eroding their software? I feel that there are a few vital pieces are missing: (1) Continuous delivery to me does not mean continuous planning. You need a highly constrained cyclic planning that feeds into iterative development with continuous delivery (learning "just in time") in order to build true value. (2) Trying to avoid constraints (e.g. #noestimates) is an attempt to avoid making decisions – shying away from innovation and creativity. We need constraints and estimates to generate ideas and make smart choices. Without a constrained system, we will forever chase the electric rabbit of the "unaccountable" customer. (3) Agile teams explore and learn about possibilities well before they need them in the product. Winning teams need to learn what they need "now".

5   Ken Power

Ken is a Principal Engineer and internal coach and consultant with Cisco Systems. He lives in Galway, Ireland and works with teams and organizations around the world. His responsibilities include leading the agile transformation for Cisco's largest software group. He also works with universities and research groups in agile, lean and software engineering research. He is currently completing a PhD in Lean Flow and understanding impediments in teams and organizations. He is a frequent speaker at the major international agile, lean and software engineering conferences, and has published numerous papers on agile and lean development. Ken is a Fellow of the Lean Systems Society, a certified Human Systems Dynamics Professional, and a trained Co-Active Coach and Organization & Relationship System Coach.

Continuous Delivery (CD) brings many advantages that enable business agility. However, CD is not solely a technology and infrastructure challenge. Not all teams and organizations are ready to adopt CD. There are a number of pre-requisites that I have found useful to articulate. These pre-requisites are both technical and cultural, and neither can be neglected without jeopardizing the overall effort. Continuous Delivery depends on several pre-requisites being in place. Firstly – the requisite foundation is a culture that supports continuous improvement and problem solving. Secondly – followed by the technical and cultural aspects of Continuous Integration

(CI) and Continuous Feedback. To be successful, these elements must work together to support Continuous Deployment.

6   Linda Rising

Linda Rising is an independent consultant who lives near Nashville, Tennessee. Linda has a Ph.D. from Arizona State University in object-based design metrics. Her background includes university teaching as well as work in industry in telecommunications, avionics, and strategic weapons systems. She is an internationally known presenter on topics related to agile development, patterns, retrospectives, the change process, and the connection between the latest neuroscience and software development. Linda is the author of numerous articles and has published several books: *Design Patterns in Communications*, *The Pattern Almanac 2000*, *A Patterns Handbook*, with co-author Mary Lynn Manns, *Fearless Change: Patterns for Introducing New Ideas* and to be released in 2015 *More Fearless Change*.

Even my very elementary understand of physics reveals that light can be viewed as a wave (continuous) or as a stream of particles (discrete). Which is "right"? Both! The useful approach is determined by context. That is so true for models! In our industry, we tend to embrace the current model and throw out everything from the past. We even denigrate past models – not realizing that we are where we are because we built on those former approaches. Perhaps it's time to become more scientific, to see the effect of context, and to consider appropriate contexts for continuous delivery.

7   Werner Wild

Werner Wild studied Computer Science and Mathematics at the University of Innsbruck and currently teaches at the Free University of Bolzano and the University of Innsbruck. Previous assignments include UNESCO, NIO Goa, ISS The Hague, UBS Switzerland, SwissRe Zurich, Joanneum Research Graz and others. He also helps organizations to build high performance software development teams from scratch, including recruiting, process establishment, project management, training & coaching, dev-ops and also creates scalable architectures. His involvement with computers started 1972; developing virtual machines, compilers, medical and financial applications – and continues with agile trends in Software Engineering. He organizes workshops at international conferences and is an elected official to the Austrian Chamber of Commerce in the Tyrol, identifying and tackling the challenges ahead of the Austrian IT industry. He loves to fly (for more than 25 years) and holds a FAA Commercial Pilot License, with a current Instrument Rating.

In a recent mission critical project (mobile payment) we were able to implement Continuous Delivery successfully. Our goal was to deliver a change within 30 minutes – to production, from code check-in to going live! By fully automating building, testing and deployment (but including a last minute manual safety check!) we were able to bring the time down to 20 minutes! For development we use eXtreme

Programming, steering the project via Kanban, and rigorously following the principles of Lean Software Development. In my opinion a highly disciplined development approach is required to succeed with Continuous Delivery and equally important we should not forget to include our "sys admins" in the process - right from the beginning! We are all in ONE team! However, I am not convinced that the business can leverage this new flexibility to the fullest – since the business has to be as agile as the development team to earn maximum value from Continuous Delivery.

8   Rebecca Wirfs-Brock

Rebecca Wirfs-Brock invented the set of design practices known as Responsibility-Driven Design (RDD) and by accident started the x-DD meme. Along the way she authored two popular object design books. In her spare time she jogs (even in the rain). In her work she helps people hone their design and architecture skills, manage and reduce technical debt, refactor their code, and address architecture risks. She is program director of the Agile Alliance's Experience Reports Program.

With continuous delivery you can perform small experiments that contribute to small steady course corrections. However, can a more significant innovation fit into a development process where the drumbeat of delivery is constant? Innovation should not be forced to fit into a cycle of continuous delivery. I don't know how to plan for big innovations but I have some experience with taking slightly innovative ideas off a continuous delivery pipeline in order to vet their feasibility and mitigate design risks before committing to them. We were able to explore unproven, intriguing ideas in small, bounded experiments or innovation spikes. These experiments were several weeks long, and they were time-limited. Some failed. Others succeeded – and through this learning we helped shaped future product innovation.

Learning from Disaster and Experience: Evolving Software Professionalism

Steven Fraser[1], Janne Järvinen[2], Erik Lundh[3], Ken Power[4],
Linda Rising[5], Werner Wild[6], and Rebecca Wirfs-Brock[7]

[1] Innoxec, CA, USA
sdfraser@acm.org
[2] F-Secure, Finland
janne.jarvinen@f-secure.com
[3] Compelcom, Sweden
erik.l.lundh@gmail.com
[4] Cisco Systems, Galway, Ireland
ken.power@gmail.com
[5] Independent Consultant, TN, USA
rising1@tds.net
[6] University of Innsbruck, Austria
werner.wild@uibk.ac.at
[7] Wirfs-Brock Associates, OR, USA
rebecca@wirfs-brock.com

Abstract. Professionalism evolves as knowledge and skills mature from craft to commercial practice – often as the result of learnings derived from failure and human hazard. Aviation, medicine, engineering, and architecture are examples of disciplines with an established knowledge base and curriculum of learning and mentorship. These disciplines often require regulated practices executed by certified professionals to ensure the safety and economic value of delivered services. This panel will debate whether we are learning effectively from our experiences and what might be done to accelerate increased software professionalism and product value.

Keywords: Professionalism · Knowledge · Skills · Craft · Practice · Learning · Failure · Certification · Value · safety

1 Steven Fraser (*Panel Impresario*)

Steven Fraser is based in Silicon Valley California and has served as an innovation catalyst with global influence for three Fortune 500 Companies serving as: Director, Cisco Research Center; Senior Staff, Qualcomm Learning Center; and Senior Manager, Nortel Disruptive Technologies and Global External Research. In addition to a year spent as a Visiting Scientist at Carnegie Mellon University's Software Engineering Institute (SEI) consulting on Domain Engineering (software reuse) processes and practices he has organized and delivered over 75 software engineering conferences, panels, keynotes, workshops, and tutorials.

© Springer International Publishing Switzerland 2015
C. Lassenius et al. (Eds.): XP 2015, LNBIP 212, pp. 334–338, 2015.
DOI: 10.1007/978-3-319-18612-2

Twenty-five years ago, CMU professor Mary Shaw wrote on "Prospects for an Engineering Discipline of Software" in IEEE Software (Nov.1990, pp 15-24). She proposed that engineering disciplines evolve from craft – with development characterized by virtuosos, talented amateurs, intuition, brute force, extravagant use of available materials and manufacture for use rather than sale. Shaw further postulated that as time progresses, a shared experience base characterized by skilled crafts people, established procedures based in science (enabling education and training) with a concern for economics and materials – scales to commercial practice and manufacture for sale. "Engineering discipline" is achieved when a cadre of educated professionals with a shared knowledge in analysis, theory, and science – including awareness for economics, ethics, human hazards and risks – evolves to develop products and services for the good of humanity. This panel brings together industry experts to share their thoughts on software professionalism and discipline.

2   Janne Järvinen

Janne Järvinen has over 25 years of experience in software engineering and software process improvement in various positions within software industry from programmer to VP Engineering in small and large software companies. Janne is Director, External R&D Collaboration at F-Secure Corporation and has also been active in academia in various research programs such as European ESPRIT (BOOTSTRAP, PROFES) and ITEA (MOOSE, FLEXI). He led the Cloud Software program (www.cloudsoftwareprogram. org), and now leads the N4S program (www.n4s.fi) under DIGILE Oy. He is an IEEE member and holds a PhD in Information processing science from University of Oulu (2000).

I am a strong believer of continuous improvement in all possible forms. I have led software teams both in small and large organizations and I have seen both successes and failures. More than often an important contributing factor to success has been the ability learn from one's mistakes. On the other hand, as making of software is largely invisible software professionals are often challenged to demonstrate aspects of their work that may bear little relevance to actual software. Or what actually is relevant for a software professional? Is it enough that one produces superior code? Finally, I would borrow ideas to develop software professionalism from digital security research where I have seen teams of analysts engage in investigations of the latest threats in close cooperation with industry partners and international and national information security authorities. We must share our experiences with a larger community more effectively and transparently than possible today.

3   Erik Lundh

Erik Lundh has more than 30 years' experience in product-technical-software development beginning as an apprentice at an innovative design and engineering firm. Erik has worked in mature firms and start-ups, from small to large (Ericsson and ABB). Erik programmed industrial just-in-time (Lean) systems in the 1980's, was a "process-management guy" in the 1990's, and spent the fun part of the 2000's as an agile evangelist-coach. Erik facilitated his first (highly successful) agile project in 2000 and helped Sweden's top e-commerce brand go agile in 2006. Erik was invited to mentor Ericsson's first major agile transformation of 2,300 staff at 10 R&D sites in 5 countries 2006-08.

We lost the ball when the Agile movement was handed "sticks": the 1990s light-weight method Scrum – reengineered as the safe haven for change-angst mediocre low level managers (in my opinion head-count reduction road-kill), Kanban – the Taylorists revenge, and SAFE – the RUP exploiters revenge. Good people turned away in disgust from third rate agile "profiles", catering to pointy-haired bosses with money in hand looking for agile storefronts on assembly line software sweatshops. Some of the best of the original agile proponents stopped caring about process and product. Their reaction was to initiate the blue collar Software Craftsmanship Movement. In my opinion, we need agile software professionals that master process, product, craft and technologies – and we need to send all scrum masters to retraining as product management support. I spent the 1980s solving – strike that – *fixing* larger and larger problems with my technical prowess, only to realize that the root causes were non-technical. Early agile methods involved programmers in business and *vice versa*, and that as what attracted me and my Swedish process improvement community to agile methods like Extreme Programming in 1999-2000. That hope and motivation has been replaced by nervous laughs when asked whether agile works.

4   Ken Power

Ken is a Principal Engineer and internal coach and consultant with Cisco Systems. He lives in Galway, Ireland and works with teams and organizations around the world. His responsibilities include leading the agile transformation for Cisco's largest software group. He also works with universities and research groups in agile, lean and software engineering research. He is currently completing a PhD in Lean Flow and understanding impediments in teams and organizations. He is a frequent speaker at the major international agile, lean and software engineering conferences, and has published numerous papers on agile and lean development. Ken is a Fellow of the Lean Systems Society, a certified Human Systems Dynamics Professional, and a trained Co-Active Coach and Organization & Relationship System Coach.

The profession of software engineering is still finding its identity, even now decades on from when the term was first coined. Referring to professional education in general, Donald Schön describes what he calls "the crisis of confidence in professional knowledge". Schön proposes that university-based professional schools should take influence from the traditions of education for practice. These influences should include art and design, music and dance conservatories, athletics coaching, and apprenticeship in the crafts. All of these have in common an emphasis on coaching and on learning by doing. He goes even further to say that professional education needs to be redesigned "to combine the teaching of applied science with coaching in the artistry of reflection-in-action". There are several options for bringing this to life in teams and organizations. Examples include job rotations, shadowing, and formal mentorship. The increasingly popular guilds, chapter and communities of practice are further opportunities, but they need to have real substance and organizational support.

5   Linda Rising

Linda Rising is an independent consultant who lives near Nashville, Tennessee. Linda has a Ph.D. from Arizona State University in object-based design metrics. Her background includes university teaching as well as work in industry in telecommunications, avionics, and strategic weapons systems. She is an internationally known presenter on topics related to agile development, patterns, retrospectives, the change process, and the connection between the latest neuroscience and software development. Linda is the author of numerous articles and has published several books: *Design Patterns in Communications*, *The Pattern Almanac 2000*, *A Patterns Handbook*, with co-author Mary Lynn Manns, *Fearless Change: Patterns for Introducing New Ideas* and to be released in 2015 *More Fearless Change*.

This topic calls to mind the *ACM Forum on Risks to the Public in Computers and Related Systems* moderated by Peter G. Neumann (*www.risks.org*) detailing software misadventures. The Forum reports accidents, injuries, and deaths as a result of software error. I always read that and I always thought that our industry didn't seem as responsive as other fields such as avionics. We don't seem to pay attention to those reports. We seem to talk about the latest buzzword and I wonder what we are carrying forward. Are we as an industry becoming like our projects – small and focused on the moment – just trying stuff without any formal approaches and leaving our mathematical and scientific history behind? As software becomes a more important part of every produce and service. This failure to learn seems to lead to a place we might not want to go.

6   Werner Wild

Werner Wild studied Computer Science and Mathematics at the University of Innsbruck and currently teaches at the Free University of Bolzano and the University of Innsbruck. Previous assignments include UNESCO, NIO Goa, ISS The Hague, UBS Switzerland, SwissRe Zurich, Joanneum Research Graz and others. He also helps organizations to build high performance software development teams from scratch, including recruiting, process establishment, project management, training & coaching, dev-ops and also creates scalable architectures. His involvement with computers started 1972; developing virtual machines, compilers, medical and financial applications – and continues with agile trends in Software Engineering. He organizes workshops at international conferences and is an elected official to the Austrian Chamber of Commerce in the Tyrol, identifying and tackling the challenges ahead of the Austrian IT industry. He loves to fly (for more than 25 years) and holds a FAA Commercial Pilot License, with a current Instrument Rating.

In aviation many systems are in place to learn from experience and to receive valuable feedback. For example, we must continually demonstrate our skills in a simulator and in flight. If there are "incidents" – these must be reported (e.g. ASRS: Aviation Safety Reporting System - http://asrs.arc.nasa.gov). Pilots frequently review incident and accident reports to learn from others. Perhaps it is time to borrow an idea or two from aviation to foster increased professionalism in our software industry.

7   Rebecca Wirfs-Brock

Rebecca Wirfs-Brock invented the set of design practices known as Responsibility-Driven Design (RDD) and by accident started the x-DD meme. Along the way she authored two popular object design books. In her spare time she jogs (even in the rain). In her work she helps people hone their design and architecture skills, manage and reduce technical debt, refactor their code, and address architecture risks. She is program director of the Agile Alliance's Experience Reports Program and co-chair of the XP 2015 Experience Reports track.

I hope I never stop learning. My technical learning has been driven by positive experiences and interactions with others as we build something together. I learn the most when I work with those who are articulate and considerate enough to explain why they want to solve something some particular way, to share what the next move we should take as well as why they are confident (or not) about what we're doing, and how they feel about our code. Back and forth communication as we build something significant and complex together is where I learn best. A highly performing, tight agile team is one of the best opportunities for professional learning. However, I have written lots of code solo, and through those experiences I have also learned a great deal. I don't believe that every bit of code is best developed by a collective mind. Sometimes solo efforts are the most productive where you get deep into the problem.

I have also worked on teams where we didn't communicate as we banged out code and as a consequence, we didn't learn much. What seems most important to me as a software professional is doing things that help me develop a wise inner critic who considers why I prefer some solution over another, why I think this is a hack and that is not, why I think this will work and that will not. And that is because software is, well, soft. There are many ways to solve a problem in code, but only a few are good enough solutions. To get really good at this profession, you need challenging work where you don't know how to solve it and lots of feedback.

Practical Applications of the Agile Fluency Model

Diana Larsen[1], Steve Holyer[2], Jutta Eckstein[3], Antti Kirjavainen[4], and Olli Sorje[5]

[1] FutureWorks Consulting LLC, 6307 NE 8th Avenue, Portland, OR, USA
Diana@futureworksconsulting.com
[2] Engage Results, Founder, Agile Coaching, Aemtlerstrasse 114, Zurich, Switzerland
coach@engage-results.com
[3] IT communication, Gaussstr. 29,38106 Braunschweig, Germany
je@it-communication.com
[4] Flowa, Department, Kaarlenkatu 3-5 B 14, FI-00530 Helsinki, Finland
Antti.Kirjavainen@flowa.fi
[5] Affecto Finland Oy, Retail and Services, Helsinginkatu 15, FI-20500 Turku, Finland
olli.sorje@affecto.com

Abstract. First published in 2011, the Agile Fluency Model (agilefluency.com) describes four stages for achieving agile team proficiency: focus on value, deliver value, optimize value, and optimize the system. Adopting agile in successive stages the model delivers benefits proportional to investments. The model fosters the identification, adaption and adoption of agile practices appropriate to the team's context and objectives. Does it reflect reality? Is it useful? Does it work when theory meets practice? This panel brings together Agile Fluency practitioners to share their challenges, successes, and future directions for model evolution.

Keywords: Agile adoption · Agile fluency · Agile practices · Team proficiency · Value delivery

1 Diana Larsen – Panelmeister

Diana consults with leaders and teams to create work processes and environments where innovation, inspiration, and imagination flourish. She is an international authority in the areas of Agile software development, team leadership, and Agile transitions.

Diana co-authored *Agile Retrospectives: Making Good Teams Great*! and *Liftoff: Launching Agile Teams and Projects*. She created the Agile Fluency™ Model with James Shore.

2 Steve Holyer — Looking for Organizational Fluency

When Diana showed the Agile Fluency™ Model to me, I recognized that it describes exactly what I've experienced when I've worked with software teams who are successfully mastering Agile development. That's why I'm so excited about it. It's not a

© Springer International Publishing Switzerland 2015
C. Lassenius et al. (Eds.): XP 2015, LNBIP 212, pp. 339–341, 2015.
DOI: 10.1007/978-3-319-18612-2

maturity model that dictates how teams must progress, it's an observation based on experience of what teams can expect in their progress. I've used the model as a tool to encourage teams that were stuck doing "by the book Scrum" (1-Star) so they could see a much richer path. The Agile Fluency™ Model has proven useful for changing the conversation with leaders about targets and KPI's so that it becomes a conversation about helping teams and the organization evolve their understanding of leadership and team learning. Diana and I used the Agile Fluency™ Model to create a set of learning objectives that we've used to train teams at each level of Agile Fluency. This broadened the focus of our training beyond the typical Agile training focus which is often focused on just one level of fluency.

The Agile Fluency™ Model is written to describe the evolution of a development team. Therefore it naturally describes the experience of delivering software from the perspective of the builders creating code. And yet, the model itself states there's a shift in organizational structure that takes place as a build team becomes a 3-star team. There's also an organizational culture shift that takes place as the build team moves from a 3-star team to become a 4-star team. This begs the question, "How does the whole organization become fluent at the 3-star and the 4-star level?" There must be more to the Agile Fluency™ Model that hasn't been described yet at the level of Agile Management. The Agile Fluency™ Model is based on anecdotal evidence from the authors and their colleagues. Now that the model is defined, I'm looking forward to expanding the body of knowledge about Agile Fluency with efforts to collect more data so we can see what new data reveals.

Steve serves as advocate, trainer and mentor for companies discovering different ways of working using Agile practices in a productive, fulfilling, and fun way. He uses the model in most, if not all, aspects of his work with teams.

3   Jutta Eckstein – The Shifts are Harder than You Think

To me, as a practitioner, the Agile Fluency™ Model mirrors what I see happening in Industry. I experience that many teams already struggle with the first stage on the model – to focus on value. They concentrate instead on the adherence to practices. Yet, I also experienced teams that not only focused on value but reached the second stage to also deliver it. They were not able to let go of their habits even when asked to switch back to waterfall. They just couldn't.

However, the model doesn't show how hard it is to move from one stage to the other. And I wonder if reaching four stars is only possible if an organization starts this way. Although I want to believe it's possible, I doubt that a cooperation doing business in a non-agile way for e.g. 30 years will be able to ever reach that stage. If only for the reason, that they won't have the patience to go through the deep culture shift which will take at least ten years.

Jutta Eckstein works as an independent coach, consultant, and trainer. She holds a M.A. in Business Coaching & Change Management, a Dipl. Eng. in Product-Engineering, and a B.A. in Education. She has helped many teams and organizations worldwide to make an Agile transition. She has a unique experience in applying Agile processes within medium-sized to large distributed mission-critical projects. She has published her experience in her books *Agile Software Development in the Large*,

Agile Software Development with Distributed Teams, Retrospectives for Organizational Change, and together with Johanna Rothman *Diving for Hidden Treasures: Finding the Real Value in your Project Portfolio.*

4   Antti Kirjavainen

Having coached software development and knowledge work teams and organizations for the past 5 years, I have found that setting goals together with the organization I'm coaching helps to carry out the coaching relationship and contributes to the relationship's success. We set the goals in terms of impact. I have used the Agile Fluency™ Model over the past 2.5 years to facilitate this goal-setting and to successfully set expectations related to the change process.

I have found Agile Fluency™ Model useful for agreeing on the current state of teams with the customer, agreeing on the desired end state with teams and their sponsors and with setting realistic expectations for the change. What I have found challenging is making the progress visible and measurable during the change. The metrics described in the model work well as lagging indicators, but we would benefit from leading indicators as well. The linear representation of the model makes it easy for sponsors to mistake it for a maturity model. There is some ambiguity in the description of the model and its stages and whether or not to focus on different stages at once. That is why I have adapted my own description of model's stages to call them dimensions instead.

Antti is an entrepreneur at Flowa (Finland). He helps organizations achieve effectiveness and excellence in software development and knowledge work through agile, lean thinking and Management 3.0. Antti is also fascinated about the potential of games for learning and facilitating collaboration.

5   Olli Sorje

For me the Agile Fluency™ Model means giving context for all Agile practices. It helps you to identify where you and your team currently are and decide where you should aim for. Not all organizations should aim for a 4-star level. This model also helps you understand why you are not maybe getting the benefits that Agile promises. I also like the concept of Fluency a lot. You might use all the practices from a specific star level, but it you devolve back to old habits under pressure it means you aren't fluent at that level! That's unfortunately what typically happens in Agile transitions. You adopt Agile practices, but then the deadline starts to get closer. You decide that these new practices are slowing you down, and you fall back to old practices.

Olli Sorje is working as Lead Developer at Affecto Finland. Olli is passionate about Agile and creating real value for customers. Olli enjoys working with teams and helping them evolve.

References

1. http://agilefluency.com (last time accessed March 20, 2015)

Doctoral Symposium Abstracts

Improving Processes by Integrating Agile Practices

Philipp Diebold[✉]

Fraunhofer IESE, Kaiserslautern, Germany
philipp.diebold@iese.fraunhofer.de

Abstract. Even though agile development has been known for many years, it is mainly used in information systems and is not common yet in embedded systems. Despite the mandatory regulations, the companies would like to increase the flexibility by the benefits of agile development. Thus, the idea is creating an Agile Capability Analysis with a subsequent Process Simulation, resulting in appropriate process extensions adhere to mandatory requirements. Because often agile methods require context-specific adaptations, we believe that the upfront investigation which agile practices to integrate into processes entails many benefits, especially in regulated domains.

Keywords: SPI · Agile SW development · Agile practices

1 Introduction and Problem

Agile development has been common for several years. Nonetheless, it is mainly used in information systems and not in embedded systems (ES), which are often restricted by regulations. The problem in these domains is their inflexible development. Thus, they want to use agile development within their regulations. This raises the research question: How to bring more agility to the regulated software domains?

2 Related Work

Even though plan-based processes, e.g. waterfall and V-model, which fit many regulations, dominate different ES domains [2], there are some approaches that try to address the problem of getting agility integrated into regulated domains. Some of the common agile methods like Scrum are already used in part in ES. But this only applies to pilot projects or to early phases of the final product, where it is possible to try things and where developers are not restricted by too many regulatory requirements. In addition, less specific approaches have also been published that try to address the issue of more flexibility in regulated domains. One is the Agile V-Model [1], developed for medical devices.

As shown in the short discussion of existing related work and the already mentioned issue of adapting the different agile methods, there is a lack of systematic Software Process Improvement (SPI) approaches in research that make use of agile practices while adhering to mandatory regulations.

© Springer International Publishing Switzerland 2015
C. Lassenius et al. (Eds.): XP 2015, LNBIP 212, pp. 345–346, 2015.
DOI: 10.1007/978-3-319-18612-2

3   Solution Approach

To address this problem, the overall solution idea is based on two parts: the **Agile Capability Analysis** and a **Process Simulation** aimed at finding the most appropriate agile practices as process extension. These two parts constitute the contribution and novelty of the idea because no such analysis is currently available and even though process simulations are widely used, none deals with the integration of agile practices.

The purpose of the **Agile Capability Analysis** is to identify the capability of extending the current development process with agile practices in terms of the context (incl. regulations). The inputs are the current process and context information, e.g., team size or team location. This analysis is built on a model containing the information about the impact of all different agile practices, which are formal described in a repository. This reveals all possible agile practices that could be potential extensions in the specific context.

The purpose of the **Process Simulation** is to simulate possible agile practices combinations and their joined impact. Therefore, the formal process description and the outputs of the analysis are used. All possible combinations of the set of agile practices are simulated in the company's process. Thus, the formalized process and the possible process extension with the necessary information, e.g. their impact, will be used to come up with the simulation model. This model will then be used for the simulation and should provide information on how the combinations might behave concerning the impact characteristics.

Based on this information, the SPI can be performed by selecting one of the possible combinations that best fits to the organizations improvement goal. This should than be implemented and further been evaluated compared to the assumed impact.

4   Conclusion and Future Work

The overall solution idea should support SPI in regulated environments by integrating agile practices into the current development processes. This is done by the Agile Capability Analysis and a simulation of the process extensions, the agile practices.

The future research agenda regarding this idea includes the following aspects: The Agile Capability Analysis will be defined in detail because only parts already exist. Additionally, the Process Simulation needs to be elaborated more detailed because currently it is rather a high level idea. Finally, the question is how to evaluate the overall idea and/or its different parts.

References

1. McHugh, M., Cawley, Q., McCaffery, F., Richardson, I., Wang, X.: An Agile V-Model for Medical Device Software Development to Overcome the Challenges with Plan-driven Software development Lifecycles. In: Proceedings of SEHC 2013 (2013)
2. Weiguo, L., Xiaomin, F.: Software Development Practices for FDA-Compliant Medical Devices. In: Proceedings of CSO 2009, pp. 388–390 (2009)

Assurance Case Integration with
An Agile Development Method

Osama Doss and Tim Kelly

High Integrity Systems Engineering Research Group,
Department of Computer Science, University of York, York, YO10 5DD, UK
{osad500,tim.kelly}@york.ac.uk

Abstract. Agile software development has had success in different domains. However there is one area where the implementation of agile methods still needs development – that is in the field of safety critical systems. In this field, the software engineering processes need to be justified against the requirements of software safety assurance standards (such as ISO 26262 in the automotive domain). We describe our ongoing research on assurance case integration with an existing agile development method – SafeScrum.

Keywords: Safety-critical systems · Assurance · SafeScrum · Assurance case · Safety cases

1 Research Problem

Whilst the use of agile methods is seen by some as attractive, and there is some evidence of increasing use in safety-critical domain, there are still many in the domain who have concerns. For example, Redmill [1] raises concerns about whether hazard identification and analysis can be carried out incrementally. The question of how to integrate agile methods and safety assurance is not new. But there is one particular area of practice that remains neglected in the existing work – namely the integration of safety (assurance) case development with an agile approach. A safety case is the argument and evidence that establishes the acceptable safety of safety-critical system [2]. It is normally prepared (by the developer) and assessed (by an independent assessor or regulator) as part of safety critical systems development. Safety cases are an increasingly widespread approach [3]. Structured argumentation approaches (such as the use of the Goal Structuring Notation – GSN - [4]) have become popular as a means of explicitly representing the arguments (and links to evidence) contained within a safety case. The research problem we are tackling is the integration of assurance case development (including the incremental development of structured arguments) with a typical agile development method.

© Springer International Publishing Switzerland 2015
C. Lassenius et al. (Eds.): XP 2015, LNBIP 212, pp. 347–349, 2015.
DOI: 10.1007/978-3-319-18612-2

2   Research Methods

- We have conducted a survey to investigate the practical problems posed by the integration of the two disciplines.
- We are developing a pattern-based approach to integrating software safety cases, SafeScrum's Safety Product Backlog, risk-based planning, and requirements-based evaluation. Software safety argument patterns describe the nature of the argument and safety claims that would be expected for any software safety case [5].
- The feasibility, and practicality of the proposed integration of safety case development with SafeScrum will be initially evaluated through an illustrative case study.
- Peer review (through structured questionnaire) of the developed approach applied to the worked case study example will be conducted.
- 1-to-1 semi-structured interviews will also be used with some of the respondents from our initial survey, the purpose of this interview study is to investigate the success proposed of safety case development within SafeScrum.

3   Results and Future Work

We have already conducted the practitioner survey (with 31 respondents). The results from this survey have provided a clear direction in terms of the importance of incremental hazard analysis, safety requirements development, and assurance case development (i.e. they indicate clearly that these activities must be performed within an increment, rather than simply being up-front or end-of-development activities). We are using the insight gained from the case study to evaluate how safety activities are currently being proposed within the Safe-Scrum method, and to help define a process model for how requirements development, hazard analysis and assurance case development can be performed as in-increment activities. With regard to assurance case development, we have identified that the existing GSN argument patterns of Hawkins et al. [5] already attempt to integrate software safety requirements development and assurance case development. At present these patterns are expressed to suit a traditional 'tiered' software development. We are currently examining how these patterns can be adapted to suit incremental development. Following development of the process model, and adaptation of the patterns we will be applying the proposed approach to a case study system to serve as the basis for further evaluation with the respondents from our initial survey.

References

1. Felix, R.: Software Projects: Evolutionary v Big-bang Delivery. Wiley Series in Software Engineering Practice. Hardcover (January 30, 1997)

2. Kelly, T.: A Systematic Approach to Safety Case Management. In: Proceedings of SAE 2004 World Congress, Detroit (March 2004)
3. Hawkins, R., Habli, I., Kelly, T., McDermid, J.: Assurance cases and prescriptive software safety certification: A comparative study, vol. 59, pp. 55–71 (November 2013)
4. Kelly, T., Weaver, R.: The Goal Structuring Notation – A Safety Argument Notation. In: Proceedings of the International Conference on Dependable Systems and Networks – Workshops on Assurance Cases, Florence, Italy (2004)
5. Hawkins, R., Clegg, K., Alexander, R., Kelly, T.: Using a Software Safety Argument Pattern Catalogue: Two Case Studies. In: Flammini, F., Bologna, S., Vittorini, V. (eds.) SAFECOMP 2011. LNCS, vol. 6894, pp. 185–198. Springer, Heidelberg (2011)

Data-Driven Decision-Making in Product R&D

Aleksander Fabijan[1], Helena Holmström Olsson[1], and Jan Bosch[2]

[1] Malmö University, Faculty of Technology and Society,
Östra Varvsgatan 11,205 06 Malmö, Sweden
{Aleksander.Fabijan, Helena.Holmstrom.Olsson}@mah.se
[2] Chalmers University of Technology, Department of Computer Science
and Engineering, Hörselgången 11, 412 96 Göteborg, Sweden
Jan.Bosch@chalmers.se

Abstract. Software development companies experience the road mapping and requirements ranking process to be complex as product management (PdM) strives in getting timely and accurate feedback from the customers. Often, companies have insufficient knowledge about how their products are being used, what features the customers appreciate and which ones will generate revenue. To address this problem, this research aims at helping the companies in closing the 'open' feedback loop that exists between PdM and customers. Moreover, the research strives at exploring techniques that can be used to involve customers in continuous validation of software functionality in order to provide PdM with the evidence needed for accurate R&D investments.

Keywords: Customer feedback · Data collection · The 'open loop' problem

1   Introduction

Due to the increasing amount of software in products and hence, the capability to connect these products to the Internet, there is a fundamental shift in how products are developed and in how the life cycles of these products are perceived [1], [2]. This implies that user feedback collected in the early phases of product development is complemented with another data source, i.e. product data revealing real-time use [3].

Despite this, product managers often struggle with getting timely and accurate feedback from customers. Typically, the feedback loops are slow and there is a lack of mechanisms that allow for efficient customer data collection and analysis [1], [5]. As a result, companies have insufficient knowledge about how their products are used and what features the customers actually appreciate. This means that there is an 'open loop' between customer data and product management decisions [4], [5].

To address this problem, this thesis project aims at exploring the existing methods and discovering new techniques that allow for (1) continuous validation of deployed software functionality through product and customer data, and (2) efficient customer and product data collection and analysis practices.

© Springer International Publishing Switzerland 2015
C. Lassenius et al. (Eds.): XP 2015, LNBIP 212, pp. 350–351, 2015.
DOI: 10.1007/978-3-319-18612-2

2   Proposed Approach and Evaluation of Results

The research presented in this proposal is conducted within a large research collaboration consisting of three universities and eight companies.

For the purpose of this research, we use a qualitative case study approach in which we engage with company representatives with various roles such as e.g. developers, product managers and product owners etc. on a continuous basis using a mix of interviews, workshops, weekly status update meetings, individual visits and validation sessions. Interview results work as a basis for workshop sessions and seminars in which we further discuss and validate our findings. It should be noted that the company collaboration is well established and results are continuously evaluated with the companies and reported every six months.

In terms of data analysis, we adopt a qualitative approach as described by e.g. Walsham [6].

3   Expected Contributions and Progress Towards the Goals

As the first phase in the research project outlined here, we have conducted a 'state-of-the-art' literature review in which we identify existing customer feedback and data collection techniques as reported in the software engineering domain, i.e. the top ranked journals and conferences [7]. The results were summarized in a structured model that provides an overall understanding for the existing feedback and data collection techniques, and that works as a support for selecting the appropriate feedback technique(s) in a specific stage of the software development process.

Moving forward, we plan to expand this model with additional feedback collection techniques, identify and complement it with the types of data collected, and to validate our model in the companies to provide also a 'state-of-practice' view.

References

1. Olsson, H.H., Alahyari, H., Bosch, J.: Climbing the "Stairway to Heaven". In: 2012 38th EUROMICRO Conference on Software Engineering and Advanced Applications Software Engineering and Advanced Applications (SEAA), Izmir, Turkey (2012)
2. Cockburn, A., Williams, L.: Agile software development: it's about feedback and change. Computer 36, 0039–0043 (2003)
3. Bosch, J.: Building Products as Innovations Experiment Systems. In: Cusumano, M.A., Iyer, B., Venkatraman, N. (eds.) ICSOB 2012. LNBIP, vol. 114, pp. 27–39. Springer, Heidelberg (2012)
4. Olsson, H.H., Bosch, J.: From Opinions to Data-Driven Software R&D. In: Proceedings of the 40th Euromicro Conference on Software Engineering and Advance Applications, Verona, Italy (2014)
5. Bosch-Sijtsema, P., Bosch, J.: User involvement throughout the innovation process in high-tech industries. Journal of Product Innovation Management (2014)
6. Walsham, G.: Doing Interpretive Research. 2006 European Journal of Information Systems (15), 320–330 (2006)
7. Fabijan, A., Olsson, H.H., Bosch, J.: Customer Feedback and Data Collection Techniques in Software R&D: A literature review. Accepted to Proceedings of ICSOB 2015, Braga, Portugal (2015)

Combining Kanban and FOSS: Can It Work?

Annemarie Harzl and Wolfgang Slany

Institute of Software Technology, Graz University of Technology,
Inffeldgasse 16b/II, 8010 Graz, Austria
aharzl@ist.tugraz.at, wolfgang.slany@tugraz.at

Abstract. Free and Open Source Software (FOSS) and Agile Software
Development(ASD) research have gained momentum over the past decade.
However, to the best of our knowledge, there exists no work about these
two phenomena combined. This thesis will show how Agile Software
Development(ASD), specifically the Kanban Method, and FOSS can be
consolidated and how they can benefit from each other's advantages. The
agile community and the FOSS community can benefit from this body
of work, as we aim at broadening the understanding of both.

Keywords: Lean · Agile · Kanban · FOSS · Open source

1 Statement of Research Problem

In 2009 Ågerfalk et al. [1] identified research about agile development in the
context of open source software as a future research area. This research intends
to take first steps to fill this gap. The knowledge if and how agile methods should
be introduced into FOSS projects can be valuable for the FOSS community
and cooperating companies, which intend to spread their agile methods to the
community, they are working with.

For the purpose of this work a FOSS project was selected, which is situated at
Graz University of Technology. One team was chosen to participate in the study,
because conducting the study with the whole project, would not be feasible. Being
at the same university as the FOSS project provides us with the opportunity to
directly observe the contributors in their natural context. The project already
applies some agile methods (for example Test-Driven Development (TDD)), but
not in a systematic way, and contributors experience some problems with agile
adoption. Hence, they contacted us and asked how they could improve their use
of agile methods. The Kanban Method [2] has been chosen by the research team,
because it is the most adaptive method [3]. It allows to take an existing process
and slowly adapt it to the specific needs of the organization. The Kanban Method
does not impose a huge set of rigid rules, which is very important, because introducing rigid rules into a system almost always requires positional power, which is
not available in a FOSS community.

© Springer International Publishing Switzerland 2015
C. Lassenius et al. (Eds.): XP 2015, LNBIP 212, pp. 352–353, 2015.
DOI: 10.1007/978-3-319-18612-2

Research Questions: My doctoral research aims at answering the questions if Agile Software Development (ASD) techniques, specifically the Kanban Method, can be successfully applied to a FOSS project and whether a FOSS project can benefit from it. I am interested in the current state of agile adoption in the studied project and how the agile process and its introduction into the project can be customized to better fit the needs of the FOSS project and its contributors.

- Research Question (RQ)1 What are the current problems with agile adoption and can they be solved through the use of the Kanban Method?
- RQ2 Can FOSS projects benefit from using agile methods like the Kanban Method?
  - RQ2.1 Do FOSS contributors, who are coached in the Kanban Method, experience this knowledge as beneficial to their work or not?
  - RQ2.2 Do interaction or communication in the team change with the use of the Kanban Method?
  - RQ2.3 Does the Kanban Method have any effect on the source code created by the coached team?

2   Research Methodology

To answer RQ1 a longitudinal single-case study was chosen as research methodology because the case study method is suitable for research of contemporary phenomena in their natural context [4]. According to [5] this method has advantages when a researcher has little or no control over the studied events and when, how or why research questions are asked. At first I will observe team meetings and coding sessions and then I will coach the team in the usage of agile methods. To answer RQ2.1 another research method will be used, namely surveys. Participants of the case study will give subjective feedback about their experience with agile methods at the beginning, throughout and at the end of the case study. They will do this through questionnaires. Surveys and observations of team meetings will be used to answer RQ2.2. This provides the opportunity to compare the perception of team members and someone outside the team. Some code metrics will be calculated for the teams' source code, for example code complexity as a measure for internal quality, to answer RQ2.3.

No results have been achieved so far.

References

1. Ågerfalk, P., Fitzgerald, B., Slaughter, S.: Introduction to the special issue: flexible and distributed information systems development: state of the art and research challenges In: Information Systems Research 20 (2009)
2. Anderson, D.: Kanban - Successful Evolutionary Change for Your Technology Business, Blue Hole Press (2010)
3. Nirenberg, H., Skarin, M.: Kanban and Scrum - making the most of both, C4Media (2010)
4. Runeson, P., Höst, M.,: Guidelines for conducting and reporting case study research in software In: Empirical Software Engineering engineering, vol. 14, 2009
5. Yin, R.: Case Study Research - Design and Methods Fourth Edition (2009)

Paradigm Shift from Large Releases to Continuous Deployment of Software: Designing a Reference Model for Continuous Deployment

Teemu Karvonen, Markku Oivo, and Pasi Kuvaja

University of Oulu, Finland
{Teemu.3.Karvonen,Markku.Oivo,Pasi.Kuvaja}@oulu.fi

Abstract. Continuous deployment (CD) is an essential method as software development companies move towards real-time business and continuous experiments. Powered by the lean and agile methods, CD aims for continuous deployment of valuable software. This doctoral research investigates what it will take to enable CD. The findings will be collected to generate a CD reference model. The research is initiated by studying existing literature and models for organisational assessment in relation to lean and agile approaches. Next, the focus is sharpened to capabilities that are required for enabling CD in information and communication technologies (ICT) industry. The research will apply literature reviews, case studies and the design science research (DSR) framework.

Keywords: Lean · Agile · Software development · Continuous deployment · Real-time business · Reference model · Assessment

1 Doctoral Research Plan

The software engineering (SE) field of research has focussed on studying multidisciplinary aspects concerning how to improve ways of developing and deploying software intensive products. Today, the development paradigm in information and communication technologies (ICT) has moved from plan-based waterfall to iterative agile methods [1]. Many software development companies have set their future goal to 'deliver value in real time'. It seems that innovation experiment systems and continuous deployment of *valuable software* are essential new capabilities which companies must develop in order to advance beyond the agile approach [2,3,4]. **Continuous deployment (CD)** [5,6] describes practices for developing and deploying software. CD has clearly built-in principles of lean [7] and agile. According to the lean principle *'flow'*, value-creating steps should occur in a tight sequence so that the value will flow smoothly towards the customer. In addition, the agile manifesto[1] describes how to deliver software: *'Our highest priority is to satisfy the customer through early and continuous delivery of valuable software'*. Moreover, it aims to *'deliver working software frequently, from a couple of weeks to a couple of months, with a preference to the shorter timescale'*.

---

[1] http://agilemanifesto.org/principles.html

C. Lassenius et al. (Eds.): XP 2015, LNBIP 212, pp. 354–355, 2015.
DOI: 10.1007/978-3-319-18612-2

Organisational assessment models are also frequently discussed in SE studies. Periodical assessments are found useful for analysing an organisation's current status. A reference model can be used together with an assessment model to define desired real-life working practices. The reference model (what to assess) and assessment model (how to conduct assessment) can also be integrated into a single 'tool', such as in Lean Enterprise Self-Assessment Tool (LESAT) [7].

The **research goal** is to develop new knowledge and methods which aid in the transition towards CD. The main research methods and questions are as follows: 1) How do ICT companies apply CD? – Case studies; and 2) How can CD capabilities be assessed? – Systematic mapping study and design science research (DSR) [8]. In the principles of DSR, the aim is to produce innovative research artefacts. Research has already started, with a wide-range study of lean and agile methods and their related assessment models. The first design artefact, *LESAT for software* [7], is an adaptation of the self-assessment tool designed for lean enterprise transformation. Next, the research scope will be narrowed to CD practices and capabilities in a real environment, following the design and validation of the CD reference model. The first results from case study interviews indicate that CD requires the involvement of multiple stakeholders and the tight integration of the customer, product management, research and development (R&D) and operations.

References

1. Dybå, T., Dingsøyr, T.: Empirical studies of agile software development: A systematic review. Information and Software Technology 50, 833–859 (2008)
2. Bosch, J., Eklund, U.: Eternal embedded software: Towards innovation experiment systems. In: Margaria, T., Steffen, B. (eds.) ISoLA 2012, Part I. LNCS, vol. 7609, pp. 19–31. Springer, Heidelberg (2012)
3. Fagerholm, F., Guinea, A.S., Mäenpää, H., Münch, J.: Building blocks for continuous experimentation. In: Proceedings of the 1st International Workshop on Rapid Continuous Software Engineering, RCoSE 2014, pp. 26–35. ACM Press, New York (2014)
4. Olsson, H., Bosch, J., Alahyari, H.: Towards R&D as innovation experiment systems: A framework for moving beyond agile software development. In: IASTED Multiconferences - Proceedings of the IASTED International Conference on Software Engineering, SE 2013, pp. 798–805 (2013)
5. Humble, J., Farley, D.: Continuous Delivery: Reliable Software Releases through Build, Test, and Deployment Automation. Addison-Wesley Professional (2010)
6. Fitzgerald, B., Stol, K.-J.: Continuous software engineering and beyond: trends and challenges. In: Proceedings of the 1st International Workshop on Rapid Continuous Software Engineering, RCoSE 2014, pp. 1–9. ACM Press, New York (2014)
7. Karvonen, T., Rodriguez, P., Kuvaja, P., Mikkonen, K., Oivo, M.: Adapting the Lean Enterprise Self-Assessment Tool for the Software Development Domain. In: Proceedings of 38th EUROMICRO Conference on Software Engineering and Advanced Applications (SEAA), September 5-8, pp. 266–273 (2012), doi:10.1109/SEAA.2012.51
8. Hevner, A.R., Chatterjee, S., Gray, P., Baldwin, C.Y.: Design research in information systems: theory and practice. Springer, New York (2010)

How to Adopt Continuous Delivery? A Research Proposal

Eero Laukkanen[1] and Casper Lassenius[1,2]

[1] Aalto University, P.O. BOX 19210, FI-00076, Aalto, Finland
{eero.laukkanen,casper.lassenius}@aalto.fi
[2] Massachusetts Institute of Technology, Sloan School of Management

1 Research Problem

Continuous delivery (CD) is a software development discipline in which software can be released to production at any time [1]. The discipline is achieved through optimization, automatization and utilization of the build, deploy, test and release process [2]. The proposed benefits of CD are increased visibility, faster feedback and empowerment of stakeholders [2]. However, when trying to adopt CD, organizations have faced numerous challenges and problems [3,4]. Even continuous integration (CI), which is a prerequisite for CD [2], has not been adopted in some cases [5].

The dissertation aims to gain deep understanding of the problems when adopting CD and build solutions to those problems. Since the already found problems have been numerous [3,4], we believe that simply finding the problems is not enough, but we need to analyze the causal structure of the problems in order to solve them. Thus, the following research questions are asked:

1. What problems are faced when adopting CD for a software product?
2. What are the causes for those problems?
3. What solutions can be used for solving those problems?

2 Research Methodology

The dissertation will consist of five empirical qualitative studies. First, a systematic literature review (SLR) [6] is executed to summarize existing research and experience reports on the subject. The SLR will include empirical studies and experience reports which are qualitatively synthesized into a theory of adoption problems and solutions. Second, the theory is refined through a single case study [7] focusing on problems perceived by individuals in a project adopting CD. Individual analysis is done, because it is believed that the perceptions between individuals differ. Third, a single case study will be performed using ARCA root cause analysis method [8] to study adoption problems in a single case and to innovate solutions to the problems. Fourth, the impact of these solutions is investigated in a follow-up study. Fifth, the root cause analysis is

© Springer International Publishing Switzerland 2015
C. Lassenius et al. (Eds.): XP 2015, LNBIP 212, pp. 356–357, 2015.
DOI: 10.1007/978-3-319-18612-2

performed in other cases too, and the results are synthesized into a generalized theory.

Data sources for the case studies are Finnish software companies in the Digile Need for Speed program that continues until 2017. Thus, there is an opportunity to conduct long-term longitudinal case studies of CD adoption. The selection of data sources for the case studies is done partly based on convenience, but also according to the research goals. The subject of the research program is tightly related to CD, so it is expected that the case companies are also valid subjects for the studies.

3 Results and Future Agenda

The systematic literature review is in writing and will complete in near future. Data collection for the single case study has been executed partially. The design for the first root cause analysis case study has been done and the data collection will begin in the near future.

The initial results of systematic literature review indicate that numerous problems when adopting CD have been identified and some of them could be solved. However, we found that there is a lack of causal analysis done on the problems. This indicates that our future agenda on root cause analysis will provide improvement on the current knowledge.

References

1. Fowler, M.: ContinuousDelivery (May 2013), http://martinfowler.com/bliki/ContinuousDelivery.html
2. Humble, J., Farley, D.: Continuous Delivery: Reliable Software Releases Through Build, Test, and Deployment Automation. Addison-Wesley Professional, 1st edn. (2010)
3. Claps, G.G., Svensson, R.B., Aurum, A.: On the journey to continuous deployment: Technical and social challenges along the way. Information and Software Technology 57(0), 21 – 31 (2015)
4. Debbiche, A., Dienér, M., Berntsson Svensson, R.: Challenges When Adopting Continuous Integration: A Case Study. In: Product-Focused Software Process Improvement. Lecture Notes in Computer Science, vol. 8892, pp. 17–32. Springer International Publishing (2014)
5. Ståhl, D., Bosch, J.: Automated Software Integration Flows in Industry: A Multiple-case Study. In: Companion Proceedings of the 36th International Conference on Software Engineering. pp. 54–63. New York, NY, USA (2014)
6. Kitchenham, B.: Guidelines for performing systematic literature reviews in software engineering. Tech. rep., Keele University Technical Report (2007)
7. Runeson, P., Höst, M.: Guidelines for conducting and reporting case study research in software engineering. Empirical Software Engineering 14(2), 131–164 (2009)
8. Lehtinen, T.O., Mäntylä, M.V., Vanhanen, J.: Development and evaluation of a lightweight root cause analysis method (ARCA method)–field studies at four software companies. Information and Software Technology 53(10), 1045–1061 (2011)

Posters

Teaching Scrum – What We Did, What We Will Do and What Impedes Us

Emil Alégroth, Håkan Burden, Morgan Ericsson, Imed Hammouda,
Eric Knauss, and Jan-Philipp Steghöfer

Software Engineering Division
Department of Computer Science and Engineering
Chalmers University of Technology and University of Gothenburg
{Emil.Alégroth,Håkan.Burden,Morgan.Ericsson.Imed.Hammouda,
Eric.Knauss,Jan-Philipp.Steghöfer}@chalmers.se

Abstract. This paper analyses the way we teach Scrum. We reflect on
our intended learning outcomes, which challenges we find in teaching
Scrum and which lessons we have learned during the last four years. We
also give an outlook on the way we want to introduce and apply Scrum
in our teaching and how we intend to improve the curriculum.

The results aggregated in this paper are a response to a crisis: we, a group of
teachers and researchers at the University of Gothenburg (GU) and Chalmers
Technical University have realized that the way we teach Scrum doesn't align
with the intended learning outcomes of our courses. These often include process
knowledge, technical knowledge, and methodological knowledge. The intended
outcome in the process area is the ability to apply the process and the agile principles in future development projects. We feel that the courses become unmain-
tainable for us and put a lot of cognitive load on our students who learn Scrum
in lectures and apply it in projects in parallel. While applying Scrum is key to
understand it, the projects' deliverables and technical aspects tend to shadow
teaching goals and reflection on agile principles and practices. This causes students to feel like the process is "overhead" instead of being a possibility to structure their work. Since we as teachers are necessarily mainly concerned about the
outcome of the project and mainly interact with the students when they present
deliverables, we also have very little opportunity to observe the application of
the process and give direct feedback on it.

The Software Engineering division is a joint venture between GU and Chalmers.
Apart from courses in different programmes at both universities, it offers a Bachelor in Software Engineering and Management and a Master in Software Engineering. Both programmes emphasise project-based learning and thus allow students
to experience work in group settings with complex case studies and fixed deadlines.
A number of these courses either include agile practices in their learning objectives
or make use of them for the project work.

As teachers at the Software Engineering division we are responsible for teaching Scrum in four courses in three contexts – *Software Processes* (first term)
and *Software Architecture Project* (third term) in the Software Engineering and

C. Lassenius et al. (Eds.): XP 2015, LNBIP 212, pp. 361–362, 2015.
DOI: 10.1007/978-3-319-18612-2

Management bachelor program; *Software Engineering Project* (second term) for various engineering and IT programs as well as *Agile Software Development* in the Software Engineering master program. The project courses in the bachelor program and the course in the master program have a focus on technical knowledge whereas the Software Processes course focuses on theoretical knowledge.

By sharing our experiences and our lessons learnt we hope to allow trainers and teachers elsewhere to benefit from our experience and to balance the cognitive load and to start the same alignment process in education and training of agile software development that has now begun for us.

To get an overview of how we teach and apply Scrum in our courses we collectively reflected on our experiences and, applying the terminology of Brookfield, evaluated our practices using a *peer lens* [1]. Following Schön the reflection was *on-action* [2] since our teaching is spread out over the academic year and the course curricula are set for each course instance. This process led us to a number of insights and best practices that we want to apply in our future teaching. Two examples are:

1. Teaching Scrum needs to have a practical element: Scrum must be applied to know it. However, the more technically advanced the practical element is, the more the students focus on learning the platform instead of the process. The platform becomes an impediment for learning Scrum.

2. Stress is an impediment for learning Scrum since the students focus on delivering before the deadline instead of using a sound process. In a workshop setting the stress creates learning opportunities since the close interaction with the teachers enables immediate and detailed feedback. This resonates with what Babb et al. report from industry where the need to meet deadlines had a negative impact on the Scrum teams possibility for *reflection-in action* during the sprint retrospectives [3].

Our suggestion is to introduce Scrum using workshops and a platform with low technical demands. When students have been introduced to Scrum they can apply the knowledge in a project with a more technical setting, thereby balancing the cognitive load among the process aspects and technical aspects of the project. We have adapted our curriculum accordingly and now offer a Scrum workshop using Lego building blocks as part of the different courses to allow students of all semesters to experience Scrum this way. In the future, every student in the first term will participate in such an exercise and therefore be prepared for the use of Scrum in the second term Software Engineering project.

References

1. Brookfield, S.: Becoming a Critically Reflective Teacher. Higher and Adult Education Series. Wiley (1995)
2. Schön, D.A.: The Reflective Practitioner: How Professionals Think in Action. Harper torchbooks. Basic Books (1983)
3. Babb, J., Hoda, R., Nørbjerg, J.: Barriers to Learning in Agile Software Development Projects. In Baumeister, H., Weber, B., eds.: Agile Processes in Software Engineering and Extreme Programming. Volume 149 of Lecture Notes in Business Information Processing., Springer Berlin Heidelberg (2013) 1–15

Agility in Dynamic Environments: A Case Study for Agile Development

Simon Brooke and Dina Allswang

Abstract. Continual technological advances require software solutions, products and platforms to be adaptable, extendible and rapidly created to meet market needs.

Software technologies must be interchangeable, environments transparent, solutions maintainable, continuously integrated and delivered with value to the customer.

This paper presents a video software solution in which architecture, design, development, quality and integration were all done in an Agile manner to meet quality requirements, functional requirements, timelines and customer needs, while ensuring adaptability to changes at continuously high quality.

1 Background

In the past, our software development was based on Waterfall methodology. Requirements and design were many months ahead of implementation and coding periods were several months. High-level management decided that Agile could improve development processes. An Agile expert was consulted. Several problematic areas in the development lifecycle were identified:

- Major code rewrites due to late requirement changes
- Several rounds of fixes due to long, serial development/QC
- Integration bugs found too late in the development process
- Functionality not always as intended due to lack of ongoing feedback

2 New Project Using Scrum

An inter-departmental team was selected, consisting of personnel with varying levels of experience and multiple areas of expertise. The Scrum methodology was adopted for the project and various roles were assigned.

The project involved development of 5 components and integrating them into a larger subsystem. High-level architecture was managed using Agile and detailed architecture for each sprint was reviewed with the product owner.

C. Lassenius et al. (Eds.): XP 2015, LNBIP 212, pp. 363–364, 2015.
DOI: 10.1007/978-3-319-18612-2

3   Sprint Activities

The product owner managed the prioritized backlog in consultation with all stake-holders. For each sprint, the team members declared their capacity and selected tasks from the product owner's prioritized sprint plan.

Daily stand-up meetings provided close collaboration between team members, to request help and prevent impediments. The team updated progress on the scrum board enabling re-allocation of resources if necessary.

Retrospectives were held to discuss successful methods and improvements.

4   Continuous Integration

The components were continuously tested and integrated into the subsystem. Auto-mated tests were run nightly and issues handled daily. This enabled completion of development and QC within sprint scope.

5   Collaboration with Project Customer

Detailed design, requirements and implementation were reviewed with the project representative including a demo per sprint enabling timely feedback.

6   Conclusion

A measure of the project success was the satisfaction level of the customers. They appreciated the potentially shippable products available at the end of each sprint in-cluding a set of expected and high quality, high-priority features enabled by continuous customer involvement and feedback.

References

1. Schwaber, K., Sutherland, J.: The Official Scrum Guide

Introducing SafeScrum

Geir Kjetil Hanssen[1], Ingar Kulbrandstad[2], and Børge Haugset[1]

[1] SINTEF ICT, Strindveien 4, 7465 Trondheim, Norway
[2] Autronica Fire & Security, Haakon VII's gate 4, 7041 Trondheim, Norway
ghanssen@sintef.no, Ingar.Kulbrandstad@autronicafire.no,
borge.haugset@sintef.no

Abstract. Safety-critical systems such as process control- and signal systems play a fundamental role in many important industries and aspects of society. Such systems, including software, must fulfill extreme demands for correct operation and integrity, meaning that development must follow strict standards (in our case IEC 61508), which has to be documented and evaluated by external certification bodies to receive necessary approval. We present recent industrial experience in applying the SafeScrum approach in a complex software organization.

Keywords: Safety-critical systems · SafeScrum · IEC 61508

1 Agile Development of Safety Critical Systems

An increasing part of the functionality of safety-critical systems, e.g. ship-control and fire-detection are implemented as software due to more standardization of hardware. This gives larger and more complex software development projects, which must meet the same strict requirements for safety operation performance as electronically based systems. This calls for efficient and flexible development processes. Present methods are tailored for hardware development, emphasizing low requirements- and design-change frequency, being plan-based and document driven. This gives low requirements change tolerance and high costs (25-50% of total project costs) for producing documentation to prove conformance to standards such as IEC 61508 (process control systems) [1].

2 SafeScrum

To challenge this trend we have proposed the SafeScrum approach [2], which is an extension of the Scrum software development methodology in combination with common XP techniques. Scrum has now been adapted to fit development of safety critical systems and has been harmonized with software lifecycle requirements defined in the IEC61508 standard. Fitting Scrum for this type of development and certification means that it has to be extended with additional activities. For example, code reviews need to be documented with full traceability in such a way that an independent assessor can

© Springer International Publishing Switzerland 2015
C. Lassenius et al. (Eds.): XP 2015, LNBIP 212, pp. 365–366, 2015.
DOI: 10.1007/978-3-319-18612-2

verify that all code has been reviewed according to the standard. Another important extension is routines for change impact analysis, meaning that changes in requirements must be followed by an analysis on whether the change may impact the safety function of the system. This must also be fully traceable and documented for external verification. The overall challenge is to utilize the benefits of an agile approach, having it aligned with the standards extensive requirements for documentation while at the same time avoiding too much extra weight.

3   Introducing SafeScrum – Early Lessons Learned

Autronica Fire & Security AS has for over a year introduced SafeScrum in a SIL3 industry project (very high safety performance). Key lessons learned are:

(1) Adaptation and adoption of a radically different process needs change agents: Although supported by external experts, the shaping of SafeScrum and the change process itself happened as a grass-root movement. Having the ones that are to be using the process implement it themselves is important to establish sufficient motivation and to build necessary hands-on knowledge on a very detailed level. **(2) A radical change costs extra resources and needs support from management:** In our case management strongly supported the change, giving the team trust, freedom and time to try and fail. Without this support and resources it would have been extremely hard to succeed bottom-up. **(3) External support and validation strengthens the change:** Although the change happened bottom-up, external input on methodology and safety assessment (researchers) as well as discussions with the certification body (TÜV in this case) has enabled the team to prioritize change actions, discuss ideas and evaluate the suitability of SafeScrum and compatibility with the IEC 61508 standard. **(4) Tools are as important as processes:** There is a need to provide extensive documentation of compliance with the process. Traditionally this results in a lot of effort spent to produce explicit documentation in addition to the development itself. SafeScrum works very much because tools automate or supports the team in creating this type of information. **(5) Change needs to be done step-by-step:** The new process was started in the simplest possible way with only the core Scrum elements. Eventually, more details were added based on constant evaluation and refinement of the process. This approach also gave the team confidence as they always had a fully working process, which was in-line with the IEC 61508 standard.

References

[1] Bell, R.: Introduction to IEC 61508. Presented at the 10th Australian Workshop on Safety Critical Systems and Software, Darlinghurst, Australia (2005)
[2] Stålhane, T., Myklebust, T., Hanssen, G.K.: The application of Scrum IEC 61508 certifiable software. Presented at the ESREL, Helsinki, Finland (2012)

Revisit – A Systematic Approach to Continuously Improve Agile Practices in Large-scale and Fast-expanding R&D Center

Peng Liu and Yuedong Zhao

Nokia Networks Chengdu Technology Center,
Building A4, Tianfu Software Park, High-tech Zone,
610041 Chengdu, Sichuan, P.R.China
{brian.1.liu,yuedong.zhao}@nokia.com

Abstract. We give an overview of our recent initiative in designing a systematic framework to help teams continuously improve Agile practices in large-scale and fast-expanding R&D centre. The framework is expected to be a closed-loop, light-weighted and sustainable one with positive business impact. To address these requirements, after several rounds of pilot, a "Revisit" framework is figured out, which consists of five major phases:1) Goal/Problem-driven planning; 2) Light-weight audit; 3) Audit result analysis and reporting; 4) On-demand Competence Development support leveraging resources across the organization; 5) Progress tracking and effectiveness check. Also, a joint-force including a Revisit team, Revisit agents, and ScrumMaster community is setup to ensure the effective execution. Initial results indicate promising evidence this approach can help teams' quality and efficiency improvement.

Keywords: Agile method · Scrum · Continuous improvement · Competence development · Light-weight audit · Software quality support processes

1   Introduction

Agile, as an effective strategy to make software enterprises more flexible and responsive to changes, has one vital focus on continuous improvement [1]. However, in large-scale software R&D center with teams in different maturity levels, immature teams are most likely to be incompetent and inefficient in inspecting the real barriers in their agile practice and corresponding root causes and therefore adapting by taking effective improvement actions [2]. On the other hand, for matured teams, they may become stagnant, and it is a challenge to reinvigorate these teams in their agile practice to make it more efficient in creating customer values. Moreover, for a fast-expanding R&D centre (e.g., in China, India and Poland), a new challenge is to ensure new hires do not introduce too much "turbulence" to the agile way of working of existing teams. Yet another aspect to consider is employee Competence Development

---

Peng Liu is now agile/engineering coach in Nokia Networks Chengdu TC, and Yuedong Zhao is the head of R&D office, Nokia Networks MBB OSS Chin.

C. Lassenius et al. (Eds.): XP 2015, LNBIP 212, pp. 367–368, 2015.
DOI: 10.1007/978-3-319-18612-2

(CoDe). The fact is, however, employee CoDe team is most likely a central function not working closely with teams, which may lead to a mismatch between teams' real training needs and the resources (e.g., training, coaching) provided by the CoDe team.

Facing all above challenges, in Nokia Networks Chengdu Technology Centre (TC), there is a high demand for a mechanism to effectively help teams across the organization to continuously improve their agile practice with major requirements as:

Requirement 1: Light-weight. Teams expect low overhead and interruption.

Requirement 2: Close-loop. The mechanism shouldn't stop with identifying problems but should form a closed Plan-Do-Check-Act (PDCA) loop to help team grow.

Requirement 3: Effectiveness. CoDe support should be based on problems identified and positive business impact are expected from team.

Requirement 4: Sustainability. Good agile practice should sustain, and team should be capable for inspecting and adapting themselves.

2   Solution

As a result, in Nokia Network Chengdu TC, after several pilots, we finally figure out the "Revisit" framework as a systematical approach to help teams continuously improve agile practice in large-scale and fast-expanding software powerhouse.

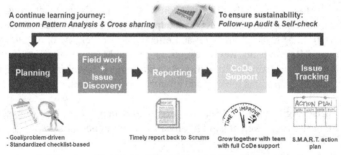

Fig. 1. Revisit framework: An overview

Highlights of lessons learnt are: First, this bottom-up initiative really gains buy-in from teams; second, refresh on Agile principle and Scrum practice is a must in fast-expanding R&D to avoid pitfalls like mini-waterfall; third, on-demand CoDe based on issues identified in Revisit is more effective in achieving positive business impact.

References

1. Meso, P., Jain, R.: Agile software development: adaptive systems principles and best practices. Information Systems Management 23(3), 19–30 (2006)
2. Beavers, P.A.: Managing a large "agile" software engineering organization. In: Agile Conference (AGILE), pp. 296–303. IEEE (2007)

Applying Randori-Style Kata and Agile Practices to an Undergraduate-Level Programming Class

Chitsutha Soomlek[✉]

Department of Computer Science, Faculty of Science,
Khon Kaen University, Khon Kaen, Thailand
chisutha@kku.ac.th

Abstract. This study adapted and applied a traditional randori-style kata to a web programming class, in order to help undergraduate students improve their programming skills. The process in the traditional randori-style kata was modified to match to the nature of XML. The results indicated that the modified randori-style kata is an effective method for the programming course and the students to enhance their programming skills. The activity also helped the students to repetitively review and reapply theories and knowledge to programming problems. The kata can stimulate the learning system, enhance self-confidence, and improve the relationships among the students.

Keywords: Randori-style kata · Coding dojo · Kata · Learning systems · Programming education

1 Introduction

A kata, also called coding dojo, is an activity designed for programmers to improve their coding skills through practices, repetition, and knowledge sharing [1]. A kata includes agile practices; e.g., pair programming, Test-Driven Development (TDD), Continuous Integration (CI), refactoring, and timeboxing; in the activity [1]. Swamidurai et al. indicated that using peer code review in the TDD context is even more effective for a programming practice than the traditional pair programming [2].

2 Procedure and Methods

In order to help our undergraduate students to improve their coding skills, a modified version of randori-style kata was created and integrated in a web programming class at the Department of Computer Science, Khon Kaen University, Thailand. The class was designed for 3rd-year and 4th-year students and focused on XML, XML-based technologies, Web technologies (e.g. HTML, XHTML, and JavaScript), and their applications (e.g. AJAX and Web services). The modified kata was assigned as one of the class activities in the Fall 2014 semester. There were 79 3rd-year students registered in this class. There were one instructor and two teaching assistants.

© Springer International Publishing Switzerland 2015
C. Lassenius et al. (Eds.): XP 2015, LNBIP 212, pp. 369–370, 2015.
DOI: 10.1007/978-3-319-18612-2

In the traditional randori-style kata, TDD is primarily used. However, writing a test before writing a code in XML is different from other programming languages that already have corresponding testing frameworks, e.g. Java and JUnit, PHP and PHPUnit, etc. Therefore, instead of writing a failing unit test on a testing framework, Document Type Definition (DTD), XML schema, and test cases were employed. For example, the instructor introduced a programming problem, a corresponding DTD/XML schema, and explained the acceptance criteria with examples to the students. The students had to write a well-formed and valid XML document according to the definitions provided in the DTD/XML schema. Sometimes, an XML document was given; then, the students had to write a DTD/XML schema that is complied with the XML document while keeping the document well-formed and valid. After the students were familiar with how to write a DTD/XML schema, they had to write a definition in DTD/XML schema first, and then, they had to create corresponding XML tags. Moreover, the instructor occasionally gave subtle hints, strategies, direct instructions, or changes of requirements during the practice sessions.

In the traditional kata, audiences are not allowed to disturbed the pilot and co-pilot, i.e. paired programmers. In this class, students were allowed to deliberate, share, and discuss their ideas with the class.

3   Results

This class was evaluated through three sets of questionnaires with open-end questions and interviews. 79 students registered in this course.

26 students participated in the modified kata ≥ 2 times. 22 students participated only once. 25 students did not participate in the kata. 6 people did not answer the questionnaires. 100% of participants agreed that the activity was an excellent activity for reviewing what they had learnt from the class, can help them understand XML, and can improve their coding skills. The activity can also motivate the students to hone their coding skills. Moreover, the modified randori-style kata can improve self-confidence and relationship among the students. However, the non-participants stated several reasons why they did not participate in the modified kata, for example, the session ended before their turns and they did not know how to solve the problems.

The modified randori-style kata could be used as an alternative method for programming practices. It can be applied to any programming courses and used for training purposes. Moreover, there are many possibilities to enhance the activity such as having multiple groups of kata working on the same programming problem.

References

[1] Martin, R.C.: The Clean Coder: A Code of Conduct for Professional Programmers. Prentice Hall (2011)
[2] Swamidurai, R., Dennis, B., Kannan, U.: Investigating the impact of peer code review and pair programming on test-driven development. In: IEEE SoutheastCon 2014, pp. 1–5. IEEE (2014)

Continuous Strategy Process in the Context of Agile and Lean Software Development

Tanja Suomalainen[1] and Jenni Myllykoski[2]

[1] VTT Technical Research Centre of Finland
Kaitoväylä 1, P.O. Box 1100, FI-90571 Oulu Finland
{Tanja.suomalainen}@vtt.fi
[2] Oulu Business School Pentti Kaiteran katu 1,
P.O. BOX 4600, FI-90014 University of Oulu Finland
{Jenni.myllykoski}@oulu.fi

Abstract. This extended abstract introduces an ongoing research which elaborates the concept of continuous strategy with an aim to better address the contemporary challenges of strategy process within the field of software development. Theoretically the research draws on the strategy process and practice -literature and on the literature of agile and lean software development when conceptualizing continuous strategy. Empirically the research examines the emerging challenges in software companies' strategy process when they are pursuing continuous practices in software development. The tentative analysis revealed that the practices that stem from the more traditional, structured strategy process are not compatible with the more "continuous planning"-oriented organisational practices. Thus, there seems to be pressure for developing more continuous strategy process and practices. Furthermore, in other organisational processes, especially in team level, the practices relating to continuity are more successfully applied, than in strategic level.

Keywords: Strategy process · Continuous planning · Software development

1 Introduction

In recent few years, the adoption of agile and lean development practices has increased remarkably in Information and Communication Technology (ICT) industry. Even though many companies have succeeded in adopting these practices, even more innovative approaches that support continuous practices throughout the organisation are needed [1]. For example, [2] emphasize continuous integration between software development and its operational deployment as well as continuously assessing and improving the link between business strategy and software development. Similarly, there is a clear need for continuous planning in which plans are dynamic open-ended artifacts that evolve in response to changes in the business environment. However, the continuous software development practices appear to be ill assorted with the traditional, rationalistic view of strategy process. Whereas the continuous software development stresses the importance of real time actions and continuous change [1], the

© Springer International Publishing Switzerland 2015
C. Lassenius et al. (Eds.): XP 2015, LNBIP 212, pp. 371–372, 2015.
DOI: 10.1007/978-3-319-18612-2

rationalistic view of strategy process is very static and future-oriented. It relies on the assumption of relatively predictable business environment that allows the rational managers [3] to create a long term future plan based on systematic scanning and positioning [4], and subsequently to implement it while having sufficient control over the consequences of actions [3]. The usefulness of such theories in the context of software development is questionable.

2   Research Method

We argue that continuous software development and planning calls for flexibility also in the strategy process and therefore the purpose of this research is to introduce and empirically investigate the concept of continuous strategy. The concept is rooted on the emerging literature on strategy process and practice that acknowledges continuous change as the inherent feature of reality and views strategy as fluxing, improvisational and temporal process [3, 4]. In addition, we draw on the literature on continuous software development, with an aim to connect the concept of continuous strategy with the practice of agile and lean software development. The research builds on a qualitative multi case study [5] in which data is collected through several interviews (altogether 22 at the moment) and analysed with the help of NVivo tool. The research is done in Digile's Need for Speed (N4S) research program (http://www.n4s.fi/en/).

The tentative analysis of an interview data revealed that the practices stemming from the "traditional", structured strategy process are not compatible with the more continuous planning practices within the organisation. Thus, there seems to be pressures for developing continuous strategy process and practices. Furthermore, in other organisational processes, especially in team level, the practices relating to continuity are more successfully applied, but in strategic level continuity is not yet achieved.

References

1. Olsson, H.H., Bosch, J., Alahyari, H.: Towards R&D as Innovation Experiment Systems: A Framework for Moving Beyond Agile Software Development. In: Proceedings of the IASTED International Conference on Software Engineering, SE 2013, pp. 798–805 (2013)
2. Fitzgerald, B., Stol, K.: Continuous Software Engineering and Beyond: Trends and Challenges. In: Proceedings of the 1st International Workshop on Rapid Continuous Software Engineering, pp. 1–9. ACM (2014)
3. MacKay, R., Chia, R.: Choice, Chance and Unintended Consequences in Strategic Change: A Process Understanding of the Rise and Fall of Northco Automotive. Academy of Management Journal 56(1), 208–230 (2013)
4. Tsoukas, H., Chia, R.: Introduction: Why philosophy matters to organisation theory. In: Philosophy and Organization Theory: Research in the Sosiology of Organisation, vol. 32, pp. 1–21. Emerald Group Publishing (2011)
5. Yin, R.K.: Case study research: design and methods, 3rd edn. Applied Social Research Methods Series, vol. 5. Sage Publications, Thousand Oaks (2003)

Automatizing Android Unit and User Interface Testing

Juha-Matti Vanhatupa and Mikko Heikkinen

PacketVideo Finland Oy, Hallituskatu 8, FI-33200 Tampere, Finland
{vanhatupa,mheikkinen}@pv.com

Abstract. In this paper we describe our efforts moving towards automatized testing in Android application development. With sophisticated combination of Android development tools and Perl scripts, we have automatized parts of the testing produce. Using the built system, unit tests are built and run automatically each time when a new build is created. In addition, we are automatizing user interface testing using Android uiautomator tool. In this automatization process we encountered several technical issues, for which Android development tools do not offer ready-made solutions, and we had to implement solutions for those.

Keywords: Test automation · Android · graphical user interface testing

1 Introduction

Mobile applications are designed to run on smartphones, tablet computers and other mobile devices. They are a challenging target for testing, many of them are web applications using resources from the Web, and they can also use data from sensors of the device. In addition they feature many different versions of operating systems and software frameworks customized for different devices [4].

The use of unit testing is generally low in mobile development community [1]. Approximately 20% of developers stated that their companies do not use any unit testing, and when performed it was mostly done manually. In addition, graphical user interface testing is challenging to automatize, and it is mostly done manually [1]. It was automatized only in 3% of the cases.

We have automatized executing unit tests with combination of Perl scripts and Android build tools. In addition we convert manual user interface (UI) tests into automatized tests using uiautomator framework [3]. The target application of this work was Twonky Beam [2], an app that lets users discover and transfer online video content from a tablet or mobile device to a television.

2 Test Automatization Approach

The purpose of automatizing unit testing is to ensure these tests are executed with each build. Natural solution was to include compiling and running unit tests

C. Lassenius et al. (Eds.): XP 2015, LNBIP 212, pp. 373–374, 2015.
DOI: 10.1007/978-3-319-18612-2

into build scripts of Twonky Beam. So they are executed, when a new feature or bug fix is pushed to the remote stream in version control and a build is launched on Jenkins. Scripts used for compiling Twonky Beam are written in Perl and we used it also for unit test automatization.

Perl has many built-in functions for shell programming and it can call operating system facilities. This enabled compiling projects (application project and unit test project), and starting Android emulator, and running unit tests on it.

We started automatization of UI testing using uiautomatorviewer tool. The tool enables taking screenshots of UI and viewing layout hierarchy of UI components. Then we implemented UI test cases. Manual UI tests are converted into uiautomator tests. Almost all of our 80 UI tests are possible to automatize using uiautomator, excluding only test cases, which required rebooting the device, or manual switching on of wireless networks.

When implementing uiautomator test cases, we encountered a problem with WebView component. Uiautomator cannot gather info about UI components inside it, since it sees WebView only as one component. We resolved the problem using coordination calculation algorithm, which calculates correct coordinates based on pixel density of the device and made a mouse click using those.

Another issue in UI testing was caused by different localization versions of Twonky Beam application (English and Japanese), because uiautomator uses text strings of UI components to locate them. To avoid failures in string comparison we included an extra step to the build process of uiautomator project. In this step files containing localized strings are copied into uiautomator project. When text string of UI component is required in the project, a separate function is called and the string is fetched from the correct file of localized strings.

3   Conclusions

Android framework offers many valuable tools, e.g. uiautomator is an excellent tool for UI test automatization. Although, as we described special cases in UI testing have to be handled separately. Overall, test automatization can save time and resources. The implemented approach can be used with other Android applications also.

References

1. Joorabchi, M. E., Mesbah A., Kruchten, P.: Real Challenges in Mobile App Development. In: Proceedings of the ACM/IEEE International Symposium on Empirical Software Engineering and Measurement. pp. 15–24. IEEE Computer Society (2013)
2. Twonky Beam application, http://twonky.com/product/beam/
3. uiautomator testing framework,
   http://developer.android.com/tools/testing/testing_ui.html
4. Wasserman, A.I.: Software Engineering Issues for Mobile Application Development. In: Proceedings of the FSE/SDP Workshop on Future of Software Engineering Research. pp. 397–400. ACM (2010)

Author Index

Abrahamsson, Pekka 52
Ahmad, Muhammad Ovais 178
Alègroth, Emil 361
Allswang, Dina 363
Ämmälä, Mikko 205
Arcelli Fontana, Francesca 3
Aro, Ismo 329

Bajwa, Sohaib Shahid 52
Barroca, Leonor 64
Berger, Christian 15
Bjarnason, Elizabeth 27
Bjerke-Gulstuen, Kristian 239
Boekhorst, Laurens 248
Borg, Markus 27
Bosch, Jan 218, 350
Brooke, Simon 363
Burden, Håkan 361

Chmelař, Martin 302
Claassen, Arjan 248
Counsell, Steve 129

Destefanis, Giuseppe 129
Diebold, Philipp 40, 345
Dingsøyr, Torgeir 239
Dönmez, Denniz 193
Doss, Osama 347

Eckstein, Jutta 339
Eklund, Ulrik 15
Engström, Emelie 27
Ericsson, Morgan 361

Fabijan, Aleksander 350
Fontana, Rafaela Mantovani 199, 310
Fraser, Steven 334, 329
Fridstrom, Josh 294

Giardino, Carmine 52
Gregory, Peggy 64
Grote, Gudela 193

Hammouda, Imed 361
Hanssen, Geir Kjetil 365
Harzl, Annemarie 352
Haugset, Børge 365
Heikkilä, Ville T. 93
Heikkinen, Mikko 373
Hokkanen, Laura 81
Holyer, Steve 339
Hunt, Johanna 254

Ilieva, Sylvia 230
Itkonen, Juha 93

Jacques, Adam 294
Järvinen, Janne 334

Karvonen, Teemu 354
Kassab, Mohamad 129
Kelly, Tim 347
Kettunen, Petri 205
Kilpela, Kurt 294
Kirjavainen, Antti 339
Kivioja, Henri 329
Knauss, Eric 361
Krchňák, Jan 302
Kulbrandstad, Ingar 365
Kuvaja, Pasi 212, 354

Larsen, Diana 339
Larsen, Emil Wiik 239
Lassenius, Casper 356
Laukkanen, Eero 356
Lehtinen, Timo O.A. 93
Lenarduzzi, Valentina 105
Lindgren, Eveliina 117
Liu, Peng 367
Lundh, Erik 329, 334
Lunesu, Ilaria 105
Lwakatare, Lucy Ellen 212

Malucelli, Andreia 199, 310
Marchesi, Michele 129

Marshall, Stuart   141
Martini, Antonio   218
Matinlassi, Mari   262
Matta, Martina   105
Md. Rejab, Mawarny   141
Meyer Jr., Victor   199
Münch, Jürgen   117, 154
Myllykoski, Jenni   371

Noble, James   141
Nybom, Kristian   166

Oivo, Markku   178, 212, 354
Olsson, Helena Holmström   350
Ortu, Marco   129
Ostberg, Jan-Peter   40

Pareto, Lars   218
Partanen, Jari   205, 262
Porres, Ivan   166
Poupko, Avraham   270
Power, Ken   329, 334

Reinehr, Sheila   199, 310
Rising, Linda   329, 334
Rissanen, Olli   154
Rodríguez, Pilar   178
Rosenberg, Shlomi   279

Salah, Dina   64
Sarkela, John   294
Schneider, Matti   287
Sennersten, Charlotte   224
Sharp, Helen   64
Siverland, Susanne   224

Slany, Wolfgang   352
Smeds, Jens   166
Šmiřák, Roman   302
Soomlek, Chitsutha   369
Sorje, Olli   339
Stålhane, Tor   239
Stavru, Stavros   230
Steghöfer, Jan-Philipp   361
Suomalainen, Tanja   371

Taibi, Davide   105
Taylor, Katie   64
Tonelli, Roberto   129
Tramontini, Ramon   310
Tripathi, Nirnaya   178
Tureček, Tomáš   302

Unterkalmsteiner, Michael   27

Väänänen-Vainio-Mattila, Kaisa   81
Vanhatupa, Juha-Matti   373
Virtanen, Risto   93

Wagner, Stefan   40
Walter, Marcelo   310
Wang, Xiaofeng   52
Wernersson, Roger C.S.   224
Wild, Werner   329, 334
Wilson, Alexander   319
Wirfs-Brock, Rebecca   329, 334

Zanoni, Francesco   3
Zanoni, Marco   3
Zendler, Ulrich   40
Zhao, Yuedong   367

Printed in the United States
By Bookmasters